WESTMAR COLLE ✓ W9-BMI-102

VLADIMIR AKIMOV
ON THE DILEMMAS OF
RUSSIAN MARXISM
1895–1903

V. P. Akimov

VLADIMIR AKIMOV
ON THE DILEMMAS OF
RUSSIAN MARXISM
1895-1903

*The Second Congress of the Russian Social
Democratic Labour Party*

*A Short History of the Social Democratic
Movement in Russia*

TWO TEXTS IN TRANSLATION

EDITED AND INTRODUCED BY

JONATHAN FRANKEL

*Vladimir Akimov, i.e.,
Vladimir Petrovich Makhnovets
///*

CAMBRIDGE
AT THE UNIVERSITY PRESS
1969

Published by the Syndics of the Cambridge University Press
Bentley House, 200 Euston Road, London N.W.1
American Branch: 32 East 57th Street, New York, N.Y.10022

Library of Congress Catalogue Card Number: 68–23178
Standard Book Number: 521 05029 4

'The Russian Institute of Columbia University is pleased
to support the publication of some of the research conducted under its auspices. While not necessarily endorsing
its conclusions, the Institute believes that this volume in
its *Studies of the Russian Institute* is a contribution to
scholarly research and public understanding'

The frontispiece is reprinted from *Deiateli revoliutsionnogo
dvizhenniia v Rossii: Bio-bibliograficheskii slovar'*, v, 35

Printed in Great Britain
at the University Printing House, Cambridge
(Brooke Crutchley, University Printer)

CONTENTS

PREFACE

The decision to publish a translation of Akimov's two major political tracts was taken some years ago, but, as is the way with such enterprises, the period between promise and fulfilment proved unexpectedly prolonged. Despite the work and time expended, I am not sorry that I made the effort if only because Akimov would seem to deserve a more substantial place in the history of Russian Marxism than has usually been assigned him hitherto. True, in the last few years there have been signs of a growing appreciation of Akimov's qualities as polemicist and historian—Dr J. H. L. Keep, for instance, in his study of early Party history certainly pays him and the 'Economists', in general, considerable attention. I hope that this trend will be sustained now that Akimov's two most important works are more accessible.

I received help from many quarters in preparing this edition. The enterprise would never have been possible if I had not received unflagging support from the faculty of the Russian Institute at Columbia University. Nearly all the work on the book was completed while I was a visiting Fellow of the Institute. The Directors —first Professor Henry L. Roberts and then Professor Alexander Dallin—encouraged and advised me throughout with great good will, in a spirit of real friendship. However, I feel that special thanks are due to Miss Louise E. Luke of the Institute (now Managing Editor of the *Slavic Review*) who devoted unlimited effort and innumerable hours to editing the manuscript in its early stages. What patience I now have for the laborious exactitudes of editing, I have learnt from her. I also received assistance from other past and present members of the Institute staff, particularly from Mrs Nora Beeson, Mrs Miriam Bergamini and Miss Constance Beezer. Last but not least, my deepest thanks are due to Miss Mirra Ginsburg, who made the first draft of the translation, an unrewarding task that was executed with great expedition and skill. It is hardly necessary to add that if despite all help given me at Columbia errors remain, then the responsibility is entirely mine.

In 1962, I visited the late Miss Lydiia Makhnovets at her home near Paris. She received me with warmth and interest, pleasantly surprised to hear that her brother's works were to be republished in English translation. She furnished me with new information about the personal and political life of the Makhnovets family. The Second Party Congress suddenly became very much alive as 'Bruker' rehearsed the events of sixty years before.

In addition, my thanks are due to Professor Ladis Kristoff, formerly Associate Director of the Inter-University Project on the History of the Menshevik Movement; Dr J. H. L. Keep of London University; Professor Allan Wildman of the State University of New York (Stony Brook); Professor Leopold Haimson of Columbia University; Mr H. Kempinsky of the Bund Archive; Mrs Iuliia Kammermacher-Kefali; and to my good friend Dr Israel Getzler of the University of Adelaide—all of whom came to my aid with advice, hospitality and information while I was in New York.

Although this is essentially a project conceived and carried through at Columbia, I would not want to leave unmentioned the help I received in England, where I am indebted to the Master and Fellows of Jesus College, who enabled me to retain my Research Fellowship at Cambridge while absent in New York; to my Cambridge teachers and friends, Mr E. H. Carr, Mr D. J. V. Fisher, Professor Charles Wilson, Mr Moses Finley, Mr Maurice Cowling and Miss Betty Behrens, whose advice and guidance have been a constant source of encouragement to me over the years; and to the Leverhulme Foundation, which financed my return visit to Columbia in order to complete this project.

Some technical details remain to be noted. Akimov's two booklets have been reproduced in complete form without any omissions. However, as was usual in works reproduced in the conditions of penurious exile, the originals are marked by an abundance of typographical and editorial errors—numbers are jumbled, names misspelt, quotations carelessly reproduced. I felt that it would be excessively pedantic to reproduce these errors only to correct them in parentheses or in the footnotes, and so I have corrected them without indicating the fact. It goes without saying that mistakes due to misinformation have been left as they are (and commented upon, when discovered, in the notes). Moreover, the report of the Union of the Russian Social Democrats Abroad which Akimov included in his booklet on the Second Party Congress has been reproduced here as an appendix. I felt that this somewhat bulky report tended to overshadow the trend of

Akimov's argument and that it would therefore be legitimate to return to it the status of an independent document. I have indicated the place where this report was to be found in the original. In general, Akimov provided the titles and subtitles as reproduced here, but in some cases breaks were marked by asterisks only. Where it seemed necessary for the sake of clarity, I sometimes added explanatory titles at such points.

Capitalization has proved a troublesome problem. But, in principle, 'Party' has been used to describe formally constituted bodies (e.g. the RSDLP from its foundation in March 1898), 'party' to describe hypothetical organizations or those in the process of formation (e.g. the Russian Social Democratic movement prior to 1898). Again 'economism' refers to the economic agitation movement in its early stages (Akimov's 'second period') and 'Economism' or 'so-called Economism' to that movement in its later, more clearly defined forms (Akimov's 'third period'). In my Introduction and the 'Short History', 'Congress' is used to describe a Party's sovereign assembly but, to avoid excessive capitalization, the form 'congress' was preferred in the work devoted specifically to this subject ('The Second Congress of the RSDLP'). Finally, I should perhaps explain that in transliterating I followed the original of the Russian text. Thus, for instance, 'sotsial' demokratiia', 'sotsial-demokratiia' and even 'sotsial'-demokratiia' crop up from time to time.

JONATHAN FRANKEL

Jerusalem,
December 1967

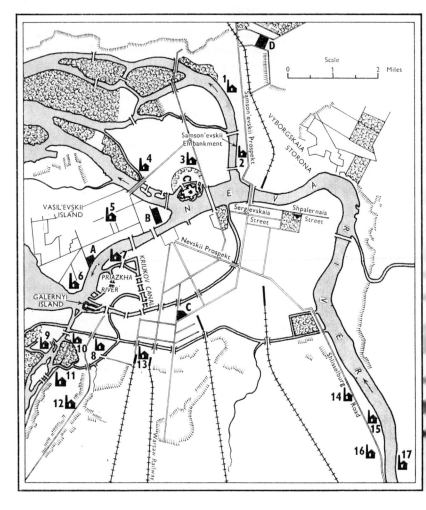

FACTORIES IN ST PETERSBURG,
1895–7

A	Mining Institute	8	Russo-American Plant
B	The University	9	Voronin Rezvoostrovskii Mill
C	Technology Institute	10	Koenig Mill
D	Forestry Institute	11	Ekaterinhof Mill
1	Voronin Mill	12	Putilov Plant
2	Lebedev Mill	13	Warsaw Workshop
3	Gol'darbeiter Mill	14	Semiannikov Works
4	Voronin Mill	15	Pal' Mill
5	'Laferm' Factory	16	Aleksandrovsk Works
6	Baltic Yard	17	Thornton Factory
7	New Admiralty Works		

INTRODUCTION

THE POLARIZATION OF
RUSSIAN MARXISM (1883-1903)

PLEKHANOV, LENIN AND AKIMOV

INTRODUCTION

Leninism: Marxist or Populist?

In the years 1902–5 Vladimir Akimov and Vladimir Lenin stood at the opposite poles of Russian revolutionary Marxism. Lenin, as the leader of the Bolshevik faction, had opted for a 'maximalist' interpretation of Marxist thought—a full-blooded socialist régime in Russia as an immediate goal. For Akimov (the major spokesman of the so-called 'Economist' faction), Marxism demanded before all else the belief that the workers must master their own fate. The 'kingdom of freedom' could only be built on the broad foundations of popular initiative. A socialist revolution, as distinct from a revolutionary coup or an anarchic jacquerie, could be carried through only by a working-class confident in its own self-made and democratically-run organizations, in its own knowledge and ambitions. And to lay such foundations required time, patience. Both men were revolutionaries because both saw in the Tsarist autocracy an insuperable barrier thrown across the road of historical advance. But profound disagreement about the post-revolutionary future led to their diametrically opposed interpretations of party history, of Marxist doctrine and of the principles of party organization.

The full implications of this dispute only became apparent after the February Revolution of 1917 when Lenin's call for the immediate establishment of a proletarian dictatorship clashed with the caution of the Mensheviks who, together with the right-wing Bolsheviks led by Kamenev, urged that a longer period of parliamentary government was required to enable the proletariat to prepare itself for power. But Lenin successfully asserted the primacy of political initiative over the dictates of socio-economic 'realities'. It was against his voluntaristic interpretation of Marxism that Bukharin, too, was twice to argue a 'deterministic' alternative. In 1918 Bukharin fought tooth and nail against a separate peace—Brest-Litovsk—and in favour of revolutionary war, because how could the Bolsheviks hope to build socialism in a peasant country without the direct aid of the European proletariat and the advanced industry of the West? And in 1928–9 he resisted the collectivization of agriculture because how could the

I-2

massive intervention of political power taken by itself make up for the crippling shortage of capital required for the frenetic tempos of Stalin's industrialization plans? Bukharin was defeated no less surely than Kamenev and the Mensheviks in 1917. The 'great leap forward' on a national scale prevailed over the right-wing Marxist faith in steady growth and over the left-wing Marxist faith in the indivisible revolution of the European proletariat. Politics triumphed over economics.

The Mensheviks saw the Leninist revolution of October 1917, with its contempt for the long-term laws of socio-economic development and its deliberate exploitation of the blind passions of the masses, as alien to Marxism. They argued that Lenin had reverted to Russia's pre-Marxist Populist (Narodnik) tradition—revolution-ary, egalitarian, nationalist, incipiently dictatorial but clearly foreign to scientific and proletarian socialism. After all, it was Bakunin (Populist and anarchist) writing in the 1860s who had argued that a few magic slogans used by the revolutionaries could work Russia's peasant masses into a holy rage of destruction and so bring the old social order toppling into ruins. And it was Tkachev (Populist and Jacobin) writing in the 1870s who insisted that the Tsarist state—lacking solid support in society and so wholly dependent on bureaucracy, landowners and army—could be snatched from the hands of the Romanovs by an ever-vigilant band of revolutionaries.

Many Soviet historians looking back over Russian revolutionary history also came to see the October Revolution as the triumphant justification of Tkachev and of his followers in the revolutionary and terrorist party, the *Narodnaia Volia*. Historians such as Mitskevich and Teodorovich gained a growing notoriety by arguing that Tkachev and the *Narodovol'tsy*, like Lenin after them, had analysed the realities of Russian life—a top-heavy state, a popula-tion predominantly peasant and downtrodden, a miserably weak urban bourgeoisie—and had come up with 'Bolshevik' con-clusions decades in advance of Lenin. Or as Mitskevich put it: 'The Bolsheviks acted according to the testament of the [Russian] Jacobin-Blanquists and we were not deterred when our opponents abused us—for them these were terms of abuse—as Blanquists and Jacobins.'[1] Such a community of views, argued these historians,

[1] S. Mitskevich, 'Russkie iakobintsy', *Proletarskaia revoliutsiia*, nos. 6–7 (18–19) (1923), p. 26.

showed that Lenin had known how to apply Marxist doctrine to Russian realities thus triumphantly vindicating both Marx and Tkachev.

Nevertheless, Mitskevich, Teodorovich and their historiographical school could be interpreted to mean that, while the October Revolution without Lenin was unthinkable, there could well have been a Lenin without Marx and Marxism. It is hardly surprising that by 1933 this entire school of Party historians had been silenced by the Stalin régime. The official orthodoxy, as developed in Stalin's history of 1938 (*The Short Course*), now became that the Bolsheviks owed all their ideas to Marxism as applied to Russia initially by Plekhanov but above all by Lenin, while Populism in all its forms was essentially reactionary and exerted a purely negative influence.

The truth of the matter is that while the revolutionary Populists as organized, for instance, in the *Narodnaia Volia*, did make plans for revolution remarkably similar to those eventually adopted by the Bolsheviks, they based these plans on radically different doctrinal premises. From the first, the structure of Bolshevism was reinforced by very specific ideological struts which had not been inherited from Populism. The Left-wing Socialist Revolutionaries, who saw themselves as the direct heirs of the *Narodnaia Volia*, supported the October Revolution and the dispersal of the Constituent Assembly, but they drew the line at Brest-Litovsk—they did not see the preservation of the 'proletarian' state as justifying the huge losses of Russian soil—and they would certainly never have acquiesced in collectivization, the enforced recruitment of Russia's peasantry to build up industrial socialism. And, of course, in recent years the developing countries have given us ample opportunity to see that not every one-party, egalitarian, socialist dictatorship is necessarily Leninist. The Bolshevik credo, their overall strategy as distinct from their specific choice of tactics at a given moment, was recognizably alien to Populism.

The doctrines which distinguished Leninism from the philosophy of Tkachev and the *Narodnaia Volia* were sufficiently clear-cut. Firstly, the Bolsheviks believed that in Marxism they had a scientific key which, if properly understood and interpreted, would enable them to understand the laws of nature and of man in nature, of history and society, of past and future. According to this law, the industrial proletariat was the instrument of historical progress at this stage of world development and upon it was laid the duty of overturning the bourgeois order and establishing a truly communist society, of carrying mankind from the kingdom of necessity to the kingdom of freedom. It was the function of the Marxist party to act as the *avant-garde* of the industrial proletariat leading it along its predestined path. In this capacity, the party had to seize power wherever it could in order to advance the interests of the world-wide proletariat. The success of the party was dependent on its ability to analyse correctly the historical forces in play at a given time and place, on its ability to apply the Marxist master-key to reality. A misinterpretation would lead to inevitable disaster—a failure to seize power when the time was ripe; a premature coup, inability to hold power once gained. Thus, the leaders of the party had to ensure that only orthodox Marxists be allowed to join its ranks and that any sign of deviation be rapidly stamped out. To maintain this degree of inner purity, the party clearly had to be highly centralized. False prophets would never be able to lead the people to the promised land.

These doctrines, then, were clearly not of Populist origin, but had they come from Marx? This was frequently denied by the Mensheviks. Of course, the basic propositions—that Marxism was an all-embracing and proven science, that the proletariat had a key rôle to play in building a radically new world—were accepted by all Marxists. But the sanctification of an élite and highly centralized party, the fear of deviation, the relegation of the masses to a passive rôle, the demand that the party seize power at the first opportunity—these were all beliefs which were repudiated over the years by most Mensheviks, as earlier by Akimov and the Economist faction.

Was, then, the Bolshevik credo essentially new, sprung fully armed from the head of Lenin? Many Mensheviks have tended to argue that it was (or at least that Leninism was) a new synthesis of Tkachev's Jacobinism and Bakunin's anarchism in superficial Marxist disguise. The study of Akimov's political career as of his writings suggests that this thesis is fallacious. The essentials of Leninism were finally forged in the years 1902–3 during the clash with the 'Economists'. But in this, the first, Party schism, Lenin was not only in the same camp as Aksel'rod, Martov and Potresov, the future leaders of the Menshevik faction, but was inspired and urged on by Plekhanov, 'the father of Russian Marxism' and from 1904–8 a major Menshevik spokesman. Until Lenin broke away from the other editors of their joint journal, *Iskra*, his central ideas were barely questioned and Akimov was therefore right to see Leninism as a logical stage in the unfolding of Russian Marxism as it had developed under Plekhanov's theoretical guidance. He opposed it and hoped that it would pass, but he never believed that it could be dismissed as a freakish imitation, a throw-back to Populism.

In his history of the Party, Akimov did not dwell at length on the early writings of Plekhanov, believing (quite erroneously as it proved) that the future of the movement lay with the working-class in Russia—as distinct from the émigré ideologists—and that the time had therefore come to trace the indigenous roots of Social Democratic action within the Empire. But an assessment of the clash between Akimov and the Economists, on the one hand, and Plekhanov and Lenin, on the other, must start with an analysis of Plekhanov's theories. He was the pioneer. The ideological roots of both 'Economism' and Leninism are to be found in Plekhanov's dialectical attempt to apply Marxism to Russia.

Plekhanov's Marxism

Plekhanov wrote his first clearly Marxist work in 1882. But even before this it had become apparent that anybody hoping to convert the Russian revolutionary movement to Marxism would have to overcome a crucial dilemma. If he emphasized that Russia had to go through the same prolonged stages of capitalist development as the West, he would be accused of weakening the faith of the revolutionaries who were fighting for equality, for socialism, not for political liberty. The revolutionary could hardly be expected to martyr himself in the attempt to overthrow the dictatorship of the Tsar if the only result would be to entrench emergent capitalism. If Marxism meant to postpone all hope of socialism for many decades or even for centuries, then such a doctrine spelt suicide for the revolutionary movement.

Yet, as against this, if it was said that Russia could avoid the capitalist stage and so pass directly to socialism, then what was the relevance of Marxism to the Russian revolutionary movement? Nearly all the Populist leaders—Lavrov, Tkachev, even Bakunin —admired Marx's socio-economic analysis of capitalist society, but they all argued that Russia as a feudal and agrarian country could learn from the West only how to avoid its errors and so find a direct road to socialism. Marxism was irrelevant.

7

This problem had bedevilled Marx and Engels before Plekhanov. In his famous open letter of 1874 to Tkachev (who was erroneously taken by Marx and Engels to be a Bakuninist), Engels had argued that it was absurd to dream that Russia's peasants could create a socialist society. Socialism was the product of a highly advanced, industrial society and could be made a reality only by the proletariat moulded and prepared by such a society. Even if, as was to be hoped, a peasant rebellion tumbled the Tsarist régime, the result would not be socialism but the consolidation of a bourgeois order of society based on peasant, or petty bourgeois, private enterprise. The much lauded peasant commune (*mir* or *obshchina*) would disintegrate under the new order even faster than hitherto.

Yet this argument, however valuable in the anti-Bakuninist feud, lost its appeal to Marx and Engels when a few years later the revolutionaries in Russia finally organized themselves into an effective and dangerous revolutionary party, the *Zemlia i Volia* (which later developed into the *Narodnaia Volia*). Both parties worked for the violent overthrow of the Tsarist régime and its replacement by a socialist order. Marx, seeing in the Romanov régime the bulwark of European reaction, followed their successive assassinations and would-be assassinations with a mounting enthusiasm. When in 1881, Vera Zasulich (who had herself attempted a major political assassination three years before and who was still a Populist) turned to Marx with an impassioned plea to give the Russian revolutionary socialists a glimmer of hope, he decided to modify the water-tight determinism used by Engels against Tkachev. True, he replied, an agrarian society could not hope to attain socialism under its own steam. But if a revolutionary victory in Russia coincided with a proletarian revolution in the West, then with the aid of the industrial countries the Russians could by-pass the later stages of capitalism, thus advancing directly to a socialist system—the *obshchina* could then be saved and act as the 'main pivot for the social rebirth of Russia'.[1] Similarly in a letter of 1885 from Engels we read that 'if ever the Blanquist fantasy—to shake a whole society by means of a small conspiracy—had any foundations then of course it is in St Petersburg'.[2]

This dualism in the Marxist attitude towards Russia was

[1] *Perepiska K. Marksa i F. Engel'sa s russkimi politicheskimi deiateliami* (Moscow, 1947), p. 242.　　　[2] *Ibid.* p. 251.

inevitable and, as we have seen, persistent. But Plekhanov came to believe that he could bridge the gap. He rejected the whole-hearted support which Marx and Engels gave in the late 1870s and 1880s to the Populist revolutionaries seeing in their uncritical attitude a form of intellectual deception or self-deception. But, equally, he could not see in the West European Social Democratic Parties a model directly relevant to Russia. Germany, the Marxist motherland, was too far ahead—a major industrial power with an entrenched trade union movement, universal suffrage, and a Social Democratic Party with millions of followers.

It was in the writings and doctrines of Marx and Engels from the late 1840s that he believed he had found a solution. The Russia of the 1880s and the Germany of the 1840s could be seen as fundamentally similar: politically backward, semi-feudal, agrarian countries just entering the stage of capitalist industrialization. For both countries, at this stage, political democracy was a thing of the future and in both there could be discovered an industrial proletariat in embryo. The Russians could, therefore, hope for no better guide than the *Communist Manifesto* and other political works of the years 1847–50. It was no coincidence that Plekhanov's introduction to a translation of the *Manifesto* was his first clearly Marxist work.

Plekhanov now developed the argument put forward in 1874 by Engels. The plans of the *Narodovol'tsy* to save Russia from capitalism were utopian. Like Tkachev, they had seen the absence of an entrenched bourgeoisie as the great tactical advantage enjoyed by revolutionaries in Russia over those in the West. 'Does it follow from this', Plekhanov ironically asked, 'that the Persians, Egyptians and Chinese will go over equally easily to the idea of "peuple souverain"? If so, then the further east we go, the nearer we come to the government of the people.'[1] As this idea seemed patently absurd, he concluded: 'Thus, it follows that the extent to which a particular country is ready for true rather than fraudulent democracy is defined by the level of its economic development.'[2] However egalitarian its intentions, a would-be socialist coup by a few Populist revolutionaries would only accelerate the disintegration of the *obshchina*. Land distribution would inevitably strengthen the acquisitive and petty bourgeois instincts of the peasant, and the *Narodovol'tsy*, having seized the

[1] G. V. Plekhanov, *Nashi raznoglasiia* (Geneva, 1885), p. 230.
[2] *Ibid.* p. 232.

state machine, would emerge not as socialists but as latter-day Robespierres, not socialist but radical and bourgeois, not liberators but dictators.

Yet there was hope. The Russian proletariat, however embryonic, had to be organized. Once even the skeleton of a workers party was in existence, it could play a decisive rôle in the anti-feudal and anti-Tsarist bourgeois revolution which was bound to break out in the foreseeable future. Marx and Engels had believed that, under these circumstances, the proletariat could ally with the bourgeoisie—democrats and radicals—against the feudal order. Taking up its stand on the extreme left wing of the democratic movement it could drive it forward to ever greater revolutionary violence. As the bourgeois revolution unfolded, the proletariat would eventually be able to seize power. This scheme, sketched out in the *Communist Manifesto*, had been further clarified by Marx and Engels in their *Address to the Communist League* of 1850. They had concluded that in Germany the struggle would be more difficult than in neighbouring and more industrialized France, but that power would nonetheless be won after a lengthy revolutionary development.

For Plekhanov this viewpoint was admirably suited to Russian conditions. In fact, in many ways it was even more applicable to the Russia of the 1880s than to the Germany of the 1840s. In Russia, the revolutionary movement had much deeper roots. 'We must not overlook the vitally important fact that with us the socialist movement began when capitalism was still in its embryo stage.'[1] It was therefore in a position to organize the industrial proletariat from its earliest years. Moreover, Russian capitalism had made a very late entry on to the stage of history and was doomed to live out its timid life caught between the Tsarist hammer and the proletarian anvil. When the anti-Tsarist revolution came, not the urban bourgeoisie but the proletariat would take the lead. Thus, the proletariat would enter the stage of bourgeois parliamentarianism well organized, tempered by victory in one revolution and ready for the next—the socialist— revolution. 'Our capitalism', he wrote, 'will fade without having fully flowered.' Just as 'in Germany the development of capitalism placed the working-class on a higher level of development than in England or in France and [just as] the resistance to capitalist exploitation was there more rapid and decisive,'[2] so now the Rus-

---

[1] G. V. Plekhanov, *Nashi raznoglasiia*, p. 212.   [2] *Ibid.* p. 299.

sian proletariat could be expected to catch up with or even to pass the German. He quoted approvingly that section of the *Communist Manifesto* which looked forward to the 'German bourgeois revolution' as the 'immediate prologue to the workers' revolution' and he explained that the Russian Marxists of 1883 had 'the right to hope that the social liberation of the Russian working-class will follow very quickly after the fall of absolutism. If the German bourgeoisie "came too late", then the Russian bourgeoisie came later still and its rule cannot last long.'[1]

By this use of Marxist dialectics, Plekhanov believed that he had overcome the dichotomy between economic determinism and socialist impatience. There was a satisfying completeness about his solution. It replaced the fundamental pessimism of much Populist thought ('If not *now*, then not for a very long time—perhaps *never*'[2]) with the confident certainty of Marxist laws—with every year the advance of capitalism brought the socialist revolution nearer. But equally it avoided the passivity so easily engendered by faith in historical inexorability and promised socialism 'in our time'. With its insistence that only the proletariat could undertake a socialist revolution it retained the first law of Populist belief— 'the liberation of the people is the task of the people itself'. And it was from this standpoint that Plekhanov attacked the plans of the *Narodnaia Volia* as fundamentally utopian and dictatorial (seeking 'to replace the initiative of a *class* by that of a *committee*, to make the task of the entire working population of the country that of an exclusive organization'[3]). But as against this, Plekhanov also reaffirmed those narrowly conspiratorial methods of organization which had characterized the Populist parties since 1876 and which had encouraged the *Narodnaia Volia* to abandon their early faith in a truly popular revolution—for the time being the most that he hoped for was 'the organization of workers' socialist circles'.[4]

His blue-print envisaged the establishment of a parliamentary bourgeois democracy, so making feasible an anti-Tsarist alliance with all the liberal forces at work in the upper levels of Russian society; but at the same time it assured the out-and-out socialists

---

[1] 'Sotsializm i politicheskaia bor'ba' (1883), in *Sochineniia*, ed. D. Riazanov (Moscow, 1923–), II, 86.

[2] P. Tkachev, *Izbrannye sochineniia na sotsial'no-politicheskie temy*, ed. B. P. Koz'min (Moscow, 1922–3), III, 70.

[3] G. V. Plekhanov, *Nashi raznoglasiia*, p. 222.

[4] 'Sotsializm i politicheskaia bor'ba', in *Sochineniia*, II, 84.

that the bourgeois régime would prove a transient inconvenience to be destroyed while still in its cradle. To the proletariat it offered all, for nothing could be achieved until the workers were conscious of their destiny, but for the time being the intelligentsia was to retain its ascendant rôle in the revolutionary movement. ('Our socialist intelligentsia must become the leader of the working-class in the liberation movement of today.'[1])

Plekhanov's writings of the mid-1880s undoubtedly represent an intellectual *tour de force* and as such they profoundly altered the character of the Russian revolutionary movement. An entire generation of revolutionaries came to Marxism as his disciples, seeing in his arguments proof that Marxism was as relevant to Russia's problems as to those of Western Europe. Early in their revolutionary careers both Lenin and Akimov were among the disciples. Yet, finally, both repudiated him. The very complexity of Plekhanov's thought—its dialectical reconciliation of opposites—gave it great initial strength but also made it ultimately unstable. His logical ingenuity could disguise but could not conjure away the basic dilemma that he had left unsolved.

If proletarian self-education was the primary goal, then bourgeois democracy and capitalism would have to be allowed to entrench themselves after the overthrow of the autocracy. But if the overriding aim was to establish a socialist régime on the ruins of Tsarism, then the emphasis on proletarian consciousness would have to be radically reduced—in a police state the possibilities for proletarian organization would always be severely limited. This dilemma was a root cause of the disputes which caught up the Marxists at successive stages. Should they merge into a united anti-Tsarist revolutionary front or should they rather establish an independent 'proletarian' movement? Should their party be highly centralized or allow room for local initiative and autonomy? Was it to be the party of an élite or of the masses? Should it seek to ally with the liberals or the peasants? Plekhanov seems never to have admitted that his plans contained any contradictions that could not be overcome by a truly dialectical, and therefore scientific, analysis. But by 1903 Akimov and Lenin at least had seen that there was a choice to be made and they made it, so irrevocably dividing up Plekhanov's intellectual inheritance.

Yet even before the Economist crisis which, in the years 1898–1902, produced the first major schism in the Party, Plekhanov and

[1] G. V. Plekhanov, *ibid.*

his Group for the Emancipation of Labour found their programme subjected to periodic attack. Criticism was provoked not only by Plekhanov's arguments in themselves but also by the enormous gap which in the 1880s divided the Group's aspirations—the establishment of an independent proletarian party capable of dominating Russia's two future revolutions—from its actual political strength. Founded in 1883 the Group for the Emancipation of Labour was made up of a mere handful of émigrés—Plekhanov, Aksel'rod, Deich, Vera Zasulich and V. I. Ignatov. Of them, Ignatov soon died of tuberculosis, while Deich was captured in 1884 by Bismarck's police and extradited to Russia, ending up in Siberian exile. His arrest was a disaster for the Group because he had been expected to act as liaison officer, to organize the transportation of the Group's publications across the frontier and to encourage the establishment of Marxist cells within the Empire. Without him, the three solitary exiles found themselves hopelessly isolated in Switzerland, unable to exert direct influence on their few scattered supporters in Russia and driven back more and more on to themselves, either to elaborate still further their theories of revolution or else (in the case of Plekhanov) to study the history of radical thought. Combined as it was with theoretical dogmatism, their organizational impotence laid them open to sharp attacks from all sides.

Not untypical was the relationship of Engels to the group of Russian Marxists in Switzerland. Pinning his hopes on a political revolution in Russia, on the overthrow of Alexander III, he failed to see why the Russian Marxists should isolate themselves from the Populist revolutionaries, from Lavrov and the remnants of the *Narodnaia Volia*. Aware of the enthusiastic support which Marx had given the *Narodovol'tsy* before his death in 1883, Engels was not impressed by Plekhanov's theory that only the proletariat organized in a separate party of its own could bring down the Tsarist régime. Ignoring the fact that his own open letter to Tkachev had supplied Plekhanov with many of his basic arguments, he explained in a letter of 1885 to Vera Zasulich why he was unimpressed by Plekhanov's attack on the Populist revolutionaries. 'Let us grant that these people [Tikhomirov and other *Narodovol'tsy*] claim that they can seize power—but so what? Let them only open a breach in the dam and the current will soon rid them of their illusions . . . what is important in my opinion is that in Russia a jolt should be produced which will start the revolution.

Whether the signal is given by one group or another, whether it takes place under one banner or another—that is not so important for me. Let it be a palace conspiracy. It will be swept away next day.'[1] A year later, Vera Zasulich wrote dejectedly that she had not been 'entirely in agreement' with Engels and had therefore torn up her original reply.[2]

Engels was simply not attracted by the attempt to transplant to the Russia of the 1880s those tactics which Marx and he had applied to the Germany of the 1840s. Excessive doctrinal disputation among the Russian émigrés would only fragment and undermine the forces pitted against the Tsarist régime. 'Everybody', he wrote in 1891 of the émigré colonies,

knows everybody else and consequently every step forward is inevitably accompanied by splits, by polemics, which take on an extremely personal character. This is typical of every political 'emigration'. We too had our share of this in the period 1849–60. But at the same time I was always convinced that the party with sufficient moral strength to rise above this atmosphere of personal scores and to refuse to be influenced by these squabbles would gain a great advantage over the other parties.[3]

If Engels really hoped to soften the disputatious nature of his Russian disciples, he hoped in vain. The tolerance which he permitted himself in the 1880s and 1890s as the revered figurehead of the great German Social Democratic Party was utterly alien to Plekhanov who saw in the correct interpretation of doctrine a key element in the shaping of revolutionary victory. After all, in *Our Disagreements*, his booklet of 1884, he had written 'There is much confusion in the heads of our "revolutionary youth". But let us hope that this confusion will give way finally to the theories of contemporary, scientific socialism and will cease to paralyse the success of our revolutionary movement.'[4]

If Engels felt it merely inexpedient to emphasize the ultimate goal, proletarian socialism, at the expense of the immediate objective, the overthrow of Tsarism, Stepniak-Kravchinskii objected on principle to Plekhanov's double-edged evaluation of parliamentary democracy. Kravchinskii, well known as a revolutionary and novelist, spoke for that school of Russian Populists who, convinced of the need for a liberal-socialist alliance against the autocracy, had come to see a democratic Russia as an impera-

---

[1] *Perepiska*, p. 251.　　　　[2] *Ibid.* pp. 257–8.
[3] *Ibid.* p. 262.　　　　　　[4] *Nashi raznoglasiia*, p. 309.

tive goal of absolute value. 'Hitherto', he wrote in 1892, 'we socialists have regarded the word "constitution" as somehow unclean . . . [But we now] recognize free speech and the free press and the free vote as adequate and—so long as they are guaranteed by an inviolable law—as the only weapons in the socialist struggle of the future[1] . . . We are repelled by the idea that we can regard freedom merely as a means to something else.'[2] In reply to this attack Plekhanov pointed out that the Marxists were fighting for parliamentary democracy and nobody could object if they warned the proletariat to prepare in advance for the defence of its own interests within the framework of such a democracy. 'How is this an insult to political democracy?'[3] he asked. Yet elsewhere in the same brochure it emerged that this self-defence of the down-trodden could include overrunning the first democratically-elected parliament (*Zemskii Sobor*). 'It could happen that the people, as at the time of the Great [French] Revolution, would *purge* the *Zemskii Sobor* with a new revolutionary sweep of the hand. But in that case, too, it would act under the leadership of the Social Democrats.'[4]

Against the Populist calls for a united revolutionary front (even if supported by Engels) Plekhanov could always reply that the intelligentsia and the liberals alone could never overthrow the autocracy, that in Russia 'political freedom will be won by the working-class or not at all'.[5] As the *Narodnaia Volia* crumbled into nothingness, as capitalist industrialism rapidly gained momentum and as Alexander III consolidated his régime quite unhampered by the liberal forces in government and society, so Plekhanov's views won mounting support. The new generation of revolutionaries who came on to the scene at the end of the 1880s turned more and more to Marxism. But Plekhanov's dialectical formula invited criticism from the left no less than from the right.

This fact was clearly illustrated during the great famine which overtook Russia in the years 1891–2. The Group for the Emancipation of Labour hoped that the enraged protests of liberal circles

[1] S. Stepniak, *Chego nam nuzhno i nachalo kontsa* (London, 1892), p. 23.

[2] *Ibid.* p. 28.

[3] *O zadachakh sotsialistov v bor'be s golodom v Rossii* (Geneva, 1892), p. 72.

[4] *Ibid.* pp. 76–7. The *Zemskii Sobor* was the advisory assembly which was called together by the Tsars during the sixteenth and seventeenth centuries. Its membership was predominantly noble, and it last met in 1684. During the nineteenth century, *Zemskii Sobor* was a term sometimes used to describe the long-expected Russian parliament of the future.

[5] G. V. Plekhanov, 'Kak dobivat'sia konstitutsii' (1890), *Sochineniia*, III, 16.

inside Russia would perhaps snowball into full-scale political revolt. Plekhanov and Aksel'rod therefore threw their support behind the Society for the War on Famine, an émigré and non-party group, and Plekhanov at once wrote a manifesto, *All Russia is Disintegrating*, an impassioned plea for revolution. Surely the liberal elements in Russia, particularly those grouped around the Zemstvos, could no longer stand idly by as disaster overtook their land? 'All those honest Russians who do not belong to the world of mere money-makers, kulaks and Russian bureaucrats [*chinovniki*] must at once begin to agitate for a *Zemskii Sobor*.'[1] But this appeal to 'all honest Russians' and their participation in a non-socialist front exposed the Group to criticism from their own more recent adherents. A number of young Russian Marxists abroad, led by Lev Grozovskii and Boris Krichevskii, denounced the policy of the Group as in fact more liberal than socialist. (They were both to maintain their hostility to the Group in future years: Krichevskii as a leader of the Economists; Grozovskii as a founder and leader, together with Rosa Luxemburg, of the Social Democratic Party of the Kingdom of Poland.) If, they now asked, the Russian Marxists had a unique mission—the organization and guidance of the pro-letariat—how could they act like mere constitutionalists? They recalled that the *Communist Manifesto*, while calling for co-operation with all opposition forces, had also insisted that the communists must 'never cease for a single instant' to emphasize 'the antagonism between bourgeoisie and proletariat'.[2] Plekhanov had surely slipped off his own tight-rope. He, of course, dismissed the criticism as showing crude ignorance of the tactics required by the dialectical method. 'In all the brochures and in all the letters,' he explained to Engels in 1894, 'we said that our comrades should exploit the situation for *constitutional* agitation. Mr Iogikhes [Grozovskii] taunted us as traitors to socialism—"For a true socialist, constitutional agitation is pointless!" You can see the profundity of his thought.'[3]

Yet, for all their scorn, the Group for the Emancipation of Labour were worried by these young critics from their own camp. They were hurt by their isolation from Russia and were vulnerable to the arguments of the younger revolutionary émigrés who com-

---

[1] Plekhanov, *Vserossiiskoe razzorenie* (St Petersburg, 1906), p. 61.

[2] Marx and Engels, *Werke*, IV, 492–3.

[3] 'Pis'ma G. Plekhanova k F. Engel'su i R. Fisheru', *Pod znamenem marksizma*, no. 12 (Nov.–Dec. 1923), p. 18.

plained that the veteran *troika* had in fact not given clear-cut political guidance to the emergent Marxist movement in Russia. Why did not Plekhanov lay down practical proposals to supplement his broad theories? He took up the challenge at once. He now tried to show how the Marxist revolutionaries could build up a broad movement among the masses without losing their own identity, without sacrificing their guiding rôle.

The Agitation Programme: Triumphs and Tensions (1892–98)

In his booklet of 1892, *On the Tasks of the Russian Social Democrats during the Famine in Russia,* Plekhanov argued that the Marxists should conduct their educational work among the proletariat on two levels—'propaganda' and 'agitation'. 'A sect', he explained, 'can be satisfied with propaganda in the narrow sense of the word: a political party never . . . A propagandist gives *many* ideas to one or a few people, while an agitator gives only one or only a few ideas but to masses of people . . . Yet history is made by the masses.'[1] 'Thanks to agitation, the necessary link between the "heroes" and the "crowd", between "the masses" and "their leaders", is forged and tempered.'[2] In short, rather than concentrate merely on 'the organization of workers' socialist circles', the revolutionaries should try to move out and arouse mass discontent on the basis of political or 'economic' slogans such as the demand for the eight-hour working day. Demands of this kind would attract all the workers towards the socialist movement. 'Thus all—even the most backward—workers will be clearly convinced that the carrying out of at least some socialist measures is of value to the working-class . . . Such economic reforms as the shortening of the working day are good if only because they bring direct benefits to the workers.'[3] It was the duty of the party 'to formulate economic demands suitable for the present moment'.[4]

With this declaration Plekhanov opened up new prospects before the Russian Marxists. Hitherto, he had emphasized the need to create the nucleus of a future proletarian party, to build up a network of 'those workers' circles which now represent the beginnings of the future Russian labour party'.[5] This skeleton

[1] *O zadachakh*, p. 58.
[2] *Ibid.* p. 81.
[3] *Ibid.* pp. 58–9.
[4] *Ibid.* p. 79.
[5] 'Vtoroi proekt programmy russkikh sotsial-demokratov', in Plekhanov, *Sochineniia*, II, 402. This programme was not made public until 1887, but

party was apparently expected to enter the struggle against the Tsarist régime as soon as the political revolution broke out and then to convert itself rapidly into a true class party. But now, in 1892, Plekhanov opened up a further prospect: the skeleton party could begin to recruit the masses under its wing even in the Tsarist police state. Partial demands could be advanced even now. As a result, a crucial question which could only be settled finally after the downfall of the autocracy took on an immediate relevance. What was to be the relationship of the party to its mass following? Where was initiative to lie? This was not, of course, a question which concerned Plekhanov at this stage, but it was revealed with the passage of time.

Meanwhile his call for 'agitation' met with a ready response from certain Marxist groups in Russia. The great famine of the winter of 1891–2 had jolted the young *intelligenty* who for almost a decade had seemed resigned to observing rather than making history. Stung by the taunts of the veteran Populists that Marxism in Russia could only be a quietist faith, a number of students in St Petersburg responded almost immediately to Plekhanov's plea for action and devised a scheme to print and distribute illegal literature for popular consumption. Despite the scepticism of many of the older Marxist students, they went ahead with their plans and only abandoned them when the police arrested the ringleaders. It was in the western areas of the Empire, however, that Plekhanov's plea for 'economic' agitation fell on the most fertile ground because there had already been a spectacular strike in Łódź in 1892 and, indeed, ever since 1889 a hard core of Polish workers had been organized in an illegal union—the *Związek Robotniczy*—for mutual aid and strike action.

Thus, a very active group of Marxist *intelligenty*, who (frequently as the result of police expulsion from university cities) were in Vilna, made a bid in the years 1892–3 to break out of the small and constricting workers' circles and to infiltrate the workshops and small factories of the town. The new tactics met with startling success if only because the agitators demanded nothing less than the enforcement of an obsolete law from the reign of Catherine II which made twelve hours the maximum legal working day. Under

N. L. Sergievskii has argued convincingly that it was actually written in 1885. See his 'Kogda i po kakomu povodu byl napisan Plekhanovym Proekt programmy russkikh sots.-demokratov', *Proletarskaia revoliutsiia*, no. 1 (72) (1928), pp. 85–7.

the cover of the law, it proved possible to encourage the workers to organize in various mutual aid societies (*kassy*) and to wage strikes, which spread to many of the major towns of Lithuania and Belorussia. Made bold by the relative economic prosperity of these years and attracted by the illegal meetings and literature (which had been switched from Russian to the better understood Yiddish), the Jewish workers proved eager to organize themselves. Each trade developed its own workers' organization which controlled the collection of funds and other day-to-day matters but which was dominated by the agitators who, in turn, met to receive instructions from the revolutionary leaders (in Vilna, such Russified Jewish *intelligenty* as Arkadii Kremer and Samuel Gozhanskii).

It was Kremer who in a small brochure written in 1894, *On Agitation*, summarized the goals of the strike movement and formulated what soon came to be known as the Vilna Programme. Kremer's arguments (which he had formulated with the help of the young Martov who had come to Vilna on expulsion from St Petersburg) followed closely the main theses of Plekhanov's booklet. It was imperative, he explained, to find ways and means to win the support of the masses, for only the workers could liberate themselves. Popular 'agitation' was the only method acceptable to a true Marxist, for 'propaganda' restricted to small circles had led to the ' degeneration of the socialist cause into nothing more than a sect'.[1] Moreover, Kremer shared the fear, central to Plekhanov's thought, that the working-class could be harnessed to bourgeois interests. Even if 'the bourgeoisie learns to be revolutionary', he wrote, 'it must not be given the chance to act as teacher and leader of our proletariat'.[2]

Nevertheless, there were nuances foreign to Plekhanov's work of 1892. There was a tendency to reduce the rôle of the leadership and to assume that the mass movement would eventually gain an autonomy of its own. Where Plekhanov had described agitation as 'the link' between 'the heroes' and 'the crowds', Kremer clearly saw the task of the leadership to be the conversion of the masses into 'heroes'. His brochure therefore did not assign separate functions to 'propaganda' (for the leaders) and 'agitation' (for the masses), but on the contrary called for the unification of propaganda and agitation in a broad campaign to educate the working-

[1] *Ob agitatsii* (Geneva, 1896), p. 20. (Although the brochure bears the date 1896, it was actually published at the end of 1897.)
[2] *Ibid.* p. 12.

class. Plekhanov had seen agitation as a way to provide the commanders—the tightly knit skeleton party—with an army. Kremer now suggested that the agitation campaign would teach the ranks how to select their own officers. This barely articulated (but potentially fundamental) divergence was typified by Kremer's confidence that the British trade-union movement would inevitably turn to political action as soon as it had exhausted the purely industrial possibilities. 'The attainment of political power', explained Kremer,

is the main task of the militant proletariat. But it is only possible to face the working-class with this task when the 'economic' struggle brings it up against the blatant impossibility of improving its position under the given conditions . . . The party . . . has nothing more to do than to choose the right moment for the transition to the political struggle and to prepare those elements within the masses themselves who alone can make it possible for this transaction to take place with minimal losses.[1]

Kremer's pamphlet thus acted as a kind of distorting mirror to Plekhanov's brochure of 1892, but it was only in 1901—six years after he had received the manuscript—that Plekhanov decided to draw attention to what he by then considered to be a fatal flaw: the deflation of the rôle of the leadership; the failure to distinguish clearly between the class (the proletariat) and the party (its *avant-garde*). Meanwhile, the agitation programme continued to run its natural course.

In the years 1893–7, the Vilna Programme gradually won almost universal approval from the leading revolutionary Marxists in Russia. Those who had seen it at work in Vilna moved out over the years to new centres: Gozhanskii to Belostok, Portnoi-Noakh to Grodno, Liakhovskii to Kiev, Mil' to Warsaw, Nikitin-Sponti to Moscow, Dushkan and Frankfurt to Ekaterinoslav, Aizenshtat to Odessa, Martov and Gorev to St Petersburg. Whether or not to change over from propaganda to agitation, from the educational circle to the factory floor, became the main point of debate among the Social Democrats of the capital towards the end of 1894. Although, as in Vilna, many of the workers were reluctant to abandon well-tried methods of work, the *intelligenty*—with one or two exceptions such as German B. Krasin—seem in principle to have accepted *On Agitation*, to have agreed that a change of tactics was essential. Thus, when a strike broke out on Christmas Eve,

[1] *Ob agitatsii*, pp. 7–9.

1894, at Semiannikov's shipbuilding and machine works, the major Social Democratic group in the capital—the so-called 'veterans'—soon responded with leaflets to be scattered through the factory.

On 19 February 1895 a small informal meeting was held in St Petersburg at which revolutionaries experienced in the Vilna system—Kopel'zon, Liakhovskii, and Sponti—met with two of the leading 'veterans' of the capital, Krzhizhanovskii and Ul'ianov (Lenin). Although the latter argued with Sponti about the exact form agitation should take, all were agreed that the time had come to go to the factories with simple slogans appealing to the immediate interests of the workers. On his return in September 1895 from a visit to Western Europe, Ul'ianov went to Vilna to seek the support of the revolutionaries there for his plan to have workers' literature published in Switzerland. And when Martov returned from Vilna to St Petersburg in October 1895 he was able to win Ul'ianov's active co-operation in applying the new methods, and his own circle of friends (which included Liakhovskii and Gorev) now merged with the 'veterans'. It was this enlarged group which issued a steady stream of popular leaflets during the autumn of 1895 and which in December took the name Union of Struggle for the Emancipation of the Working Class.

The Union's leaflets were usually addressed to the workers of a given factory and played upon their particular grievances. Its appeals coincided with a mounting wave of industrial unrest—the characteristic result of appalling economic conditions meeting a period of economic boom—and its leaflets were eagerly snapped up and read in the factories. The Union was able to heap fuel on the smouldering discontent and must have been at least partially responsible for the growing boldness of the workers during the early months of 1896 and even for the massive strike of May, when some thirty thousand textile workers were out. So menacing did these developments appear to the authorities that on 2 June 1897 the government finally agreed on the terms of a statute which fixed the legal maximum for the working day at eleven and a half hours. The Marxist underground had won a remarkable moral victory. What had hitherto appeared to be a harmless, even anachronistic doctrine in such a backward country as Russia, was now seen as a threat of intimidating dimensions.

Nevertheless, despite—or, rather, because of—their success, the strike period, the Vilna Programme and 'economic' agitation eventually led to the disruption of the movement. As long as the movement had confined itself to laying down contingency plans for the hypothetical revolution, disputes had tended to be purely theoretical, acrimonious certainly, but restricted to a tiny circle of protagonists and without practical application. Now, however, the movement was growing fast in numbers and influence, was facing complex day-to-day problems, and was making new and rising demands on all its members. Tactical questions thus took on an immediate, as well as long-term, significance and became all the more explosive. There were two key organizations in which the breaking-point was eventually to be reached—the St Petersburg Union of Struggle and the Union of Social Democrats Abroad.

Disputes among the Russian Marxists abroad had occurred at increasingly frequent intervals since 1887. These disputes occasionally took an ideological form—the criticism, for instance, of Plekhanov's *All Russia is Disintegrating* or of his Polish policy— but their frequency was a symptom of a basic clash between two generations. The members of the Group saw themselves, quite rightly, as the theoretical founders of Russian Marxism. They believed that their main function should be to act as ideological guides to the Russian movement and even perhaps (after the death of Engels) to the international socialist fraternity. Equally, they felt that they had a right to expect assistance from junior recruits and that they should be free to employ such assistance in the way they considered most useful.

But the 'youngsters', who had come abroad either to study or else on various missions from the revolutionary committees in Russia, tended to see the situation in a different light. They were ready to assist the Group, but they expected to have a measure of control over the work they did: fund-raising, the publication and transportation of illegal literature, the maintenance of communications with Russia. They were ready to help as equals in one organization but not as technical assistants. In principle, the Group agreed in 1887–8 and again in 1892–3 to create a Union of Russian Social Democrats Abroad, but negotiations broke down on this central point of discord. To the 'veterans' it seemed absurd that they should have to surrender any control of publications to 'people who have not been through the revolutionary school'[1] or

---

[1] See the letter of Aksel'rod to Plekhanov, 1887, in *Perepiska G. V. Plekhanova i P. B. Aksel'roda*, ed. P. A. Berlin, V. S. Voitinskii, and B. I. Nikolaevskii (Moscow, 1925), I, 27.

who had not proved themselves 'true-believing Marxists'.[1] To the 'youngsters' it seemed equally absurd that any revolutionary organization abroad, where there was little danger from the police, should be based on the principle of built-in privileges.

The 'youngsters' usually arrived straight from Russia, full of confidence after their illegal adventures, brash, narrow in outlook, better read in Marxism than in the other classics of European thought and literature. And all this led them to clash disastrously with Plekhanov's severely correct, ironic, cultivated and somewhat fastidious style. One furious collision followed another, and as early as 1894 a number of the most energetic and brilliant young Marxists had quarrelled irrevocably with the Group: Ermanskii, Riazanov, Parvus, Grozovskii, Mil', Krichevskii, Teplov, Kurnatovskii and Rosa Luxemburg were only the most prominent on the list.

A constantly recurring factor in these disputes was the problem of popular literature for the Russian workers. The Group accepted the vital importance of such publications but, in practice, was reluctant to involve itself too deeply in work so mundane and exhausting. They saw their primary duty as the production of more searching and original works which would blaze new tactical paths, win over student recruits or serve as 'propaganda' for the worker élite. (Plekhanov reputedly said that the Russian worker was 'not stupid but poor'.[2]) The Group suggested that agitation could not be effectively aided from abroad but had to be organized and run by men on the spot. But these arguments failed to convince—Plekhanov, after all, had proclaimed that the first priority was to win a mass following among the workers—and it was on the failure of the Group to publish popular literature that criticism centred even as early as 1887. In 1894 some of the 'youngsters', unable to reach an agreement with the 'veterans', started two independent popular publication projects, one headed by Ermanskii and Kurnatovskii, the other by Grozovskii and Krichevskii.

So long as these disputes were confined to émigré circles they

---

[1] In a letter of March 1893, Zasulich wrote to Aksel'rod that she was opposed to the Group's joining the Union of Russian Social Democrats because it was impossible to find 'true-believing' (*pravovernye*) Social Democrats among the younger generation. This letter is in the Aksel'rod Archive at the International Institute for Social History, Amsterdam, to which I was very generously given full access.

[2] O. A. Ermanskii, *Iz perezhitogo (1887–1921 gg.)* (Moscow and Leningrad, 1927), pp. 33–4.

acted as mere pin-pricks easily ignored by the Group, but the rapid growth of the 'agitation' movement in Russia tended to alter radically the existing balance of forces. In a letter of 1894 to Engels, Plekhanov had dismissed Krichevskii as a man 'entirely unknown'[1] in Russia, but from early 1895 revolutionaries from Russia on missions to Switzerland were found to be pleading those same arguments which had long become commonplace abroad. During their visits of 1895 both Ul'ianov and Nikitin-Sponti urged that the time had come to increase the output of popular and semi-popular literature. The former brought the manuscript of *On Agitation* to be published by the Group, while the latter was particularly aggressive in his demands and accused the Group of hostility to 'economic' agitation, an accusation which Aksel'rod denied but which seemed to find support in the list of the Group's publications.

Under pressure from Russia, the Group eventually agreed in 1895 to form a small Union of Russian Social Democrats Abroad to assist it in its publication work. The choice of membership was to be in the hands of the Group, which in 1896, urged on by Ul'ianov, began to publish a semi-popular miscellany, *Rabotnik* [*The Worker*]. Later in the year, after consultations with Potresov and Struve during the London Congress of the International, it was decided to publish in addition the *Listok Rabotnika* [*The Worker Supplement*], to be devoted primarily to news of the labour movement and industrial unrest in Russia. Yet another concession was the agreement of 1897 that anybody who had been a member of a leading Social Democratic committee in Russia should have the right to join the Union Abroad.

Thus, the long-awaited expansion of the movement in Russia had not brought the 'veterans' authority or prestige, but merely a growing load of laborious responsibilities. True, Plekhanov refused to take part in the publication of popular literature, but this simply meant that even more work devolved on the over-burdened Aksel'rod, the highly-strung Vera Zasulich and their main assistant, Kol'tsov. From 1896 the letters of Aksel'rod and Zasulich revealed an irritable dissatisfaction with the type of work for which they were responsible and a lack of trust in the ability of the younger revolutionary generation to guide the workers along the correct path. In a letter of late 1896, Vera Zasulich complained that she 'began to revolt' as soon as she set

---

[1] *Pod znamenem marksizma*, no. 12 (1923), p. 16.

eyes on 'the hopeless, incredible phrases'[1] of the articles presented for *Listok Rabotnika* and at the same time Aksel'rod was writing that 'of course, it is possible to publish such literary caricatures without me'.[2] This note recurred time and again. In the spring of 1898 Aksel'rod admitted in a letter to Plekhanov that 'for reasons beyond our control we have treated our functions abroad more than casually' and that Vera Zasulich and he were 'eager to escape having to edit illiterate and semi-literate publications'.[3] Or as she put it: 'And if we could only believe that this hard labour of ours is of use to the Russian movement! But I am convinced that it is not. What we have done so badly, they [the youngsters] can also do.'[4]

Yet there were numerous factors—personal income, prestige, distrust, a sense of duty—which deterred the pair from resigning the responsibilities which they found so futile and burdensome. For example, they had assured those of the younger generation, such as Lenin and Potresov, with whom they had established friendly relations, that they would supervise publishing activity abroad and they did not want to go back on this promise. (From a letter of 1895 to Aksel'rod it emerges that Lenin expected the Group to counteract such negative influences as the provincialism he had just met in Vilna.) Again, they were afraid that if left to themselves, the 'youngsters' might upset the balance of the dialectical Marxism which they had taught since 1883.

And developments in the St Petersburg Union of Struggle only increased their suspicions. Ul'ianov, Martov and many other founders of the St Petersburg Union had been arrested in the winter of 1895–6, and increasingly the agitation movement had come to depend on the factory workers themselves. Thus, the grandiose strikes of the summer of 1896 were not controlled but were merely urged on by the Union of Struggle. While the Union had been emasculated by a series of arrests, the workers had discovered that through the sheer weight of numbers they were a power to be reckoned with. What conclusions were to be drawn from this development? The time had come for the St Petersburg revolutionaries to reassess the tactics employed by their agitation campaign.

One opinion, forcibly advocated by Stepan Radchenko, was

---

[1] *Gruppa Osvobozhdeniia truda*, ed. L. Deich (Moscow, 1928), VI, 174.

[2] *Perepiska G. V. Plekhanova*, I, 166.

[3] *Ibid.* p. 32.   [4] *Gruppa*, VI, 205.

that their overriding concern must be to maintain intact the central core of the movement, the revolutionary nucleus, the small group of *intelligenty* which constituted the Union of Struggle. A strike could succeed without the aid of the *intelligenty*, but not a revolutionary organization. The leadership had first and foremost to safeguard its own existence, even if it had to withdraw into its shell.

In opposition, innovators such as Konstantin Takhtarev and Apolinariia Iakubova argued that if the *intelligenty* were in constant danger of arrest and if the workers were becoming more self-confident, then it followed that the load of responsibility had to be broadened, power shared. Throughout the 1890s the workers and *intelligenty* had usually organized their own circles independently of each other. True, the *intelligenty* had visited the workers' circles as propagandists in charge of education classes or discussions, and whenever the workers had established a central executive body, representative of all their circles in the city (the Central Workers' Circle of 1890–2 or the Central Workers' Group of 1895) the *intelligenty* had always had the right to be represented at its meetings. But now Takhtarev and Iakubova proposed to make this right reciprocal. They urged that two delegates from the Workers' Group be invited to join the Union of Struggle.

Finally, there were those in the centre, like Gorev, who supported the *status quo*, who wanted the Union to remain a small group of revolutionary *intelligenty* willing to throw itself into every industrial battle, but unwilling to surrender any of its autonomy to the workers' organizations. It was this position which Ul'ianov (Lenin) and Martov strongly defended when in February 1897 they were released from custody for a few days prior to their journey to Siberian exile. Lenin in particular made it absolutely clear that he was opposed to any changes in the structure of the Union. He granted that individual workers might be suitable candidates for the Union, but he insisted that on no account should their organizations be yielded the right to automatic representation. Control had to come solely from above.

Echoes of this conflict were carried beyond St Petersburg when late in 1897 a group of workers in the capital began to bring out *Rabochaia Mysl'* [*Labour Thought*]. (From 1898 it was published abroad as the official organ of the St Petersburg Union, which had now passed completely under the control of new recruits—the original leaders had nearly all been arrested since 1895.) The new journal manifested an ill-concealed hostility and condescension to the revolutionary intelligentsia. 'The labour movement', read the programme of *Rabochaia Mysl'*, 'owes its vitality to the fact that the worker himself has finally snatched his fate from the hands of his leaders and has taken it into his own hands. This is easily understood. So long as the movement was only a means to quiet the guilty conscience of the repentant intellectual, it was alien to the worker himself.'[1] Such sentiments could only disturb the Group. Although they saw the independent action of the worker as ultimately crucial, his independence was valueless unless reinforced by political consciousness and for this he was meanwhile dependent on the educated Marxists, the revolutionary *intelligenty*.

Moreover, in the summer of 1897 Plekhanov had fallen out with two leaders of the agitation movement in Russia, Arkadii Kremer from Vilna and Takhtarev from St Petersburg. At their brief and acrimonious meeting, Takhtarev and Kremer asked Plekhanov why the Group which published so little itself—only one number of *Listok Rabotnika* appeared between November 1896 and November 1897—should have refused to publish popular workers' literature written in Russia. For its part, the Group pointed out that the Marxists in Russia had still not created that unified revolutionary organization which had been envisaged by the Draft Programme of 1885 and which had again been advocated by the Russians who had attended the London Congress of the International in 1896.

Thus, by the end of 1897 the 'economic' agitation movement had become the cause of increasing tensions and doubts. Technical issues began to take on ideological dimensions. A number of the 'youngsters' abroad—Kuskova, Prokopovich, Grishin-Kopel'zon (all of whom lived in Berlin) and Peskin—identified themselves whole-heartedly with the strike movement in Russia. They considered the emphasis on day-to-day industrial disputes to be a necessary stage in the growth of a large, powerful labour movement and believed that even under Tsarism this stage might well continue for a lengthy period. In contrast, the 'veterans' showed themselves increasingly anxious that the movement pass rapidly on to a more militant 'political' and revolutionary stage. They were afraid that the worker might be tempted to rest on his laurels. Their concern made itself felt in the private letters of Vera Zasulich and in a number of articles of Aksel'rod.

---

[1] *Rabochaia mysl'*, no. 1 (October 1897), p. 1.

In a letter of February 1898, Zasulich described Prokopovich and his friends as 'narrow Marxists' for whom 'economics works in such a way that it forces them and the workers to accept the idea that under present conditions the workers can by strikes alone achieve the prosperity and political *rights* which the Russian bourgeoisie *has already achieved*'.[1] Such theories could lead the workers astray. 'What torments me', she wrote, 'is the repellent epidemic of the "ultra-economist" psychology which fills the heads of the Russians . . . Among the intelligentsia it is only a fad. It will pass. But in my way of seeing things, I assign tremendous importance to those ideas which will enter the heads of the masses at that moment (now imminent) when the age-old natural-economy way of thinking is destroyed.'[2] Or as she put it in another letter: 'But when the economists reign, they will teach the workers to croak according to their own tune.'[3] The future achievements of the workers were seen as dependent on the quality of their teachers.

It was Aksel'rod who undertook to reveal publicly the danger of allowing the labour movement to become bogged down in the swamp of narrow economic demands. In a series of articles written in 1896–7 and published in the winter of 1897–8 he pointed out that 'economic' agitation represented only one aspect of Russian Marxist tactics (the necessity to organize the proletariat), and that there had always been another aspect (the necessity to ally with all other constitutional and anti-Tsarist forces). In a critique of Kremer's brochure *On Agitation* he pointed out that the brochure spoke in terms of proletarian self-sufficiency. It painted a naive—even Bakuninist—picture of social relations. To all the wealthy and privileged classes, it opposed all the labourers. Over-simplified, it failed to distinguish between total enemies and enemies who were also temporary allies. Aksel'rod placed high hopes on the enlightened Russian landowners and on the intelligentsia—the 'third element'—grouped around the Zemstvos. The proletariat would be handicapped in its attempts to spur forward all potential rebels unless it avoided two possible extremes: the temptation to bury itself in purely 'trade-union' affairs (Aksel'rod accused Kremer of overestimating the political awareness of the British trade-union movement) and the temptation to fight alone, to make a direct 'Bakuninist' or 'Blanquist' revolution. The workers

[1] *Gruppa*, VI, 194.   [2] *Ibid.* p. 196.
[3] *Ibid.* p. 242.

required not only strikes but also 'education and organization'.[1] Aksel'rod's strictures clearly revealed the tensions which from the first had been the concomitant of the Group's tactical theories. The working-class was the primary force called upon to overthrow the Tsar but not the only force and it had therefore to be self-sufficient but not too self-sufficient, ready to defend its immediate and intermediary interests but also to retain its long-term vision. Like Plekhanov in his *All Russia is Disintegrating* of 1892, Aksel'rod had tipped the scales sharply towards a constitutionalist alliance—perhaps even further than Plekhanov now wished and certainly much too far for Lenin and Martov, who read his articles in eastern Siberia.

But the admonitions of Aksel'rod, the irritation of Vera Zasulich with the 'economist' exaggerations of certain of the 'youngsters', the inability of Plekhanov to establish any kind of friendly relationship with the majority of the underground leaders from Russia, and Ul'ianov's tiff with the successor generation of the St Petersburg Union—these strains and stresses were not regarded before March or April 1898 as indicative of a major crisis in the movement. For example, in *Tasks of the Russian Social Democrats*, which Lenin wrote in 1897, he selected the St Petersburg Union as the perfect model for the Russian Marxists. In the same year, a pamphlet of Plekhanov described the 'agitation' movement in glowing colours. ('If, earlier, the Social Democrats using propaganda won control of our revolutionary world in a relatively short time, what is to be expected now that they have taken up agitation with such success?'[2]) For all their complaints, Aksel'rod and Zasulich did not even consider the possibility of an open break with the 'youngsters' abroad, still less with those in Russia. Certainly they had criticized and would continue to criticize 'in a friendly way'[3] (as Zasulich put it in a letter of 1898) but they would continue to work with the younger generation.

In fact, early in 1898 there were ample grounds for the view that the relations between the veterans and their wayward 'economist' disciples were entering a period of tranquillity. Vera Zasulich had given *Rabochaia Mysl'* (no. 2) a warm welcome, while Aksel'rod had acceded to the most pressing demand of the Berlin group

---

[1] Aksel'rod, *Istoricheskoe polozhenie i vzaimnoe otnoshenie liberal'noi i sotsialisticheskoi demokratii v Rossii* (Geneva, 1898), p. 28.

[2] Plekhanov, *Novyi povod protiv russkoi sotsial'demokratii* (Geneva, 1897), p. 32.

[3] *Gruppa*, VI, 194.

(Prokopovich, Kuskova, Grishin and Bukhgolts)—that Kol'tsov be replaced as secretary of the Union Abroad. Kol'tsov, who was a devoted admirer of Plekhanov and shared the Group's doubts about the strike movement, was widely considered to have acted both inefficiently and in a highly authoritarian manner as secretary. Now, in February 1898, Aksel'rod had agreed to ally with the 'Berliners' in a 'revolution' against Kol'tsov and to give them a larger share in the control of the *Listok Rabotnika*.[1] Prokopovich and Kuskova were to come to Switzerland to settle the details of the new arrangement and Kuskova was then to join Vera Zasulich for a holiday in Florence.

Developments within Russia also promised well for a growing rapprochement between the veterans abroad and the leaders of the movement at home. The Social Democratic movement in St Petersburg was divided for and against the *Rabochaia Mysl'* and was tending to splinter into various factions, but in the southern and western areas a new enthusiasm for unification, organization, and political action was emerging. In September 1897, representatives from the major Jewish Social Democratic committees of western Russia met in Vilna and established the centralized General Jewish Labour Union in Russia and Poland—the Bund. It is true that Kremer, who was the prime mover in this development, revealed again, as in his *On Agitation*, a faith in the possibility of creating a genuine workers party even in Tsarist Russia and, at his suggestion, the designation 'Social Democratic' was omitted from the title of the organization. 'A Social Democratic group', Kremer is reported to have argued at the congress, 'is only a handful of people who adhere to Social Democratic principles and are the leaders of the labour movement of one town or another, of one region or another. A union of such groups would be a union of the "summits"' . . . There would be no room in it for all the labouring masses, and this would be deplorable, for the Bund will only become strong when all the working masses in the struggle join it.'[2] Nevertheless, a major step had been taken towards greater centralization and at the same time (the autumn of 1897) a firmly entrenched and energetic Social Democratic group in Kiev began to publish the *Rabochaia Gazeta* [*Workers Gazette*] which in its second number urged the necessity to unite the scattered groups of Russian Marxists in one organization and to place a greater

[1] *Perepiska G. V. Plekhanova*, I, 206.
[2] *Die Arbeter Shtime*, no. 6 (17 October 1897), p. 2.

emphasis on the political aims of the movement. This delighted the veterans in Switzerland, who had strongly advised the journal to fight parochialism and over-emphasis on strikes.

Then in March 1898 the Party—the creation of which the Group had urged for some fifteen years—was finally established at a small Congress in Minsk. Among those present were representatives of the Bund (including Kremer), of the *Rabochaia Gazeta* (Eidel'man and Vigdorchik), and of the St Petersburg Union (Radchenko, an old comrade of Lenin and Martov). The Party took the name of Russian Social Democratic Party (almost immediately changed by the survivors of the Central Committee to the Russian Social Democratic Labour Party, or RSDLP), appointed the Union of Russian Social Democrats (still controlled by the Group) as its representative abroad, and decided to ask the Marxist intellectual and theoretician, Peter Struve, to draw up the Party's first official proclamation. Struve's *Manifesto*, published in April 1898, declared boldly that the first necessity of the proletariat was political freedom and that 'the Russian proletariat *alone* can win for itself that political freedom which it needs'.[1] Almost immediately after the founding of the RSDLP, another revolutionary Marxist party, the Russian Social Democratic Party, was founded. Very short-lived, it still bore witness to the growing concern with co-ordinated organization and political action which was then prevalent among the *praktiki*[2] in Russia.

Manoeuvres (1898–9)

In the spring of 1898 the halting but still united growth of the movement which had culminated in the foundation of the RSDLP came to a stop. The Union of Russian Social Democrats Abroad divided, the 'veterans' against the 'youngsters', and the split gradually overtook the Party as whole. By mid-1900, the dispute had hardened into a formal rift, the first Party schism. Plekhanov, outvoted in the Union, with little support in the RSDLP, nevertheless staked a claim to leadership—the right of the most proficient Marxist theorists to command obedience from the orthodox. The equation was simple: whoever questioned the

---

[1] [P. Struve], 'Manifest rossiiskoi sotsial-demokraticheskoi partii' (1898), *Pervyi s"ezd RSDRP* (Moscow, 1958), p. 80.

[2] The revolutionaries who ran the organizations in Russia as distinct from the theoreticians who were usually abroad for long periods of time.

authority of the Group was endangering the Party's orthodoxy
and had therefore placed himself among the heterodox. This
equation was one of Plekhanov's gifts to Lenin who proved much
more adept in using it to consolidate a strong following. The
'youngsters' tried at first—1898–1900—to rely simply on the
principle that the leadership must be chosen by the majority, but
ultimately (1901–4) they were forced to question the entire policy
of Plekhanov and even more of Lenin. An organizational feud
developed into a major ideological confrontation.

Arriving in Zürich in March 1898, Kuskova and Prokopovich
proved unexpectedly to be in a mood not of accommodation but of
defiance. Prokopovich was an impulsive and able young man who
had been abroad for some years, had lived for a time in Belgium,
where he had been highly impressed by the local labour and
co-operative movements, and had later moved to Berlin where he
had come under the influence of the probing, iconoclastic Eduard
Bernstein. With his wife, Kuskova, he had early joined the Union
of Russian Social Democrats Abroad, and in Berlin they helped
Bukhgolts and (from 1897) Grishin to maintain communications
with Russia. He had written two works in 1897 on the tactical
problems of the Russian labour movement, and, although these
had been criticized by Aksel'rod and Zasulich, Plekhanov had
insisted that one of them—on agitation—should be printed. 'In
my opinion', Plekhanov had written in January 1898, 'it is not
bad and it is essential to encourage "the young talents". You
yourself know that everyone is accusing us of keeping them down.'[1]
Nevertheless, the editorial rigour of Aksel'rod and Vera Zasulich
had irked the young Prokopovich. Zasulich, who was an excellent
judge of character, had already warned Plekhanov that he had to
be handled carefully for fear that 'he will not just quarrel but will
raise the flag of revolt—he will consider it his duty to do so. I do
not know if you have gained a conception of the full depths of
that gentleman's vanity? Very probably not. You did not argue
with him, and his excellent court manners do not permit him to
reveal this conceit at once.'[2]

Now, on his visit to Switzerland, her forebodings were proved
all too accurate. Prokopovich and Kuskova evidently launched a
full-scale attack on the Group, Aksel'rod's brochures, and Plekhanov's Draft Programme of 1885. Their honourable intentions

---

[1] *Perepiska G. V. Plekhanova*, I, 182.   [2] *Gruppa*, VI, 186–7.

were beyond doubt. They could no longer bear either the arrogance of Kol'tsov or the censorship of Aksel'rod and Zasulich, and had come to suspect that there were multifarious dangers hidden between the lines of Plekhanov's theses. However, it is doubtful whether they had considered the full implications of a direct challenge to Plekhanov. The internal stability, such as it was, of the Union Abroad, depended primarily on the fact that Plekhanov stood above day-to-day affairs and was regarded by himself and by others as a kind of ultimate authority on questions of ideology and tactics. To attack any of his writings was to change entirely the nature of the discussions which Aksel'rod and Vera Zasulich had been conducting with the 'youngsters' abroad. The fact is that Plekhanov could not tolerate open criticism within the Union Abroad, the very *raison d'être* of which he considered to be the defence and advancement of his own ideas.

Prokopovich was asked by his opponents to formulate his position in a brochure to be studied at leisure by members of the Union Abroad and then published. The manuscript, soon presented for perusal, opened a new phase in the history of Russian Marxism, not because it won an enthusiastic following—on the contrary, its outspoken and extreme views antagonized nearly all the close comrades of Kuskova and Prokopovich—but because its mere appearance brought to the fore a new type of question. Since the establishment of the Union Abroad there had been disagreements about tactics—about the type of material to be published, about the future of the strike movement, about the value of creating a unified party at that particular juncture—but now the emphasis shifted to the question of how decisions were to be made and who was to make them.

In his brochure Prokopovich discussed the themes developed by Plekhanov (in 1892) and by Kremer (in 1894) in their works on agitation. Like Plekhanov (and unlike Kremer) he made a firm distinction between propaganda (education of workers in small circles) and agitation (the attempt to rally the masses). He considered the time ripe for political propaganda and for 'economic' agitation but not for 'political' agitation, which would have to await a more opportune moment, perhaps in ten years. Thus, he accepted both the necessity for a political revolution and also the tactics employed in that period by the *praktiki* in Russia. The startling innovations in his manuscript lay elsewhere.

He attempted to analyse and criticize the concept of revolution advanced by the Group. He pointed out that the veterans seemed to think in terms of a political revolution controlled by a tiny party which would either command a few thousand workers in arms or else would ride to power on an elemental storm of popular rage. But in Prokopovich's view this pattern of revolution did not allow for conscious action by an appreciable section of the proletariat, let alone by the proletariat as a class. It was simply a modified version of the Blanquist revolution which, as expounded by the *Narodovol'tsy*, had been so bitterly attacked by Plekhanov himself. Prokopovich maintained that the revolution, if it was to be effective and not end up in a senseless massacre of the workers, had to be a 'planned, organized struggle'.[1] Such a revolution—the work of the 'conscious' proletariat—would only be possible if the workers had learned to organize themselves, to take the initiative, to retaliate *en masse* and in a purposeful way. He therefore demanded that the Social Democrats encourage the workers to form and enter all types of labour and educational 'societies' and 'unions', even legal organizations. The Draft Programme of 1885, which had envisaged a revolution under the control of a revolutionary network, was hopelessly outmoded now that the Russian proletariat was developing 'a mass movement not confined within the limits of plots or conspiracies'.[2] The Group, living its fantasies, had not thrown its weight behind the strike movement. 'The literature published abroad', he wrote scornfully, 'must stop talking about that "wonderful future" when we shall "overthrow the autocracy" and must help the comrades in Russia in these immediate and most urgent tasks of the Russian labour movement.'[3] Nevertheless, he concluded with a plea for mutual tolerance. 'We are not a sect, but a party and various disagreements cannot prevent us from going hand in hand in a common cause.'[4]

Prokopovich's brochure came almost ten years too soon to have any positive influence within the Social Democratic ranks. The advocacy of legal workers' organizations only began to win support after the partial success of the 1905 revolution. Until then it was left to Zubatov, Gapon and other employees or associates of the Ministry of the Interior to explore the possibilities of a legal

---

[1] 'We are not talking, of course, of an elemental revolution which nobody can "prepare" beforehand; we are talking only of a planned, organized struggle.' Prokopovich's brochure, in Plekhanov, *Vademecum dlia redaktsii 'Rabochego dela': Sbornik materialov* (Geneva, 1900), p. 51.
[2] *Ibid.* p. 53.   [3] *Ibid.* p. 59 n.   [4] *Ibid.* p. 60.

labour movement. On only two occasions were ideas similar to those of Prokopovich publicly developed in the 1890s: once in Kuskova's declaration of faith hurriedly written in 1899—subsequently known as the 'Credo'—and again in the supplement to *Rabochaia Mysl'*, no. 7 (September 1899), with which Prokopovich was probably also directly associated. The 'Credo' carried the ideas of Prokopovich's brochure to their logical conclusion: the organizational divorce of the 'economic' labour movement from the liberation movement led by the radical intelligentsia. A separation along these lines, argued Kuskova, would prevent the exploitation of the workers by the revolutionary élite and, equally, the submergence of the liberation movement in a sea of uncontrolled mob passions and anarchy. Thus, from the 'Credo' it was only a very short step to the non-socialist but radical *Soiuz Osvobozhdeniia* [Liberation Union] inspired by Struve, in which Prokopovich and Kuskova were to play a prominent part from 1903.

But although Prokopovich's ideas were unacceptable for one reason or another to almost every Russian Marxist, they were enough to split the movement if only because their reception was to show that Plekhanov's writ did not run unchallenged. Thus, the first practical issue created by the rebel manuscript was whether or not to expel Prokopovich, Kuskova and their friends from the Union Abroad. Plekhanov insisted that Prokopovich had proved himself an 'arch-swindler and a supreme rogue'[1] and that 'S.N. [Prokopovich] must be punished: one does not talk with such insolence about the Programme of the Union'.[2] There were two alternative methods which Plekhanov—backed up by his personal followers, Kol'tsov, Bliumenfel'd and Polinkovskii—suggested for the expulsion of Prokopovich and Kuskova. As the Group's Draft Programme of 1885 had been accepted in the Statutes as the basis of the Union Abroad, it could be maintained that to criticize the Draft involved automatic exclusion from the Union. All that would be required was a circular letter declaring invalid the membership of the rebellious couple. Alternatively, they could be voted out of the Union, although in order to maintain their small majority, the Group would have to oppose the admission of two influential newcomers from Russia (Ivanshin from St Petersburg and Evgeniia Etinger from Kiev)—and such a policy of discrimination would have entailed a breach of the agreement reached in 1897 on the election of members.

[1] *Perepiska G. V. Plekhanova*, II, 39.   [2] *Ibid.* p. 18.

Thus, unwilling to use an administrative *diktat* or to break an explicit agreement, Aksel'rod and Vera Zasulich reluctantly decided not to support Plekhanov's demands for decisive action. They were acutely aware of the widespread feeling that the Union Abroad and the movement as a whole could never flourish unless room was allowed for differences of opinion and free discussion. As Grishin put it in a private letter of this period: 'Who, one can ask, does not suffer from passions and theoretical excesses? This, nevertheless, does not prevent us from working together or from valuing a man as active and sincere.'[1] It was Grishin who, for the sake of peace in the movement, persuaded Prokopovich not to permit the publication of his brochure. Vera Zasulich, too, pressed for a settlement. 'You are mistaken,' she wrote sadly to Plekhanov,

when you think that we are opposed by only two fools who must be removed. Against us is practically the entire young 'emigration' allied with those elements of the student body who have worked or intend to work in a serious way. They are full of energy and behind them is Russia in the form of Vilna, Minsk and Kiev (Etinger) . . . The administrative letter [of expulsion] would help them greatly in this agitation. S.N. [Prokopovich] is not a serious problem. It is very probable that one could finish off his theoretical fantasies with one or two brochures. That is, if he would only come out with these fantasies soon and categorically in print. But this general rise in the spirit against us is only outwardly connected with S.N. . . . It cannot be chained down but must be lived through.[2]

For the time being, the forces of compromise, Aksel'rod, Vera Zasulich, and Grishin won the day. Prokopovich did not publish his brochure, but, on the contrary, left the Union Abroad, for which Kuskova and he now felt a real loathing. In a parting letter to Grishin, she wrote:

I have no right to take part in this dictatorship of brainless and fossilized émigrés. I have to remember that my duty is to the labour movement, which above everything else needs to be purged of dictatorships . . . In its present form, I regard the activity of the Union Abroad as harmful. To change it all is impossible. Only one way remains—to leave and to work alone. That I shall do[3] . . . [But] I suffer unbearably for Russia, for all its back-room education and for its entire underground, trained for nothing but dictatorship.[4]

---

[1] Quoted in Plekhanov, *Vademecum*, p. 35.   [2] *Gruppa*, VI, 207.
[3] 'Materialy k istorii pervogo s"ezda', *Proletarskaia revoliutsiia*, no. 74 (March 1928), p. 160.
[4] *Ibid.* p. 162

True to her word, Kuskova soon arrived in St Petersburg, where her ideas spread a wave of confusion among the Marxists.

Deprived of his most conspicuous target, Plekhanov decided to postpone the implementation of his plans, which were described at one stage by Aksel'rod as 'the making of war—and war alone—regardless of us, without us'.[1] In fact, during the summer and autumn of 1898 the *status quo ante* seemed to have been more or less restored. The compromise envisaged at the beginning of the year was now partially carried through—Kol'tsov was replaced by Grishin as secretary of the Union Abroad; the 'youngsters' were given a much larger share in the preparation of *Listok Rabotnika*, while ultimate control remained in the hands of Vera Zasulich as representative of the Group. However, the truce was now very shaky because among the 'youngsters' there was still resentment at having to play the rôle of mere subordinates, while among Plekhanov's disciples there was a conviction that accounts had to be settled with the insubordinate.

In response to these pressures, a congress of the Union Abroad was summoned to meet in Zürich in November 1898. It was evident beforehand that the 'youngsters' would have a majority and Plekhanov did not go. For an entire week the members debated theoretical, tactical, and administrative questions in a heated and discordant atmosphere, but eventually decisions were taken on the major issues. First, as predicted, control of the Union now passed to the 'youngsters'. Aksel'rod and Zasulich retired from all administrative functions, for they were not prepared to accept anything less than unfettered control of publication activity. The 'youngsters' now decided to replace *Rabotnik* and *Listok Rabotnika* with a new journal and supplement—*Rabochee Delo* [*The Workers' Cause*] and *Listok Rabochego Dela* [*Supplement to the Workers' Cause*]—and Krichevskii, Ivanshin and Sibiriak-Teplov were elected editors. Finally, the congress was able to formulate an ideological statement, which was considered binding even by the minority voting against it and which received the vote of the only member of the Group present at the time, Vera Zasulich.

In its programme, the congress accepted the absolute necessity to fight for political freedom. Echoing Struve's *Manifesto*, the programme declared that the most immediate needs of the working-class in Russia were the basic liberties of the individual, which were as 'essential to the Russian proletariat in its struggle

---

[1] *Perepiska G. V. Plekhanova*, II, 35.

for freedom as light and air'.[1] It described the 'economic struggle' as the 'most effective method to gain broad political influence over the masses', but also gave 'unqualified sympathy to attempted political demonstrations'.[2] It endorsed Aksel'rod's thesis that 'every enemy of the autocracy is an ally for the time being of the working-class in its struggle for liberation'.[3] Although the programme rejected the idea that total political victory was an immediate possibility, it claimed the Russian 'revolutionaries of the 1870s and 1880s as [its forerunners]'[4] and declared the historical task of the Russian Social Democrats to be 'the overthrow of the autocracy and the complete economic and political liberation of the working-class'.[5]

Thus, *Rabochee Delo* was launched with a programme which repudiated the various extremes detected by Aksel'rod in the strike movement and avoided the militant intransigence of Prokopovich and Kuskova. The central planks of the Group's ideology had been endorsed, but its control rejected. Although Plekhanov, Zasulich, and Aksel'rod remained officially members of the Union Abroad they actually regarded its new leadership with deep hostility, and this hostility was inevitably directed not only at the 'young' émigrés but also at the movement in Russia which had produced them. From November 1898, if not earlier, the committees in Russia, particularly the Bund (centred in Vilna and Minsk), the St Petersburg Union of Struggle, and the Kiev, Odessa and Ekaterinoslav committees were all anathema to the Group.

Throughout 1899 the veterans sought ways of escape from this situation which threatened to relegate them to rank-and-file membership in the movement which they had fathered. At first it was assumed that *Rabochee Delo* would soon founder on the rock of internal dissension, but in practice the editors avoided public disagreement, and the journal, together with its supplement, was generally counted an improvement over its predecessors. Again, the veterans expected the new journal to lapse into various heretical outbursts, but this expectation was belied. As a result, from late 1898 a number of the Group's supporters—frequently encouraged by Plekhanov—advocated desperate measures: an official split in the movement, the seizure of the press of the Union,

---

[1] *Programma periodicheskogo organa Soiuza Russkikh Sotsialdemokratov,* '*Rabochee delo*' (Geneva, 1899), p. 3.
[2] *Ibid.* p. 4.   [3] *Ibid.* p. 6.   [4] *Ibid.* p. 5.
[5] *Ibid.* p. 7.

a thoroughgoing ideological exposure of the 'youngsters'. Vera Zasulich characterized the plan to take over the press as 'an act of impotent malevolence',[1] and she insisted that an official split would simply highlight the contrast between 'our unproductivity [and] the activity of the other group . . . one-and-a-half invalids (Pavel and I) as against all the Social Democrats abroad'.[2]

The two moderates in the Group believed that in time the movement would once more come to accept their guidance and that meanwhile they should satisfy themselves with occasional sallies against *Rabochee Delo* and the 'youngsters'. It was just such tentative criticism which marked two essays published by Aksel'rod in 1898–9—his introduction to Lenin's booklet sent from Siberia to be published abroad, *Tasks of the Russian Social Democrats*, and his open *Letter* to *Rabochee Delo*. Aksel'rod insisted that Lenin's ideas represented a welcome sign of health in the Russian labour movement which unfortunately was not evident in the approach of certain 'young comrades who had been a relatively short time abroad . . . and who stand at quite a distance from the views' expounded by Ul'ianov's brochure.[3] In reply, *Rabochee Delo*, no. 1, warmly welcomed the brochure and wondered which comrades could be hostile to this uncontroversial work; *Rabochee Delo* knew of no such comrades. In his *Letter*, written in the summer of 1899 and published in December by the press of the Union, Aksel'rod insisted that even if heresy was no longer prevalent among the youngsters, it had been when Ul'ianov's brochure was being prepared for the press in 1898. Not everybody had then understood that the policy of the proletariat had to be based on 'the objective conditions and needs of that *epoch* through which the Russia of today is passing as seen from the point of view of its interests as a class' and not on 'local or industrial interests' nor on 'the momentary interests of the various elements which constitute our proletariat'.[4]

With this statement, Aksel'rod had made explicit a paradox which had always been implicit in Plekhanov's Marxism—only the proletariat could liberate itself but, equally, the proletarians *en masse* could not be relied upon to understand their true class interests. Social Democrats, Aksel'rod now insisted, had to act in

---

[1] *Gruppa*, VI, 218.   [2] *Ibid.* p. 232.

[3] Introduction to Ul'ianov's (unsigned) *Zadachi russkikh sotsial'demokratov* (Geneva, 1898), p. 3.

[4] Aksel'rod, *Pis'mo v redaktsiiu 'Rabochego dela'* (Geneva, 1899), p. 17.

accord with the universal interests of the proletariat and not with the whims of the proletarians at a given moment. This thesis was to take on central importance in later ideological developments but for the time being it aroused no comment. (It could, after all, always be backed up by reference to the *Communist Manifesto*.[1]) The editors of *Rabochee Delo* avoided controversy realizing as they did that the Group was waiting to pounce on any statement that could be construed as a deviation. Both sides were now engaged in a life-and-death struggle to win over the as yet uncommitted exiles in Siberia and eastern Russia who had played no active part in the movement for some years; who had no detailed knowledge of what was taking place in it, and who were dependent on the occasional delivery of long outdated journals, brochures and private letters. Theoretical discussion was their major interest and they waited eagerly for news of disputes in the Russian or European socialist movements, disputes which they inevitably tended to see in predominantly ideological terms. The stand taken up by Potresov, Lenin, and Martov was bound to be of crucial importance. It was not clear for which side they would opt. Potresov had been on friendly terms with the Group since 1892 and Lenin since 1895, but then, too, both Lenin and Martov had been intimately associated with the strike movement and might be expected to sympathize with the *praktiki* who had founded the RSDLP in 1898.

The first reaction of Lenin and Martov to Aksel'rod's attacks of the winter of 1897–8 on 'economism' was, in fact, hostile. In letters of September 1898 and January 1899, Lenin wrote that he considered Aksel'rod to have gone too far in stressing the community of interests tying the proletariat to its liberal allies. 'In my opinion', he wrote to Potresov in January, '"to use" is a much more exact and more apt word than *Unterstützung* and *Bundesgenossenschaft*. This latter suggests the equality of the *Bundesgenossen* when in fact (here I am in full agreement) they must go to the rear . . . The author has tipped the stick too far in the opposite direction . . . In fighting the "economists" he played down *praktische* immediate demands (*Forderungen*), important alike for the *industr.[ielle] Arb.[eiter]* and for the *Hausindustrielle* and *Landsarb.[eiter]*.'[2]

---

[1] I.e. 'The Communists are distinguished from other proletarian parties . . . by the fact that at the different levels of development through which the struggle of the proletariat against the bourgeoisie passes they always represent the interests of the movement taken as a whole.'

[2] *Sotsial-demokraticheskoe dvizhenie v Rossii: Materialy*, ed. A. N. Potresov and B. I. Nikolaevskii (Moscow, 1928), p. 36.

Lenin's preference for the peasants to the liberals as comrades-in-arms for the proletariat was already hardening. For his part, Martov, as he himself has recorded, was even less favourably impressed than Lenin by Aksel'rod's exposition and he actually planned to write a brochure attacking it. (Indeed, such authoritative Marxists as Steklov and Riazanov described Martov when in Siberia as a 'typical economist'.[1]) In contrast, Potresov from the first seems to have been outspokenly in support of the Group, and as early as 1898 he wrote to the veterans attacking *Rabochaia Mysl'* and urging them 'to raise [their] mighty voice and to clear out the Augean stables of the Russian Social Democratic movement'.[2] Even Potresov, however, was not entirely in tune with the Group, for he placed very high hopes on the newly created RSDLP and considered that 'economism' was on the wane among the Russian workers.

A reversal in the attitude of Martov and Lenin came in the spring of 1899, when they heard that the Group had resigned from all its editorial responsibilities and that Kuskova on her lone mission had arrived in St Petersburg, and, even more, when they received copies of *Rabochaia Mysl'*, no. 4, and of Kuskova's manuscript, the 'Credo'. Lenin wrote to Potresov in April 1899 that he was 'deeply shocked' and that he had 'no idea how matters stand there and what disasters the future holds'. He deplored the fact that the 'arguments with the ultra-economists had not entered *fully* and in entirety into print' and concluded that 'now there is total chaos'.[3] Immediately on receipt of Kuskova's 'Credo' divorcing the labour movement from the liberation movement, he issued a sharp protest drawn up at a meeting of seventeen Siberian exiles. (Martov, isolated in Turakhansk, added his signature later.) Again, the contempt shown by *Rabochaia Mysl'* no. 4 for 'the abstract writings of the *intelligenty*' roused Lenin to compose an acid article in defence of the revolutionaries. However, in themselves these protests did not constitute a commitment to support the Group against the 'youngsters', for *Rabochee Delo* also condemned *Rabochaia Mysl'* no. 4, and Kuskova's 'Credo', and was the first to publish the protest of the seventeen exiles. Conspicuous in Lenin's article on *Rabochaia Mysl'* was his praise of

[1] D. Riazanov, *Materialy dlia vyrabotki partiinoi programmy*, vol. II: *Proekt programmy 'Iskry' i zadachi russkikh sotsial'demokratov* (Geneva, 1903), 143–4; and Iu. Steklov, 'V ssylke i v emigratsii (ideinye konflikty)', *Proletarskaia revoliutsiia*, no. 5 (17) (1923), p. 203.

[2] *Gruppa*, v, 151.   [3] *Sotsial-demokraticheskoe dvizhenie*, p. 41.

the Bund and of the RSDLP—both of which the Group now counted among its major enemies.

Towards the end of 1899, when his exile was coming to an end and he was preparing to re-enter the fray, Lenin struck a new note. He was now feeling his way towards an all-embracing condemnation of the opponents of the Group, towards a clear-cut division between the sheep and the goats:

> The public declaration by Bernstein that the majority of the Russian Social Democrats agree with him; the schism between the 'young' Russian Social Democrats abroad and the Group for the Emancipation of Labour which founded, perpetuates and most faithfully guards 'the old trend'; the labours of *Rabochaia Mysl'* to say something new, to revolt against 'broad' political aims . . . finally, the total chaos of legal Marxist literature . . . all this, in my opinion, clearly shows that to reinforce and energetically *defend* the 'old trend' undoubtedly constitute the order of the day.[1]

While throughout 1899 Lenin (advised by Potresov and followed by Martov) was thus attempting to mark off allies from enemies within the movement, Plekhanov's policy continued to oscillate violently. His position was unenviable. The 'youngsters' clung to the ideological safety of the middle way, while he himself was engaged in a bitter and highly emotional campaign against Eduard Bernstein, who since late 1897 had been developing his uninhibited critique of hallowed Marxist doctrine. If Plekhanov were to attack the 'youngsters' as followers of Bernstein, he would only confirm the latter's assertion that the majority of Russian Marxists were his supporters; and if he denied Bernstein's claim, he would forfeit a major weapon in the fight for ideological hegemony within the Russian movement. Even more complex was the problem which arose when the Group, on Plekhanov's advice, refused to transfer to the treasurer a large sum of money sent from America to Aksel'rod for the Union Abroad.

Caught in this web of unenviable alternatives, Plekhanov advocated now one policy, now another. In March he was anxious to deny the fact of Bernstein's influence over the Russian Marxist press, and in May he was equally anxious to make a full and dramatic exposé of that influence. In the summer negotiations began between Plekhanov and the 'youngsters' for a formal

---

[1] Lenin, 'Pis'mo k redaktorskoi gruppe', in *Sochineniia* (2nd ed. Moscow–Leningrad, 1927–32), II, 489–91. Unless otherwise stated, all references to Lenin's *Sochineniia* will be to the second edition.

settlement which would give both sides regular access to the printing press, grant membership in the Union Abroad to a number of the Group's nominees, and make the 'American money' available to the Union. In July, Plekhanov wrote to Aksel'rod urging him 'to tone down the sharp expressions'[1] in his *Letter* to *Rabochee Delo,* and in August he is reported to have said that there were 'no differences of principle between the "old" and the "young" Social Democrats'.[2]

However, in September, personal relations between Plekhanov and Ivanshin rapidly deteriorated. Although negotiations were renewed and actually carried to a successful conclusion—a settlement was reached on 9 January 1900—Plekhanov no longer intended to fulfil its terms. He had made up his mind that formal schism was essential, and he was simply manoeuvring for the most advantageous position. As he wrote indignantly to Aksel'rod in December 1899: 'Do you think that I will somehow come to terms with them? That is impossible! For me the question is only how to force them (at their cost) to print a number of [our] things.'[3] He was now preparing a full answer to *Rabochee Delo*—a conclusive proof that Aksel'rod was justified in accusing the 'youngsters' of heretical sympathies—and in February 1900 he once again explained his viewpoint to his friend: 'If we do not bring out the brochure, it means that we recognize that you are wrong. But in your capacity as a member of the Group for the Emancipation of Labour *you are innocent and cannot err* (you know that I am beginning to incline towards Jacobinism).'[4]

Polarization (1900–3)

The conflicts in the Union Abroad and in the St Petersburg Union of Struggle had thus brought forth new and interlocking questions. How far was it possible even under the Tsarist régime to transform a party of leaders into a party of the masses? Should the movement be organized according to a hierarchical or a democratic pattern? In his booklet of 1892 Plekhanov had called for the creation of a 'party' as opposed to a 'sect', but this demand had been understood to mean both that the acquisition of a mass following was

---

[1] *Perepiska G. V. Plekhanova,* II, 93.
[2] Quoted in *Otvet redaktsii 'Rabochego dela' na 'Pis'mo' P. B. Aksel'roda i 'Vademecum' G. V. Plekhanova* (Geneva, 1900), p. 51.
[3] *Perepiska G. V. Plekhanova,* II, 110.
[4] *Ibid.* p. 118.

enough to make the sect into a party and, alternatively, that the sect should begin to transform itself into a 'democratic' organization representative of the mass will. Now, with the publication in March 1900 of his *Vademecum*—addressed to the editors of *Rabochee Delo*—Plekhanov began to clarify his position on this issue. And just as his clarification of 1892 had been the ideological jumping-off point for the agitation movement, so his *Vademecum* opened the period of ideological and organizational polarization. Centrifugal forces had begun to tear asunder the Russian Marxist movement and, with it, Plekhanov's dialectical constructions.

The central thesis of the *Vademecum* was that catastrophe awaited the Russian Marxist party unless it kept itself orthodox in its policies, its beliefs and, equally, in its membership. Plekhanov had already mapped out the fundamentals of this position during the controversy with Eduard Bernstein which had engulfed the German Social Democratic Party since 1897. Karl Kautsky, the leading ideologist of the German Party, had insisted that the Party condemn Bernstein's revisions of Marxism, but did not demand that he and his supporters be expelled from the Party. They had raised important questions and for this at least the Party had to be grateful. If Bernstein were prepared to remain in a Party which rejected his arguments what could be done about it? Plekhanov was fundamentally opposed to this toleration. A revolutionary party, he argued, could not permit its members to question the fundamentals of its faith. He could not understand why Kautsky had permitted Bernstein's articles to be published in the Party's leading journal, *Neue Zeit*. 'Why Should We Thank Him?' was the title which Plekhanov gave his open letter of protest in 1898. 'If Bernstein is right we can bury our programme and our entire past . . . The question now is, will Bernstein bury the Social Democratic movement or will the Social Democrats bury Bernstein?'[1] In Plekhanov's eyes, the 'orthodox' Kautsky was hardly less guilty than the 'revisionist' Bernstein, the toleration of treason hardly less fatal than treason itself. The necessity to exclude all doubters now became for him a major principle of revolutionary organization. (It was, of course, this principle which would inspire the famous twenty-one conditions of membership formulated by the Bolsheviks in 1920 to save the Third, or Communist, International from the internal dissension characteristic of the Second.)

[1] 'Za chto nam ego blagodarit'?', *Sochineniia*, XI, 35.

And it was this principle which imbued Plekhanov's *Vademecum*. The Russian Party, too, had its heretics and here too heresy was compounded by toleration. Kautsky at least understood the dangers of Bernstein's criticism and had the German Party condemn it. In the Russian movement, however, the majority had at first simply denied that heresy existed and had so taken upon themselves a full share of the guilt. It is true that in 1904—after his quarrel with Lenin—Plekhanov was to point out that 'a veritable abyss divided . . . the "practical" Economists [*Rabochee Delo*, the Bund] on the one hand, from the "theoretical" Economists [Prokopovich, Kuskova, *Rabochaia Mysl'*, no. 7] on the other.'[1] But in 1900 it was just this 'abyss' which Plekhanov was determined to bridge. Only by discrediting the majority in the Union could Plekhanov justify the Group's decision to break away and establish a separate 'orthodox' Social Democratic organization abroad.

With its publication of Prokopovich's manuscript (hitherto known only to a handful of émigrés) and of private letters from Kuskova and Grishin, Plekhanov's *Vademecum* demonstrated that in 1898 the accepted principles of the movement had been called into question. The 'Berliners' had said that the Party should not agitate for an immediate political revolution to be led by the proletariat, that 'it is absurd to talk in Russia about the abolition of capitalism, or about socialism'.[2] By their silence, the majority of Social Democrats abroad had given these theories their tacit support. 'The young comrades', wrote Plekhanov in his introduction,

have regarded themselves as representative of a new trend in the Russian Social Democratic movement but at the same time in this would-be trend there was neither *socialism* nor *democracy* . . .[3] We have remained true to the sacred traditions of our revolutionary movement. We are proud of this fact, and shall always remain proud, however much this may infuriate blinkered pedants, political castrates, sophisticates of Marxism . . .[4] And all these are *comrades*! And all these are *Social Democrats*! Is not this anarchy? Is not this chaos? Is not this infamous?[5]

What Plekhanov saw as so outrageous was that the 'youngsters' had not rallied round the Group early in 1898 and had not expelled Prokopovich. They had revealed a lack of theoretical insight and,

[1] 'Nechto ob "ekonomizme" i ob "ekonomistakh"', *ibid.* XIII, 20.
[2] Grishin quoted in Plekhanov, *Vademecum*, p. 31.
[3] Plekhanov, *Vademecum*, p. xxx.
[4] *Ibid.* p. xli.   [5] *Ibid.* pp. li–lii.

as a result, were fundamentally unfit to lead the movement. The point, as he put it, 'was not the ideas which Mr G[rishin] now supports, but that we have many people who call themselves Social Democrats and who have not even learned the alphabet of contemporary socialism'.[1]

The first moral which the *Vademecum* drew from the events of 1898–9, then, was that the theoreticians were now duty-bound to save the Party from the leadership of an unlettered majority. The second lesson—organically bound to the first—was that the Party could not tie its policies to the given level of its proletarian following but had to press ahead. The ultimate aim (socialism) and the penultimate (the overthrow of the autocracy) had to play as large a rôle in Party thinking as the immediate aims (strikes, May Day celebrations, organization). The 'revolutionary bacillus'— the Marxist intelligentsia—had constantly to reveal to the workers their 'real interests'. Only quality as against mere quantity could ensure the success of the Party in this, its pathfinding, rôle. Here the Populist revolutionary parties could serve as a model, for though poor in numbers, they had been rich in revolutionary energy. In fact, a limited alliance between the 'orthodox' Social Democrats and the remaining Populist revolutionaries was no longer beyond the realms of possibility. (The *Vademecum* was, after all, printed with the remains of the 'American money' on the press of the Old *Narodovol'tsy*.[2]) 'At this moment it is the obligation of the Social Democratic press to emphasize and stress those elements and practical aspirations which are common to our movement and to revolutionary Populism.'[3]

In an article prepared later in the same year, 1900, Plekhanov elaborated still further on the theme of the élite party. The fundamental error of Kremer's *On Agitation*—an error that had made it the 'Bible of the "pure" Economists'—was its underestimation of the independent rôle to be played by the leadership.

---

[1] Plekhanov, *Vademecum*, p. lii.

[2] The Group of Old *Narodovol'tsy* (*Gruppa starykh narodovol'tsev*) was composed of revolutionary émigrés who strove to perpetuate the principles of the *Narodnaia Volia*. It was centred in Paris but had its printing press in Geneva. Among its publications were the journals *S rodiny i na rodine* (1893–6) and *Vestnik russkoi revoliutsii* (1901–5). Its name distinguished the group from both the *Narodnaia Volia* organizations (of the 1880s and early 1890s) and from the Young *Narodovol'tsy*, who controlled the press of the *Gruppa Narodovol'tsev* in St Petersburg during the years 1895–6 and produced *Letuchii listok* [*Express Review*], nos. 3–4.
Vademecum, p. 66.

Kremer's work, he argued, had failed to draw a firm line between the party of the proletariat and the proletariat itself. It was a misconception to assume, as the author had done, that the policies of the party should be tied to the level of the workers. 'The entire working-class is one thing and the *Social Democratic* party is another, for it forms only a column drawn from the working-class —and at first a very small column . . . I think that the political struggle must immediately be started by *our Party* which represents the *advance guard* of the proletariat, its most conscious and revolutionary stratum.'[1] As the Party was not to be bound by the narrow horizons of the labour movement it could freely champion all anti-Tsarist causes, even those remote from the average workers. 'Our Party will become the *liberator* par excellence, the centre attracting all democratic sympathies and producing all the most powerful revolutionary protests . . . [Such] tactics will inevitably give the Russian Social Democratic movement . . . the hegemony in the anti-Tsarist struggle for liberation.'[2]

That the orthodox *teoretiki* should control the Party and that the Party—the 'revolutionary bacillus'—should march ahead of the proletariat were, of course, ideas implicit from the first in Plekhanov's Marxism. Yet they had never been formulated so unequivocally as now. Lenin took up these theses and made them his own. They cemented the alliance between the two men (until Lenin developed them further than even Plekhanov considered justifiable). Yet, for all this common ground and despite Lenin's immense veneration for Plekhanov, the long hoped-for orthodox bloc was established only hesitantly in 1900. United on fundamentals, the two men were divided in their assessment of the immediate steps to be taken. Plekhanov engineered a schism in the movement, confronting the Union Abroad in May 1900 with his own new Social Democratic Revolutionary Organization. He sought immediate and total polarization. At one stage, his supporters even impounded the press of the Union Abroad claiming that the agreements of 1895 were no longer binding. The time had come for the orthodox to rally their own forces and to refurbish their weapons. Here were tactics born of isolation and despair.

But Lenin, released from Siberian exile in 1900, was full of optimism in the ability of the 'orthodox' wing to reconquer and

---

[1] 'Eshche raz sotsializm i politicheskaia bor'ba', *Zaria* (Stuttgart), no. 1 (1901), p. 21.
[2] *Ibid.* p. 32.

rebuild the movement. In Martov and Potresov, now also at liberty, he had reliable and experienced comrades-in-arms. He was convinced that his own 'troika', allied to that of Plekhanov, would prove invincible. What was required was a joint journal to present their views decisively and uncompromisingly, 'to clear out the Augean stables'. Such a journal would provide the movement with a new centre to replace that created by the First Congress in March 1898, but immediately destroyed by arrests. At first this 'orthodox' nucleus would be weak and in dire need of all the support it could find, whatever the source. However, it would only accept aid without ideological strings. Whoever wanted to help could. Those who wanted to join would have to adopt the principles of the old guard.

Lenin saw that the Group for the Emancipation of Labour was opposed not, as Plekhanov maintained, by a single line-up of out-and-out heretics, but by multifarious and divergent interests: the declared enemies (*Rabochaia Mysl'*, Kuskova, Prokopovich); the scholarly critics of Marxist theory (Tugan-Baranovskii, Struve and Bulgakov), who sympathized with Bernstein but called for anti-Tsarist political action and had no time for narrow 'economic' action; the *Rabochee Delo* group, which was revolutionary and Marxist but which had failed to take a clear stand on ideological issues. Like the veterans, Lenin saw all three groups as outsiders but, unlike Plekhanov, he did not see why he should treat them all alike. He had already declared his unqualified hostility to Kuskova's 'Credo' and to *Rabochaia Mysl'*, but he intended to treat the Legal Marxists and 'youngsters' (who controlled the Union Abroad and the most active committees in Russia) with greater subtlety.

Thus, early in 1900, on his return from Siberia, he gave Struve, Tugan-Baranovskii and Grishin-Kopel'zon all an amicable welcome and, in return, received information from Grishin and promises of financial support for the proposed journal from Struve. He agreed to attend the congress, organized by the leading committees in Russia, which was to be held in Smolensk in May 1900 to form anew the executive organs of the Party. Although the congress had to be abandoned because of arrests, Lenin joined the Union Abroad when he arrived in Switzerland in the summer of 1900. His first draft of the announcement for the new journal was conspicuous for its failure to criticize *Rabochee Delo*. And when the journal finally appeared (under the title *Iskra*), it carried an article by Lenin which—despite Plekhanov's objections—praised 'the services of *Rabochee Delo*, which has done so much to produce [illegal] literature and to organize its delivery [to Russia]'.[1]

Early in 1900, Vera Zasulich, who had spent the winter of 1899–1900 in Russia, wrote to Plekhanov that Lenin considered himself 'not only orthodox but, what is more, Plekhanovite'.[2] Yet it is hardly surprising that throughout the year Plekhanov lived in the fear that Lenin intended 'to fight without us'.[3] United on principle, the two were divided in mood and, as a result, their first reunion in August 1900 almost ended in utter disaster. Plekhanov could not understand why Lenin was handling the revisionist Struve and the Economist 'youngsters' with kid gloves. He declared that the Union Abroad was guilty of 'spying, of *geschäftsmacherei*, of rascality' and that 'he would "shoot" such traitors without hesitation'.[4] He announced that the Jewish Bund (allied to the Union) was 'not a Social Democratic organization but simply an organization of exploitation, to exploit the Russians ... that a Russian [*russkaia*] party must be Russian and not give itself into captivity'.[5] The stream of intransigent abuse infuriated Lenin who did not consider the 'orthodox' yet strong enough for a total break with all other Russian Marxists and he jotted down in his personal report that 'we do not want to be pawns in the hands of this man. He does not permit and does not understand the meaning of a friendly relationship.'[6] Nevertheless, Lenin's project for rebuilding the movement had to have that stamp of orthodoxy which only Plekhanov, its founding father and most brilliant ideologist, could provide. Lenin swallowed his pride. He pressed ahead with the plans to launch the joint venture. (In order to calm Plekhanov he added criticism of *Rabochee Delo* in his proposed announcement of the new journal.) And in December 1900 *Iskra* first appeared, edited in Munich where the younger "troika" could maintain a measure of day-to-day independence from Plekhanov in Switzerland.

Now it became clear why Lenin had not wanted an immediate total schism in the summer of 1900. With Plekhanov, he saw such a schism as inevitable. A now famous sentence of his *Iskra* announcement read: 'Before we unite and in order to unite we must first mark ourselves off decisively and clearly.'[7] But he was

---

[1] Lenin, *Sochineniia*, IV, 65–6.   [2] *Gruppa*, VI, 249.   [3] *Ibid.*
[4] Lenin, *Sochineniia* (5th ed. Moscow, 1959–), IV, 337.   [5] *Ibid.* pp. 338–9.
[6] *Ibid.* p. 344.   [7] *Ibid.* p. 358.

determined to stand the ideological principles of the Group on solid organizational foundations. Plekhanov believed in the ultimate power of argument, of theory. After all, Marx and Engels, living abroad and removed from its day-to-day affairs, had come to dominate the German socialist movement. His own almost single-handed crusade against the Populist tradition had conquered only because his Marxist writings had won over an entire revolutionary generation and he saw no reason why they should not do so again. In contrast, Lenin believed it his personal duty to ensure that the existing Social Democratic organization in Russia—united in name, atomized in practice—be replaced by a new organizational structure built brick by brick according to the specifications and instructions of *Iskra*'s editors in Munich. The execution of such plans would take time, care, patience and it clearly would not do to antagonize all the *praktiki* in Russia and abroad before they had even been announced.

It was not until May 1901—with *Iskra* already being carried in fairly satisfactory quantities into Russia, in part along the transportation network of organizations allied to the Union Abroad—that Lenin first published a preliminary organizational sketch. The Party, he wrote, had to be mobile and ready to put itself at the head of all the discontented strata of society. 'We must set up a platform which will speak for the entire people in its exposure of the Tsarist régime.'[1] Moreover, it was to the journal that all 'orthodox' Social Democrats would give allegiance and from the journal that they would take their lead on all points of ideology. So far, of course, Plekhanov had already gone, but Lenin had his own contribution to make. The *Iskra* office would become the headquarters of an entirely new organizational network. Its Social Democratic supporters throughout Russia would devote their time largely to distributing *Iskra* and expounding its ideas and supplying it with inflammatory news. They would follow the instructions of the editors who would form them into a nation-wide framework welded together in one faith and acknowledging a single authority. Thus, *de novo*, *Iskra* would create that unified Party organization so long dreamed of but as yet never attained:

The journal is not just a collective propagandist and collective agitator. It is also a collective organizer . . . The technical problem alone—to guarantee that the journal be supplied with material, that it be regularly distributed—will necessitate the establishment of a network of local

[1] 'S chego nachat'', *Sochineniia*, IV, 10.

agents ... This network of agents will form the skeleton of that organization we need: large enough to encompass the entire country; sufficiently broad and many-sided to ensure a strict and detailed division of labour.[1]

Only an organization as strong and purposeful as this could plan the overthrow of Tsarism, could give 'the call for the decisive battle and lead that battle'.[2]

As a first step, the selected supporters—or agents—of *Iskra* in Russia were told to demand from the leading Social Democratic committees that they recognize it as the leading Party journal. At the same time, under pressure from uncertain allies (Riazanov and Steklov), the *Iskra* editors entered into negotiations for the unification on a federal basis of the Russian Social Democratic organizations abroad. With its enthusiastic response to the student protests of February and March 1901, the Union Abroad had clearly demonstrated its commitment to political action, and this fact smoothed the path to a provisional agreement, drawn up in June and hopefully to be ratified in October. Lenin had delayed a final break with the Union, but his own plans clearly went against a formal peace treaty. As *Iskra*'s links with Russia grew, so dependence on the transport routes of the Bund and other pro-Union organizations decreased. In May, Lenin had written to Aksel'rod explaining that he wanted the negotiations out of the way as soon as possible 'in order to launch our own organization [abroad] the sooner and so to be ready for a decisive war against the Union ... The war is bound to be transferred to Russia during the summer.'[3] The surprising success of the preliminary negotiations demanded in Lenin's view that severer conditions now be put to *Rabochee Delo*. 'The aim of *Iskra*', explained Krupskaia in a letter of June 1901, to one of the 'agents' in Russia, 'is to become the controlling organ. At the [October] congress, the question will probably arise whether *Rabochee Delo* should not cease altogether the publication of its *Listok*.'[4] And in a letter of the following week, she wrote: 'Unification is hardly likely to take place. The editorial board has decided to make changes in the original project which will guarantee the interests of *Iskra*.'[5]

Paradoxically enough Plekhanov, who a year earlier had denounced the leaders of the Union as 'traitors' and had contemplated an alliance with the Populists, now made an abrupt *volte-*

---

[1] *Ibid.* pp. 11–12.
[2] *Ibid.* p. 13.
[3] *Leninskii sbornik*, III, 172.
[4] *Ibid.* VIII, 167.
[5] *Ibid.* p. 172.

4-2

face in favour of a reconciliation with the 'youngsters' against the emergent Populist (or Social Revolutionary) movement led by Chernov. But Plekhanov, ill in Geneva and out of touch with his co-editors in Munich, had failed to appreciate not only Lenin's real intentions, but also the temper of the *Rabochee Delo* group. Throughout 1900, as earlier, the 'youngsters' had declared that although they were at one with the orthodox Marxist principles of the Group they could not tolerate further its disruptive inclinations, its rejection of the democratic organization of the Union Abroad. Plekhanov's attempts to categorize them as Economist sympathizers they dismissed as a deliberate and totally unfounded smear campaign. 'Is it not obvious', they had asked in their reply to the *Vademecum*, 'that he [Plekhanov] is transferring the dispute to grounds of principle simply in order, with the pretext of saving the "purity of principles", to destroy the democratic organization? . . . Thus "saviours of society" in bourgeois states encourage or invent plots with the aim of breaking up democratic elections.'[1] The dispute, they had said, was based on a fiction, was artificially engendered.

But with the appearance of Lenin's articles in *Iskra*, many of the Union's leaders began to reappraise their position. They saw these articles (together with Plekhanov's sustained critique of *On Agitation*) as something new, a shift in Russian Marxist policy, a change of emphasis and even, perhaps, of fundamentals. Within the Union, too, enthusiasm for the ratification of the June agreements began to wane and when *Rabochee Delo*, no. 10, appeared shortly before the October 'unification' congress, it was found to contain two articles sharply attacking Lenin's plans for the reorganization of the Party. Thus, by the time the congress finally assembled it no longer had the slightest chance of success. Lenin took the opportunity to develop a reasoned exposé of *Rabochee Delo* and, on the second day, Plekhanov, Lenin and their supporters demonstratively left the hall after their spokesman, Dan, had read out a declaration of independence. Shortly afterwards they set up their own League of Russian Revolutionary Social Democrats Abroad (into which was merged Plekhanov's Social Democratic Revolutionary Organization). The schism in the movement was complete.

For the next two years, until the Second Congress finally met in July 1903, the dispute between *Iskra* and the Union was waged on

[1] *Otvet*, pp. 51–2.

both the organizational and ideological fronts, both inside Russia and abroad. *Iskra* emerged triumphant, thanks mainly to Lenin's unsurpassed energy and administrative ability, but the prolonged campaign demonstrated as never before that totally conflicting conclusions could logically be drawn from Plekhanov's Marxism. The dispute between Lenin and *Rabochee Delo* thus paved the way for the split at the Second Congress between Bolsheviks and Mensheviks.

The arguments against *Iskra* were first marshalled for a coherent and broad counter-offensive in the Union's publications of late 1901 and early 1902. The traditional complaint against the authoritarian attitudes of Plekhanov and his faction was, of course, maintained. The organized walk-out from the October 'unification' congress was branded as typical medievalism with *Iskra*'s spokesman, Dan, 'playing the rôle of papal nuncio and solemnly reading out the bull which excommunicated the Union Abroad from the church'.[1] Hitherto, Plekhanov's authoritarianism had plagued the émigré organizations alone but now, *Rabochee Delo* complained, *Iskra* had declared its intention to carry this principle into the movement in Russia, to establish its new skeleton party independently of the existing Social Democratic committees. This attempt to face the organizations in Russia with a *fait accompli* engineered from abroad would only fan the flames of dissension. The Social Democratic movement in Germany led by Wilhelm Liebknecht had always decided its own tactical policies looking to Marx for general guidance alone. 'How then', asked the Union, 'will our Party react to its *total* subjection to this autonomous editorial board which, while it may share the intolerance of the genius, Marx, certainly does not possess the genius of that intolerant man?'[2]

But now—in *Rabochee Delo*, nos. 10 and 11—Krichevskii and Martynov placed the argument against the narrow hierarchical organization in a much larger context. *Iskra*, with its 'network of agents', was planning to lead all the discontented social strata of Russia, to make itself into the journal of 'all the people'. In fact though, Martynov objected, it was hardly possible at one and the

---

[1] *Dva s"ezda: Tretii ocherednoi s"ezd Soiuza i 'ob"edinitel'nyi' s"ezd* (Geneva, 1901), p. 28.

[2] Martynov, 'Oblichitel'naia literatura i proletarskaia bor'ba', *Rabochee delo*, no. 10 (1901), p. 63.

same time to represent all the discontented elements and also to act as a party of one particular class, the proletariat. In their anxiety to hurry the overthrow of Tsarism, Lenin and Plekhanov had forgotten the first law of Russian Marxism: 'The Russian revolutionary movement will triumph as a movement of the workers or not at all.'[1] Certainly, the 'agents' could stir up discontent here, there and everywhere but little time would then be left to build up a labour movement confident in its own power, tried and tested by its own experience. 'The struggle against the existing order', wrote Martynov, 'will only begin to triumph when the masses not only lose faith in that order but also develop faith in their own revolutionary strength.'[2] Thus, the place of the Social Democrats was within the working-class, giving direction and aid to the proletarian protest movement. As the dimensions of that protest grew, so automatically the Social Democrats, as its leaders and spokesmen, would come to dominate the political stage.

What is more, it was argued, *Iskra*'s belief in the omnipotence of the Marxist headquarters, marshalling and directing all the anti-Tsarist forces, extended even to its conception of the coming revolution. Lenin clearly believed that it was possible to plan the insurrection, to overthrow Tsarism by a 'regular siege or an organized assault'.[3] For Krichevskii there could be no shadow of doubt that the Russian revolution, like all its great forerunners, would come unexpectedly. The dam could hold back the waters for a long time but eventually—and suddenly—it would collapse. It was thus the task of the Social Democrats to build up the mass movement from one clash to the next, confident that eventually the rivulets would combine to produce that overpowering torrent which would seek out the weaknesses in and smash through the Tsarist defences. But of course here, too, a different evaluation demanded a different type of organization. If the revolution was to be planned like a battle between two regular armies then a quasi-military hierarchy complete with general staff made sense. But if revolution would eventually come of itself, the result of gradual social transformations, of new movements within the opposition classes—above all, within the proletariat—then such a network was redundant, even harmful. 'The organization of a *Social*

---

[1] Plekhanov's speech in 'Mezhdunarodnyi rabochii sotsialisticheskii kongress v Parizhe', *Sotsial-Demokrat* (Geneva), I (1890), 29.

[2] Martynov, *Sotsial'demokratiia i rabochii klass* (*Prilozhenie k no. 11 'Rabochego dela'*) (Geneva, 1902), p. 30.
Lenin, *Sochineniia* (5th ed.), v, 13.

Democratic party is pointless', wrote Krichevskii, 'without ties—
alive, tight, broad—which bind it to the working masses and so it
can grow . . . only *from below,* from *the local organizations* and from
unification between them . . . A journal, which stands *over* the
Party and *beyond its control* and independent of it thanks to its
own "network of agents", can be the organ of an individual, of a
separate group, of a conspiratorial society but not of a Social
Democratic party.'[1]

In sum, *Iskra* was accused of going further than Plekhanov alone
ever had in its belief that the revolutionary party, dependent on
nobody, could be everywhere and do everything. It was a basic
error, said Krichevskii, to overestimate the rôle played by the
conscious intervention of the planners, of the 'heroes', in history
and to underestimate the 'objective' and 'spontaneous' forces.
In his earlier years, Plekhanov had written that Social Democratic
aspirations 'represent merely the conscious expression of an unconscious, blind historical process'.[2] And now Krichevskii, following the master, concluded that 'the task of the revolutionary
Social Democrat . . . is only to *accelerate* an objective development
. . . and not to substitute subjective plans for it'.[3]

It was characteristic of Lenin that these objections, cogently
argued though they were, simply encouraged him to reinforce and
extend the positions he already held. Thus, in a memorandum
sent in September 1902 to one of his supporters in St Petersburg,
he gave a much sharper definition of his plans for the reorganization of the Party. To the 'network of agents' he now attached
innumerable dependent sub-sections each with a specialized
function of its own. Each town would have its small committee
of professional revolutionaries which would establish subordinate
committees in each industrial district and form cells in every
factory, in every student or radical circle. The Party would thus
learn what it needed to know, say what it wanted to say to each
and everyone, and show itself only when it wanted to be seen. The
urban committee would be in complete control of all activity in its
own city but totally subordinate to the Party's central executive.

For its part, the central executive was to be composed of two
sections: the Central Committee which would run the movement
in Russia and the Central Journal abroad which would be 'beyond

[1] B. Krichevskii, 'Printsipy, taktika i bor'ba', *Rabochee delo,* no. 10, p. 30.
[2] Plekhanov, *O zadachakh sotsialistov v bor'be s golodom,* p. 89.
[3] B. Krichevskii, 'Printsipy, taktika i bor'ba', *Rabochee delo,* no. 10, p. 18.

the grasp of the Russian police and so guaranteed consistency and continuity'.[1] The émigré group would thus be dominant and the members of the Central Committee would have to be selected in order to ensure that 'in all essentials they will always be at one with the Central Journal'.[2] What Lenin sought was to put a highly disciplined leadership group in a position to control a vast but as yet barely organized mass following. Ideally, the chain of command would run from *Iskra*'s editors abroad down to every factory floor and every anti-Tsarist group in Russia, while information would constantly flow back through the same system. The leaders would learn 'who is playing which violin where, who has learned and is learning to play each different instrument, . . . who is off key and where and why and who must replace whom to correct the dissonance'.[3] And what of the danger that such a system could place the wrong man in a position of immense power? This, of course, was possible, but could be prevented, not by the elective principle or decentralization, but only by the application of 'comradely influence' and appeals to the Party leadership.

On the theoretical level, Lenin showed the same enthusiasm for taking his (or Plekhanov's) premises to their logical and admirably frank conclusions. As with the organizational issue, he disarmingly admitted that his opponents had understood him perfectly, but that their resulting condemnation revealed a complete misreading of Marx and of Russian realities. Krichevskii had been right, he wrote in his *What Is to Be Done?* of early 1902, to see that the Social Democrats had to decide whether conscious political intervention by the few or 'objective' socio-economic developments would ensure the downfall of Tsarism and socialist victory. It was Krichevskii's belief that the Social Democrats had to guide events as they went along, coax history forward along its predestined course. But, Lenin now insisted, this view was fallacious and pernicious. History if 'left to itself' would not reach its appointed destination. The labour movement had not, and could not, produce the theories of scientific socialism. These had been discovered, formulated and developed by outsiders, intellectuals of bourgeois origin. In *On Agitation*, Kremer had noted that the English trade-unions were of themselves entering the political arena. This was correct, Lenin admitted, but they were not becoming revolutionary

[1] Lenin, *Pis'mo k tovarishchu o nashikh organizatsionnykh zadachakh* (Geneva, 1904; written 1902), p. 6.
[2] *Ibid.* pp. 6–7.   [3] *Ibid.* p. 22.

nor truly socialist and, if left to their own devices, they never would. The labour movement could only run into prepared ideo-logical moulds—'either bourgeois or socialist'—and the way of least resistance was to accept those reformist doctrines already prevalent in the dominant bourgeois society. Only intervention 'from without' by the Social Democrats could make the labour movement change course: 'Therefore our task is to fight the natural run of things, to divert the labour movement from its natural drift towards trade-unionism under the wing of the bourgeoisie and to draw it under the wing of the revolutionary Social Demo-cratic movement.'[1] Very similar views had, of course, been expressed from at least 1896 by Aksel'rod and Vera Zasulich who, as we have seen, were haunted by the fear that the emergent Russian labour movement would be enticed away by reformist doctrines. However, it had never occurred to them to formulate a general rule stating that, but for the intervention of the socialist *intelligenty*, the proletariat would permanently acquiesce in capitalism and Lenin's booklet caused eyebrows to be raised in the closed circle of *Iskra*'s editors. Yet for Lenin this thesis was of crucial importance. If correct—if the Marxist intelligentsia was the sole source of socialism—then clearly *Iskra* was duty-bound to keep its waters pure, to build a party one hundred per cent 'orthodox'. ('Freedom of criticism . . . means the freedom to introduce bourgeois ideas and bourgeois elements into socialism.'[2]) Equally, it was this thesis which justified *Iskra*'s conception of the Party as an organization controlled by a few leading *teoretiki* but geared to exert the maximum influence on the Russian masses. Marxism, Lenin concluded, 'places at the Social Democrats' disposal—if one can so put it—the mighty force of millions and millions of the working-class who rise up instinctively to fight.'[3]

Lenin's single-minded persistence made itself felt with equal force on the administrative front. In anticipation of the long-awaited Second Party Congress he was determined to win control of the Social Democratic committees in Russia with all possible speed. Equally, until *Iskra* enjoyed such control, he was deter-mined to sabotage any attempt by others to assemble the Congress. Thus, in March 1902, when delegates from the leading Marxist committees assembled in Belostok, the representative of *Iskra*, Dan, was able to persuade those present to designate the meeting

---

[1] Lenin, *Chto delat'?* (Stuttgart, 1902), p. 24.   [2] *Ibid.* p. 3.
[3] *Ibid.* p. 34.

a mere conference rather than a full-scale Party Congress. It is true that an Organizational Committee was formed to make the arrangements for the Party Congress, but the arrest of most of the delegates rendered the Committee impotent.

The inability of the Organizational Committee even to begin to fulfil its rôle left the stage open for the followers of *Iskra*. An increasing number of committees, thirsting for strong leadership, now began to render it allegiance. Those which did not, such as the St Petersburg Committee, were eventually split by the followers of *Iskra* who, even when in a minority, declared themselves the legitimate committee. As Martov explained to *Iskra*'s agents in St Petersburg, the policy was to gain control at all costs, including schism. 'On no account', he wrote in September 1902, 'let the entire question of schism be reduced to a question of majority rights, to a question of who has a right to the constitutional trademark. From experience we know that the "Economists" will put the question on that basis. You, on the other hand, must put the entire question on the basis of principle.'[1]

With growing support, the temptation increased for the editors of *Iskra* simply to call a congress of its followers, to declare it to be the Second Party Congress (or the founding congress of a new party) and to elect its own central committee. In April 1902, for instance, Plekhanov was considering the possibility of a break with 'the infamous Russian Party' (the RSDLP), and he repudiated what he termed 'legitimism', the policy of conformity not, it is true, to the spirit, but at least to the formalities of Party constitutionalism. 'If we were not legitimists we would probably have behind us a complete although not a large party.'[2] And in November Martov was thinking along similar lines. Since a Congress genuinely representative of the revolutionary committees in Russia would still not yield the necessary majority, he felt it only reasonable to call a congress 'of all "our" committees' which would declare *Iskra* 'the central organ' of the Party and elect an executive body. Such a course would enable *Iskra* to outmanoeuvre 'the Ekaterinoslav, Odessa and Bundist organizations which will defend the cause of "autonomy", "decentralization", local journals, mass newspapers, democratization, etc., etc. . . . The course I propose is not constitutional, but it can only accelerate the war with those who want to fight.'[3]

However, as in 1900, Lenin was more patient than most of his

---

[1] *Leninskii sbornik*, VIII, 283–4.   [2] *Ibid.* III, 290.   [3] *Ibid.* IV, 178.

comrades-in-arms. Anxious to preserve formalities, he did not despise the trappings of 'constitutionalism' and 'democratism'. Rather than have *Iskra*'s 'agents' publicly declare themselves the orthodox Russian Marxist party, he advised them to set up a new Organizational Committee which, although dominated by supporters of *Iskra*, would preserve the outward form of its forerunner elected in March at Belostok. Given the conspiratorial conditions prevailing in Russia, such a coup could easily be carried through without arousing any but the mildest protests, and the agents of *Iskra* duly gathered on 2–3 November at Pskov to set up this new Organizational Committee. In order to preserve proprieties, the Bund—now faced by an accomplished fact—was invited to send its representatives to work on the Committee. In its first public announcement, the Organizational Committee claimed to be formed from representatives of the previous Committee and, for all its disingenuousness, this plea served to forestall and to confuse potential criticism. To the Organizational Committee fell the laborious task of ensuring that opponents of *Iskra* should not appear at the forthcoming Congress. With Martov, Lenin sought a Congress which would present a solidly 'orthodox' face to the world, but he preferred to marshal his forces with as little outward fuss and bother as possible.

Impressed by the sudden reappearance of an official Organizational Committee and anxious to reunite the movement, more and more committees now subscribed to *Iskra*'s declaration of principles and were told to assign delegates to the forthcoming Congress. But coups in the local committees were often followed by counter-coups. Victories and defeats were rendered equally unstable by the frequent arrests. At one point in 1903 Krupskaia even wondered whether the Congress might not have to be postponed yet again: 'We were doing everything to hurry on the Congress, but now things have changed radically. The split in St Petersburg has sparked off a whole series of scandals. Everywhere the *Rabochee Delo* supporters are raising their heads and turning the workers against the intelligentsia.'[1] However, the final obstacles were somehow ironed out. And in July 1903 the delegates duly arrived in ones and twos in Brussels. Of the forty-seven delegates, *Iskra* controlled thirty-nine. The Bund had been assigned five, *Rabochee Delo* two (Akimov and Martynov). From Russia only one non-*Iskra* delegate had been allowed through the net ('Bruker',

---

[1] *Ibid.* VIII, 308.

Akimov's sister). Three years of unbroken effort had thus justified Lenin's belief of 1900 that given a firm and undeviating lead the committees in Russia could be reconquered by the 'orthodox' camp.

'Iskra' and the Coming Revolution (1901–2)

Prokopovich in 1898 and Krichevskii in 1902 had both tried to foresee the nature of the coming anti-Tsarist revolution. Prokopovich had accused the Group of hoping for a revolution to be made by an armed socialist band ready to seize power at an appropriate moment and at a given signal. This was childish, he argued, for not until the proletariat possessed its own large-scale organizations could planned revolution even be contemplated. Krichevskii went one step further with his theory that revolutions, unlike coups, could never be planned and that given time and coaxing the revolution would flare up of itself. This was conceded by Lenin as one possibility, but he argued that the Social Democrats could take no chances and had to marshal the people for the siege and storming of the Tsarist fortress. However, in general, the revolution-to-be was a subject barely touched upon in the public discussions of the Russian Marxists before 1903. For most, the revolution still remained an abstraction, a dream. The experience of 1905 was, of course, enough to unleash a flood of revolutionary contingency plans. Trotsky and Parvus came up with their theory of permanent revolution, Lenin with his demand for 'the democratic dictatorship of the peasantry and the proletariat', Martov with his plans to undercut the power of central government. But in earlier years, Plekhanov's broad and highly unspecific outline still held sway. Tsarism was to be overthrown by a revolutionary uprising dominated by the proletariat but given active support by peasants and liberals. A constitutional régime would be established after a struggle of indeterminate length and this in turn would be replaced by the dictatorship of the proletariat after an interval, again of indeterminate duration.

Among the editors of *Iskra*, Lenin alone showed himself eager to fill in this bare outline, to foresee the revolution in concrete terms in order the better to make and master it. The private correspondence which in the years 1901–3 flowed back and forth across Europe between the editors clearly reveals the fact that he was consumed by impatience, ever anxious to put the most explosive and intransigent interpretation on the accepted doctrines of Russian Marxism. For the most part, his colleagues watched his progress with admiration, but every now and again they found that, despite themselves, they were shocked by his brutal frankness. At this stage, however, there was little danger that his daring would isolate him from the others. Martov and Potresov felt themselves bound by ties of personal loyalty to the leading member of the younger and more energetic 'troika', while Aksel'rod and Vera Zasulich, now as ever, saw it as their primary duty to restrain their own leader, Plekhanov. And Plekhanov, too, found himself in a difficult situation. He saw in Lenin his most powerful and brilliant disciple. He was proud and jealous at the same time; grateful to Lenin for having saved the Group from oblivion, but afraid that he would overshadow his master. More than any of the others, he understood and sympathized with Lenin's 'maximalist' and 'Jacobin' inclinations. He was well aware that his own writings could be interpreted along these lines, but he also saw that, if pushed too far in any given direction, his carefully constructed system would topple off balance.

Thus, the editorial discussions about Lenin's major writings of 1901–2 and about the phrasing of the new Party programme to be presented by *Iskra* to the coming Second Congress, were punctuated by highly emotional clashes between Lenin, growing in self-confidence, more and more headstrong, but still bound to his teacher by ties of respect and interest, and Plekhanov, the domineering but highly vulnerable father figure. ('To make personal overtures to him now', wrote Plekhanov at the height of one editorial feud, 'I would feel beneath my dignity. I have treated him too well to behave towards him with indifference . . .'[1] And in a letter from Lenin at this same time, we read: 'Of course, I am no more than a "horse", one of the horses of the coachman, Plekhanov, but the fact is that even the most patient horse will throw an over-demanding rider.'[2] Yet when this particular clash was settled—Plekhanov yielded on this occasion—Lenin could with heartfelt relief write: 'Dear G.V. [Plekhanov], a great stone was lifted from my shoulders when I received your letter.'[3]) In short, to take up the metaphor, Lenin was pulling hard at the bit, now urged on, now hauled back by Plekhanov, while the four bewildered passengers anxiously followed the tumultous progress of horse and coachman.

[1] *Perepiska G. V. Plekhanova*, II, 171. [2] *Leninskii sbornik*, III, 395.
[3] *Ibid.* p. 433.

In Lenin's view, the Social Democrats had to face squarely up to the facts of their situation—they were pledged to overthrow Tsarism and establish a proletarian dictatorship in a land which was predominantly peasant (or petty bourgeois) and in which even the industrial workers often thought in the primitive terms of the Russian village. The Party leaders and the Party programme had to locate and solve the peculiar difficulties of this situation. And this, in Lenin's opinion, was just what Plekhanov's proposed version of the Party programme—presented in January 1902—had failed to do. Plekhanov was too anxious to sit on the fence.

Thus, Plekhanov had written that 'in Russia capitalism is more and more becoming the dominant form of production',[1] and to Lenin this seemed miserably equivocal. Without capitalism, after all, there could be no socialism, and Marxism in Russia would be impotent. Lenin wanted the programme to say that capitalism 'has already *become* dominant. If I say that 60 is more than 40 this does not imply that 40 does not exist . . . And if capitalism has still not become the dominant form then should we not, perhaps, postpone the Social Democratic movement?'[2] This retort drew from Vera Zasulich a typically pedagogical comment: 'Wait, while somebody else could corrupt the awakening proletariat?'[3] And in defence of his tentative description Plekhanov wrote: 'Frei [Lenin] wanted to find a formula which would eliminate every difference between Russia and the West. I understand the *psychological* basis of this attempt but I also know that it leads straight to major ideological and sociological errors.'[4] The final version of the programme—drawn up by Martov, Dan and Vera Zasulich as a compromise between the two leaders—in this case accepted Lenin's plea: 'In Russia . . . capitalism has already become the dominant method of production.'[5]

This fundamental question apart, Lenin certainly could not be accused of ignoring the peculiarities of the Russian situation. Thus when Plekhanov wrote that the proletarians constitute the majority in capitalist society, Lenin reminded him that 'the proletariat is not the majority in many countries'.[6] And to Plekhanov's statement that capitalism reduces the number of peasants and artisans, Lenin objected that 'in Russia especially capitalism does not always reduce the *number* of small-scale

---

[1] *Leninskii sbornik*, II, 60. [2] *Ibid.* p. 84. [3] *Ibid.* (note).
[4] *Ibid.* p. 93. [5] *Ibid.* p. 155. [6] *Ibid.* p. 24.

producers—it leads to a relative but not necessarily to an absolute reduction'.[1] In both cases, Lenin clearly had in mind the crucial position which in the foreseeable future the peasants would always occupy in Russia. Plekhanov, he decided, had written not a programme but a text for students 'and first year students at that, to whom one talks of capitalism in general and as yet not of Russian capitalism'.[2] (But, again, account was taken of Lenin's qualifications and the final version of the programme said that 'the vast majority of the population consists of proletarians and semi-proletarians'.[3])

Infuriated by Plekhanov's tame and academic style, Lenin complained, too, that his description of the cruel and degrading effects of capitalism lacked all force. Plekhanov had said that capitalism produces 'growing inequality, a widening gulf between haves and have-nots and increasing economic dependence of the workers on the capitalists'.[4] In his own alternative version Lenin said that 'insecurity and unemployment, the yoke of exploitation and abasement in every form become the lot of ever wider sections of the working population'.[5] This description, in turn, was attacked within the editorial circle as simply 'not true',[6] but Lenin insisted that it was essentially accurate. 'It is absolutely imperative', he wrote, 'that we point out the "poverty and privations suffered by the masses" under capitalism.'[7] After all, Kautsky in opposition to Bernstein had declared that to stress the growing impoverishment of the masses was the very hall-mark of an orthodox Social Democratic programme. Lenin did not claim that there was an 'absolute growth of poverty', but that the Russian Marxists had to pledge themselves to root out and destroy capitalism: 'In its programme the Russian proletariat must make a totally unambiguous indictment of Russian capitalism; it must declare war on Russian capitalism.'[8] The final version tried to have the best of both worlds. For Lenin, it spoke of 'increasing insecurity, unemployment and deprivations of every kind', and for the more cautious Plekhanov (who was anxious not to lay himself open to irrefutable criticism from Bernstein's camp) it described 'the relative or even absolute deterioration in the condition of the working-class'.[9]

From Lenin's passionate conviction that capitalism in Russia

[1] *Ibid.* p. 25.　　[2] *Ibid.* p. 65.　　[3] *Ibid.* p. 152.
[4] *Ibid.* pp. 16–17.　[5] *Ibid.* p. 44.　　[6] *Ibid.* p. 76.
[7] *Ibid.* p. 77.　　[8] *Ibid.* p. 88.　　[9] *Ibid.* p. 154.

as in the rest of Europe was ripe for destruction by the prole-tariat—a conviction only half-heartedly shared by his fellow-editors—there stemmed his own lukewarm assessment both of the benefits to be derived from Western forms of parliamentary government and, even more, of the part likely to be played by the Russian liberals in the overthrow of Tsarism. His controversial approach to this subject had first been clearly revealed when in 1901 he submitted an article on the prospects of Russian liberalism. Among other things he had there declared that even in democratic countries, co-operatives and trade-unions were incapable of produc-ing any significant improvement in the lot of the workers, and Plekhanov had taken him up on this: 'You say such organizations can do something. I would say they can do *much*. If you knew the Belgian co-operatives you would willingly agree that "economic" organizations—under certain conditions—can do more than some-thing.'[1] Now, in their proposed programme, Martov, Dan and Vera Zasulich spoke of 'the political and civil freedom which has long existed in the advanced capitalist countries as the natural com-plement of [capitalism]'.[2] This was too much for Lenin who wrote indignantly that 'it smells, stinks of some kind of liberalism'.[3] (The offending phrase was dropped in *Iskra*'s published version of the programme.) Not, of course, that Lenin was any less anxious than anybody else to see a parliamentary régime replace the autocracy, but he alone was genuinely possessed by the vision of a social revolution waiting to destroy the capitalist system and all that went with it.

In consequence, his attitude to the Russian liberals became increasingly unyielding. Their minimal duty he felt was to demand a fully fledged democratic régime and out-and-out war against Tsarism. He was merciless in his criticism of Struve who (finally leaving the socialist camp in 1901) had come out with the idea that the liberals could use the revolutionary threat from the left to win moderate political concessions from the Tsarist régime. Piecemeal reforms were welcome, Lenin wrote furiously, if they were seen as peripheral victories in a major war, but Struve seemed to think they were of real value in themselves. This was a deception. To flirt with the régime was to betray genuine liberalism and to divide the opposition camp against itself. The task of the liberals, Lenin concluded, was to join forces with the revolutionary army, to aid the Social Democrats.

---

[1] *Leninskii sbornik*, III, 204. [2] *Ibid.* II, 117. [3] *Ibid.* p. 129.

While still in Siberia, Lenin (it will be remembered) had privately accused Aksel'rod of excessive trust in the forces of Russian liberalism and so it was hardly surprising if, for their part, the 'veterans' now deplored the hectoring tone used towards these possible allies by Lenin. Of course, Plekhanov's hatred for Struve was unequalled, but this was a personal matter and the liberals in abstract had an important part to play according to his scheme of things. 'You talk like an enemy,' Plekhanov complained, 'when you should sound like an ally (albeit only a potential ally). And what is more, one cannot say straight out: we want the liberals to *work for* us. Naturally, this is what we really do want very much . . . but you must express yourself more diplomatically.'[1] And Aksel'rod went further still, declaring that Struve's conception of the liberals as honest brokers playing off the revolutionaries against the autocracy was realistic: 'That the "moderate" parties gain first and foremost from the existence of an extreme revolutionary party is not "a slip of the tongue", as our friend [Lenin] seems to think, but a well thought out, fully calculated lesson for the liberals and this lesson is very useful both for them and for us.'[2] After all, the revolutionaries, too, could exploit the concessions made by the Tsarist régime to the Zemstvos and, in actuality, 'were not all the "reforms" in the West half-hearted concessions to "public opinion" deliberately calculated to divide the opposition?'[3] On this occasion, Lenin did give ground somewhat, even adding a conciliatory reference to Aksel'-rod's pro-liberal brochure of 1898, but his uncompromising attitude to the liberals retained its central place in his picture of the Russian world and the coming revolution.

In his view, the peasantry would have a far more decisive rôle than the liberals to play in the overthrow of Tsarism. The Russian Marxists had never overlooked the peasantry and Plekhanov in the 1880s had described the anti-Tsarist army as 'the revolutionary intelligentsia together *with* the workers and followed by our peasantry',[4] but this was not a line of thought which had ever been developed far. The mass of the peasants, as small-scale proprietors, were generally presumed to favour full-scale and egalitarian land distribution and this is what the Populists had always promised them. But the Marxists believed that capitalism

---

[1] *Ibid.* III, 204.   [2] *Ibid.* p. 210.   [3] *Ibid.* p. 209.
[4] G. V. Plekhanov, 'Sovremennye zadachi russkikh rabochikh' (1885), *Sochineniia*, II, 363.

was naturally producing ever greater inequality in the village, that this process of enrichment for the few and impoverishment for the rest was historically progressive, that the larger units were more efficient and so ultimately more easily adaptable to socialist principles than the fragmented peasant holdings. The Social Democrats wanted peasant support but felt that to offer them what they most wanted—land, all the land—would be to adopt a Populist, a petty bourgeois and anti-proletarian programme.

Determined to find a way out of this cul-de-sac, Lenin came up with the idea (raised by Plekhanov in 1892 but not since) that a social revolution in the village—land distribution in one form or another—was after all acceptable as an immediate possibility. The goal of the coming bourgeois revolution was, he now argued, the final destruction of feudal and quasi-feudal power in Russia. In the city this meant that the bourgeoisie and the proletariat were both interested in the overthrow of the autocracy and the establishment of a parliamentary régime. In the village this meant, before all else, that the hold of the landowning nobility, hardly weakened by the Emancipation, had to be broken once and for all. Nothing less, Lenin claimed, than the return of the lands—the *otrezki*—taken by the landowners from the peasants in 1861 could put the Russian village on a post-feudal, capitalist footing, level with that to be attained by the cities. Thus, Lenin was determined to have his cake and eat it, to agitate for an immediate and violent revolution of the land-hungry peasants and also to attack as reactionary the Populist demand for total, rather than limited, land distribution.

Aware that hitherto the Russian Marxists had lacked a convincing land policy, Lenin's fellow-editors allowed him to press ahead with his radical explorations but, unable to work up enthusiasm for them, they sought to make modifications wherever possible. Aksel'rod wrote that Lenin's proposal 'shocked' him 'not by its radicalism but by its utopianism',[1] for it was an undeniable fact that over a period of forty years the lands (*otrezki*) confiscated by the landowners had been divided up, rented out, sold piecemeal. To try to return them would be an impossibly tangled enterprise. In order to guard against criticism along these lines, Vera Zasulich, Dan and Martov suggested that the programme leave the way open to two complementary methods for the return of the land: expropriation and financial compensation.

---

[1] *Leninskii sbornik*, III, 169.

But Lenin violently rejected the idea of compensation: 'In our programme we present our "maximum", our "social revolutionary" demands . . . To allow compensation is to contradict the social revolutionary character of the entire demand. Compensation . . . leaves a very specific taste in the mouth of some half-baked charitable and bourgeois measure.'[1] On this point, however, the final draft of the programme went against Lenin.

Yet, in reality, Lenin was concerned not with the practicality of his demand for the return of the confiscated land, but with the necessity to win peasant support for Social Democratic leadership in the revolution. If this demand could give the Marxist a foothold in the village it would have served its purpose: 'Our agrarian programme is meant in practice mainly for the immediate future, for the period until the fall of the autocracy'. During the revolution, it would be possible to offer the peasants either more or less, as circumstances dictated. 'The political revolution in Russia', he wrote in an explanatory article, 'will in any case lead inevitably to such fundamental changes in our *highly backward agrarian system* that we will immediately have to review our agrarian programme.'[2] This was too much for Lenin's fellow-editors. 'If the programme', argued Plekhanov, 'is intended for the period before the fall of absolutism, that is before the (bourgeois) revolution— then it cannot have that social revolutionary character which you ascribe to it and which it really has. I suggest that you cut out this entire [passage].'[3] Plekhanov thus accepted the highly inflammatory nature of Lenin's proposal but believed that it was therefore of no immediate relevance. The others tended to see the *otrezki* proposal as one which would eventually be embodied in a highly complex law to be drawn up by the hoped-for post-revolutionary parliament. Only Lenin saw it as a weapon for immediate use against the autocracy to be discarded as soon as the revolution was under way.

The weakness of Lenin's position—a necessary concomitant of its strength—was, of course, that while the Populists could attack his proposal as a mere half-measure, his Marxist opponents could, and did, condemn it as an essentially Populist demand only just short of the Bakuninist call for total and equal land distribution, the 'black repartition'. Here too, though, Lenin had his reply ready at hand. A centralized and fully orthodox Marxist party could afford to compromise with other classes knowing that, when

---

[1] *Ibid.* II, 150.   [2] *Ibid.* III, 334 n.   [3] *Ibid.* p. 371.

necessary, it could halt, or even reverse, the flow of concessions. Thus, the nature of the Party organization would be of crucial significance in the post-revolutionary no less than in the pre-revolutionary period, for the Party alone would then be able to ensure that tactical compromise did not degenerate into a perman-ent surrender of principle. For Lenin it was, then, doubly import-ant that the programme state boldly and clearly that the Party was an organization of leaders responsible for the interests of the working-class. 'The Russian Social Democrats', read his proposal for the programme, 'explain to the proletariat the historical significance of that social revolution which it has to carry out . . . and organize a revolutionary class Party which is able to direct all phases of the proletariat's struggle against the entire social and political order of our day.'[1]

But this thesis, so central to Lenin's political philosophy, had by now become a sensitive issue among the editors. In 1901 Aksel'rod had restrained Plekhanov from criticizing *What Is to Be Done?* but, nevertheless, Potresov had felt duty-bound to tell Lenin that he had a major reservation about the booklet. Had not Lenin from 'polemical and practical' motives gone 'too far in his war against "spontaneity" and in the direction of "consciousness"? It seems to me that it is far from completely and always true that "a spontaneous labour movement means trade-unionism" . . . You stress too much the *outside influence*, which undoubtedly exists in the history of socialism, but which comes to meet the general negation of the social structure that already exists *within* the working-class.'[2] This nagging doubt was clearly shared in varying degrees by the other editors. Thus Martov, on reading Lenin's suggested wording, came up with an alternative very different in tone. 'The Social Democrats', he wrote, 'give conscious expression to [the] aspirations of the proletariat . . . and organize the proletariat for an uninterrupted struggle against the entire bourgeois society.'[3] Plekhanov's version, too, stated that the Social Democrats 'organize the workers' forces'[4] and this roused Lenin to protest that they, in reality, 'create an organization of revolu-tionaries to lead the struggle of the proletariat'.[5] Again Plekhanov said that among the proletariat 'the consciousness grows that only by its own efforts can it throw off its yoke'[6] and Lenin responded with the demand that all mention of working-class 'consciousness'

---

[1] *Leninskii sbornik*, II, 45. [2] *Ibid.* III, 286. [3] *Ibid.* II, 53.
[4] *Ibid.* p. 18. [5] *Ibid.* p. 29. [6] *Ibid.* p. 17.

be dropped. The version finally adopted represented a compromise. With Plekhanov it said that the Social Democrats 'organize the proletariat into an independent political party', but with Lenin it said that they 'direct all phases of [the proletariat's] class struggle'[1] and it made no mention of class consciousness.

The implications of Lenin's interpretation of Russian Marxist theory were most fully revealed, however, when the discussions moved on from the questions of Marxist land policy and Party organization to the related problem of how to reconcile the bid for peasant support in a predominantly peasant country with the ultimate goal of a proletarian dictatorship. Nowhere was the gap between Lenin and his fellow-editors so marked. Thus, to Plekhanov it seemed obvious that after the overthrow of Tsarism the Social Democrats would try gradually to win over the peasants— or at least the poorer among them—to socialism. 'The point', he explained, 'is not that the proletariat carries through the revolution in the interests of these [petty bourgeois] strata but that it can and must draw some of them into the *common struggle against capital*.'[2] After all, he argued, the Paris Commune had received support from the petty bourgeoisie and yet Marx had considered the Commune a form of proletarian dictatorship. Again, in parts of Italy, peasant representatives had voted for the socialization of the land. 'This is a fact which we must take into account and which can repeat itself in other countries.'[3] If, as Plekhanov hoped, the Russian peasants would after all prove amenable to socialist propaganda, then the demand for a proletarian dictatorship really presented no particular problem. True, Plekhanov's description of the dictatorship sounded menacing enough—the proletariat needs 'political power which will make it master of the situation [and] enable it to suppress mercilessly all obstacles which bar the way to its great goal'.[4] But with peasant support for socialist agriculture, the proletarian government or dictatorship—Plekhanov explained that the terms were interchangeable—would not have to face very serious opposition and could count on the backing of the vast majority of the people.

It was just this kind of comforting but clearly fictitious solution of a real and fundamental problem which Lenin could not accept. Certainly, the revolutionary Marxists should do everything they

[1] *Ibid.* p. 155.
[2] *Ibid.* p. 94.
[3] *Ibid.* p. 95.
[4] *Ibid.* pp. 17–18.

could to win over the peasants for the war on the Tsarist régime, and Lenin was ready to go as far as anyone to promise them what they wanted to hear but, while the interests of the proletariat and peasantry would coincide during the bourgeois anti-feudal revolution, they would surely clash violently during the subsequent socialist revolution. For the Marxists, unlike the Populists, socialism meant the collective ownership and administration on the most efficient lines of all the means of production, including the land. Some poverty-stricken peasants could be expected to come over to this doctrine out of sheer desperation, but the peasants as a petty bourgeois class would hardly accept it voluntarily. The peasant was both a revolutionary (in his demand for more land) and a reactionary (in the defence of his own land). Only the proletarian was revolutionary through and through because only the proletarian had nothing to lose.

But it was just this fundamental clash of interests between peasant and worker which was glossed over by Plekhanov when, in his draft of the Party programme, he wrote that 'the dissatisfaction of the labouring and exploited masses grows [and at the same time] they—particularly their foremost representative, the proletariat—intensify their struggle'.[1] This, for Lenin, was simply a misrepresentation of the true situation. 'The struggle of the small producer', he protested,

is very often directed *against* the proletariat, for his very situation in many ways brings his interests into conflict with those of the proletariat. Generally speaking, the proletariat is in no way the 'foremost representative' of the petty bourgeoisie . . . The 'foremost representative' of the small-scale producer is very often the anti-semite, . . . the nationalist and populist, the social reformer and 'critic of Marxism'.[2]

The Social Democrats could therefore stand not, as Plekhanov put it, 'at the head of the liberation movement of the labouring and exploited masses', but only 'at the head of the working *class*, of the labour movement alone and if certain other elements join this class, then these are elements only but not classes'.[3] Lenin noted that the *Communist Manifesto*, normally the ultimate authority for Plekhanov, had made this very point describing the peasants as 'not revolutionary but conservative and what is more reactionary. If they are revolutionary [if!—Lenin], then only to the extent that they are about to be transferred into the ranks of the proletariat, to the extent that they *abandon* their own point of view and take

---

[1] *Leninskii sbornik*, p. 59.   [2] *Ibid.* pp. 78–9.   [3] *Ibid.* p. 79.

up that of the proletariat.'[1] (Lenin's italics.) This appeal to writ hardly impressed Plekhanov, however, who argued that, as capitalism was now much more advanced than in 1848, the peasantry was dividing much faster into hostile strata and that 'we do not have to think like Marx where Marx would have thought differently'.[2]

For Lenin this was no mere debating point but the crucial issue facing Marxism in Russia. To wait for the peasants to adopt socialism voluntarily would mean to wait indefinitely. If, as he passionately believed, however, a socialist régime was not a remote dream but an objective obtainable even, perhaps, in the near future then it was clear that a head-on clash with the peasants could not be indefinitely postponed. And surely it was his awareness that just such a situation could face the socialist revolution which had prompted Marx to speak of a proletarian dictatorship. As the proletariat was the only class fully committed to thoroughgoing socialism it, and it alone, would ultimately have to employ all means, including coercion and violence, to defend the emergent socialist system from the potential opposition of all other classes. It was, presumably, for this reason that Lenin now suggested that in the revolutionary period the Social Democrats would have to demand the nationalization of all land, including that of the peasants. State ownership of the land would, he apparently hoped, provide the proletariat with an important weapon when the time came to put agriculture on a fully socialist basis. To Lenin's co-editors, this demand for land nationalization seemed senseless, for they were thinking far more in terms of the coming constitutional régime than of its proletarian successor. 'Nationalization of the land', complained Aksel'rod, 'even as a slogan of revolt is for the moment anti-revolutionary.'[3] Or, as Plekhanov put it: 'In a police state the *nationalization* of the land is harmful and in a constitutional state it will be treated as a part of the demand for the nationalization of *all the means* of production.'[4] Once again, there was no sign of that sense of urgency which drove Lenin.

In his view, the proletarian Party had to prepare itself alike for the initial alliance with the peasantry and for the ultimate break with it. 'It is beyond doubt', he wrote in a key passage,

that the term 'dictatorship' is incompatible with positive belief that outsiders will support the proletariat. If we were really positively sure

---

[1] *Ibid.* p. 80.　　　　　　　　[2] *Ibid.* p. 95.
[3] *Ibid.* iii, 385.　　　　　　　 [4] *Ibid.* p. 306.

that the petty bourgeoisie would support the proletariat in its own—the proletarian—revolution, there would be no need to speak of dictatorship, for then we would be guaranteed an overwhelming majority and could manage perfectly well without the dictatorship (as the [Bernsteinian] 'critics' indeed wanted to argue). The recognition of the necessity for the *dictatorship* of the proletariat is linked in the tightest and most inseparable way to the proposition of the *Communist Manifesto* that the proletariat alone is the truly revolutionary class . . . [We will have to say to the peasantry]: 'If you accept our point of view then everything will be fine, but if you reject it, then do not complain. With our "dictatorship" we will say of you: "there is no point in wasting words when force has to be used".'[1]

This statement, remarkable for its unflinching directness, typically aroused almost no comment. Only Vera Zasulich formulated her reservations. Even if backed by the majority, she said, the proletarian dictatorship would still be necessary because 'only the proletariat is familiar with communal forms of production but [it is in accord with these forms that] the petty bourgeoisie has to be organized and settled'.[2] The threat of force she simply laughed off: 'On millions! Just try! You'll have to take the trouble to persuade them and that's all there is to it.'[3] The programme finally adopted accepted Plekhanov's reasoning calling on 'all strata of the labouring and exploited population' to embrace the Social Democratic programme and join the Marxist Party.

Surveying the discussions of 1901–2 among the *Iskra* editors one can hardly escape the conclusion that Lenin was actively seeking a way to foreshorten the coming constitutional interlude and to hurry on the advent of the proletarian dictatorship. His almost exclusive concentration on the negative aspects of capitalist development; his belief that capitalism was 'dominant' in Russia and that war had immediately to be declared against it; his domineering criticism of the Russian liberals; his determination to work for immediate social revolution in the village; his conception of the Party as a mobile flexible band of leaders; and, above all, his definition of the proletarian dictatorship as the imposition of socialist measures by a minority class—all these added up to a picture not unlike the theory later formulated by Trotsky as that of 'permanent revolution' and close enough to what actually happened in the years 1917–20. It was not easy for Plekhanov to formulate a coherent criticism of Lenin's theoretical progress because he had always left the way open for just such an inter-

[1] *Leninskii sbornik*, ii, 80–1.   [2] *Ibid.* p. 81 n.   [3] *Ibid.* p. 83 n.

pretation and it could come as no surprise when in June 1902 he told Lenin that 'on 75% [of the issues] we are closer to each other than to the [remaining editors]'.[1] Whether aware of it or not, the other four clearly thought too much in terms of Western models to be able to grasp that Lenin was contemplating something very different, 'something new'.

Lenin, in these years, thought of politics on a national scale as a macrocosmic version of internal Party politics. Once the leading group was formed and clearly marked off, it could afford to accept help from outsiders certain that eventually it would outwit and overpower them. Objective circumstances might appear overwhelmingly hostile, but a small band determined to reach its destination could master the 'objective' hurdles for, as he put it in *What Is to Be Done?*, 'the whole art of politics lies in finding and taking a firm grip on that link . . . which guarantees the possession of the entire chain'.[2] On an all-Russian scale this meant exploiting the anti-Tsarist bourgeois revolution to establish a régime dominated by the proletariat but supported by the peasantry as a prelude to the pure proletarian dictatorship. And victory in Russia would, as he wrote in 1902, even 'make the Russian proletariat the *avantgarde* of the international revolutionary proletariat'.[3] (This idea he erroneously attributed to Marx who, in reality, had spoken not of the proletariat but of Russia as 'the *avant-garde* of revolutionary action in Europe'.[4])

Early in 1905—by now leader of his own Bolshevik movement and so unshackled—he could at last describe, in final form and with characteristic boldness, the programme which he advocated:

The proletariat must carry through the democratic revolution to the end and draw to itself the peasant masses in order with them to break the resistance of the autocracy and paralyse the politically unstable bourgeoisie. The proletariat must carry through the socialist revolution and draw to itself en masse the semi-proletarian elements of the population [the poor peasants—J.F.] *in order to break the resistance of the bourgeoisie and paralyse the politically unstable peasantry and petty bourgeoisie.*[5]

[1] *Ibid.* III, 430.   [2] Lenin, *Chto delat'?*, p. 126.   [3] *Ibid.* p. 18.
[4] Marx and Engels, 'Predislovie k russkomu izdaniiu 1882 goda' in *Manifest kommunisticheskoi partii* (first published in 1848) (Moscow, 1948), p. 12.
[5] Lenin, 'Dve taktiki sotsial'demokratii' (1905), *Sochineniia* (5th ed.), x, 90.

Akimov

In 1897 Aksel'rod had declared that Russian Marxism had to choose one of three different routes. It would, he hoped, continue along the path laid down by Plekhanov, but it might deviate either to the right and immerse itself in trade-unionism or to the left in search of a Blanquist or Bakuninist short cut to socialism. Time proved him right and it is hardly fanciful to see Aksel'rod, Akimov and Lenin as coming over the years to personify this tripartite division. Lenin lived to telescope together the proletarian–peasant and bourgeois revolutions and, in the period of War Communism at least, he clearly dreamt that Russia could take a direct road to socialism. Aksel'rod, in exile and forever seeking Plekhanov's middle way, condemned Lenin's revolution as Blanquist, Bakuninist and anti-Marxist. Akimov (Vladimir Petrovich Makhnovets) died in Soviet Russia in 1921, an obscure citizen active in the people's co-operative movement and workers' education.

Akimov, like many revolutionaries, including Lenin, came from a family which, apparently of solid middle-class status, yet seemed destined to breed rebellious children. In the quiet provincial town of Voronezh, the Makhnovets family was, perhaps, somewhat unusual.[1] The father, Petr Makhnovets, was a self-made man of Lithuanian and Roman Catholic origin, the son of a blacksmith. His medical training he received at the out of the way University of Kazan. He was once described by his son as a conscientious and devoted doctor, who for many years worked mainly among the poor peasantry around Voronezh. In contrast, the mother of the family was the daughter of landowners, of Russian nobility, and was born into the Russian Orthodox Church. She grew up in St Petersburg where she was given an excellent education in the major European languages and where she attended lectures on foreign literature at the university. Although, like her husband, an avowed freethinker, she retained strong emotional attachments to the ceremonies of the Russian Church.

On graduation from the Realschule (Scientific High School) in Voronezh, their son Vladimir went to St Petersburg to study engineering at the famous Technology Institute, a breeding

---

[1] Much of the following information was supplied or confirmed by Miss Lidiia Makhnovets, who very generously gave me a long interview at her home in Cormeilles-en-Parisis in July 1962.

ground for revolutionaries. After two years there, 1891–3, he abandoned his plans for an engineering career, convinced by Populist ideas—and much to his father's annoyance—that a qualified engineer was doomed to participate in the exploitation of the workers. He now hoped to become a lawyer and to specialize in the defence of the poor. In order to reach the level in Greek and Latin demanded by the law faculty, he returned home for a year of private study. Immediately he became involved in revolutionary activity in Voronezh, where the first socialist workers' circles were being formed, and he was soon put under observation by the secret police (*Okhrana*),[1] which had already included him while in St Petersburg in its list of suspects.

For the time being, however, he escaped arrest, and in 1895 was back in St Petersburg as a student of the law faculty. In the capital, students were now for the first time attempting to agitate among the industrial proletariat and Vladimir Petrovich was soon caught up in this experiment. Although as yet not a Social Democrat, he was closely connected with the illegal printing-press run by the group of self-styled Young *Narodovol'tsy* which published some of the leaflets of the Union of Struggle and a brochure by the young Lenin[2] (also at the law faculty and until recently of Populist inclinations). Akimov survived the raid on the press made by the police in June 1896, and took part in attempts to re-establish illegal publication, but he was eventually arrested in March 1897. Confined for more than a year in the Peter and Paul Fortress in St Petersburg and sentenced to five years' penal exile, he was dispatched to Antsyferova, a small settlement in Eastern Siberia.[3] In September 1898 he escaped to European Russia and from there to Geneva.

In Switzerland he entered the Union Abroad in which he was generally regarded—and apparently saw himself—as an enthusiastic disciple of Plekhanov. He advocated an amicable settlement between the veterans and the 'youngsters' and was selected to participate in the peace negotiations which took place in the latter half of 1899. For a time he pressed hard for an agreement, but

---

[1] L. P. Menshchikov, *Okhrana i revoliutsiia: k istorii tainykh politicheskikh organizatsii, sushchestvovavshikh vo vremena samoderzhavia*, I (Moscow, 1928), 214.

[2] P. Kudelli, *Narodovol'tsy na pereput'i: Delo Lakhtinskoi tipografii* (Leningrad, 1925), pp. 7–28.

[3] V. Vilenskii-Sibiriakov and others (ed.), *Deiateli revoliutsionnogo dvizheniia v Rossii: Bio-bibliograficheskii slovar'* (Moscow, 1927–34), v, 37.

with him, as with so many others, personal contact with Plekhanov proved to be a disillusioning experience.[1] He rapidly
became convinced that reunion with the Group was impossible
and that the 'youngsters' would have to retain at least a measure
of independence. When, in January 1900, it seemed that Grishin-
Kopel'zon had finally attained the long sought-for settlement,
Akimov expressed heated disapproval of the many concessions
which had been made to Plekhanov. In a letter circulated to
members of the Union, he maintained that 'the proposals of the
Group, adopted by the vote of 9 January 1900, are not only
extremely dangerous to our cause but actually fatal to it'. He
insisted that the secretary, Grishin, had not kept the members
adequately informed about the course of the negotiations and
accused him of 'appeasement politics'.[2]

Akimov now did what he could to turn the Union into an
organization broadly based but with a clear-cut policy of its own.
He sought to win *Rabochaia Mysl'* away from its timid attitude
towards anti-Tsarist political incitement and in January 1900 he
was in London where he met with its editors, Takhtarev, Alekseev
and Apolinariia Iakubova. It was essential, Akimov argued, that
their policies be bolder, more daring. Although Takhtarev yielded
little, Iakubova proved to be in broad agreement with Akimov,
and after the congress of the Union Abroad in April, the editors
of *Rabochaia Mysl'* surrendered responsibility for editorial policy
to the Social Democratic Committee in St Petersburg.

Akimov insisted, too, that the Union should attack the ideas
rather than the character defects of its opponents. In July 1900,
for instance, at a meeting of Social Democrats in Zürich, he
introduced a resolution which called for an end to personal abuse—
'a fruitless waste of the strength and resources of the Party'—
and demanded that the Union ignore those 'polemical attacks
which have nothing to do with questions either of principle or of
tactics'.[3] (His later publications confirm the impression that for
him the debate was futile unless it elucidated fundamental
differences of political principle.)

---

[1] An unpublished satirical poem written by Akimov and addressed to Plekhanov attests to the bitter disappointment experienced by the former when
he came to know the latter. This poem is in the Archive of the Bund, New
York, to which I was generously given access.

[2] *Sotsial-demokraticheskoe dvizhenie*, pp. 291–2.

[3] The report of the police agent Rachkovskii, 14 September 1900, in L.
Menshchikov, *Russkii politicheskii sysk za granitsei*, I (Paris, 1914), 73–4.

Inevitably, his total lack of confidence in the Group earned him Plekhanov's scorn. Thus, early in the summer of 1900, Akimov demanded an apology from Bonch-Bruevich, a young supporter of the Group, who had sparked off a rumour that he was no more than a pliant tool in the hands of police agents abroad. Bonch was ready to explain his words before a Party court, but Plekhanov opposed so pusillanimous a solution. 'Akimov's behaviour is such', explained Plekhanov, 'that every revolutionary has the right to—and must—ask himself: Is not this (somewhat deranged) gentleman in the hands of a spy! Such an idea is so natural that I consider it strange that it has not occurred to everybody familiar with Akimov's behaviour. If I were in your place, I would *state this opinion* in print. As for the abusive remarks addressed to you by Akimov, you could simply reject them in your public statement and thenceforward pay them no more attention.'[1]

Nevertheless, in the following year, it was Akimov who, together with Krichevskii, represented the Union in those negotiations for a federal unification of the Social Democratic organizations abroad[2] which surprisingly produced a preliminary agreement. *Iskra*'s representative in these talks was Martov and it is possible that the perplexed honesty attributed to him in Akimov's writings of later years dates back to their meeting of June 1901. Opinion, of course, hardened against ratification during the summer months and Akimov himself clearly placed few hopes in *Iskra* which at this time he reportedly described as a non-proletarian, 'liberal paper'.[3]

Now that the battle for control of the committees in Russia was finally unleashed, Akimov and indeed almost the entire Makhnovets family emerged as a real obstacle to the plans of the *Iskra* group. Akimov's sisters were all determined supporters of *Rabochee Delo*, were full of energy, dedicated revolutionaries and situated at important strategic points. In Voronezh itself, the family home had long been the accepted meeting-place for all the radicals and revolutionaries in the city. Even a convinced follower of *Iskra* has recalled that around the Makhnovets family 'which then [1900] consisted of a mother and two sisters—Iuliia and Liudmila— . . . grouped all those who were considered politically "suspect". Here one could meet not only Social Democrats but old *Narodovol'tsy*

---

[1] V. D. Bonch-Bruevich, *Izbrannye sochineniia* (Moscow, 1961), vol. II: *Stati, vospominaniia, pis'ma (1895–1914)*, p. 235.

[2] *Leninskii sbornik*, III, 186–7 n.   [3] *Ibid.* p. 265.

and even *narodniki*. The family was distinguished by its warmth and hospitality.'[1] Thus, when, in 1900, Iuliia Petrovna returned from Switzerland as a firm opponent of Plekhanov, she was well placed to rally the *intelligenty* and workers in Voronezh to the support of *Rabochee Delo*, to begin to publish leaflets on a clandestine press, and to maintain contact with the Union Abroad.

Voronezh was an important transit point in the communications system of the Russian Marxist underground and Iuliia Petrovna's success there proved a source of considerable embarrassment to the agents of *Iskra*. In particular, intimate familiarity with the plans of *Iskra* enabled the Voronezh Committee, under her lead, to publicize the partisan origins of the Organizational Committee established at Pskov in November 1902. In an open letter, printed on its hectograph, the Voronezh Committee protested bitterly that the new Organizational Committee was

constituted in an extremely tendentious and nepotistic fashion which promises no good . . . To play the bodyguard of the Social Democratic movement—the rôle taken upon itself by *Iskra*—is very dangerous and readily lends itself to heresy hunting . . . whoever dares to have his own opinion is immediately whipped . . . We realize that, in response to our views, the blows of the whip may rain down upon us in the form of every kind of insinuation and accusation. But it seems that we Russian citizens have accustomed ourselves to whips, and so we dare to say that we most certainly do not consider *Iskra* worthy of prerogative powers.[2]

The letter concluded with the demand that representatives of the largest group in St Petersburg and of the Union Abroad should be included in the Organizational Committee. *Iskra* did not publish this letter, but it did publish the reply of the Organizational Committee which dismissed the complaints from Voronezh as 'illiterate and illogical'[3] and concluded that nobody was trying to compel the Voronezh Committee 'to use our services'.[4] The Voronezh Committee was ruled ineligible to send a delegate to the Second Party Congress.

While Iuliia Petrovna marshalled support in Voronezh, another Makhnovets sister, Lidiia, a medical student, was active in the socialist movement in the capital and she was elected as a delegate to the Second Party Congress by the anti-*Iskra* St Petersburg Labour Organization. A third sister, Liudmila, who was a student

---

[1] D. A. Varentsova, *Severnyi rabochii soiuz* (Moscow, 1935), p. 28.
[2] *Vtoroi s"ezd RSDRP: Protokoly* (Moscow, 1959), p. 731.
[3] *Ibid.* p. 733.   [4] *Ibid.* p. 735.

at the Warsaw Music Conservatory, assisted in the transport across the frontier of illegal literature, particularly of *Rabochee Delo*. She was the only one of the four to escape arrest and imprisonment during these years. Prior to the Second Congress, Akimov lived in Belgium, where for a time he worked in the mines in order, according to one contemporary, 'to be nearer the workers, to learn about their way of life and their conditions of labour'.[1] Later, in the winter of 1902–3, he played a leading rôle (together with Martynov and Kolokol'nikov) in a new journal, *Krasnoe Znamia* [*Red Flag*], which was intended for the Russian worker and which presented the Marxist ideology of the Union Abroad in a popular and non-polemical style.

At the Party Congress, both Akimov and his sister from St Petersburg, Lidiia Petrovna, were delegates with full voting rights. Their dogged criticism of the official leadership demanded considerable courage because they had to face a wall of contemptuous hostility from the selected delegates who—Martynov and the six Bundists apart—were all in varying degrees committed to support *Iskra*. In the third week of the Congress, at the twenty-eighth session, Akimov and Martynov finally walked out in protest against the decision taken at that stage to close down the Union Abroad. But, by then, it had become clear that the unity of the *Iskra* majority so impressive in the early stages was already a thing of the past. Akimov and Martynov—together with the Bundists, who also subsequently left—had helped to defeat Lenin and to carry Martov's fateful definition of what qualifications were required to be a Party member. Lenin's hard-earned and monolithic unity withered in the fierce heat of prolonged and open debate. Before he left, Akimov had time to note sardonically that although the Union had been abolished, the ideological disputes would clearly continue unabated,[2] albeit between unexpected contestants. 'So-called Economism' was dead; Menshevism and Bolshevism were already alive and kicking.

Given little chance to speak at the Congress, Akimov decided to publish the criticism of the Party programme which he had hoped to expound at the Congress itself and in the same year, 1904, he wrote his short history of the Social Democratic movement in Russia. These two works are republished in this present volume and will be discussed below.

[1] N. Valentinov, *Vstrechi s Leninym* (New York, 1953), p. 179.
[2] *Vtoroi s"ezd RSDRP: Protokoly*, p. 315.

As soon as the news of the 1905 revolution reached the West, he left Switzerland for Russia, full of hope that Tsarism was about to crumble. In the copy of his newly published history which he left behind in the library of his close friend, Mark Liber—the young Bundist leader who was already in Russia—he wrote excitedly: 'You are now on the field of battle! As I too am about to depart, I am leaving this booklet for you among your books for the day when we have conquered.'[1] In Russia, he first travelled extensively in the west and south and addressed many meetings of workers and peasants. From September he was very active in the Shoe Workers' Union in St Petersburg, which he represented both in the secretariat of the Central Bureau of Trade-Unions and in the St Petersburg Soviet. At the same time, he was the most productive contributor to the workers' weekly, *Rabochii Golos* [Labour Voice]. Although he was still a member of the RSDLP he remained critical of the Party leadership, which he felt had been excessively slow to support the unrest among the intelligentsia, the peasantry, and even the workers. This was not the wisdom of hindsight—a plan for giving far greater initiative to the elected representatives of the workers had been drawn up in the last part of his *Short History*, which he completed in the winter of 1904–5. (It is surely not a coincidence either that he left for Russia many months earlier than most of the revolutionaries—Lenin and Rosa Luxemburg only went at the end of the year.) He was convinced from the first that the armed uprising planned during the last months of 1905 was bound to end in disaster, although, subject to Party discipline, he was not free to express his doubts within the Soviet. Again, he believed that the Social Democrats should have played a full part in the Duma elections. The Bolsheviks had erred in their decision to boycott the elections, the Mensheviks in their decision, albeit hesitant, to boycott the Duma itself.

Akimov was able to expound these views, first, at the Fourth (Unification) Congress of the RSDLP, which was held in Stockholm in April 1906 and, second, in a series of articles which he published in 1907 (and again, in book form, in 1908). Resident in Stockholm at the time of the Congress, Akimov asked leave to participate despite the fact that he was not a delegate of any committee. His unusual request met with a varied response. A number of delegates wanted to refuse him admission. Others—almost half those present —wanted to permit him to attend without the right to speak. It

---

[1] This autographed copy is in the Archive of the Bund, New York.

was Lenin who proposed that he be invited to play a full part in the discussions of the Congress, and it was Lenin's resolution which was carried.[1] There was an element of rough justice in this unexpected intervention of the Bolshevik leader on behalf of Akimov. Since 1903 Lenin had, after all, come to regard Akimov as his most consistent opponent, his most stimulating sparring partner. Valentinov (Vol'skii) has recorded in his memoirs of Lenin, with whom he was on extremely close terms in the years 1903–4, that the name of Akimov was always on his lips. 'In [these] years . . . if ever anybody differed in anything from Lenin's ideas, he would at once drag in Akimov as a symbol of scorn: "This smells of Akimov"; this is "Akimovism"; "You have conquered, comrade Akimov"; this is "Akimov's revenge"; "an alliance with Akimov"; "a concession to Akimov", "the triumph of Akimov", etc.'[2] If, in 1906, Lenin wanted to permit his old opponent to speak, it was doubtless in order to enable the Bolsheviks to illustrate dramatically their thesis that the Mensheviks were merely muddle-headed allies of Akimov. Thus, during the subsequent debates, the Bolsheviks—Aleksinskii, Lunacharskii, Leonid Krasin, and Lenin—outdid one another in their ironic praise of Akimov as 'more consistent, more logical, more daring in his conclusions' than the wavering leaders of the Menshevik bloc, who, they declared, shared—whether consciously or not— the views of the renegade.

Yet these barbed compliments did not deter Akimov from insisting that it was essential to support the Kadets in their constitutional demands. He protested that this policy had been rejected by the Bolsheviks and pursued with insufficient enthusiasm by the Mensheviks. 'If', he said, 'the proletariat does not support the demands of the Kadets which are progressive—although not in themselves sufficient for its needs—then it risks being defeated by the reactionaries . . . Thus, if the position of the Mensheviks seems to lack consistent principles, the principles of the Bolsheviks seem to be harmful to the movement[3] . . . Our fight is not in any special way socialist or proletarian. Other forces also have a right to take part in it.'[4] Such were the arguments which he again developed in the following two years when, going still further, he demanded the liquidation of the narrow revolutionary organization

---

[1] *Chetvertyi (ob"edinitel'nyi) s"ezd RSDRP: Protokoly* (Moscow, 1959), p. 50.
[2] Valentinov, *Vstrechi s Leninym*, p. 180.
[3] *Chetvertyi s"ezd*, p. 290.   [4] *Ibid.* p. 364.

of the RSDLP and its voluntary submergence in those broader associations which the workers could now legally organize for themselves.

It was now, too, that Akimov pursued his study of specific problems of Party history—the First Party Congress, the development of May Day—and the resultant articles were to be recognized by the early Soviet historians as the most authoritative prerevolutionary source. When discussing the Party in general rather than in detail, his researches only reinforced his earlier belief that as yet the Russian Marxists had failed to meet the genuine needs of the labour movement and the following passage can be seen as his farewell to the Party in which he had worked since its creation:

It is called the party 'of the entire Empire' [*rossiiskaia*], but in practice it contained for a long period only organizations dominated by Great Russians. The Social Democratic organizations of the Polish, Jewish, Lithuanian, Latvian, and Finnish nations had not come to any accord with our party. It is called 'Social Democratic', but nine-tenths of its members have so hazy an idea of the basic principles of Social Democracy that with equal right they could be termed Social Revolutionaries or even anarchists. On the other hand, the great majority of the Socialist Revolutionaries could be members of our party with no less success than its present members. Our party is called a party of workers. But in practice, it usurped this title, just as a handful of reactionaries usurped the title 'truly Russian' [the Union of the Russian People].[1]

Henceforward, he devoted himself to the workers' co-operative movement—legal work—but he was still not able to escape the persecution of the *Okhrana*, which in 1911 instituted proceedings against him for his relatively moderate writings of 1907 and which succeeded in having him sentenced to a year's imprisonment. Once again he escaped abroad, and it was from Zürich that in 1912 he wrote a letter to the leading Russian daily, *Russkie Vedomosti*, urging the Social Democrats to ally with the liberal progressive bloc in the coming elections to the Fourth Duma.[2] When in 1913 the Tsar proclaimed an amnesty for certain political offenders, Akimov returned to Russia, where he resumed his activities in the co-operative movement. It was this work which occupied him under Tsarist and Soviet régimes alike, and which at one period led him to act as a lecturer in the Workers' Shiniavskii University. He died in Russia in 1921.

[1] Akimov, 'Stroiteli budushchego', *Obrazovanie*, no. 6 (1907), pp. 82–3.
[2] *Russkie vedomosti* (13 June 1912), p. 2.

In subsequent years his work as a pioneer historian of the Party was often discussed, his political rôle rarely. Martynov, writing in 1925 as a prominent Soviet Communist, did mention his former comrade 'whom during long nocturnal conversations I vainly tried to familiarize with the ABC of Marxism until eventually I washed my hands of him as a helplessly stupid and wilful man.'[1] More charitable and more plausible was the Menshevik exile, Valentinov, who met him in 1919 and found him little changed: 'I could not but admire his broad learning and great modesty. Of course, there was much eccentric in him, but he was a transparently honest man, a democrat to the marrow of his bones, a man who devoted himself unswervingly to work for society, devoid of all arrogance and of any tendency to indulge in eloquent phrase-mongering . . . convinced to his last breath that he should serve the common good . . . And this man who, with his democratic view, had anticipated by a decade many of his Party comrades, was considered by Lenin "practically an idiot" [*poluidiot*].'[2] Akimov died in obscurity mourned neither by Mensheviks nor by Bolsheviks, but from 1907 at least he does not seem to have wished for anything else. He had always hoped that one day, as he put it, 'to be a socialist will no longer mean to be a committee-man, an editor, an agitator, an illegal transport man, a printer, or an agent of the Central Committee'.[3]

Akimov's Marxism (1903–4)

Akimov did for the dying Economist faction what Lenin had tried to do for *Iskra* and would do for Bolshevism: he developed its ideas into a logical, unambiguous and uncompromising version of Marxism. Totally opposed to each other, Akimov and Lenin were united in their impatience with the equivocations on which Plekhanov had built and yet they both remained recognizably Plekhanov's pupils, armed with weapons from his armoury.

In the case which he developed against *Iskra*, Akimov took as his starting-point the thesis that socialism could be built only by a proletariat consciously ready for this, its ultimate mission in history. This concept he knew could be counted upon to unite

[1] Martynov-Piker, 'Vospominaniia revoliutsionera', *Proletarskaia revoliutsiia*, no. 11 (46) (1925), p. 275.
[2] Valentinov, *Vstrechi s Leninym*, p. 180.
[3] 'Stroiteli budushchego', *Obrazovanie*, no. 6 (1907), p. 87.

his own side (Martynov and Krichevskii had already made much of it) and to cause the maximum discomfiture in the rival camp. At the Second Congress Akimov argued, correctly as we now know, that a programme which omitted all mention of proletarian class consciousness and spoke of the proletariat in the objective rather than the subjective case clearly revealed the hand of Lenin. In Plekhanov's thought, after all, the gradual awakening of the proletariat had always been a favourite theme. It was this idea which in the 1880s had inspired his anger against Tikhomirov and the *Narodnaia Volia* who, in his view, had believed that the working-classes were necessary for the revolution rather than that revolution should be made for the working-class and, therefore, by the working-class. In 1892 Plekhanov had even declared passionately that if God offered mankind prosperity as a gift from on high, a socialist would have to answer: 'Creator, keep the well-being for yourself and permit suffering and thinking mankind, the proletariat of our day, to free itself by its own power. Give it a chance to reach the happiness open to it through a struggle which will develop its mind and call forth its moral sense.'[1]

Believing this how, asked Akimov, could Plekhanov have endorsed a programme which gave no independent rôle to the working-class as such, but concentrated all initiative and all consciousness in the hands of the Social Democratic party? In actual fact, he noted ironically, Plekhanov's own published commentary contradicted the spirit of the programme it was ostensibly written to explain. Plekhanov had written that, according to the programme, the Social Democratic movement does everything to '*accelerate* the development of the class consciousness of the proletariat',[2] but this idea, clearly abhorrent to Lenin, was nowhere to be found in the programme itself. Lenin believed that class consciousness was not acquired by an organic process which could be 'accelerated', but that it was the monopoly of the party which had to 'divert' the proletariat when necessary on to the right track. Akimov was laughed down at the Congress, but through the jeers he foresaw that the alliance between Plekhanov and Lenin could hardly survive so radical a disagreement for long. Their partnership, in practice, outlasted the Congress, but Plekhanov's 'Bolshevik' career came to an end a few months later,

---

[1] Plekhanov, *O zadachakh*, p. 61.
[2] Plekhanov, 'Proekt programmy Rossiiskoi Sotsial-demokraticheskoi Rabochei Partii', *Zaria*, no. 4 (1902), p. 30.

in November 1903. In his booklet on the programme of 1904, Akimov wrote that Plekhanov would now doubtless come out with a critique of *What Is to Be Done?* (as he had once lambasted *On Agitation* years after its publication), and such an attack did in fact appear later in 1904. Among the Russian Marxists of the time, Akimov was distinguished by just this ability to move freely and surely from the analysis of an apparently insignificant choice of words to the clash of personalities which lay behind that choice and thence to its ultimate implications—ideological and political.

As for Lenin so for Akimov, the question of the rôle of the Marxist intelligentsia—of conscious intervention from outside the labour movement—was the pivot on which all else hinged. In Lenin's scheme of things, the party was moving in one direction, the labour movement in another, and only constant vigilance by the revolutionaries could save the proletariat for socialism. This analysis, Lenin was convinced, was truly Marxist, for Marx had said that philosophy should not merely describe but should change society, and the decisive intervention of the few, the philosophers, had therefore to be seen as an essential component of genuine determinism. Nevertheless, pessimism played almost as central a rôle in Lenin's thought as in that of Tkachev.

In contrast, Akimov was very much the optimist. Following Kremer's *On Agitation*, he believed that the labour movement steadily acquired a growing appreciation of its place in society and of the need for concerted political action to transform that society. The development of capitalist industry guaranteed that the workers would unite and gain constant experience in the problems of organization and economics, politics and power. This was not to say that the Marxist intelligentsia had no rôle to play: they, after all, knew the function for which history was educating the masses and they had to hurry on the process of education. But this was a two-way process. Certainly the Social Democrats had to lead, explain and organize, but they had also to learn from and adjust to the transformations taking place within the working-class. They had to keep only one pace ahead of the labour movement or, as Plekhanov had once put it, 'give conscious expression to an unconscious, blind historical process'.

The clash of Lenin's pessimistic analysis with Akimov's optimism was strikingly illustrated in their conflicting interpretations of Party history. From Lenin's theory it clearly followed that the Russian Social Democratic movement had been created by the *teoretiki* 'in total independence of the blind growth of the labour movement and as the inevitable result of the way in which the revolutionary socialist intelligentsia was developing its ideas'.[1] It had made its great advance when the two branches were first successfully married in the mid-1890s, when the St Petersburg Union of Struggle—the orthodox Marxists—had taken the strike movement under its wing. The St Petersburg Union of 1895 had understood that it had to give a firm lead to the workers and inspire them with 'a very broad programme and militant tactics'. Yet the fate of this entire experiment had always hung in the balance and it did not survive the arrests which constantly carried off the leaders. Their replacements, ill-versed in Marxist theory, were unable to give a firm lead and found themselves pulled off their own track and on to that of the labour movement. They encouraged *Rabochaia Mysl'* which pronounced the disastrous, 'trade-unionist' philosophy that the workers had to run their own affairs and could not leave their fate to the intelligentsia. Thus, the second period, the mid-1890s, when the Social Democrats had finally begun to take the proletariat in tow, had given way to the third period, 1898–1902, when the intelligentsia had drifted rudderless amidst the currents of the labour movement. *Iskra* had opened the fourth period in which the revolutionary Marxists would again assert their legitimate authority, taking as their goal 'the liquidation of the third period'.[2]

In his *Short History*, Akimov accepted Lenin's periodization, but nothing else. As for the origins of the Party it was a truism that Marxist theory could only have been developed by men with a very high level of education, by the intelligentsia. But this did not mean that Lenin (or, indeed, Aksel'rod) was right to see the gestation of Russian Marxism as a process of pure intellectual speculation among a 'small group of émigrés'. The fact was that years before Plekhanov had become a Marxist he had been confronted in St Petersburg by an emergent proletarian organization, the Northern Union of Russian Workers, and had been immensely impressed by the independence, courage and political maturity of its leaders, all workers. Plekhanov, in later adopting Marxism abroad, had merely given theoretical form to the concrete reality he had met in St Petersburg years earlier: 'The embryo of the future workers party', wrote Akimov, 'was the mass labour movement. And the Russian Social Democratic movement . . .

---

[1] Lenin, *Chto delat'?*, p. 21.   [2] *Ibid.* p. 140.

was born in the large industrial centres, the centres of socio-
political life, and its first attempt at organization was the Northern
Union of [Russian] Workers.'[1] Ironically enough, this clash of
interpretations was reproduced in the Soviet Union of the 1920s,
with the leading Communist historian of the time, Pokrovskii,
arguing—like Akimov, but with no acknowledgment to him—that
'Marxist philosophy began to form in Russia on the basis of the
labour movement' and with Lev Deich, now suspect as an old
Menshevik, defending the thesis of Lenin and Aksel'rod that
Russian Marxism was the product of Plekhanov's intellectual
exploration alone.[2]

Again, Akimov tried to show that throughout the 1880s and
early 1890s, Lenin's 'first period', revolutionaries within Russia
had found their way independently of Plekhanov's Group to
Marxism, albeit often of a primitive kind, and had doggedly sought
contacts among the industrial workers. The St Petersburg Union
of 1895 had thus not appeared out of the blue but was the culmina-
tion of innumerable experiments in various Russian cities during
the previous decade. This theme, too, was developed much further
by such Soviet historians as Sergievskii and Nevskii who in the
1920s had access to and were able to publish important document-
ary material unknown to Akimov. Sergievskii, who did acknowledge his debt to Akimov, summed up the results of his research
with the suggestion that the origins of the Party had to be traced
back less to Plekhanov than to 'the "native" Social Democratic
movement which was already forming in the 1870s'.[3]

In his analysis of the 'second' and 'third' periods, Akimov
sought further support for his evolutionary concept of Party
history which he was ready enough to call the 'theory of stages'.
This was a term used with derision by *Iskra* to characterize the
philosophy of *Rabochee Delo* but, then, Akimov was distinguished
by an unusual ability to ride out ridicule and isolation. For him,
the 'theory of stages' did not mean—as implied by *Iskra*—that
the proletariat had been left to progress at its own speed with the
revolutionaries taking their place at the tail of the labour move-

---

[1] See below, pp. 351–2.
[2] M. N. Pokrovskii, *Ocherki po istorii revoliutsionnogo dvizheniia v XIX i XX
vv.* (Moscow, 1924), pp. 83–6; L. Deich, 'Kak G. V. Plekhanov stal marksistom', *Proletarskaia revoliutsiia*, no. 7 (1922), pp. 97–140; 'Kto prav (otvet
M. N. Pokrovskomu)', in *Gruppa Osvobozhdenie truda*, v (1926), 255–72.
[3] N. L. Sergievskii, *Partiia russkikh sotsial-demokratov i gruppa Blagoeva*
(Moscow, 1929), p. 115.

ment, but that the Social Democrats had always been forced to pitch their propaganda and agitation at various levels in order to meet the given needs of each particular stratum of the proletariat. Anyone trying to write Party history was duty-bound to understand that the Social Democrats, unable to go faster than the leading workers and determined to exert their influence on the proletariat as widely as possible, had inevitably advanced at different speeds in different places and at different times. Looked at from this point of view, the St Petersburg Union of 1895 appeared much less glamorous than in Lenin's description. The Union of Struggle had certainly put itself at the head of the labour movement in a period of upsurge, but in order to do so it had presented the workers not with Lenin's 'very broad programme and militant tactics' but with leaflets embodying the most simple demands for 'a penny on the pound'. This was all it could do at a time when the Social Democrats were first trying to gain the confidence of the workers and when the labour movement itself was first finding its feet. Lenin was right to describe the St Petersburg Union as the symbol of the movement in the mid-1890s, the second period, but in reality this was the period of pure 'economism' when the Social Democrats had fed the workers with primitive agitation of a purely 'trade-union' nature. In this sense, 'the first economists and indeed the only real economists were none other than the members of the Union of Struggle in 1895—the subsequent founders of *Iskra*'.[1]

In comparison, the next, the 'third period', marked a definite advance at all levels. The Social Democrats had everywhere made their agitation more sophisticated, moving from purely 'economic' wage claims to demands for civil rights and then, eventually, to the call for the overthrow of the autocracy. For their part, the leading workers had thrown themselves into the work of revolutionary organization and had even taken it upon themselves to produce illegal newspapers. If, in response to this initiative from below, some Social Democrats had sought ways to permit representatives of the workers' groups into their own organizations—into the St Petersburg Union, for instance—then this simply demonstrated that the movement for the proletariat was at last becoming a movement of the proletariat. In adopting the workers' journal, *Arbeter Shtime*, the Bund had shown an imaginative approach notably lacking among the veteran leaders, who regarded

[1] See below, p. 247.

any independent action by the workers as a sign of trade-unionism and any concession to them as a surrender of leadership, as *khvostizm*—following at the tail end. Of course, Akimov wrote, the workers' ideas were as yet 'untutored, clumsy, unsubtle! . . . Such newspapers [as *Rabochaia Mysl'*] are [therefore] not enough, but they are enormously important and necessary, for the thinking of the workers can develop only on the condition (though not the sole condition) that the workers have an opportunity to formulate their ideas.'[1] This was exactly what Plekhanov had so often said in earlier times only to forget when his ideas at last became reality.

In his *What Is to Be Done?*, Lenin reproduced or quoted a number of programmes drawn up in Russia which were designed to admit workers' representatives into the Social Democratic organizations and which he saw as typical of the degeneration of the 'third period'. But, answered Akimov—and this was the central argument of his *Short History*—Lenin examined these programmes in the light of ideal standards. He had no feeling for the relativity of things, no understanding of the experimentation and errors which must accompany all growth. Certainly, Akimov's own work, however partisan, is distinguished by a genuine interest in the details of history, in the specific as well as the general, in opponents hardly less than in allies, but then, this broad sympathy went hand in hand with the relativisitic and optimistic 'theory of stages'. Lenin's pessimistic evaluations permitted no toleration of the provincial, the backward, the idiosyncratic and he was not to be shaken by Akimov's accusation that he argued 'outside time and place'.[2]

However, in the last resort, for Akimov as for Lenin, Party history had to serve to underpin his own conceptions of how the Party should be organized in the present and of how it would develop in the future. He shared Lenin's dislike of the traditional type of organization in which there were two committees at the urban level, the dominant committee of the Social Democratic *intelligenty* and the subordinate committee of the Social Democratic workers. As we have seen, Lenin planned on each city having its one leading committee which would be composed of a few reliable Social Democrats—whether *intelligenty* or workers was irrelevant—and which would run all Party work in the area. And, in turn, this local committee would be entirely subordinate

---

[1] See below, pp. 273–4. [2] See below, p. 310.

to the Party's central executive. On the other hand, Akimov wanted the dual committee system replaced by a single committee to be elected, if only indirectly, by all the Party members in its area.

As a functioning, but as yet primitive, prototype of what he had in mind, Akimov took the local organizations of the Bund. In each town the Bundist organization was composed of three tiers: the workers organized at factory level in 'trade councils'; the 'agitators' drawn from these factory organizations; and the urban committee elected by the agitators' council. This was certainly not a truly democratic system because the 'trade councils' and the agitators were selected from above, while the urban committee once elected tended to perpetuate itself. Nevertheless, Akimov saw here the possibilities of evolution and he looked forward to the time when the factory groups—the 'trade councils' —would be 'given the right to co-opt new members and to elect their delegates to the agitators' council'[1] and to the time when 'the members of the committee would be elected for specific terms [of office]'.[2] In turn, the urban committees would naturally form themselves into unions covering large geographic areas (Siberia, for instance, or Northern Russia) and these, finally, would be guaranteed representation on the Party's Central Committee.

At the Second Congress, Akimov only had time to hint at this scheme of things, but he did intervene a number of times to warn against endowing the Party's central executive with the right to disperse the local committees at will. An all-powerful Central Committee would instantly engineer yet another round of costly splits and expulsions. He was, of course, overruled and Trotsky explained to him that *Iskra*'s Statute was consciously drawn up as an expression of that 'organizational distrust [with which the] Party as a whole [has to regard] all its parts'. Not that Akimov was against centralization, but now *Iskra*'s organizational Statute clearly gave the Central Committee sufficient power to pack the Congresses to which alone it was formally responsible. Such unfettered control by the small leadership group could, he was convinced, seriously delay the natural evolution of the Party into an organization firmly grounded on a proletarian base and the elective principle.

By the time he came to write his booklets in 1904, Akimov could point to the disastrous effects of the attempt to place a

---

[1] See below, pp. 227–8.   [2] See below, p. 230.

narrow hierarchy of orthodox and professional revolutionaries over the workers' organizations. The initial result, as predicted by the Economists, had been to alienate many workers from the Social Democratic movement. (Even Plekhanov had complained to Lenin in a letter of April 1903 that 'to many it seems that *Iskra* wants the workers to give unconditional obedience to the intelligentsia . . . We must dispel this view. But to do so we must moderate the excessively centralistic fever of our followers.'[1]) And its ultimate result had been to split the Party from top to bottom. 'Our Party', Akimov could write, 'has never been in such a state of anarchy as today.'[2] The concept of a party totally unified, totally centralized and free of all ideological impurities had encouraged *Iskra*'s adherents to define all dissent as deviation. For Akimov, the root of the problem thus lay in the fact that '"the organization of professional revolutionaries" was transformed from a means by which the proletarian movement could find expression into a self-sufficient end in itself'.[3]

Nevertheless, in accordance with his philosophy of history—his 'theory of stages'—he saw the *Iskra* period not as some random throwback to Populism, but as an exaggerated response of the Marxist movement to the genuine need of the years 1901–2 for revolutionary action more politically oriented. The mistake of the veterans—Plekhanov and Lenin alike—had been to think that the new tactics demanded a return to the narrow organizational principles of five or twenty years before, to the structure of the St Petersburg Union in 1895 or, even more, to that of the *Narodnaia Volia*. In reality, a mass movement once formed could not be crushed into a strait-jacket and the experiment had therefore ended in disaster. Where the leaders had failed, however, the workers would find their own way. A 'mighty force', he concluded, 'is building up unnoticeably and constantly in the proletariat [and] will result in an explosion unexpected by enemy and friend alike'.[4]

Up to this point Akimov had built his case, albeit more fully and more pungently, from arguments put forward in the years 1901–2 by Martynov and Krichevskii. But among the Party's thinkers, Akimov shared with Lenin the rare urge to go beyond the problem of organization, of how to build a Marxist party, in

---

[1] *Gruppa Osvobozhdenie truda*, IV, 338.
[2] See below, p. 107. [3] See below, p. 322.
[4] See below, p. 284.

order to consider the ultimate question of what the Party would be required to do once the autocracy had been destroyed. As his starting-point, he took the programme worked out by *Iskra* and adopted without real debate by the Second Party Congress. And, with a sharp eye for the essential, he selected just those ambiguous points in the programme which, when discussed in the privacy of the editorial circle, had roused Lenin to make his utterly unambiguous counter-proposals. Thus, in his booklet on the programme (*The Second Congress of the RSDLP*), Akimov examined systematically the problems of working-class impoverishment under capitalism; of the Party's relationship to the peasantry; and of the meaning of proletarian dictatorship.

Akimov wanted the programme to state clearly whether or not advancing capitalism produced an absolute decline in the working-class standard of living. Bernstein had said that it did not. Bernstein's opponents, however, rarely claimed with confidence that it did. They tended rather to argue that essentially the situation of the workers was deteriorating if only because their share of the growing communal wealth was in decline and if only because the workers had periodically to suffer the effects of ever more severe economic crises. Lenin was eager to drive this line of argument to its utmost limits and had demanded that the programme give an unmistakable impression of constant and growing impoverishment. But, as we have seen, in its final version the programme presented a compromise and now Akimov took up the issue, pouring scorn on Plekhanov's timid formula: 'Crises . . . hasten the relative or even absolute deterioration in the condition of the working-class.' This was not an abstruse point of theory, Akimov declared, for it has practical implications of central political importance. If the proletariat was subject to ever more severe impoverishment then certainly it was unreasonable to expect that the victims—like Roman slaves degraded, harried, half-starved— would organize, take the initiative and prepare themselves to run a socialist society. If this was the effect of capitalism then, of course, Lenin was right and the Party, a band of leaders, had to hold itself aloof from the enslaved and, in that case, who was more suitable than Lenin to head such a band? At any rate the Congress 'could not have selected anyone else'.[1]

Yet, more and more, Western Marxists were coming over to the view that the deterioration was only relative or, in other words,

---

[1] See below, p. 182.

that there was an actual rise in the standard of living. This attitude had characterized the most recent Marxist programme— that adopted in 1901 by the Austrian Social Democratic Party under Viktor Adler—which clearly saw the primary condition for a socialist society as the progressive transformation of working-class thinking from the 'penny on the pound' mentality to the realization that the total transformation of society was imperative. If this standpoint were correct, then clearly the decision to place a revolutionary hierarchy outside and over the working-class was a grotesque irrelevance. Now, in 1904, the Mensheviks were at last, inch by inch, beginning to criticize the extremities to which Lenin had taken Plekhanov's conception of the Party, but they had yet to realize that what was at stake was not a minor organizational issue but an entire philosophy. For them, the programme remained a shining example of orthodox Marxism.

Again, Akimov—like Lenin in the private discussions of 1902— attacked that passage in the programme in which Plekhanov deliberately blurred the differences between the proletariat and the peasantry. ('The Party invites into its ranks all strata of the labouring and exploited population.') To Lenin this was unacceptable because he believed that eventually the Party— and the proletarian minority it represented—would somehow have to impose its will on the alien, petty bourgeois, majority. To Akimov it was unacceptable because he saw the Party as an organic part of the proletariat. Its function was to speak for a specific class and it could not do that if the Party was inundated by a mass of peasant members who, ostensibly accepting the Marxist programme, would, of necessity, reject those demands which threatened their own interests. Lenin was thinking in terms of a violent clash of wills and Akimov in terms of the gradual emergence of a mass proletarian movement on the model of the German Social Democratic Party, but they were at one in their rejection of a fictitious solution. A proletarian Party, argued Akimov, could not adopt the historically retrograde Populist programme—total and egalitarian land distribution—nor half-hearted variations of that programme. As Marxists they could not deliberately seek to unleash a flood which (as it was put in one unsigned article by Akimov) 'would throw Russia back for a long period into the Middle Ages'.[1]

---

[1] 'Sotsialdemokraticheskaia partiia i partiia sotsialistov-revoliutsionerov', *Krasnoe znamia*, no. 2 (1902), p. 2.

But, as Lenin had realized, it was at this point that the Russian Marxists had to make their crucial decision. They had only three alternatives. They might live in the hope that, despite all the evidence, the peasants could be won over to their Marxian form of socialism. They could hold the Party ready to coerce the peasantry. Or they could reconcile themselves to the idea that the Social Democratic Party would be tied to one class in a democratic system in which it would have to share power or even yield it to other parties representing other classes. Lenin had opted for the second solution and Akimov for the third, but the vast majority of Russian Marxists still preferred the easy way which enabled them to hope for a proletarian dictatorship supported by the majority.

At this point too, Akimov pointed out, the programme evaded the issue, for, describing the 'dictatorship of the proletariat' as the 'conquest by the proletariat of such power as will permit it to suppress all resistance put up by the exploiters', it failed to specify whether the Party was for or against the imposition of minority rule. Akimov, probing at this spot during the Second Party Congress, was scornfully brushed aside by Trotsky who gave him a typical gloss on the programme: 'The dictatorship of the proletariat frightens him [Akimov] as an act of Jacobinism. [But] . . . the dictatorship of the proletariat will not be a conspiratorial "seizure of power" but the political rule of the organized working-class which will then constitute the majority of the nation.'[1]

If it were really so simple, asked Akimov, then why did the programme have to mention the proletarian 'dictatorship' at all, considering that no previous Marxist programme had ever done so? To ensure that the programme was orthodox, to repudiate Bernstein's gradualist concept of socialist construction, it would have been enough to say that in order to create a socialist society the proletariat has to hold political power. Here, as elsewhere, the programme glossed over the crucial question. But where the programme remained silent, Plekhanov's writings occasionally yielded a more definite answer—although he advocated the establishment of a parliamentary régime, he would not necessarily object to the destruction of constitutional government and its replacement by a one-party minority dictatorship. And, in a moment of unusual boldness, he had said just this at the Second Party Congress: 'If, in an upsurge of revolutionary enthusiasm,

[1] See below, p. 171, note 1.

94

the people elected a very good parliament—a new kind of "chambre introuvable"—we would have to try to make it into a Long Parliament; but, if the elections were a failure, we should have to try to disperse parliament not after two years, but after two weeks.'[1] He had, it will be remembered, stated this view even more forcibly in the past, but it was a prospect which he conjured up only rarely. (It was not for nothing that Akimov called him 'the diplomat of the revolution'.[2]) As a result, his speech at the Second Congress came as a surprise to the delegates and was greeted with an uproar, some cheering, some whistling in protest. As already revealed in *Iskra*'s editorial discussions, there was a general reluctance to pry too deeply into this point and Plekhanov's statement was barely debated. And it came as no surprise when a few months later, at an émigré conference, Martov tried to bury the issue once and for all. 'Of course', he explained, 'it is impossible to contemplate a state of affairs so tragic that the proletariat, in order to consolidate its victory, would have to trample on [the major] political rights'[3] and Plekhanov should have made this clear. Plekhanov did not disturb the burial and his only response was a laconic 'Merci!'

In Akimov's judgment, though, it was here that the Party had to clarify its intentions and make a stand one way or the other. 'Our answer to the problem of dictatorship', he wrote, 'will affect every single step of our activity.'[4] Here there could be no doubts. For his part, he demanded that the Party declare its faith in majority rule, in democratic processes and in the inviolability of the citizen's elementary freedoms. Certainly Marx and Engels had, at one point, contemplated the seizure of power by a minority party. But Bernstein was probably right to see this approach as the product of a passing phase when Marx and Engels were still very much under the influence of Blanqui. A far better guide to their ultimate position was the key phrase in the *Communist Manifesto* which declared that 'the proletarian movement is the independent movement of the majority in the interest of the vast majority'. As the only concrete example of the 'proletarian dictatorship', Marx and Engels had taken the Paris Commune but, as they themselves described, the Commune was based on universal suffrage and respect for the rights of the individual. In

[1] See below, pp. 179–80.   [2] See below, p. 175.
[3] *Protokoly 2-ogo ocherednogo s"ezda Zagranichnoi ligi* (Geneva, 1904), p. 50.
[4] See below, p. 153.

his *State and Revolution* of mid-1917 Lenin, of course, would use the same text, with at least equal justification, to support his campaign for the destruction of parliamentarianism in its traditional Western forms and its replacement by the direct rule of the masses guided by the Party. Aware that, in the last resort, the texts yield what the reader seeks, Akimov insisted that the Party drop the demand for 'proletarian dictatorship' and make it absolutely clear that it would limit itself by democratic 'laws which it will recognize as inviolable'.[1]

Conclusion

In its initial stages, the Economist crisis has to be seen as the last and most dramatic of those essentially personal disputes which since the 1880s had periodically ensnared Plekhanov's Group for the Emancipation of Labour. But the character of the dispute was totally transformed by Lenin's decision of late 1899 to rescue Plekhanov's forces from their helpless isolation and to rally the Marxist revolutionaries in Russia around the banner of an embattled orthodoxy. Lenin deliberately provoked an escalating debate which eventually produced a major ideological confrontation. Relentlessly, he selected the 'maximalist' and voluntarist aspects of Plekhanov's thought and rejected those aspects which lent themselves to a deterministic and gradualist interpretation. And what Lenin cast out Akimov took up and built into a coherent and cogent counter-interpretation of Russian Marxism. In this clash of two diametrically opposed philosophies—both claiming Plekhanov's inheritance—we see unmistakably mirrored that political and ideological division which in the years 1917–20 would split irrevocably first the Russian and then the entire European Social Democratic movement into enemy camps.

In 1917, the Menshevik leadership included many of Akimov's one-time opponents—Martov, Dan, Aksel'rod, Plekhanov, Potresov—but in essence this section of the Party acted in accord with what Akimov had preached. They denied the immediate possibility of a socialist revolution in Russia and proclaimed the necessity to defend the new constitutional régime at all costs. Yet it is a fact that, in general, Akimov has received hardly more recognition from the Menshevik exiles than from the Bolshevik rulers and, historically, this is understandable. Akimov and Lenin

[1] See below, p. 136.

had both unforgivably torn aside the veils of Plekhanov's dialectics exposing as unresolved the very dilemma which Russian Marxism had ostensibly been founded to overcome.

In her letter of 1881, Vera Zasulich, then still a Populist, had asked Marx whether his doctrines of economic determinism really meant that the revolutionaries in Russia would have to wait decades for the downfall of the autocracy and ages for the socialist revolution. Marx had evaded a definite answer, but he clearly wanted nothing less than that his doctrines should sabotage the revolutionary efforts of the terrorist and Populist *Narodnaia Volia*. However, against the *Narodnaia Volia* Plekhanov advanced the argument that only the people could make a people's revolution and that a revolutionary committee would only replace one tyranny by another. With his adoption of Marx's German strategy from the 1840s Plekhanov believed that he had overcome the double problem: Russia could have a genuine socialist revolution made by the people, by the industrial proletariat, and it could have that revolution in the not too distant future.

Yet now Lenin was clearly tending to substitute revolution by a committee for revolution by a class and Akimov no less clearly was relegating all hope of proletarian rule to the indefinite future. In retrospect, it is clear that there was no middle way for the Russian Marxists, but Plekhanov and his Menshevik disciples were naturally reluctant to recognize this fact and, still more, to thank those who had tried to make the choice crystal clear. After all if this was the choice, then Plekhanov, in line with Marx and Engels in their Russian policy, should have given his support to the Populist revolutionaries who argued that Marxism in its classic form was not applicable to Russia, that the revolutionary movement in a backward and predominantly peasant country had no room for a separatist proletarian party. The only possible escape route open to Plekhanov and the Mensheviks (as indeed to the economic determinists of Bolshevism, Kamenev, Trotsky and Bukharin) was their belief in the world revolution of the proletariat but here, too, Lenin and Akimov all but closed the door. Lenin persistently adapted Marxism to the specific conditions of Russia and tended to see the world through very Russian glasses, while Akimov made it clear enough in his writings that the leaders of the European Social Democratic movement were wedded to parliamentary methods and would hardly risk all to rescue a 'premature' Marxist coup in Russia.

The line of thought developed here could be taken to imply that Leninism was simply a return to the doctrines of the *Narodnaia Volia* but, as Akimov understood, this argument was fallacious for it ignored the fact that from Plekhanov alone Lenin acquired his fundamentalist approach to Marxist doctrine, his concept of a party led by a closed circle of ideologists and his belief that the revolution was to be made in the interests of a minority class. Populism, after all, claimed to represent the peasants; Lenin's Marxism was avowedly hostile to the peasants as a class (exempting only the very lowest stratum of so-called 'poor peasants'). In that sense, Leninism was a more 'Western' (and less Populist) form of Marxism than almost any other, for it was pledged to modernization *à l'outrance*.

In many ways, indeed, Lenin's pessimistic appraisal of historical trends and of the mass psychology seems today far more realistic than Akimov's classical nineteenth-century belief in the inevitability of steady progress. A strand of complacency runs through Akimov's writings. True, in the short run, his predictions proved remarkably accurate. At the beginning of the Second Party Congress, Akimov had said that the *Iskra* leaders would soon turn against each other and by the end of the Congress they had done so. The 1905 revolution, like the February Revolution of 1917, did come as a violent explosion from below, unplanned and yet immensely powerful. The workers did succeed in producing in the Soviets a genuine organ of popular expression and it was somehow only right that Akimov should have been in Russia ten months earlier than Lenin to witness this upsurge of proletarian creativity which was initially regarded with great suspicion by the Bolsheviks. In later years, the Mensheviks did, for the most part, move close to his standpoint however loth they were to admit the fact. The Social Democrats of the West could not and would not come to the aid of the Bolsheviks in 1917 and even Rosa Luxemburg—in accordance with Akimov's analysis of her views—proved hostile to Lenin's concept of the proletarian dictatorship when actually faced with it in October 1917. And, of course, nobody else predicted so early as Akimov what Leninism in action would mean. Nevertheless, in his heart of hearts, he did not believe that Lenin could succeed and here his optimism betrayed him. In the last resort, though, the debate between Lenin and Akimov was not so much a contest of predictions as a clash of moralities, of ethical absolutes, and both sides have therefore to be heard out.

98

THE SECOND CONGRESS OF THE RUSSIAN SOCIAL DEMOCRATIC LABOUR PARTY

BY VLADIMIR AKIMOV

The Second Congress of the Russian Social Democratic Labour Party was published in Geneva in 1904, under the title *K voprosu o rabotakh vtorogo s"ezda Rossiiskoi Sotsial-Demokraticheskoı Rabochei Partii*. Hitherto it has not been republished.

Most of the footnotes are editorial and are keyed into the text by numerical indicators. Akimov's notes to the Russian edition of 1904 are keyed into the text by symbols. Where it was found necessary to enlarge upon Akimov's notes, the additions are enclosed in brackets.—*Ed.*

PREPARATORY MANOEUVRES AND
THE SPLIT

In June 1902 the *Iskra* group published in its newspaper a draft programme for the Russian Social Democratic Labour Party (*Iskra*, no. 21). During the following year, no 'critical comments' or 'proposed amendments' were published by anyone (with the exception of a short article by the Latvian comrades in *Zhizn*').[1] However, 'resolutions' expressing full agreement with the views of *Iskra* were passed by some fifteen committees. This in itself showed that the comrades did not approach the complex, difficult, and important matter of drafting a Party programme with sufficient care and attention.

In publishing the draft programme, its authors wrote, quite properly, that 'the Party programme should embody the collective thought of the Party'. 'This means', they went on, 'that all the active Party groups should help to draft it.'[2] Yet the fact is that for the whole year no other group took any part in the preparation of the programme, and the work which should have been collective remained individual.

All that remained was to wait for the congress. There was reason to hope that there, at any rate, the collective thought of the Party, starting with criticism of the draft, would formulate its credo.

But very soon these hopes also began to fade. The Organizational Committee, formed in October 1902 in order to convene the congress, was composed solely of extreme *Iskra* adherents; all opponents were excluded from it, and it was therefore natural to fear that the ideological interests of the numerous and varied opponents of *Iskra* would not be adequately represented at the congress.

According to the resolution adopted at the Belostok conference in [March] April 1902 the Organizational Committee was to consist of two sections, one in Russia, one abroad. The latter, incidentally,

---

[1] I.e., 'Redaktsionnaia zametka po povodu proekta programmy *Zari i Iskry*' (translated from the Latvian *Sozialdemokrats*, no. 7), *Zhizn*' (London), no. 4 (July 1902), pp. 165–70.

[2] *Iskra*, no. 21 (1 June 1902), p. 2.

included a delegate of the Union of Russian Social Democrats [Abroad], which was known to entertain a viewpoint differing from that of *Iskra*. But the Union of Russian Social Democrats was not invited to the October conference, which reconstituted the Organizational Committee; it was thus arbitrarily excluded from important work which concerned the entire Party.

The Organizational Committee's report to the congress stated that 'the Petersburg Committee sent invitations to the organizations which had taken part in the first conference'.[1] This is not true, since the Union of Russian Social Democrats received no invitation.

Another participant in the April conference was a delegate of the Petersburg Committee, which differed sharply from *Iskra* at that time. The *Iskra* adherents in the Petersburg Committee, convinced that they could not turn the committee on to 'the true path', carried out a coup in the summer of 1902 which led to a split. In the autumn of 1902, there were therefore two organizations in Petersburg, each calling itself the Party committee.

But the October conference was attended only by a representative of the *Iskra* organization (*Protokoly*, p. 20). Who had the right to exclude the second organization, and on what grounds? And who was brought in to decide which of the two Petersburg organizations had the right to be called the Party committee? The October conference was run by the *Iskra* group, and so these questions did not come up there.

'No representative of the Bund came' to the October conference, states the report of the Organizational Committee. Thus, all the anti-*Iskra* elements were excluded from the preparations for the congress.

'It was decided', we read further in the report, 'to make up the Organizational Committee from representatives of the same bodies that had become members of the Organizational Committee by vote of the April conference.' 'The April Organizational Committee consisted of representatives of three organizations: *Iskra*, the Bund, and the Union of Southern Committees.'

This is again incorrect, in two respects. First, the April conference elected *persons*, and not representatives of organizations, to the Organizational Committee. Second, the Union of Southern

---

[1] The report of the Organizational Committee is in *Vtoroi ocherednoi s"ezd Ross. Sots.-Dem. Rabochei Partii: Polnyi tekst protokolov* (Geneva, 1903), pp. 20–5; hereafter cited as *Protokoly*.

Committees no longer existed at the time—a fact which, according to the report, became known to those responsible for the new Organizational Committee only during the October conference.

Whatever the case may be, the Organizational Committee did not include a single representative of the anti-*Iskra* persuasion.

The Voronezh Committee immediately protested against these obvious violations of the resolution of the April conference, demanding that representatives of the Union of Russian Social Democrats Abroad and the St Petersburg Union of Struggle [*Soiuz Bor'by*] be added to the Organizational Committee. It paid a heavy price for this daring—it was not admitted to the congress. The report of the Organizational Committee gives a page-long account of how much time and effort the Committee expended on the Odessa group, the Workers' Will [*Rabochaia Volia*], 'which came into existence, it is true, before 1 May of last year [1902] but was almost inactive until the autumn ' (*Protokoly*, p. 23). The organization which is now called the Voronezh Committee was formed as early as 1894; it has worked consistently since then, has several times been broken up by the police, and has issued nine proclamations during the past year. Besides, it is the only committee composed of workers. Nevertheless, it was given short shrift.

Seventeen organizations were informed by the Organizational Committee that they could not send delegates to the congress; the Voronezh Committee was listed as one of these. In fact, it never received this communication and was therefore unable to resort to arbitration, as did nine other organizations.

Foreseeing the danger of being excluded from the congress, the Voronezh Committee had long before the congress requested the Union of Russian Social Democrats to demand arbitration for it in the event of retaliatory action by the Organizational Committee. But the Union of Russian Social Democrats was itself not told until the last moment which organizations were invited to the congress and which were excluded; nor was it notified in advance of the date of the congress.

Similar treatment was accorded to the *Bor'ba* group abroad. This was the only group which, prior to the congress, published several pamphlets dealing with the question of the Party programme. The group had only one feature in common with the Voronezh Committee—it was anti-*Iskra*. Hence, there was not a single anti-*Iskra* group that was not barred, in greater or lesser measure, from the work of the congress or from its preparation.

Protests were futile, since the credentials committee was made up solely of *Iskra* members, with the single exception of Comrade Iudin of the Bund.

However, the rules of the congress, drawn up by the Organizational Committee, contained a 'liberal' point which left a chance even for dissenting elements to get into the congress. Every committee was allowed two mandates, to make it possible—as the rules explained—to present to the congress the minority as well as the majority views. An advocate of anti-*Iskra* positions could thus be sent to the congress as a delegate of an organization which was predominantly pro-*Iskra*.

However, in their conviction that it was necessary and useful to do all they could to exclude representatives of 'sedition' from the congress, the *Iskra* partisans in the Organizational Committee were actually surpassed by their fellows in the various Party committees. Comrade Kostich commented on this at the congress as follows: 'I have looked into this question particularly, and have found that all the committees which have a majority and a minority have sent both delegates from the majority.' In the *Protokoly* (p. 259), Kostich is reported to have said: 'The majority will always elect two of its own delegates.' Nevertheless, the earlier quotation, taken from my personal notes at the congress, is confirmed in the *Protokoly* by the speeches of those who immediately referred to Kostich's words (see the speeches of Gol'dblat, Liber, and Akimov, pp. 260, 261; also *The Second Congress of the RSDLP: the Report of the Bund Delegation* [*Vtoroi s"ezd RSDRP: Otchet delegatsii Bunda* (London, 1903)], p. 52).

Finally, there was still another way to give the Party minority an opportunity to defend its views at the congress. According to the rules of the congress, the Organizational Committee was empowered to invite, in a consultative capacity, comrades who had rendered special services to our movement and who represented different positions. But again, with the sole exception of one member of the Bund, these especially honoured comrades were all *Iskra* members. The Bund was thus allotted as much honour as influence—ten per cent.[1]

The Organizational Committee did not consider it its duty to invite to the congress and hear the views of such a man, for

---

[1] Akimov is here referring to the fact that the Bund delegation was permitted to cast five votes (out of a total of fifty-one) at the congress, while a Bundist, Arkadii Kremer, was one of the eight delegates invited in a consultative capacity as guests of honour.

example, as Comrade Krichevskii. Krichevskii was already active in Social Democratic work in Russia in the late 1880s. Compelled to escape abroad after release from prison, he immediately attained prominence as a contributor to international Social Democratic publications. As early as 1890 he was writing for the *Sotsial-Demokrat*, published by the Emancipation of Labour Group [*Gruppa 'Osvobozhdenie Truda'*], and contributed a number of articles to *Die Neue Zeit*. Later, parting company with the Emancipation of Labour Group, he assumed direction of the publications of the Social Democratic Library. In 1894–5 he wrote several pamphlets, which enjoyed wide success. He also translated Kautsky's *Erfurt Programme* and Marx's *Wage Labour and Capital* and *The Eighteenth Brumaire*. In 1898 he became a member of the editorial board of the Union of Russian Social Democrats, and for a time he was its sole editor. It was thus under his direction that the Union published seventy-two pamphlets, leaflets, and issues of *Rabochee Delo* [*Workers' Cause*]. The extent to which he was the spokesman of the views held at that time by Russian Social Democrats may be seen from the fact that the campaign which *Iskra* launched against these views was directed primarily at Krichevskii. At the same time Krichevskii continued to write for several German newspapers. For seven years he was a regular contributor to the central organ of the German Social Democrats, *Vorwärts*, and also continued to write for the party's theoretical journal, *Die Neue Zeit*. Even when *Iskra* had carried its polemic with Krichevskii into the Western European press, Kautsky again invited him to write for his organ. Krichevskii replied that he would, but only on condition that his articles appeared without any editorial changes. Kautsky agreed. In addition, Krichevskii was, at the time of the congress, the representative of the Russian Social Democratic Labour Party in the International Socialist Bureau; his election had been ratified in 1900 by all our Party committees.

But all this was evidently nullified by the fact that Krichevskii actively opposed *Iskra*-ism, and his presence at the congress was adjudged superfluous. For our part, we did not raise the question of Krichevskii for two reasons: first, because it would have been futile—our proposal was bound to be rejected; second, because it would have been too painful for us to hear Krichevskii subjected to the same kind of insults and ridicule that Comrade Riazanov had to suffer from the delegates and particularly from the chairman of the congress, Comrade Plekhanov. The fight that flared up over Comrade Riazanov showed that the leaders of the congress would stop at nothing in their determination to 'throw out', to use Lenin's expression, all elements that displeased him.

The same thing occurred in connexion with another comrade, K. (see the pamphlet by Pavlovich): 'One of the representatives of *Iskra* in the Organizational Committee, Comrade Z. [Aleksandrova —*Ed.*] proposed inviting a certain K., a member of *Rabochee Delo*, who was known to the organization only for his shifts of position. Z. based the case for inviting K. on . . . the fact that Z. shared all those opinions in which K. differed from *Iskra*' (pp. 7–8).[1] According to Pavlovich, 'this statement astonished and angered all the members of the *Iskra* organization'. Martov 'protested vigorously' (p. 7). From the minutes of the League congress[2] we learn (p. 56) that Z.—a representative of *Iskra* in the Organizational Committee—felt that Comrade K. was thoroughly familiar with the problems involved in the programme and therefore insisted on his being invited. At the same congress Martov explained the reasons for his 'vigorous protest' against inviting K.: 'I disagree with the appraisal of this man; I have grounds for thinking he is closer to the *Rabochee Delo* group than to *Iskra*.'

Martynov and I submitted a proposal to Comrade Kol'tsov, chairman of the Credentials Committee, urging that Comrade Parvus be invited to the congress in a consultative capacity. This proposal was also rejected. Evidently, our ringleaders had so little faith in their followers that they were afraid to have their ideological opponents at the congress even without the right to vote. And so, this final means of drawing all of the Party's forces into the common cause was also rejected. The cause of the Party was turned into that of one group.

[1] Pavlovich (P. A. Krasikov), *Pis'mo k tovarishcham o vtorom s"ezde RSDRP* (Geneva, 1904). The 'Z.' in this passage is clearly Ekaterina Aleksandrova; 'K.' is I. V. Chernyshev. Lenin, *Sochineniia* (4th ed. Moscow), VII (1946), 509.

[2] *Protokoly 2-go ocherednogo s"ezda Zagranichnoi ligi russkoi revoliutsionnoi sots.-demokratii*, ed. I. Lesenko and F. Dan (Geneva, 1904). The congress referred to here was that held in October 1903 by the League of Russian Revolutionary Social Democrats Abroad—the organization formed in 1901 by the *Iskra–Zaria* group. In October 1903 the League was split between the supporters of Martov and those of Lenin. At the time Plekhanov was still allied with Lenin, and together they edited *Iskra*, but immediately after the League congress, Plekhanov opened negotiations with Martov's camp (known, since the split in August 1903, at the Second Party Congress, as the Minority, the Mensheviks). *Iskra* now became a Menshevik journal and was often referred to as the 'new' *Iskra* to distinguish it from the original journal, of which Lenin was an editor.

The congress was to have settled two cardinal problems. It had to draft the Party programme and to set up the Party organization. It performed neither task. As for the Party organization, the congress failed utterly to establish it. Our Party has never been in such a state of anarchy as that we see today. It is clear to everyone that the Central Committee formed at the congress enjoys neither the authority nor the power essential to this important Party institution. It—together with the other Party institutions and the links between them—will have to be reconstructed by life itself. This has happened, without question, because the *Iskra* school, represented at the congress by the majority of the delegates, could not and would not respect the historic process of our Party's development. The *Iskra* school, accustomed to treating 'elemental, spontaneous' processes with hatred and contempt, wanted to counter them with its own plan of development. Comrade Martov went so far as to speak of the rapid and powerful growth of the Bund and the forms assumed by the organization of the Jewish proletariat as a historical anomaly. Comrade Martov at this point was like a man looking at a magnificent sunset and commenting: 'Such vivid colours! It's unnatural!'

What have been the basic features of our Party's development? What tasks has this development set before 'those who consciously express this unconscious process'? What type of organization was being shaped historically by the course of this development?

It would have been impossible for the *Iskra* school even to ask such questions. And the only elements within our Party which could ask and at least make an effort to answer them were, as I have said, excluded from the work of building the Party.

I shall attempt in another pamphlet to give my own answers to these questions and so contribute to the extent of my ability to this vital task. The present pamphlet will be devoted to questions involved in the programme.

To begin with, I shall present here my report on the work of the Union [of Russian Social Democrats Abroad]. The congress refused to hear this report, even while it adopted a resolution to abolish the Union. The reports to the congress were not appended to the *Protokoly* either, and I do not know whether they will ever be published. I shall therefore include my report in the present pamphlet. The report was prepared under the same conditions that dictated the subject matter of my speeches: I had no hope of

convincing the congress of anything! The congress not only enter-
tained a prejudiced view of the position of the Union delegates,
but did not wish to listen to us. Hence, any attempt to report on
the enormous work accomplished by the Union during the past
four years would have been superfluous. In the eyes of the delegates, the more the Union had accomplished, the worse—since
everything it did was evil. In view of this, I aimed in my report
merely to provoke a discussion of the Union's theoretical position.
I might have succeeded, had it not been for the 'firm policy' of
the 'mailed fists'.

Further, I shall discuss three points in the theoretical part of
our programme which I feel are particularly important. Extraneous
reasons, such as insufficient financial and technical resources,
compel me to limit myself to these three points. The entire programme seems to me to be extremely unsatisfactory. It was
adopted only because it is not *comme il faut* to be without a programme, but the congress adopted it in an utterly mechanical way.

In the minimum programme there are also very important
deviations from the international programme, but these cannot be
discussed briefly. It will suffice here to point to one example, the
question of proportional representation. In Belgium, a special
Party congress was called to discuss this question alone. The
enemies of the Social Democrats predicted a near-split in the
Workers Party on this score. At our congress, Comrades Posadovskii and Plekhanov quite correctly discussed this question on
the basis of principle, expressing highly interesting and consistent views.[1] However, the only delegate to oppose them in
principle, in a few brief words, was Comrade Egorov (although
Comrade Gol'dblat did voice his disapproval). The rest of the
congress was silent and silently supported the views of Comrades
Posadovskii and Plekhanov, as amended by Martov. I am deeply
convinced that Russian Social Democrats will repeal this decision
and that Comrade Martov will renounce his amendment.

The section on labour legislation contains demands that will
certainly not be supported by the authors of the programme
themselves. This will show how carelessly and hastily the draft
programme was prepared, merely for the sake of the bombastic

[1] The now famous Posadovskii–Plekhanov episode is discussed both in my
Introduction, pp. 94–5, and by Akimov in the conclusion to this work,
pp. 179–80.

phrase: 'The party of the class-conscious proletariat henceforth has its own programme.' Thus, for example, the demand concerning factory courts that is voiced in paragraph 15 was put into practice by Millerand in France and Thiébaud in Switzerland, and was defended by *Vorwärts*. But it was strongly opposed by orthodox Social Democrats. Another paragraph, 3, urging a total ban on overtime work, will be considered entirely unfeasible by anyone at all familiar with the problem.

Thus, our entire programme must be rewritten, from basic principles down to the smallest practical demands. By this I do not mean to say that the Second Congress of our Party has made no contribution to the formulation of a programme. On the contrary, it was the first important step. Today every member of the Party is inevitably regarded as a supporter of the Party's programme. Every thinking Party member must therefore begin to study it. A great many comrades will now start to evaluate its theses, and it is this critical work alone that can produce the formula which will correctly express the collective thought of the Party. My pamphlet is therefore meant not to belittle the work of the congress but, on the contrary, to continue the work just barely begun. It is this molecular work of the vital forces within our Party that constitutes the strength of Social Democracy.

[In the 1904 edition, the 'Report' of the Union to the Second Party Congress was reproduced here. However, its subject matter is peripheral to Akimov's central arguments in this work, and it has therefore been included separately as Appendix I, pp. 183–92.]

PROBLEMS OF THE PROGRAMME

Now I want to examine three of the most important questions involved in the programme: the theory of 'priming', the theory of pauperization, and dictatorship. Unless specified otherwise, the italics in the quotations are mine.

The *Iskra* programme is constructed along the lines of the Erfurt programme. The Erfurt programme consists of three parts: a characterization of contemporary society and its course of development, a statement of Social Democratic goals, and a discussion of how these goals are to be attained. The *Iskra* draft adds to these an introduction on the international character of Social Democracy.

Modern society and its development are characterized in the Erfurt programme in four theses: (1) The development of modern society is in the direction of division into two camps, capitalist and proletarian; (2) the wealth of some and the poverty of others both increase; (3) there is also growing antagonism between the proletariat and the bourgeoisie; (4) crises intensify this antagonism and expose the internal contradictions and bankruptcy of the existing order.

In the Vienna programme, the first thesis of the Erfurt programme is further subdivided; the programme first states the fact that society is divided into classes, and then notes the tendency toward a deepening of this division. The *Iskra* programme is at this point close to the formulation of the Vienna programme.

The second paragraph of the Erfurt programme answers the question of how the process of the development of society affects the individual classes. The third paragraph notes the antagonism between the interests of the bourgeoisie and the proletariat. In the *Iskra* draft we no longer see the clarity of formulation found in the Erfurt programme. On the one hand, the factor of dissatisfaction and struggle is entirely absent from these theses; it is transferred to subsequent paragraphs and interpreted differently than in the Erfurt programme. On the other hand, the effect of social development on the interests of the proletariat is noted not only in this paragraph, but three times, in three separate theses. Nevertheless, it is not clearly formulated and remains

110

vague and indefinite. Moreover, this vagueness results from the fact that the authors have sought here to formulate an antiquated view, which can no longer withstand criticism and which is at variance with the modern tactics of international Social Democracy.

And yet this paragraph touches upon a most important question, which has been debated in the foreign socialist press as the theory of pauperization, *Verelendungs-theorie, théorie de la misère grandissante*.

It seemed to me that it was especially important to point this out to the congress. In my introductory speech, I managed only to state the problem, but was given no opportunity to develop my ideas. Yet my opponents ascribed to me a position which I cannot leave without refutation. I shall state in this pamphlet what I wished to say at the congress.

The final paragraph of the first part of the programme corresponds to the text of the Erfurt programme. At the congress, I also proposed an amendment to the point concerning crises. However, since this amendment bears only indirectly on the tendencies in the programme which I oppose, I shall not return to it in the present work. Nor will I discuss most of my other amendments.

Further, the second part of the programme, dealing with the Party's goals, again deviates from the Erfurt programme. It was evidently meant to follow the scheme of the Vienna programme. However, the similarity to the Vienna programme is only in form. In substance, its approach to the proletariat is very different not only from the spirit of the Vienna programme, but also from that of the Erfurt programme, as well as from the most fundamental principles of scientific socialism. My statement to this effect was distorted by Comrade Lenin. And since I was unable to answer him then, I shall answer him now.

The third part of the Erfurt programme, dealing with the Party's tasks, falls into five points. Formally, the *Iskra* programme follows the same pattern.

The first and last paragraphs of the German programme, corresponding to the last paragraph of the Russian programme, discuss our Party's attitude toward non-proletarian classes. The second paragraph deals with the conquest of political power. The third, dealing with the rôle of Social Democracy with respect to the proletariat, defines the relationship between the concepts of party and class. Each of these theses is also discussed in the *Iskra* programme. The fourth paragraph proclaims the international character of our movement. In the *Iskra* programme, this point appears in the beginning, in the form of an introduction. In essence, however, every one of these theses diverges most sharply from the ideas of the Erfurt programme. Sometimes, only the terms are new, only the shades of meaning; the distinctions seem only semantic—yet what a vast difference they make in these two programmes! As a result, the two programmes emerge as remarkably complete expressions of two sharply divergent philosophies.

I cannot analyse all these points at this time, but I shall discuss at least one of them: the question of the conquest of political power. Finally, I shall analyse the arguments with which my opponents disposed of my brief, ten-minute speech, knowing that I would not be permitted to defend my position.

The Premises of Socialism

The goal of the international Social Democratic party is to replace the present capitalist system with a socialist system, under which 'large-scale production will be transformed from a source of poverty and enslavement into a source of the highest welfare'.[1] This is what the Erfurt programme states and this should be the idea set forth in every Social Democratic programme. But the Vienna programme points out that the capitalist system itself will inevitably produce the forces and the means for its own destruction and the creation of a new world. These forces lie in the proletariat, which becomes conscious of its class interests and ideals, the theoretical expression of which is scientific socialism. And the means are the technical advances which permit the organization of collective production. Here, too, the *Iskra* programme deviates from the Erfurt programme and follows the order of the Vienna programme, but only the order, not the ideas.

'The necessary material and spiritual conditions for new forms of collective production are created', says the Vienna programme. The material conditions reside in the fact that, already within the capitalist system, production becomes collective, 'individual production is squeezed out', and therefore 'individual ownership becomes superfluous and harmful'. The right of private property becomes a harmful legal institution, a privilege which is at variance

---

[1] 'Programm der Sozialdemokratischen Partei Deutschlands', in *Protokoll über die Verhandlungen des Parteitages der Sozialdemokratischen Partei Deutschlands Abgehalten zu Erfurt, 14.–20. Oktober 1891* (Berlin, 1891), p. 4; henceforward cited as *Erfurt*.

with actual relationships and the requirements of further social development. It becomes possible and necessary to transform the instruments of collective labour into collective property.

As for the spiritual conditions, they lie in the fact that 'the greater the expansion of the proletariat, resulting from the development of capitalism, the more it is compelled to launch a struggle against capitalism, and the more capable it becomes of waging this struggle . . . The proletariat begins to realize that it must further hasten the development [of society] and that its goal should be the transfer of the means of production to common ownership by the entire people.'[1]

The *Iskra* draft offers a good formulation of the process which creates 'the material conditions for the replacement of capitalist by socialist productive relations'. I would say, however, that the draft speaks *only* about material conditions. The proletarians are regarded here merely as the *instrumentum vocale*; these instruments become sufficient in number ('the proletarians . . . grow in number').[2] Just as giant machines are made up of individual mute tools and implements which were formerly separate units in the artisan's workshop, so do modern plants and factories muster within themselves whole collectives of human instruments, once scattered through outlying districts ('the proletarians grow in number and solidarity'). The draft also states that 'the labouring and exploited masses become increasingly dissatisfied' and that the struggle between the proletarians and 'their exploiters becomes ever sharper'.[3] But these were precisely the characteristics of the slaves of ancient Rome—mere 'speaking instruments'. They too constituted a 'labouring and exploited mass' whose 'dissatisfaction' grew and whose 'struggle against their exploiters became ever sharper'. However, this was merely a technical flaw in the instruments. The exploiters took account of this flaw just as we today take into account imperfections in machines. Neither the exploiters nor the exploited thought of abolishing the institution of slavery as such.

Are these the qualities of the proletarians which make us

---

[1] 'Programm der Sozialdemokratischen Arbeiterpartei in Oesterreich', in *Protokoll über die Verhandlungen der Sozialdemokratischen Arbeiterpartei in Oesterreich Abgehalten zu Wien, 2.–6. November 1901* (Vienna, 1901), p. 3; henceforward cited as *Vienna*.

[2] 'Proekt programmy Rossiiskoi Sotsial-demokraticheskoi Rabochei Partii', *Zaria* (Stuttgart), no. 4 (August 1902), p. 4; see below, Appendix ii, p. 194.

[3] *Ibid.*

certain of the victory of the working-class? Are these the conditions assuring the coming of a socialist system? What of the
creative spiritual forces of the proletariat? What of its class
consciousness?

Let us take a look at Plekhanov's comments. He writes on p. 31:
'Our draft programme says that, as the contradictions inherent
in capitalist society develop, "there is also an increase in the
dissatisfaction of the labouring and exploited mass and the
proletariat's revolutionary struggle against the exploiters becomes
ever sharper".'[1]

In quoting the text, Plekhanov amends it. In the quotation as
he gives it, he inserts the word 'revolutionary' before 'struggle'.
He also uses the term 'proletariat' (i.e., a class) instead of 'they'
or 'proletarians' (i.e., a sum of individuals). These are highly
significant corrections. In Plekhanov's formulation, the scattered
individual struggles of proletarians are seen as the molecular
movement of a single, powerful social force. In the draft's formulation, the proletarians are 'human dust' flying into the eyes of the
exploiters.

Plekhanov's amendment is essential, but insufficient. After the
passage quoted above, Plekhanov continues his commentary and
amendments as follows:

These words, it seems to us, correctly express the attitude toward
capital of the various classes of the people oppressed by it. Its yoke is felt
today not only by the proletariat, and the proletariat is not alone in
resenting this yoke. But only the proletariat *consciously rebels* against it;
the proletariat alone wages a *revolutionary* struggle against capital, i.e.,
a struggle aimed at the *abolition of capitalist relations in production*
[all italics Plekhanov's].[2]

And so, in Plekhanov's opinion, the draft has reference to
'various classes of the oppressed people'. Dissatisfaction grows
among the entire 'labouring and exploited mass', including the
proletariat. But, in contrast to other classes, the proletariat is not
only dissatisfied; it 'consciously rebels' and 'wages a revolutionary
struggle'.

'It seems' to Plekhanov that this entirely correct idea is
'correctly expressed' by the wording of the draft programme.
Plekhanov wants to convince his readers that the words of the

[1] *Zaria*, no. 4, p. 31. Plekhanov's commentary (pp. 11 ff.) follows the draft
programme in this issue.
[2] *Ibid.* p. 31.

draft—they 'became increasingly dissatisfied', and 'their struggle against their exploiters becomes ever sharper'—mean the same as the 'conscious rebellion' and the 'revolutionary struggle' of a *class*, the 'proletariat'! Here, too, Plekhanov is amending the draft, in which there is no reference whatever either to the conscious or the revolutionary nature of the proletariat's struggle or to its class character.

Plekhanov categorically, tirelessly, eulogizes the new draft, calling it 'fully orthodox'[1] and 'a photographically exact picture of reality'.[2] And if anyone 'does not like' 'orthodoxy', 'he does not have to read the draft; it was not written for him'.[3] But there are several places in the draft programme where it glaringly deviates from 'orthodoxy'. In such cases, Plekhanov declares that '*it seems*' to him that the draft expresses such and such an idea, and then proceeds to formulate his own emendation.

I endorse Plekhanov's emendations. I want our programme to state that 'as the contradictions inherent in bourgeois society grow' (*Iskra* draft),[4] 'there is also an increase in the *conscious, revolutionary class struggle, the rebellion* of the proletariat'[5] (Plekhanov's amendment). Instead, it speaks merely of '*their* (the proletarians') struggle with *their* exploiters'. Such a struggle has been characteristic of all oppressed people, under all systems of productive relations in past eras.

But how did it come about that an orthodox Social Democratic programme, stating the basic premises of socialism, did not find it necessary to note the conscious, revolutionary, and class character of the proletarian struggle? This cannot be, and is not, accidental. It fully corresponds to the view of one of the authors of the draft, Comrade Lenin, who regards the proletariat as a passive medium in which the bacillus of socialism, introduced from without, can develop.

In his book, *What Is to Be Done?*,[6] Comrade Lenin offers the following view:

The theory of socialism grew out of the philosophic, historical, and economic theories that were developed by the educated representatives of the propertied classes, the intellectuals. The founders of modern scientific socialism, Marx and Engels, were themselves, in social position,

---

[1] *Ibid.* p. 21. [2] *Ibid.* pp. 24, 27. [3] *Ibid.* p. 21.
[4] *Ibid.* p. 4. See below, Appendix II, p. 194.
[5] *Zaria*, no. 4, p. 31.
[6] N. Lenin, *Chto delat'? Nabolevshie voprosy nashego dvizheniia* (Stuttgart, 1902).

members of the bourgeois intelligentsia. Similarly, in Russia the theoretical doctrine of Social Democracy arose *entirely independently* of the spontaneous labour movement; it arose as a natural and inevitable outcome of the development of the thought of the revolutionary-socialist intelligentsia (p. 21).

Taken by themselves, these strikes [of 1896] were trade-union struggles, but not yet Social Democratic struggles. They marked the *awakening of antagonism between workers and employers*, but the *workers were not and could not be* conscious of the irreconcilable conflict of their interests with the entire modern political and social system. They still lacked Social Democratic consciousness . . . This consciousness could only be brought to them from without. The history of all countries shows that, by its own efforts alone, the working-class is able to develop only trade-union consciousness, i.e., realization of the necessity for combining into trade-unions, *waging a struggle with the employers*, and seeking to press the government to pass . . . laws (p. 20).

They imagine that a pure and simple labour movement can and will evolve its own independent ideology . . . But this is a profound mistake (p. 26) . . . There can be no talk of an independent ideology, developed by the labouring masses in the process of their movement. [In creating an ideology] the workers take part not as workers, but as socialist theoreticians, as Proudhons and Weitlings (p. 27). Spontaneous development of the labour movement leads precisely to its subordination to bourgeois ideology . . . The spontaneous labour movement is trade-unionism, it is *Nur-Gewerkschaftlerei*, and trade-unionism means the ideological enslavement of the workers by the bourgeoisie (p. 28).

Thus, the expressions we see in the draft programme were taken almost *in toto* from the above lines by Lenin. The draft tells us that 'their [the proletarians'] struggle with their exploiters becomes ever sharper'. Lenin says: 'These strikes [of 1896] . . . marked the awakening of antagonism between workers and employers.' Plekhanov comments: 'It seems to me . . . these words say . . . that the proletariat *consciously rebels*, wages a *revolutionary* struggle . . . aimed at the *abolition of capitalist relations in production*' [all italics Plekhanov's]. But Lenin explains that 'the workers *were not and could not be conscious of the irreconcilable conflict of their interests with the entire modern . . . system.*' How, then, could Lenin agree that what 'it seems' to Plekhanov should actually be said in the programme?

Of course, Lenin is not against consciousness and revolutionary ideas; however, in his view, these excellent qualities belong not to the proletariat but to the revolutionary-socialist intelligentsia. It is the latter which, having organized the Social Democratic Party, will 'introduce' them into the 'labouring masses'. Therefore, this entire problem is discussed later, in that section of the draft which deals with the tasks of the Party.

And the paragraph under discussion formulates Lenin's view that, to make 'social revolution possible', there must be 'technological progress, growth in the number and solidarity of the proletarians, and a sharpening of their struggle against their exploiters'. All the rest will be done by the 'social-revolutionary intelligentsia', the 'professional revolutionaries'. They will form the party, which will be 'the conscious spokesman of the proletariat's class movement', 'basing itself' on a large number of massed proletarians. In support of his view concerning the rôle of the intelligentsia, Lenin quotes in *What Is to Be Done?* (p. 27) Kautsky's speech at the Vienna Congress. Kautsky said:

It is absolutely untrue that socialist consciousness is a necessary and direct product of the proletarian class struggle.[1]

Socialism and class struggle arise side by side, and not one out of the other; they arise out of different premises. Modern socialist consciousness can arise only on the basis of profound scientific knowledge. And the vehicle of science is not the proletariat but the *bourgeois intelligentsia* [Kautsky's italics]. Thus, socialist consciousness is something introduced into the proletariat's class struggle from without, and not something that arose from it spontaneously.[2]

Kautsky's view is absolutely wrong. I shall confine myself here to a quotation from Adler's reply to Kautsky's words, since Lenin's position, as I shall try to show, goes far beyond Kautsky's. Besides, if Kautsky may have had some grounds for saying that these disagreements with Adler were a *Doktorfrage* rather than programmatic differences, in Lenin's formulation the theory of priming the proletariat with socialism (*Erfüllungstheorie*) runs counter to the basic principles of scientific socialism.

Adler replied to Kautsky as follows:

In his criticism, Kautsky asserted, among other things, that the draft contains a contradiction, since it says in one place that Socialist Democracy must seek the emancipation of the entire people from the shackles of economic slavery, etc., and, in another, that this consciousness, this striving, arises in the proletariat spontaneously . . . I consider the text of the draft entirely correct, and find no contradiction in it. It says here

---

[1] *Vienna*, p. 124.
   Quoted in *Chto delat'?*, pp. 26–7, from Karl Kautsky, 'Das Programm der Sozialdemokratie in Oesterreich', *Die Neue Zeit*, xx, no. 3 (1902), 79–80. (In *Chto delat'?* the page number is incorrectly given as 97.)

that the proletariat arrives at an understanding of this entire development, that it becomes aware that the goal of the struggle for the liberation of the working-class must be communism. The vehicle of this
development, as the draft goes on to say, can be none other than the
organized proletariat itself. As for awakening the proletariat—this, in
turn, can only be the task of Social Democracy. Thus, as I have already
stated, I find no contradiction here; moreover, I maintain the view that
the whole development of the theory of socialism relates to the labour
movement as an ideological superstructure relates to material economic
development generally. I am convinced that the entire progress of
socialist thought can be explained by the economic movement of the
proletariat itself . . . I believe that the socialist idea is the product of the
working-class . . . Social Democracy is its brain . . . The birthplace of
Social Democratic thought is the proletariat; Social Democracy is the
product of this thought, and it brings the proletariat to self-knowledge.
(*Protokoll* [Vienna], p. 108.)

However, although Kautsky considers that 'socialism and class
struggle arise side by side', he also holds that they develop along
parallel lines, and that the rivulet of 'consciousness' finally flows
into the current of the proletarian movement. This image has been
used repeatedly as a figurative description of the development of
the socialist labour movement.

'The theory of socialism,' says Vandervelde (*Socialism in
Belgium*, 1898, p. 14), 'born of compassion, remained divided
from day-to-day socialism, born of suffering. It required long
years, full of heavy ordeals, for the thinkers and proletarians to
join forces and extend a hand to each other.'[1]

But in Vandervelde's thought, too, the intellectuals and proletarians are merely the theoreticians and the practical elements
of the same movement—socialism. In Lenin's view, however, the
'intelligentsia' develops in one direction. The 'theory of socialism'
'grows out' of 'philosophic, historical, and economic theories'.
But the proletariat moves in a different direction, it moves toward
'its subordination to bourgeois ideology'; the spontaneous labour
movement is trade-unionism. Hence, the intelligentsia must
launch a struggle against spontaneous development and '*divert*
[Lenin's italics] the labour movement from this spontaneous
striving'.[2]

No Social Democrat has, to my knowledge, ever attained such
paradoxes!

[1] J. Destrée and E. Vandervelde, *Le Socialisme en Belgique* (Paris, 1898).
[2] *Chto delat'?*, p. 28.

It is enough to pick up any work of Marx or Engels to see how widely this basic view of Lenin's, which is so fully reflected in the *Iskra* draft programme, diverges from the views of the founders of scientific socialism.

I shall not attempt here to compare Lenin's views with those of Marx and Engels. This was done before me, and better than I could do it, by Comrade Martynov in his report to the congress in the name of our organization. Comrade Martynov confined himself to a single correction of the draft programme (excluding minor ones), selecting precisely this paragraph as the most important. And rightly so. But it seems to me that Comrade Martynov was mistaken not to review all of the programme's theses, and not to show how the basic error of the programme was reflected in each of them.

In his *Anti-Dühring*, Engels graphically traces the process of development of new ideas and principles of action, using the example of military tactics. An example is not proof; however, I shall cite it, not as proof, but as illustration.

We have seen how the introduction of technological improvements has always, almost forcibly, led to changes and even revolutions in the methods of warfare, *often against the will of the military authorities.*[1]

In the Franco-Prussian War two armies met for the first time armed with breech-loading rifles, but each employing substantially the same tactics, which were a carry-over from the times of the old smooth-bore flintlocks. The Prussians, it is true, attempted to find in their company columns a formation more appropriate to the new weapon . . . But all attempts to expose closed formations of any type to enemy fire were abandoned, and from now on the Germans fought exclusively in dense skirmish lines. This was the type of line into which the columns—despite the resistance put up by the officers to this new form of 'indiscipline'—have normally broken up of themselves as soon as they came under the murderous hail of bullets. Similarly, the only movement now possible under the enemy's rifle fire was the run. *The soldier once more showed himself cleverer than the officer: he instinctively found* the only form of fighting possible under the fire of breech-loading rifles, and he managed it successfully *despite the stubbornness of his commanders.*[2]

The influence of brilliant generals was at best confined merely to the adaptation of the method of warfare to new weapons and new troops.[3]

But although the leaders have only to adapt 'the method of warfare to the troops', their rôle nevertheless remains not only necessary to the movement but also of prime importance.

[1] F. Engels, *Herrn Eugen Dührings Umwälzung der Wissenschaft* (Zürich, 1886), pp. 163–4.   [2] *Ibid.* pp. 161–2.   [3] *Ibid.* p. 159.

In issue no. 41 of *Iskra*, Plekhanov says that *Iskra*'s draft programme is indeed the only programme that could have been adopted by the Emancipation of Labour Group.[1] But every reader of his works must be impressed by Plekhanov's purely Marxist view that the ideology of the proletariat is developed 'by the labouring masses themselves in the very progress of their movement'.

All that is left to the ideologists is to formulate the ideology and to establish its theoretical foundation; then—proceeding from the theory thus established—to point out the best ways toward achieving the goal and predict the conditions under which the struggle will have to be waged in the future: *Le but de toutes les sciences est savoir pour prévoir et pourvoir.*

Such is the purpose and rôle of scientific socialism. And because this idea permeates all of Plekhanov's works, from the first to the very latest, including, as I have shown, his commentaries, I shall limit myself here to only two points.

'Ideas, notions, conceptions, in short, man's entire outlook, change with changing conditions of existence, social relations, and social life.' This, according to Marx, is how the 'independent ideology' of a class is developed. Citing the above lines from the [*Communist*] *Manifesto*, Plekhanov remarks quite justly that this theory impregnates the whole *Manifesto* 'and comprises what may without risk of error be called its *fundamental* idea'.[2]

The proletariat's philosophy is thus created by the conditions of its existence. As the proletariat evolves into an independent class, its ideas form themselves into an orderly theory.

This superstructure of independent ideology lags behind its base, behind the conditions of its existence which have changed in the course of a given period of time. This is why the proletariat remains for a time under the sway of the ideology of the class whose dominance historically precedes the rule of the proletariat. But it finally liberates itself from this ideology.

On 1 May 1891 a group of workers celebrated this international proletarian holiday in Petersburg. Four speeches were delivered. They were published abroad with an introduction by Plekhanov, in which he wrote:

Among the most advanced circles of Russian workers, that vanguard of the Russian revolutionary proletariat, awareness of the socio-political

---

[1] Plekhanov, 'Ortodoksal'noe bukvoedstvo', *Iskra*, no. 41, pp. 2 ff.
[2] Plekhanov, Foreword to *Manifest Kommunisticheskoi Partii K. Marksa i F. Engel'sa* (Geneva, 1900), p. lvi.

tasks of the working-class has already attained such clear-cut forms that all that is left for us, the revolutionary 'intellectuals', is to take note of them and guide ourselves by them, abandoning for all time our long search for the best of all possible programmes . . . This means that the workers have outstripped the bourgeoisie, and that all truly progressive people must come under the banner of the workers.[1]

Rabochaia Mysl' [*Labour Thought*] went no further in narrowing the rôle assigned to 'us, the revolutionary "intellectuals"'—perhaps because there was no further to go.

Today, twelve years after the writing of those lines, we revolutionary 'intellectuals' might say to Plekhanov: 'We are ready to take note of and guide ourselves by the ideas of the vanguard of the Russian revolutionary proletariat, but allow us, for the time being, not to abandon our long search!' In reply, we hear with astonishment that the programme of the Emancipation of Labour Group can be nothing but that of the author of *What Is to Be Done?* who says that the revolutionary-intellectual (this time, without the quotation marks) will not only 'develop the theoretical doctrine of Social Democracy entirely independently of the spontaneous labour movement', but must also divert this movement from its false path.

A pamphlet by the editors of the *Sotsial-Demokrat*, presented in 1891 at the International Socialist Congress, had this to say, among other things (the quotation is from the American newspaper *Progress*, no. 7):

It would be superfluous to seek to convince you, who represent the revolutionary proletariat, of the revolutionary rôle assigned by history to the modern proletariat. It would be equally superfluous to say that where there is no proletariat, there can be no socialist movement worthy of the name. Each of you knows all too well that *modern socialism is nothing else—to use the words of Engels—than the theoretical expression of the movement of the proletariat.*[2]

Nothing else! Socialism is only the theoretical expression of the movement of the proletariat! And so 'the movement of the proletariat' is socialist. At a given period, of course, the 'movement of the proletariat' may not yet present socialist demands. Specific forms of the 'movement of the proletariat' may, of course, 'in themselves', not be socialist. But in the direction taken by the

---

[1] *Pervoe maia 1891 goda: Chetyre rechi rabochikh proiznesennye na tainom sobranii v Peterburge* (Geneva, 1892), p. vi.

[2] 'Programma russkikh sotsial'demokratov', *Progress* (New York) (15 Jan. 1892), p. 3.

growing 'movement of the proletariat', in the goals which will *inevitably* sooner or later *be proclaimed* by the proletariat, in the significance of the particular acts of the proletariat in its class struggle—this movement is socialist. It develops spontaneously in the direction of socialism, and Social Democracy merely consciously elects as its goal that which will be the inevitable outcome of the initially unconscious 'movement of the proletariat'.

Social Democracy has no need to '*divert*' the proletariat from its path; it can and must seek only to accelerate its movement. Social Democracy has no reason to fear *this* spontaneous element—it is our own element. We are the 'firelighters'. Are we then to fear 'the beneficial, purifying flame'? We are the 'stormy petrels'—are we to fear the storm? We are the 'waves', the children of 'the hoary ocean'! With fire, we call up rebellion. With storm, we call the revolution. With turbulent ocean, we invoke the movement of the people.

In his note explaining the programme, Plekhanov says: 'Carefully, and not without "orthodox" intent, we have underlined in our draft the rôle of Social Democracy as the advance unit of the workers' army and, at the same time, as its leader.'[1] Plekhanov goes on to show how the authors of the programme have emphasized this rôle. Without using quotation marks, he cites almost verbatim the text of the draft on page 30 of his commentary, giving the reader the illusion that everything said here by Plekhanov is indeed to be found in the programme. But the programme does not contain the most important things said by Plekhanov. In this case, too, he corrects a word in quoting a passage, and inserts several words of his own. Then he breaks into a philippic against the 'critical' 'sedition' which, supposedly, 'has created a thick fog, leading the Russian Social Democrats of the "Economist" school to imagine that the duty of Social Democracy is not indefatigably and as rapidly as possible to stimulate the class consciousness of the proletariat, but solely to express that which has already been created without any assistance from the revolutionary bacillus'.[2]

But all these charges are nothing but 'fog'! Russian Social Democrats, whether of the 'Economist' or any other 'seditionary' tendency, have never imagined what Plekhanov attributes to them. Even when it was said that the rôle of the intelligentsia was 'to express that which has already been created', this was con-

---

[1] *Zaria*, no. 4, p. 30.   [2] *Ibid.*

sidered necessary precisely in order to stimulate 'indefatigably and as rapidly as possible the self-awareness of the proletariat'. As for the fog, Plekhanov needed it so that he might, under its cover, present not the idea expressed in the programme, but an entirely different (and quite correct) idea, sharply at variance with the programme.

Plekhanov defines the meaning of the programme as follows:

It [Social Democracy] organizes the working-class into an independent party, which opposes all the parties of the exploiters. It exposes to the working-class the irreconcilable contradiction between the interests of the exploiters and those of the exploited. And generally, by all the means available to it, it seeks to *accelerate* [Plekhanov's italics] the development of the class consciousness of the proletariat and to clarify for the latter the necessity and the character of the coming social revolution.[1]

On the whole, this quotation differs from the text of the programme no more than a translation differs from the original, except that the phrase 'and generally, by all the means available to it, it seeks to *accelerate* the development of the class consciousness of the proletariat' was inserted by Plekhanov himself.

In the entire quotation, Plekhanov underlines only one word —*accelerate*; evidently, he quite justly invests it with special importance. But this word is not in the programme, as indeed it could not be. For anyone who says that Social Democracy accelerates the development of the proletariat's class consciousness obviously expresses an idea diametrically opposed to the idea of the man who finds it necessary to bring socialist consciousness to the proletariat 'from without' and who feels that 'by its own efforts alone the working-class is able to develop only trade-union consciousness'. Under such conditions, it is natural that Plekhanov wants to 'accelerate' the development of the proletariat's self-awareness, while Lenin wants to 'divert' the proletariat from its path. Both are right from their respective points of view. But the points of view are poles apart.

I certainly did not insist—as Plekhanov says I did—that he divorce Marshal Lenin. But let him first openly divorce the old Plekhanov, the author of the above quotations. There is no alternative!

But we cannot do without the *services* of consciousness. 'The proletariat must attain self-knowledge' (Adler); the proletariat

[1] *Ibid.*

must 'give birth to the system of socialism' (Engels); the theory of socialism will be 'nothing else than the expression of the movement of the proletariat'. *Consciousness* within the movement of the proletariat is the *essential precondition* of social revolution, and this must be stated in our programme. As long as only 'professional revolutionaries' approach the struggle consciously, we shall see repetitions of the sad events of 1848.

'The movement existed', says Engels in the preface to *The Class Struggles* (p. 9, Russian translation):

It was instinctive, spontaneous, irrepressible. It was this fact which gave us faith in the inevitable victory of the revolution, which, though it was to take place under the leadership of the minority, would this time be most genuinely in the interest of the majority. If the broad popular masses have, during all the more or less extended revolutionary periods, responded so easily to the illusory promises of the leading minority, why should they have been less open to ideas which reflected with utmost exactness their own economic condition, which were nothing but the clear and conscious expression of their own still unrealized, still vaguely sensed needs? True, this revolutionary mood of the masses has almost always—and in most cases very quickly—given way to fatigue or even reactionary moods, as soon as illusions vanished and disappointment came. But this time it was a question not of promises but of the satisfaction of the most vital interests of the vast majority. It is true that this majority was still far from a clear awareness of its own interests; but the actual satisfaction of those interests—the lesson of experience—should quickly have opened its eyes. Could it be doubted, then, that the revolution of the minority would be transformed into the revolution of the majority as well? History did not bear out our expectations and the expectations of all those who shared our views.[1]

The material and spiritual conditions for socialism were absent: (1) 'The economic development of the continent was still far from the abolition of capitalist production' (*ibid.* p. 10). (2) 'The mass of workers did not have any definite plan of action before it' (*ibid.* p. 9). The proletariat's movement was 'instinctive, spontaneous, irrepressible', but it lacked consciousness, and it remained without result.

It is these conditions for the victory of the proletariat, which were lacking during the revolution of 1848 and which proved to be necessary, that we must note in the paragraph of the programme under discussion here. I therefore propose to revise it as follows:

[1] Engels, 'Vvedenie', in K. Marx, *Klassovaia bor'ba v Frantsii ot 1848 do 1850 g.* (Geneva, 1902), pp. ix–x (a translation of *Die Klassenkämpfe in Frankreich 1848 bis 1850*).

As all these contradictions characteristic of bourgeois society grow and develop, so the material and spiritual conditions for social revolution and the establishment of new forms of collective production are created. Technological advances, concentrating the means of production and distribution, and socializing the process of labour in capitalist enterprises, create the material basis for the replacement of capitalist by socialist productive relations. At the same time, the dissatisfaction of the labouring and exploited masses with the existing order also grows. There is an increase in the number and solidarity of the proletarians. The proletariat comes to realize that it must further the natural development of society and hasten the coming of the socialist order.

The Theory of Pauperization

In his commentary on the programme, Plekhanov says:

> The most important of the burning questions of our time, which agitate the Social Democrats of the whole world . . . a question upon which all the others depend, has been, as we well know, the problem of whether social inequality is growing or diminishing. In other words, does the economic distance between classes widen or narrow as capitalist society develops? The ideologists of the bourgeoisie have been very anxious to prove that it is narrowing . . . The theoreticians of socialism have demonstrated that . . . the distance . . . is constantly growing. And, of course, the authors of the draft programme have felt it their duty to present in the proper light this important result of the debate—a result which fully confirms the correctness of Marx's theory.[1]

The theoreticians of socialism and the bourgeoisie did indeed engage in such a debate. But it began—as Plekhanov himself showed in nos. 2–3 of *Zaria*—back in the days of Carey and Bastiat.[2] Is it that the socialist theoreticians have only just reached their conclusions, so that the authors of the Russian text of the international Social Democratic programme saw it as their particular duty to present the result of the debate? The results of *this* half-century-old debate have already been expressed in all the programmes of the Social Democrats. And, it would seem, it is sufficient for us simply to state them, as have the other programmes. But the point is that other programmes presented these results in different ways, since there were also disagreements within the ranks of the Social Democrats themselves.

What Plekhanov failed to point out was that, although these

---

[1] *Zaria*, no. 4, pp. 20–1.
[2] See Plekhanov, 'Kritika nashikh kritikov', *Zaria*, nos. 2–3 (December 1901), pp. 101 ff.

'burning questions'—including that of the theory of pauperization —were first raised by the Social Democratic press in its polemics [against the bourgeois theoreticians], they were subsequently given, and are still being given, conflicting answers by the socialists themselves. And it is the result of *this* debate that should have left its imprint on the Russian formulation of the truth, unquestioned by any Social Democrat, that the antagonism between the interests of the proletariat and the bourgeoisie is growing. However, this is not said either in the draft or in the commentaries.

This debate was carried from the pages of the press to the Vienna Congress of the Austrian Social Democratic Party (1901), which discussed a draft for a new programme.

The old Hainfeld programme of 1886 had the following to say on this problem: 'Private ownership of the means of production . . . implies the growing poverty of the popular masses, the growing impoverishment of ever wider strata of the people.'[1]

In the new [Austrian] programme, this passage is replaced by the following: 'The degree of exploitation increases and . . . the living standard of ever wider sections of the labouring people becomes more and more out of line with the rapidly growing productivity of their own labour and the growing wealth created by their own hands.'[2] Thus, instead of absolute worsening of the position of the working-class, the new Austrian programme speaks of relative worsening, increasing contradiction between what the proletariat receives and what it could and should receive.

The 1864 Statutes of the International said: 'The economical subjection of the man of labour to the monopolizer of the means of labour, that is, the source of life, lies at the bottom of servitude in all its forms, of all social misery, mental degradation, and political dependence.'[3]

The Gotha programme read (1875): 'In modern society the means of production are monopolized by the capitalist class. The resulting dependency of the working-class is the cause of poverty and enslavement in every form.'[4]

[1] *Verhandlungen des Parteitages der Österreichischen Sozialdemokratie in Hainfeld, 30. Dez. 1888—1. Jan. 1889* (Vienna, 1889), p. 3.
[2] *Vienna*, p. 3.
[3] *Address and Provisional Rules of the International Working Men's Association* (London, [1864?]), p. 12.
[4] 'Das Programm der Partei', in *Protokoll über die Verhandlungen des Parteitages der Sozialdemokratischen Partei Deutschlands Abgehalten zu Halle,*

The Erfurt programme, drawn up in 1891, after the Hainfeld programme, states: 'To the proletariat and the declining middle strata, this transition [of the means of production into the hands of the capitalists] means an increase in insecurity, poverty, oppression, enslavement, degradation, and exploitation.'[1]

Thus, the old Austrian programme was in strict accord with all the other programmes. Therefore, the change introduced at Vienna is all the more important. And it is all the more essential for the Russian text to express categorically the position of either the Vienna programme or the Hainfeld programme. But the *Iskra* draft fails to do so.

If we were to combine all the statements relating to this question, which, as we have pointed out, are scattered in three paragraphs of the *Iskra* draft, we would obtain the following text:

Hired labour becomes increasingly dependent on capital, and the level of its exploitation rises . . . Crises . . . encourage an even greater dependence of hired labour on capital. They hasten the relative or even absolute deterioration in the condition of the working-class. Thus, advancing technology, which leads to an increase in labour productivity and social wealth, results, in bourgeois society, in growing social inequality, a widening gulf between the haves and have-nots, and increasing insecurity, unemployment, and deprivations of every kind for ever wider sections of the labouring masses.

Thus, we find no definite answer in the programme adopted by the congress to the 'burning question of our day'. This is why Comrade Plekhanov is wrong when he says that the authors of the draft have 'presented in the proper light the important result of this debate'. The question is not illuminated, but obfuscated, and presented in a form that cannot satisfy anyone.

This is what the 'orthodox' Riazanov says on the subject:

If you are convinced that the condition of the working-class is deteriorating, then say simply and clearly, without stammering, 'It is *deteriorating*' [italics Riazanov's]. An idea . . . should be expressed clearly and definitely, and this cannot be said of the proposed draft. In one place it speaks of the increasing dependence of hired labour on capital and the rise in the level of exploitation; in another place, it speaks of relative *or even* [italics Riazanov's] absolute deterioration in the condition of the working-class.[2]

12.–18. Oktober 1890 (Berlin, 1890), p. 1; translated as 'Programme of the German Workers Party', in K. Marx, *Critique of the Gotha Programme*, ed. C. P. Dutt (New York, 1938), p. 89.   [1] *Erfurt*, p. 3.

[2] N. Riazanov, *Materialy dlia vyrabotki partiinoi programmy* (Geneva, 1903), II, 81.

Comrade Riazanov suggests that 'it should be stressed that the condition of the working-class cannot *improve* [italics Riazanov's] while capitalism exists' (p. 80).

My view, on the contrary, is that the programme should note that the condition of the working-class *can* improve *even* while capitalism still exists. But we are both dissatisfied with the draft's formulation: 'Why the wavering in the programme? Why this timidity? Why the "*or even*"?'[1]

And yet 'the result of the debate' is not only of great interest theoretically but also determines the basic character of our agitation. This is expressed in graphic form by the author of the new Austrian programme, Comrade Adler:

I am an agitator. I have addressed hundreds of meetings. And I did not say to my listeners: 'Your lives are becoming more and more wretched every day; the good days are gone!' I'll leave to others this Philistine wailing about evil times. My rebel cry was this: 'Look what is happening in the world! Look how great the wealth has grown that you created. But see what they give you: some crumbs at best, to let you live just a tiny bit better. And there is no comparison between these crumbs and what you could get . . .' In addition to this, I say: 'But if you live even a little better, it is because you are organized, because you are Social Democrats!'[2]

And so, to Adler, the answer to the question of whether there is an absolute worsening in the condition of the working-class determines the solution to another question: '*How do we raise a rebellion?*' This is why Comrade Plekhanov was right in saying that this question is the core around which all the others fall into place. This is why the authors of the draft programme were right in considering it 'their duty to present . . . the result of the debate' and why, in failing to present 'this important result' in 'the proper light', they have not fulfilled their duty.

To illustrate a view antithetical to Adler's both on the 'theory of pauperization' and the question of 'how to raise a rebellion', I shall cite the view of the anarchist journal *Les Temps Nouveaux* (no. 13, 1901):

Almost everyone agrees that a strike brings no material benefits. Can we describe as benefits the paltry increases in earnings, which, as soon as they go up, go down again, or are counterbalanced by a corresponding rise in unemployment? From the viewpoint of revolutionary socialists, the sole virtue of a strike is its educational effect. If a strike is a true means of emancipation, it is not because it can compel the employer to

[1] N. Riazanov, *Materialy*, ii, 81.   [2] *Vienna*, p. 103.

yield . . . but because it gives the worker an opportunity to realize his economic position as well as his duties and rights as a toiler, an opportunity to be aware of himself precisely as a worker, and, as such, an independent force . . . an opportunity to express his initiative and his organizational abilities, his social instinct, and the impulse of mutual aid.

It is obvious that the author of this article will 'raise a rebellion' very differently from Adler. And the position of *Les Temps Nouveaux* is by no means specifically anarchist. When Millerand introduced strike legislation in the French parliament, the socialist press of every country heatedly discussed the bill. And it was argued, incidentally, that there was great harm in the long interval set by the bill between the moment of the announcement and the actual start of the strike. *Vorwärts* wrote the following on this subject (16 December 1901): 'Those who still believe that the sole purpose of strikes is agitation will deplore this loss of time. But the experience of economic struggle teaches us that unprepared strikes, provoked by enthusiasm, end in failure. The freedom to strike is already limited in all big unions by strike regulations.'

In Russia there are also different views on the significance of economic struggle in general and of strikes in particular, and the differences of opinion greatly affect our tactics. I belong to those who believe that a *workers* party should assume leadership in the workers' struggle for *all* their interests. And this applies all the more to the *Social Democratic* workers party. Hence, to me every victory in the workers' economic struggle is of independent significance in itself, *in addition to* its tremendous agitational and educational value. It is significant, to begin with, because the workers will receive an additional 'penny on the pound' and because they will 'start the machine when the whistle blows, without hurrying too much'.

I feel that only with such an attitude toward the 'purely labour' struggle can we be a workers party and not a party basing itself on the workers. The difference between Social Democrats and trade-unionists is not that the former assign less importance to the workers' direct gains. The Social Democrats are as interested as trade-unionists in winning for the workers under the capitalist system the maximum of what this system can give them, and they are more capable of achieving this aim. But, above and beyond this, they want what the trade-unionists do not want—to abolish

129

the capitalist system itself. And this is the only reason why trade-union organization is not only insufficient, but is superfluous when there is a Social Democratic party.

Comrade Riazanov sees it differently. He complains that 'the author of *The Workers' Cause in Russia* is a typical economist ... He fails utterly to grasp that the economic struggle can be advocated by a man who believes that it can yield no "tangible" results apart from educational influence' (p. 143).*

Comrade Riazanov is not opposed to economic struggle, but he would like to utilize its every action *solely* for pedagogic, educational ends:

There is, and there can be, no workers' need, no workers' demand too 'petty' for Social Democracy to defend, if it is to remain true to its banner. There is no 'purely economic' demand—be it only the demand for a rise of 'a penny on the pound'—that cannot be placed within the framework of general political conditions, that cannot be utilized to awaken political and class consciousness among the labouring masses (p. 144).

Obviously, Comrade Riazanov and I will lead strikes very differently from each other. Yet both Comrade Riazanov and I are equally anxious that the programme should formulate the tactics which the Party considers necessary. And this depends on the Party's view concerning the possibility of improving the condition of the working-class as a whole while still under the capitalist system.

This is why both Comrade Riazanov and I are dissatisfied with the *Iskra* draft. The vagueness of the draft's formulation is due to the fact that its authors, or at any rate one of them, Plekhanov, believe in the unacceptable 'theory of pauperization'.

In his article in *Zaria* (nos. 2–3), Plekhanov argues that the absolute worsening of the workers' lot is an observable fact. He cites the book of the anarchist Pelloutier and studies by bourgeois economists of England and the United States. At almost the same time that the programme was being drafted, Plekhanov gave support to Lassalle's 'iron law' of wages. In the pamphlet by Lafargue and Guesde, *What the Social Democrats Want* (published by the League of Russian Revolutionary Social Democrats Abroad, 1902), we read on page 11 that the results of capitalist development are:

* Riazanov, *Materialy*, ii, 143. [The author of *Rabochee delo v Rossii* was Martov.]

On the one hand, accumulation of wealth in the hands . . . of the capitalists and, on the other, the poverty of the unpropertied producers
increasing with the growth of production itself.

Their (the workers') share of production is only the amount absolutely
required to maintain their lives and the reproduction of their race. But
the capitalists are continuously and inevitably striving to reduce even
these indispensable expenditures, which constitute the workers' wages.

Plekhanov commented on this statement as follows:

Similar definitions of the 'natural price of labour' can be found in the
writings of Turgot, Smith, Say, and every 'serious economist', to use
the words of Lujo Brentano. However, since the days of Lassalle's
agitation, bourgeois economists have realized that the above law of
wages must appear to the workers as one of the major indictments of
bourgeois social relations. This is why 'serious economists' today are
making 'serious' efforts . . . not toward changing social relations in such
a way as to make them more favourable for workers but toward finding
a new, less candid and sharp *formulation* of this law [italics Plekhanov's].[1]

Naturally, after this Plekhanov could not use in the draft the
'less candid and sharp formulation of the law' long since rejected
by the theoreticians of socialism. But, on the other hand, it was
also impossible to offer the theory of 'poverty . . . increasing with
the growth of production itself'.

This is what Kautsky says on the subject in his reply to Bernstein:

In the most advanced capitalist countries it is no longer possible to
discern a general increase in physical poverty [absolute worsening—
V.A.]. On the contrary, everything indicates that physical poverty is
decreasing. The working-class today lives better than it did fifty years
ago. There is a steady increase, not in physical poverty [not absolute
worsening—V.A.], but in social poverty [relative worsening—V.A.]; in
other words, in the contradiction between the worker's needs, depending
on the cultural level, and the means for their satisfaction at the command of the worker. In short, the *quantity* of commodities received by
the worker may increase, but the *share* of the output received by the
worker becomes smaller [italics Kautsky's].[2]

Bebel also takes Bernstein to task, in his speech at the Hanover
Congress (published by *Zhizn'*,[3] pp. 42, 44), for attributing to Marx

[1] *Chego khotiat sotsial'demokraty*, annotated by G. Plekhanov (Geneva, 1902),
p. 11 n.
[2] Kautsky, *Bernstein und das Sozialdemokratische Programm* (Stuttgart, 1899),
p. 116.
[3] *Bebel' o Bernshteine: Rech' Avgusta Bebel'ia proiznesennaia na Gannoverskom
parteitage 10 oktiabria 1899 goda* (London, 1902).

the view of 'absolute pauperization'. He asserts that Social Democrats recognize as a fact only the relative worsening in the proletariat's condition—the growing contrast between its want and the luxury of the exploiters. He says:

Of course, the condition of the majority of the working-class, judged from an absolute point of view, has improved and risen. But has it also improved *relatively*, as compared with the condition of the ruling classes?

If Marx had subscribed to the theory of pauperization as in Bernstein's interpretation, he would have been guilty of a colossal contradiction, which could have been proved to him. If the theory of pauperization were correct, then Marx could not have waged his polemic against the iron law of wages.

The extent to which Plekhanov's views on this question are at variance with the most fundamental principles of international Social Democratic tactics is shown even more graphically by another of his remarks in the same booklet [*What the Social Democrats Want*]. On page 16, Guesde expresses the entirely retrograde view that 'trade education or any other education' 'merely increases the quantity' of manufactured 'products, to the detriment of the producers, who are condemned to new unemployment'. This corresponds entirely to the old view, long ago abandoned by everyone, that everything in the world is continually becoming worse and that only the temporary dictatorship of some revolutionary organization can divert the world from its catastrophic course. This view logically leads to the position that no constructive work is possible in modern society and that, specifically, cultural activity is futile and even harmful, because it deflects energies from destructive activity. To mitigate this conclusion, Plekhanov says:

We must not, however, conclude that Social Democrats are *against* the trade and general education of the people. They merely say that general education *will not improve* the material condition of the working-class, and that trade education will *worsen* it. But if this is the *direct* economic effect of education, its *indirect*, historic effect is, on the contrary, most beneficial to the working-class. The more educated and developed the proletariat becomes, the more successful will be its struggle against the bourgeoisie. [Italics throughout the quotation are Plekhanov's.—V.A.][1]

And so Social Democrats must *tolerate* the spread of education, just as they tolerate the introduction of machines, despite the

---

[1] *Chego khotiat sotsial'demokraty*, p. 16 n.

harmful direct effect of both! This comparison is made by Plekhanov himself later in the same commentary.

Just as Plekhanov's views regarding the 'priming theory' are diametrically opposed to Lenin's views, so his views concerning the 'pauperization theory' are diametrically opposed to, say, Adler's (I name him only as the most typical and thoroughgoing representative of the other school of thought). And if the choice of either position in regard to the 'priming theory' can change most radically one's view of the rôle and significance of a revolutionary party in relation to the proletariat, so can either approach to the 'theory' of pauperization alter by 180 degrees the direction of the party's activity in all spheres, beginning with its leadership in the daily struggle of the workers for 'a penny on the pound' and ending with its political tasks in 'the street' and in parliament. This is why Plekhanov was right, and right again, and a thousand times right in saying that this is the central question in all debates.

And it is precisely because the views of the authors of the *Iskra* programme differ from those of the majority of theoreticians of international Social Democracy, and from all its tactics, that the *Iskra* programme was bound to be not only wrong but also evasive, in dealing with the 'theory' of pauperization.

How, then, should it be changed?

Comrade Riazanov would like to change it in the spirit of the old Austrian programme (and all the other programmes too). For my part, I would like to see our programme formulated in the spirit of the new Austrian programme. I should therefore offer the following version of this thesis:

Technological advances, as they raise the productivity of labour, bring about an increase in social wealth. But the benefits of this increase are appropriated by the class of capitalists and large landowners who have monopolized the means of social production. For the proletariat, this progress intensifies the oppressive dependence upon the capitalist class, raises the level of exploitation, increases the distance between the exploiters and the exploited, the disparity between growing needs and their satisfaction, between what the proletariat creates and what it receives.

The Dictatorship of the Proletariat

The aim of Social Democracy is to destroy the foundation of the existing order, private property, by expropriating all the means of production and placing them at the disposal of society as a whole.

This latter step presupposes the existence of a body representing society as a whole. Such a body would, on the one hand, assure the rights of the individual members of society and, on the other, see to it that they fulfilled their obligations to society.

To perform its essential function, this body must possess extraordinary authority; it must have government power. We regard the transition from the capitalist to the socialist order 'as a historical process, which may take a more or less extended period of time; and the difficult struggle may last entire decades'.* Before this struggle is begun, it is necessary to take over power. The act of transfer of political power from the class governed by bourgeois ideals to the class governed by socialist ideals will be the social revolution of the proletariat.†

The act of transfer of political power to the proletariat will be a matter of creating a specific form of government—a specific mode of organization of power.

The *Iskra* draft states that the proletariat must win political power. This idea strictly conforms to one of the fundamental tenets of Social Democracy, and I had no objection to it. The version of this thesis, as I proposed it, read as follows:

The struggle of the working-class against capitalist exploitation must necessarily assume the form of political struggle. The working-class cannot successfully conduct its economic struggle and develop its economic organizations without political rights. It cannot carry out the transfer of the means of production to social ownership without first gaining control of political power.

I deliberately formulated this idea almost verbatim in the words of the Erfurt programme in order to forestall debate over terminology. The corresponding passage in the draft programme is, in my view, inexact and erroneous. It reads: 'A necessary condition for this social revolution is the dictatorship of the proletariat, that

---

* Kautsky, *Sotsial'naia revoliutsiia* ([Geneva], Izd. Ligi R.R.S.-D. [1903]), p. 96.

† 'This universally used term', says Kautsky about social revolution (*ibid.* p. 7), 'is invested with different meanings not only by different people, but even by the same person at different times.' It seems to me that this applies to Kautsky himself as well. I use the term in the sense which Kautsky gave it on page 10: 'Political revolution is the conquest of state power by the hitherto subjugated class.' A political revolution aimed at 'social emancipation' is defined by Kautsky as a social revolution. Hence, it seems to me that he uses words loosely when he subsequently applies the term 'social revolution' to the whole period when the proletariat, armed with power, will introduce its reforms and gradually transform the old social order.

is, the conquest by the proletariat of such political power as will permit it to suppress all resistance put up by the exploiters.'[1]

The authors of the draft have used the expression 'dictatorship of the proletariat', which does not appear in any Social Democratic programme or, to my knowledge, in any draft programme. At any rate, it does not appear in the Gotha, Erfurt, Hainfeld, Vienna, Guesdist, Belgian, Swedish, or Italian programme. Nor is it to be found in the Statutes of the International, in any of the four draft programmes offered at the Erfurt congress, or in the two drafts offered at the Vienna *Parteitag*. The drafts of the Emancipation of Labour Group also contain no mention of the word 'dictatorship'.

Thus the term 'dictatorship', employed by the authors of our present programme, is entirely new in the programme of international Social Democracy, and such an innovation demands justification. The authors of the draft should prove that the terminology of all other programmes is unsatisfactory and that, consequently, we Russians are obliged in this case to disregard the request of the Paris International Socialist Congress which obliges us to formulate our programme to correspond as closely as possible to other programmes. This was not done either in Plekhanov's commentary or at the congress. None of the delegates of the committees found it necessary to inquire as to the reasons for this departure from the usual terminology. And this paragraph of the programme, like so many others, was adopted without discussion.

Let us see, then, whether the new term (new to the programmes) is at least well chosen. The word 'dictatorship' denotes a special form of government. It was created by Roman law and had the following characteristics:

(1) The dictator was always elected. His power was dictatorial only in relation to the people who elected him. Since the dictator was elected, his power was inalienable. Suppose, now, that the proletariat as a collective entity attains absolute power. This would come about not by the will but against the will of those over whom this power would be wielded. Such a government might be called autocracy, despotism, or tyranny, but not dictatorship, if we use words according to their meaning, rather than their impressive sound.

[1] See the draft programme, in *Zaria*, no. 4, p. 5. See below, Appendix II, pp. 194–5.

Moreover, the proletariat as a whole cannot be the vehicle of power. Hence, when people speak of the rule of the proletariat, they have in mind the persons empowered by the proletariat to exercise such rule. Let us assume that the proletariat will elect a council of its most favoured persons (made up of ten, a hundred, or a thousand individuals) and will delegate to it the absolute power which 'will permit it to suppress all resistance put up by the exploiters'—*rei opprimendi omnem resistentiam exploatatorum causa* [sic]—according to [*Iskra's*] noteworthy formula proclaiming the dictator. Such a government might be called a dictatorship. But whose dictatorship, and over whom? It would be a dictatorship of the revolutionary government over the proletariat, albeit set up to save the proletariat from its exploiters. Is this what our congress wanted when it adopted the *Iskra* draft? I believe that it did not, and therefore I consider that the congress adopted this paragraph unaware of what it was doing. However, I believe that the authors of the draft understood dictatorship precisely in this sense, and it is against such Blanquism in our Party that I wanted—and still do want—to fight.

(2) The second feature of dictatorial rule was the fact that the dictator was not limited by anything in exercising his power, except by the interests of the business in hand. Must the proletariat become the Sulla of modern society? I believe that this is not necessary, and that it will not occur.

We consider that the autocracy, which deprives us of freedom of speech, press, assembly, organization, and participation in government, is reactionary. But do we think so only because it is we who are the victims? Do we think it possible and necessary that the proletariat, having overthrown despotism, should itself become an 'enlightened despot'? That it should, in the name of saving mankind, even temporarily deprive the people of its freedom? This is not our view. We do not seek 'such' power for the proletariat. The power that is sought by the proletariat will be limited by laws which it will recognize as inviolable. The proletariat will guide itself in its actions not only by the interests and needs of the cause but also by its views concerning the rights of the individual. This is not how a dictator behaves.

The International Working Men's Association declared, first and foremost: 'All societies and individuals adhering to it [the IWMA] will acknowledge truth, justice, and morality as the basis of their conduct toward each other and toward all men . . . And in this spirit they have drawn up the . . . provisional rules of the International Association.' (See the Statutes of the IWMA.[1])

The Vienna programme states: 'The party will seek to realize its programme by all suitable means, in accordance with the people's natural sense of right.'[2]

This was how the international Social Democratic movement limited itself both in its first and in its most recent programme. In the same manner, it will limit its future revolutionary government, and it will therefore not invest this government with dictatorial powers.

I have said earlier that the term 'dictatorship' of the proletariat is new (new to programmes), and that no justification for this innovation is given. I said further that this term is inept, because it expresses either an idea which cannot be realized—the direct rule of an entire class over another class—or a Blanquist idea alien to Social Democrats—the investment of absolute, unlimited power in a provisional revolutionary government after the proletariat has made the revolution. Now I shall turn to Plekhanov's commentaries to see how he explains this paragraph of the draft programme.

When the bourgeoisie fought against the aristocracy, it consciously sought *political* supremacy, for it understood that only thus could it realize its socio-economic aspirations. It achieved such supremacy and took measures to secure its social order from the encroachments of the proletariat. It resorted to *force*. In short, it understood that its *dictatorship* was a necessary *political condition for its social emancipation and its supremacy*. But now it declares that class dictatorship is a malicious invention of narrow '*dogmatists*', an absurd notion of revolutionary '*doctrinaires*'. It is the duty of all adherents of revolutionary Social Democracy to explain to the proletariat that it must strive toward dictatorship if it wants to abolish *capitalist* relations in production and replace them by *socialist* relations [italics Plekhanov's].[3]

These commentaries argue—however weakly—the same idea: namely, that the proletariat must conquer political power, as the bourgeoisie has done in the past. Plekhanov does not argue that this power must assume the form of the dictatorship of a class, and generally uses the term 'dictatorship' as synonymous with 'political power'. But if Plekhanov called all political power dictatorship, there would have been no need for him to use this

---

[1] Quoted here from *Address*, p. 13. Akimov's Russian-language version contains insignificant variations.

[2] *Vienna*, p. 3.   [3] *Zaria*, no. 4, pp. 28–9.

new term (new to programmes) instead of those generally used. In fact, however, both Plekhanov and the authors of our programme have usually, and rightly, distinguished between the concepts of 'dictatorship of a class' and 'political supremacy of a class'. By dictatorship, they understood—and quite correctly—*one* of many different forms of political rule, a form they considered necessary to the social revolution.

When they wrote 'dictatorship', the authors of our programme realized that its meaning remained extremely vague, and therefore found it necessary to explain it then and there, in the programme itself. It reads: 'The dictatorship of the proletariat, i.e., the conquest by the proletariat of *such* political power as will permit it to suppress all resistance put up by the exploiters.' Consequently, the authors held that there may also be *another* mode of political power besides dictatorship, or, to be precise, other forms of power, which are insufficient for the proletariat if it is to suppress resistance. This is all that their explanation says, for it still leaves unclear just what is meant here by 'such' political power. To this question, we get only one answer, dictatorship—an altogether vague answer, as I have already pointed out. Hence, all we can gather from the text of the programme is that dictatorship is one form of rule and that it is precisely this type of rule that is considered necessary for the proletariat.

Plekhanov offered a better explanation of what he understands by 'dictatorship' in his introduction to the *Manifesto of the Communist Party*: 'The dictatorship of any given class means the *rule* [italics Plekhanov's] of this class which enables it to wield the organized force of society in order to defend its own interests and to suppress directly or indirectly all social movements which clash with those interests' (p. 67).

Plekhanov adds: 'This was already very well understood by Mignet.' However, the passages he cites show only that Mignet considered it 'well known that a force which achieves dominance always assumes control of institutions'.[1] This, indeed, is well known. But a political force which takes control of institutions transforms them in accordance with its principles. The important question to us is how the proletariat will transform institutions when it achieves power. Plekhanov assumes that it will transform them into the form of a class dictatorship, and adds at once that 'this was already understood by Mignet'. But Mignet said nothing of the sort.

---

[1] Foreword to *Manifest*, p. lxvii n.

Plekhanov's definition of dictatorship which I quoted above is still unclear. It may seem that here, too, Plekhanov means by dictatorship every type of class dominance, and hence all political rule. In that case, the term 'dictatorship' would simply be superfluous, obfuscating the generally accepted idea that the proletariat must win for itself political power. However, the addition of the phrase, 'rule which enabled it to wield force in order to defend and suppress' *may* mean that not every kind of rule makes such action possible and that the author desires for the proletariat a particular form of rule permitting such action—namely, dictatorship.

On the next page, Plekhanov explains his idea, and there it becomes clear that the earlier quotation not only *may* be understood as I did understand it, but indeed cannot be understood in any other sense. Offering a new definition of dictatorship, Plekhanov adds, 'As we have said'. But he speaks differently now— more clearly and specifically: 'The dictatorship of a given class is, as we have said, the rule of this class which enables it to wield the organized force of society in order to defend its own interests and to suppress all social movements which directly or indirectly threaten these interests.'[1]

Instead of the direct or indirect suppression of movements which clash with the interests of the proletariat, Plekhanov now speaks of the suppression of movements which *directly or indirectly* threaten these interests. And so, the revolutionary government will have to keep an eye on the movements which may *threaten* the interests of the proletariat, if only *indirectly*, without actual infringement of these interests. All such movements must be suppressed.

Yes, this indeed is a dictatorship of the revolutionary government which can bring the proletariat nothing but disasters. Such a government would inevitably regard as most 'dangerous' those movements which threatened it, which resisted one aspect or another of its policy, but after the revolution such movements might well be first and foremost those formed within the proletariat itself. They will then be branded 'not truly proletarian', 'not conscious', and so on, and to them will be opposed the 'enlightened despotism' of the revolutionary government.

Such a view on the possible course of events is by no means hypothetical. This was the ideal of Blanquism, and even much earlier was put into practice by the government of 1793. Both

---

[1] *Ibid.* p. lxviii.

Plekhanov and Lenin, whose influence was unquestionably dominant in the drafting of the programme, have generally retained a good deal of Blanquism in their views, and their idea of how the proletariat is to win political power is but one manifestation of their philosophy. 'We are terrorists, in the sense of the terror of 1793!' declared Plekhanov in a paper delivered in Geneva. But the terror of 1793 brought to the guillotine not only enemies of the revolution but also its best friends: Camille Desmoulins, Danton, and finally Robespierre himself. If, at least, this price had bought the victory of their ideas! But on the contrary, the terror of 1793 did not achieve its purpose, and we must make every effort not to repeat the mistakes of the past.

But the expression 'class dictatorship' was introduced by Marx. Bernstein wrote against 'dictatorship'. And this gave the advocates of our draft programme the chance to label as Bernsteinism my refusal to accept their formulation of the political tasks of the proletariat. Let us, then, turn to Marx and Bernstein.

In *The Class Struggles in France*, Marx often uses the word dictatorship to denote the political dominance of the bourgeoisie, on the one hand, and of the proletariat, on the other. Following the events of 1848–51, step by step, Marx sharply criticizes the activities of all parties, including the socialists of that time. His sympathies are only with Blanqui and his supporters, whom he calls in the *Eighteenth Brumaire* 'the true leaders of the proletariat' (p. 15).* The socialism to which the proletariat was moving was, in Marx's words, 'revolutionary socialism, communism, for which the bourgeoisie itself invented the title of *Blanquism*' (*The Class Struggles*, p. 121).† 'A constitutional republic is a dictatorship of the united exploiters; a red republic is a dictatorship of friends and allies. This was said by the socialists in pamphlets, almanacs, a variety of handbills and brochures' (*The Class Struggles*, p. 115), and Marx accepts this terminology.

He did not have to look far for an example to explain what he meant by the 'dictatorship of the bourgeoisie'. What he denoted by these words was a terrible fact, which he described as follows: 'From 25 June to 10 December 1848—a dictatorship of the pure bourgeois republicans. From 13 July 1849 to 31 May 1850—a dictatorship of the "party of order"' (*Eighteenth Brumaire*, pp.

---

* *Vosemnadtsatoe briumera Lui Bonaparta* [translated by B. Krichevskii] ([Geneva], 1894).
† *Klassovaia bor'ba v Frantsii* ([Geneva], Izd. Soiuza R.S.D. [1902]).

103, 104). Before these periods, between them, and after them, various bourgeois factions carried on a struggle for power, for dictatorship.

Let us see, then, what kind of power this was.

'A bourgeois republic in Europe means the unlimited despotic rule of one class over another' (*Eighteenth Brumaire*, p. 17).

'Cavaignac represented the dictatorship of the bourgeoisie by the sword' (*Class Struggles*, p. 61).

'The unity of the two powers of the constitutional republic (legislative and executive) begins when it is a question of repression of all the classes which rise against the dictatorship of the bourgeoisie' (*Class Struggles*, p. 117).

'Has not the party of order consistently made unconstitutional use of its parliamentary prerogative?' (*Eighteenth Brumaire*, p. 78).

'The constitution naturally prohibited any attack on the freedom of other peoples; but, in the eyes of the ministry, the French army in Rome was attacking not "freedom" but the "despotism of anarchy". The interpretation and application of the constitution belongs to those who adopted it' (*Class Struggles*, p. 91).

'The foundation of the constitution is [universal] suffrage. Abolition of universal suffrage—such is the last word of the party of order' (*Class Struggles*, p. 125).

'Repudiating universal suffrage, of which it had made a great show until then, the bourgeoisie admitted openly: "Our dictatorship has existed until now by the will of the people; henceforth it will be consolidated against the will of the people"' (*Class Struggles*, p. 126).

'Bonaparte demanded the restoration of universal suffrage . . . the assembly rejected it. Thus it tore up its mandate once more; it confirmed once more that it had transformed itself from a freely elected body of representatives of the people into a *usurpatory parliament of a class*; it admitted once more that it had itself severed the muscles connecting the parliamentary head with the body of the nation' (*Eighteenth Brumaire*, p. 100).

'The party of order is saying its last word: "the iron ring of legality which is throttling us must be broken"' (*Class Struggles*, p. 125).

'The bourgeoisie revenged itself for the mortal fear it had suffered by unheard-of brutalities and subjected three thousand prisoners to severe beatings' (*Class Struggles*, p. 50).

'For the entire duration of the rule of the Constituent Assembly, continuous sacrificial rites were held backstage—the constant sentencing of captured June insurgents by courts-martial or their deportation without trial. The Constituent Assembly had the tact to admit that, in dealing with the June insurgents, it was not trying criminals but destroying enemies' (*Class Struggles*, p. 57).

'The rule of the bourgeoisie inevitably had to be transformed into the terrorism of the bourgeoisie . . . and the dictatorship of the bourgeoisie was officially proclaimed' (*Class Struggles*, p. 53).

'The Constituent Assembly agrees that the royalist factions of the bourgeoisie are the natural masters of the republic established by it . . . that violation of the constitution is its realization . . . that the passive alliance of the republic with European peoples fighting for liberation, an alliance proclaimed at the height of the revolutionary intoxication, means active alliance with European counter-revolution' (*Class Struggles*, p. 83).

The bourgeoisie worshipped the sword . . . it destroyed the revolutionary press . . . it placed popular meetings under the surveillance of the police . . . it dismissed the democratic (petty bourgeois) National Guard . . . it resorted to a stage of siege . . . it replaced jury courts by military commissions . . . it deported without trial . . . it suppressed every movement of society by government force . . . France had evidently rid itself of class despotism only to find itself under the despotism of an individual.

This is dictatorship! And is it *such* power that the proletariat seeks? Is it sufficient to substitute the word 'proletariat' for 'bourgeoisie', and 'bourgeoisie' for 'proletariat' in order to attain our ideal social order?

Cruel, ruthless, and merciless suppression of a conquered adversary is not devoid of a certain dark grandeur and poetry. But 'the social revolution cannot derive its poetry from the past; it must derive its poetry from the future' (*Eighteenth Brumaire*, p. 10).

'The bourgeoisie admitted openly: Henceforth, our dictatorship will be consolidated against the will of the people!' From that moment, at any rate, the dictatorship of the bourgeoisie was transformed into tyranny over the people. Who will deny this? But we are told that the proletariat must begin with this! Is this what the proletariat needs? No, the proletariat needs exactly the opposite.

'All the previous movements were movements of minorities, or in the interest of minorities. The proletarian movement is the independent movement of the majority in the interest of the vast majority' (*Communist Manifesto*, pp. 14–15). Under such conditions, the form of power necessary to the proletariat is antithetical to the form of bourgeois power. The proletariat needs a broadly democratic organization of power and a guarantee of non-intervention by this power into the sphere of individual and social freedom. It needs what is embraced by a single term—democracy.

As I have said earlier, Marx used the term 'dictatorship' to denote both the bourgeois and the proletarian forms of power. I have tried to show the form of bourgeois rule—bourgeois dictatorship—as Marx saw it. Now I shall try to discover how Marx envisaged the form of proletarian rule—the dictatorship of the proletariat.

Several passages in *The Class Struggles* suggest that Marx generalized his views and attributed to every victorious class that which had characterized the triumph of the bourgeois class. Bernstein may have been right (*horribile dictu!*) in assuming that at this time Marx's views concerning the form of the proletariat's political rule were, under the influence of Blanqui, different from what they were later. Marx says:

> When a class arises in which the revolutionary interests of society are concentrated, it does not look for material for its revolutionary activity: it destroys enemies, takes the steps dictated by the requirements of the struggle, and is driven forward by the results of its own actions. Such a class does not engage in theoretical inquiries into its own tasks. The French working-class was not in such a situation; it was not yet capable of accomplishing its revolution [*Class Struggles*, p. 36].

> Revolutionary socialism is the revolution without halt [permanent revolution—*Ed.*], the *class dictatorship* of the proletariat, necessary as the transitional stage on the way to the *abolition of all class distinctions*, the abolition of the productive relations on which these distinctions rest, the abolition of all social relations that correspond to these productive relations, the overthrow of all ideas that result from these social relations [*Class Struggles*, p. 121].

However, these references to the tasks of the proletariat when it becomes capable of accomplishing its revolution are altogether inadequate. This is so because the proletariat was still too far from power at the time of the events dealt with in this pamphlet.

But if Marx had more than sufficient grounds for his description of the rule of the bourgeoisie, it did not come within the scope of his historical work to describe the forms that were to characterize the rule of the proletariat. He says so himself on p. 121: 'The scope of our exposition does not permit us to dwell on this subject in greater detail.'

It was a long time before Marx had occasion to describe, rather than to forecast, the forms of proletarian rule. Indeed, it took twenty years before the occasion finally arose, and the stern critic of the 'dictatorship of the bourgeoisie' was able to offer a description of the 'dictatorship of the proletariat'.

Would you like to know, my dear sirs, what this dictatorship is like? Take a close look at the Paris Commune. This was the dictatorship of the proletariat—as Engels says in his introduction to *The Civil War*.[1] Let us turn, then, to Marx's remarkable picture of the Commune.

The moderation of the Commune during its two months of unquestioned dominance can be compared only with the heroism of its defence.[2]

From 18 March until the Versailles troops broke into Paris, the proletarian revolution was so free of any of those acts of violence in which revolutions, and particularly the counter-revolution of the upper classes, abound that its enemies could not charge it with anything except the execution of Generals Lecomte and Clément Thomas and the clash at the Place Vendôme.

One of the Bonapartist officers who participated in the nocturnal expedition against Montmartre, General Lecomte, had four times ordered the 81st line regiment to fire at an unarmed crowd at the Place Pigalle. When the soldiers refused to obey his order, he showered them with violent abuse. Instead of shooting women and children, his own soldiers shot him.[3]

'And quite right too!' will be the response of every reader. Lecomte was evidently to the Frenchmen what von Wahl or Bogdanovich, who has already been assassinated, are to us. If only we had been able to do the same with them! But Marx says something else:

The habits acquired by the soldiers under the training of the enemies of the working-class could not, of course, disappear the moment these soldiers changed to the flag of the workers. The same men shot Clément Thomas as well [*Civil War in France*, p. 16].

The Central Committee and the Paris workers were as responsible for the deaths of Clément Thomas and Lecomte as the Princess of Wales was for the people crushed to death in the crowd on her arrival in London [*Civil War*, p. 17].

We cannot help asking ourselves how this unquestionably excessive desire on Marx's part to clear the Commune of the slightest reproach for cruelty is to be explained. Marx evidently felt that it was necessary to suppress every movement which even indirectly threatened the interests of the proletariat.

[1] Engels, in Marx, *Grazhdanskaia voina v Frantsii* (*1870–1871*) (Geneva, 1893), Introduction, p. xvi.
[2] Marx, *ibid.* p. 49.　　　　　　　　　[3] *Ibid.* p. 16.

The panic of the bourgeois was their only punishment. Even the police, instead of being disarmed and arrested, as they should have been, had the gates of Paris thrown open before them for their flight to Versailles. The 'men of order' were not only left alone; they were allowed to entrench themselves in many strong positions in the very centre of Paris. This indulgence of the Central Committee, this magnanimity of the armed working men, so strangely at variance with the customs of the 'party of order', was interpreted by that party as symptoms of conscious weakness [*Civil War*, p. 18].

Where, then, does one find here '*such* a power as would permit', and so forth? After all, there had been *such* a power in the hands of the bourgeoisie when it was carrying out its revolution, when it set up its dictatorship. Marx recalls this time when he says of 1848:

Dufaure rushed a number of new repressive laws through the National Assembly. There were mass arrests and mass deportations; terror reigned. The lower classes behaved differently. The Central Committee of 1871 simply ignored the flight of the heroes of the 'peaceful demonstration', so that only two days later they were able to undertake another demonstration, this time an armed one, under Admiral Saisset, ending in the famous flight to Versailles. Persistently refusing to engage in the civil war opened by Thiers' nocturnal expedition against Montmartre, the Central Committee this time committed a fatal error. It should have marched immediately against Versailles, for the moment without sufficient means to defend itself, and put an end once for all to the conspiracies of Thiers and his 'rural deputies' [*Civil War*, p. 19].

Marx sees the error of the Central Committee solely in its avoidance of the civil war opened by Thiers, at a time when it should not have been avoided.

After the decree of the Commune of 7 April, the Commune threatened reprisals, declaring it to be its duty to 'defend Paris from the cannibalism of the Versailles bandits, and to demand an eye for an eye, a tooth for a tooth'.[1]

But Thiers and his generals learned that the reprisals decreed by the Commune were no more than an empty threat, leading to no action, and that even the gendarme spies, caught in Paris disguised as National Guards, and the policemen, seized with incendiary bombs, were spared. As soon as they became aware of this, the mass shooting of prisoners was resumed and continued uninterruptedly to the end.[2]

The Communards could hardly have thought that the Versailles bandits did not threaten the interests of the proletariat, even indirectly.

But where is the dictatorship? We have looked for it in vain!

[1] *Ibid.* pp. 20–1.   [2] *Ibid.* p. 20.

It may be said that the Commune was defeated precisely because it did not suppress all social movements which threatened it directly or indirectly, because it did not exercise '*such*' power. Why, then, does Engels point to the Commune as a model for the 'dictatorship of the proletariat'?

Engels points to the Commune because, despite its faults and errors, it was indeed a model of that form of power which the proletariat should create, whatever the name attached to it—even the inappropriate one of dictatorship. The term dictatorship can be used here only figuratively, as one does in speaking of the 'dictatorship of the heart'. (The Minister [M. T. Loris-Melikov—*Ed.*] to whom this title was applied was, of course, entirely undeserving of it.) In reality, it was the opposite of class dictatorship; it was democracy in the broadest sense of the word:

The Commune was composed of municipal councillors, elected on the basis of universal suffrage by the districts of Paris. Its members were accountable and subject to recall. The majority of them were, naturally, workers or acknowledged spokesmen for the working-class [*Civil War*, p. 26].

Universal suffrage would cease to serve the people as a means of electing every three or six years some member of the ruling class to represent and oppress it in parliament. Rather, the people, organized into communes, would be able to use universal suffrage as every employer uses his right of free choice in the selection of workers, overseers, and book-keepers for his business . . . In its very spirit, the Commune was hostile to the replacement of universal suffrage by hierarchic investiture [p. 28].

The antagonism between the Commune and state power was erroneously interpreted as a distorted form of the old struggle against excessive centralization [p. 29].

The Commune gave the republic purely democratic foundations [p. 30].

Such was the 'dictatorship of the proletariat'!

Let us see now how Bernstein approaches this question. In the chapter on the political and economic conditions for the realization of socialism, he says:

A certain level of capitalist development is the first condition for the general realization of socialism. The second condition is the transfer of political power to the working-class party, the Social Democratic Party. The form in which this power will be employed during the transitional period will, according to Marx, be the dictatorship of the proletariat [p. 151].*

* Bernstein, *Istoricheskii materializm*, trans. Kantsel' ([St Petersburg], Izdanie 'Znaniia', 1901).

After stating his ideas regarding the first condition and declaring that this development has still not gone far enough to be counted on, he proceeds to the second condition. In this connexion he speaks, first, about the general idea of the 'transfer of political power to the working-class party' and, second, about 'the form in which this power will be employed'—about dictatorship. His views on both of these are negative. He writes about dictatorship:

Is there any sense in repeating the phrase about dictatorship of the proletariat at a time when the representatives of Social Democracy are wherever possible taking their stand on parliamentary activity, proportional popular representation, and popular legislation—methods which are in direct contradiction to dictatorship? The phrase concerning dictatorship has outlived its time to such an extent that it can be linked to reality only by divesting the term 'dictatorship' of its actual significance and toning down its meaning [p. 228].

But Bernstein repudiates not just the given form of government but the entire principle of the conquest of power by the proletariat in general. He says:

Marxist activity is predominantly political in character and is aimed at the seizure of political power [p. 169].

We must abandon completely the idea that the state can immediately take over production and distribution. The state cannot undertake to operate even medium-size and large industries [p. 167].

No sensible socialist in England dreams any longer of the coming victory of socialism by means of a decisive coup; no one thinks of the seizure of Parliament by a revolutionary proletariat [p. 301].

I proposed the insertion in our programme of a statement that, in order to carry out a 'decisive coup', the party of the revolutionary proletariat must 'seize the parliament' and conquer political power so that society may 'take production and distribution upon itself'. Thus, I differ from Bernstein in principle regarding the question of the conquest of political power, and am in no way his supporter.

It is true, however, that I am at one with Bernstein in my hostility toward one of the forms of power—dictatorship. But let us see whether on this point I conflict with the most eminent representatives of the international Social Democratic movement.

Rosa Luxemburg was, I believe, the first to reply to Bernstein's book in a series of articles in the *Leipziger Volkszeitung*, in February 1899.* Her third article is devoted specifically to the

* These articles were published in 1899 as a pamphlet, under the title *Sozialreform oder Revolution?*

question of 'the conquest of political power'. Rosa Luxemburg, of course, expresses herself strongly in opposition to Bernstein, arguing that the proletariat must conquer political power. However, she never uses the word 'dictatorship'. Since she is obliged, in the course of her argument, to speak of the conquest of power by the proletariat literally some twenty times, she varies her terminology to avoid repetition, using such expressions as *Eroberung der politischen Macht, Gebrauch der politischen Macht, Ergreifung der politischen Macht, Ergreifung der Staatsgewalt, Eroberung der Staatsgewalt, Machtergreifung, Machteroberung* . . . But she obviously and deliberately avoids using the term 'dictatorship of the proletariat' even a single time, despite the fact that the entire article is an attempt to refute the section of Bernstein's book which argues against this concept. She had not forgotten the term, for she cites it. In reference to a certain phrase of Marx, which Bernstein interpreted in the sense of a repudiation of the idea of the conquest of power by the proletariat, she says: 'What Marx may have had in mind here is that the dictatorship of the proletariat can possibly be attained peacefully rather than that capitalist social reforms can replace such a dictatorship.'[1]

Bernstein held as a matter of principle that the transfer of political power into the hands of the proletariat was impossible and useless. Rosa Luxemburg refutes him in principle, asserting that such a transfer is both essential and possible.

Furthermore, Bernstein considers dictatorship to be a bad form of government. Rosa Luxemburg does not argue with this, but speaks of another form, which she regards as essential to the rule of the proletariat:

For the bourgeoisie, democracy has become partly superfluous and partly restrictive. But it is all the more necessary and essential to the proletariat. It is necessary because it prepares the political forms that will serve the proletariat as the starting point in its transformation of bourgeois society. And it is essential because only in a democracy and in the struggle for it—in the realization of the proletariat's rights in practice—can the latter attain an awareness of its class interests and its historical tasks.[2]

Thus, Rosa Luxemburg feels that the 'political form' which the rule of the proletariat must assume is democracy.

Several months after the appearance of Rosa Luxemburg's articles, Bebel also replied to Bernstein. On 10 October 1899 he

---

[1] Rosa Luxemburg, *Sozialreform oder Revolution?* (Leipzig, ed. of 1908), p. 42.
[2] *Ibid.*

delivered a long speech at the Hanover Congress. In this speech, which lasted several hours, he analysed the principal positions of his opponent and sharply condemned them. In conclusion, he proposed a resolution, which the congress passed by 216 votes to 21. This is what the resolution says on the question of the conquest of political power by the proletariat:

The party continues to base its position on the principle of the class struggle, according to which the emancipation of the working-class can come about only by its own effort. Hence, the party considers it the historic mission of the working-class to conquer political power and, through it, to socialize the means of production and establish a socialist mode of production and exchange, for the greatest possible good of all.[1]

Thus Bebel, and the entire congress with him, voiced in the resolution a clear, precise, and well-argued opposition to Bernstein's views on the conquest of power. But neither the resolution nor Bebel's speech has anything to say about the form of power— dictatorship—against which Bernstein had been writing. In this matter, they do not argue with Bernstein.

Kautsky also hurried to complete his long work against Bernstein before the Hanover Congress. He intended to deal with the problem exhaustively in his book, declaring that he would not return to it again. What does he say about dictatorship?

Bernstein indignantly rejects the idea of the dictatorship of the proletariat. Does he think it possible to get rid of the Prussian Junkers, the Stumms, the Kühnemänners, etc., by maintaining a friendship with them? I do not wish to assert that the rule of the proletariat must necessarily assume the form of a class dictatorship. But experience has not shown and, so far as can be predicted, does not promise for the future that democratic forms will remove the need for the proletariat to rule in order to emancipate itself.[2]

In this book, Kautsky does not suggest what form of power, if not dictatorship, the proletariat needs. To learn Kautsky's views on this subject, let us look at another of his works, *The Day after the Social Revolution*. Here, our best theoretician hastens, first of all,

to clear himself of the grave suspicion that may arise in the minds of many people when they see the title of his work. *The Day after the Social Revolution*! Does it not prove that 'orthodox Marxists' like ourselves

---

[1] *Bebel' o Bernshteine*, p. 69.   [2] Kautsky, *Bernstein*, p. 172.

are in essence no more than disguised Blanquists, who assume that one fine day they will succeed in seizing social dictatorship in one bold stroke?[1]

Kautsky feels that the 'suspicion' that Social Democrats hope one fine day to 'seize social dictatorship' would be a 'grave' matter. He dismisses such a suspicion.

I hasten to state that I regard revolution as a historical process which may last a considerable time; and its difficult struggles may extend over decades . . .[2] But if we want to present it in the simplest form, we must start with the assumption that one fine day all political power, free of any limitation, will come all at once into the hands of the proletariat, and that in using it the proletariat will guide itself solely by its class interests, and employ it in the most rational manner.[3]

The possibility that all political power might be transferred instantly into the hands of the proletariat is admitted by our scholar only schematically, for the sake of the analysis and study of this phenomenon; but he expects its outlines to be somewhat less sharp in the actual situation. However, let us see how Kautsky envisages the rule of the proletariat in its ideal, extreme form:

To begin with, the proletariat will, of course, complete what the bourgeoisie left unfinished. It will sweep off the face of the earth all remnants of feudalism and will put into practice the democratic programme which the bourgeoisie had itself at one time advocated. As the lowest of all classes, the proletariat is also the most democratic of all classes. It will institute universal suffrage in elections to all institutions and assure complete freedom of the press and association. It will make the state independent of the church. It will abolish all hereditary privilege, give every community the right to self-government, and abolish militarism [p. 99].

Replying to Bernstein, Kautsky says that he does not maintain that class dictatorship will be the form of proletarian rule. In the same passage he takes it for granted that the form will be democracy, and democracy complete with its two component parts: broadly democratic organization of state power and non-interference in the sphere of individual and social freedom.

Thus, Kautsky regards proletarian rule in the same light as Rosa Luxemburg.

At the Vienna Congress in December 1901 the Austrian Social Democratic Party re-examined its programme. Neither the old Hainfeld programme nor the new draft said anything about the

---

[1] Kautsky, *Sotsial'naia revoliutsiia*, p. 95.   [2] *Ibid.*
[3] *Ibid.* pp. 96–7.

conquest of political power. This provoked numerous comments. Adler said the following in this connexion: 'And now about the dictatorship of the proletariat. The draft programme says nothing about it, but only Comrade Brod can reproach me for this. On the other hand, I am much more concerned over the reproach that the draft says nothing about the conquest of political power' (p. 107).* Here Adler makes a clear distinction between the question of the conquest of political power and that of dictatorship. Concerning the former, he merely tries to explain how the programme happened to omit the question and expresses his readiness to rectify the omission. The latter question only provokes Adler to a contemptuous remark. He returns again to the term 'dictatorship' later: 'Bernstein comes and slays us with an old slogan, now totally lifeless, and starts a hue and cry about the dictatorship of the proletariat. Should we, then, include this idea of dictatorship in the programme for fear of being branded Bernsteinians?'[1]

And then once again—as in the lines quoted above—when faced with the problem of introducing the term 'dictatorship' into the programme, he raised the question of whether the programme should not proclaim the necessity to conquer power. As the author of both the old programme and the new draft, neither of which contained such a statement, Adler naturally assumed that this necessity was taken for granted by, and was implicit in, the programme. But he was ready to make an addition to the text of the programme (and, in fact, made it):

Should we now . . . when our party, far from being indifferent to politics, is actually too political, put in the programme something that goes without saying? However, if you wish, I have nothing against it [p. 108].

It is entirely clear to every Social Democrat that the means for attaining our goals is conquest of political power. None of the authors of the draft—and myself least of all—has questioned this. But since many comrades feel that this should be stated in the programme, we are meeting their wish [p. 191].

The insertion in the programme reads: 'The conquest of political power is to be the means by which the working-class struggles for its emancipation.'[2]

---

* See the minutes of the Vienna *Parteitag* [cited herein as *Vienna*].

[1] *Vienna*, p. 108. Akimov has mistranslated the first sentence, which reads in the original: 'Jetzt ist Bernstein gekommen und hat alte Schlagworte, die oft gar nicht mehr am Leben sind, tot geschlagen und hat uns auch ein bisschen mit der Diktatur des Proletariats geuzt.'

[2] *Vienna*, p. 3.

To return to our programme. Its authors will provoke an argument over a mere word if, intending to express nothing but a generally accepted idea, they insist on a term which is obviously inept and obviously avoided in all the programmes and in the speeches and articles of our best theoreticians and agitators. But if the authors of the draft, which has become our programme, meant by 'such' rule a form of political power that is not broadly democratic, then they deserve to be reproached on two counts: first, for attempting to introduce into our programme the idea of a conspiratorial seizure of power, which is alien to Social Democratic thought; and, second, for smuggling it in as contraband, in vague and indefinite form, hiding behind an expression which Marx borrowed from Blanquism at a time when Blanquism was the most progressive trend. And yet, the authors could have conveyed this hardly novel idea quite plainly. As a relevant example, I should like to cite the words of an old manifesto:

We are firmly convinced that the revolutionary party which will head the government if the movement succeeds will have to retain the existing form of political, although not of administrative, centralization. For, by making use of such centralization, it will in the shortest possible time be able to put economic and social life on new foundations. It will have to seize dictatorial powers and stop at nothing. The government should influence the elections to the national assembly and make sure at the outset that no adherents of the present order (if any remain alive) should enter it. What happens when a revolutionary government does not intervene in elections is demonstrated by the French Assembly of 1848, which destroyed the republic and gave France no choice but to elect Louis Napoléon as Emperor.

Here is the idea simply, clearly, precisely, and eloquently expressed! Its only shortcoming is that it is somewhat obsolete—these lines are from *Molodaia Rossiia* [*Young Russia*] of 1862 (see Burtsev, *One Hundred Years*).[1]

If *this* is the view of the authors of our programme regarding the conquest of political power, then—and only then—can we understand their statement that even universal suffrage and freedom of the press will not always have their support. We can also understand how they could refuse to include the demand for proportional representation in the programme; how they could demand an organization of professional revolutionaries instead of

[1] V. Burtsev, *Za sto let* (*1800–1896*) (London, 1897), p. 44. Young Russia was the Russian Jacobin organization of P. G. Zaichnevskii.

a revolutionary organization of the proletariat, in which professional revolutionaries would merely serve in the ranks; how they could brand as bourgeois the demand for a democratic organization of the Social Democratic Party; and how they could urge the necessity of suppressing any social movement that might even indirectly threaten us . . . All this was characteristic of the bourgeoisie when it won power, but 'the lower classes do not behave in this way'. They do not have to suppress anyone; they need political power only to avoid being suppressed themselves. Having freed itself of the 'class despotism' of the bourgeoisie, the proletariat will counter it, not by its own despotism, but by a broadly and genuinely democratic order.

When it comes to this debate about dictatorship, some people may quote Kautsky's reply to Bernstein: 'We can calmly postpone to the future the solution of the problem of the dictatorship of the proletariat. For the time being, it is still useless for us to tie our hands on this score.'[1]

But it behoves us to concern ourselves with the problem. First, because, in contrast to the authors of the Erfurt programme, the authors of our programme have forced our hand by inserting the word dictatorship in our credo. And, second, because this question is highly significant as a matter of principle and, like every principle enunciated in the programme, is reflected in the entire tactics and organization of our Party. If we must prepare for the conquest of 'such' power, then we must create 'an organization of revolutionaries' and train the masses of the people to act in obedience to the 'conductor's baton'. But if we are to seek democracy, and if our future revolutionary government is merely to serve the proletariat—as 'the worker, the overseer, and the book-keeper serve their employer'[2]—then we must at once create the kind of organization, and adhere in all our actions to the kind of tactics, which will educate the broad strata of the working-class and train them to express their will through their party. Our answer to the problem of dictatorship will affect every single step of our activity.

[1] Kautsky, *Bernstein*, p. 172. [2] See above, p. 146.

ISKRA-*ISM*

The Attempt to amend Iskra*'s Programme*

The vast majority of delegates at the congress was on the side of *Iskra* in the matter of the programme. The authors of the programme might, therefore, have been expected to welcome criticism from their opponents. This would have given them an opportunity to justify their position without the risk of yielding an iota. And it would have lent the programme at least some semblance of a collective work. But the authors of the programme refused to give the floor even to those few isolated representatives of the opposing wing of the Social Democratic movement who had managed to find their way into the congress.

'I considered it necessary', said Comrade Lenin at the congress of the League, 'to elect a bureau which could pursue a firm and steadfast policy, and, should the need arise, even employ the so-called "mailed fist".'[1] Lenin had his way. The [Second Party] Congress obediently supported its bureau, but even the congress itself was astonished at times at the 'steadfast policy' and the 'mailed fist'. The agenda established for the discussion of the programme was correct enough. First, there was to be a general discussion of the programme, with each delegate allowed three ten-minute speeches. This was to be followed by discussion of individual paragraphs. And, again, on each point—that is, on each particular question of our *profession de foi*—every delegate had the right to speak three times, i.e., to state his views and then to defend them. But this procedure was soon forcibly violated.

Martynov was the first to speak about the programme. And it became clear at once that the delegates had no intention of even listening to their opponents. The majority, in fact, the vast majority of delegates had even left the hall. The rest were busy with 'their own affairs'. Only the chairman, Comrade Plekhanov, listened to Martynov with demonstrative attention.

I am certain that the readers of the minutes of the congress will note that Comrade Martynov's speech was the only one dealing with the programme. But there was no discussion of his speech. A few words by Comrade Martov (*Protokoly*, p. 122), several jocular

---

[1] *Protokoly 2-go ocherednogo s"ezda zagranichnoi ligi*, p. 44.

remarks by Comrade Plekhanov (p. 122), and a few 'philosophical' comments by Comrade Gorin (p. 119) were sufficient for the congress to consider Comrade Martynov completely demolished. Under such circumstances, it was only a formality to listen to those of us who were dissatisfied with the draft programme. And, naturally, the bureau of the 'mailed fist' could not have been expected to hesitate before violating 'formalities'. My speech (p. 127), it seems to me, served as the immediate pretext for the application of the 'firm, steadfast policy'. Since I had only ten minutes, I was of necessity compelled in *this* speech to indicate only the general features of the objections I wished to make. But already from this first speech of mine it was clear that I would raise a number of problems which could not be dismissed with jokes and laughter. Most of the delegates were under the happy delusion that they had to choose between the programme of revolutionary Social Democracy and opportunism, Economism, Bernsteinism, and so on, and so on. In this delusion they were systematically supported by the authors of the programme. However, I would have proved that this was a mere delusion, since I was defending the programme of the international Social Democratic movement, and countering the *Iskra* programme, not with Bernstein's book, but with the Vienna or Erfurt programme. I would have shown, moreover, that various theses in the programme had been interpreted differently by other representatives of revolutionary Social Democracy; and so when it accepted or rejected this or that statement in the programme, the congress would have to choose between the views of Guesde and Bebel, Kautsky and Adler, Plekhanov and Lenin. Had these questions been put to the congress, then—unless it wished to sign its own bankruptcy statement—it would have been obliged to consider them. It would have had to listen to long debates about the programme before deciding to reject the positions, not of Akimov, Martynov, or Liber, but of Kautsky, Bebel, Adler, and Plekhanov. Yes, Plekhanov, too, because he would then have been compelled to admit his profound disagreement with Lenin on one of the most essential points of the programme.

Of course, this would have prolonged considerably the time spent on 'point three' of the agenda. But there was a time when *Iskra* was not afraid to devote as much time as necessary precisely to this 'point'. I recall Lenin's words at the 'unification' congress of 1901: 'Let us devote our entire time to matters of principle. If we agree on these, we shall then be able to decide the organizational questions in half an hour.' There was a good deal of truth in this hyperbole. And if the congress had appreciated the full importance of the central principles behind the position chosen, if it had realized that the programme *implicitly* contained all tactical and organizational decisions, it would have curtailed to a minimum all the other points on the agenda and devoted itself above all to the programme. The congress did exactly the opposite.

If the programme had really been discussed at the congress, instead of merely being put to the vote, the clash between the 'hards' and the 'softs' would in all probability have taken place on the ground of principles. This would have been a great step forward in the development of our Party. The Party will take this step, and is indeed already taking it today, but it is still groping its way forward. Its criticisms are directed initially at particular deductions from, and at particular applications of, the general principle which had characterized the old *Iskra*—a slow and painful process, condemned to 'zigzags', which saps our Party's strength.

My first speech was opposed by Martov, Karskii, Plekhanov, Gorin, Lenin, and Trotsky. I must now answer their arguments, since I was not permitted to do so at the congress itself. With the exception of Martov and Karskii, those who argued against me were already aware that I would have no opportunity to reply to them. Under these conditions, it did not require too much skill to 'crush' me. Comrade Lange, whose specialty was the introduction of motions to close debate, hastened to suggest a clever method to put a speedy end to debates on the programme. He proposed voting on the entire programme at once and then turning it over to a committee for final revision. This efficient method of curbing critics was, of course, supported by no one. However, Comrade Trotsky, supported by Comrade Martov, proposed that the list of speakers be closed. This meant that the floor would be given to Plekhanov, Gorin, Lenin, and Trotsky, to excoriate the 'critics', and that the latter would be deprived of the opportunity to defend their positions. Comrades Martov and Trotsky justified their proposal with the argument that there would still be enough time for debate when the programme was discussed point by point after its return from committee (*Protokoly*, p. 127). The congress agreed to this, and the list of speakers was closed.

And then the draft was returned from committee (p. 162).

The first point of the programme was placed under discussion.

Comrade Martynov proposed an amendment. Then I argued for an amendment, similar to Martynov's. Immediately after that Comrade Rusov moved for the application of a 'mailed fist' measure; he urged that all my amendments be combined into one and submitted to a single vote. Comrade Martov 'could find no way out, but pointed out the tremendous inconvenience of turning the congress into a debate between academics'. The chairman, Comrade Plekhanov, was more quick-witted than Comrade Martov. He declared that he 'interpreted the rules to mean that delegates were allowed ten minutes for comment on the entire programme'. This shameful violation of the rules was immediately put to the vote by Plekhanov, despite my protests and my demand that the text of the rules be read before a vote on his deliberately false interpretation. At that time Plekhanov was still one of the 'hards'. But the congress, to its honour be it said, was even then lacking in the requisite degree of 'hardness', and did not accept Plekhanov's 'interpretation'.

At that point Martov finally 'found a solution'. He proposed that delegates be allowed to 'speak on each point once for five minutes'.[1] The value of this system had already been demonstrated to Comrade Martov in the committee; at the committee sessions my amendments were all distorted beyond recognition and then ridiculed and 'crushed'. I was compelled to watch this mockery quietly and did not have the right to speak out against it. I found myself, in rapid succession, a Millerandist, a Bernsteinian, a *khvostist*, and a Philistine.

Several delegates later expressed astonishment at the composure with which I listened to all these compliments. But, on the one hand, I was given no opportunity to reply before the committee (where protest would have been futile in any case). On the other hand, I hoped—and here I must confess to *naïveté*—that I would be given an opportunity, in strict conformity with the congress rules, to prove before the congress the full absurdity of my opponents' arguments.

My hopes had been naïve indeed. Had my opponents thought that I would be given the right to reply, that they would have to repeat and defend their arguments on the congress floor, and later see them in print in the *Protokoly*, they would not have replied in a way which they themselves knew to be preposterous. I had not taken this into account.

[1] *Protokoly*, p. 164.

After the tactless motions of Comrades Rusov and Plekhanov, Martov's politic proposal seemed more suitable to the congress, which proceeded to adopt it. At once, all difficulties vanished. No one deemed it necessary to reply either to Comrade Martynov or to me, and the first point of the programme was immediately put to a vote and adopted by forty-two votes.

From then on, it was plain sailing. The 'discussion' by the congress of those sections of the programme which deal with principles is reported in the *Protokoly* on *one page* (pp. 165–6). None of the fifty disciples of 'scientific socialism', who had converged from all ends of Russia and Western Europe, found it necessary to make a single remark, a single amendment in matters of principle to the draft programme. Not a doubt, not a question arose in any mind. No one felt the need to add a single word, to change a single expression, to delete a single term. All of the most complex problems of international socialism, collected in the theoretical part of our programme, took the congress as much time to decide as the single question of whether or not it was necessary to establish nurseries for children of factory workers (pp. 184–5).

'The party of the class conscious proletariat, the Russian Social Democratic Party, now has its own programme . . . We can say with all due pride that the programme we have adopted gives our proletariat a sound and trusty weapon in the struggle with its enemies.' This is how Comrade Plekhanov saw fit to sum up the work of the congress on the programme (p. 235).

Party and Class

I shall now attempt to analyse the brief replies I received during the general discussion of the programme.

The first speaker to answer me was Comrade Martov (p. 125). He began with the statement that he was 'entirely at a loss to see where in the draft Akimov could have discerned a tendency to minimize the significance of the labour movement'. 'I do not know', he says further, 'what Akimov has in mind when he says that the programme expresses a scornful attitude toward the economic struggle of the workers.' 'Where has Akimov found evidence of our excessive trust in other social movements?'

If it is true that Martov did not know what I had in mind when I criticized the programme, if he was really asking where I had found evidence of misplaced trust, if it was indeed unclear to him what errors I saw in the programme, then it was Comrade Martov's first duty to oppose Comrade Trotsky's motion to close the list of speakers. Yet he supported this motion. In fact, it was he who in the end introduced a change in the congress rules which made discussion of the programme impossible.

Of course, Comrade Martov could simply have refrained from answering me. He could have said that my speech did not merit argument. But if he undertook to answer, he should have begun with an attempt to find out what he 'did not know', to clarify to himself what he was 'at a loss to see'. Instead, Comrade Martov preferred simply to voice his conjectures, completely unfounded and designed—as I have said earlier—solely to suggest to the congress that the opponents of the draft were opportunists. A good illustration of this is the following phrase: 'Does he want us, then, instead of fighting for the general economic goal of the entire labour movement—social revolution—to deal with the specific problems of various sections of the proletariat?'[1] Comrade Martov knew very well that this was not what I wanted.

In themselves, Comrade Martov's questions were entirely valid. And this is true for two reasons. First, in my initial ten-minute speech I could only state 'the general considerations by which I was guided in proposing' my amendments (p. 123). This was all I intended to do, and all I did. Therefore, the questions as to 'where Akimov found' and 'what Akimov had in mind' were entirely natural. These questions were anticipated in my speech; indeed, my speech was designed to raise them. For it was only the *first* speech, and was limited to ten minutes. It achieved its purpose; it raised the questions I intended it to raise, and my two subsequent speeches were to answer them. However, I made a mistake in one thing: these questions arose in Martov's mind, but not in the minds of the majority of delegates to the congress, who showed themselves completely unprepared to discuss the principles embodied in the programme.

Secondly, there was another reason why Comrade Martov, and precisely he, should have responded *in this way* to my speech. He did so because he actually does not see those faults in the programme which I had intended to point out. If he had realized the profound meaning which was in reality put into the programme, and which is already manifesting itself to some extent in

[1] *Protokoly*, p. 125.

the tactics of the 'hards', he would not have accepted this programme. And I am deeply convinced that he will come to see this meaning, and then he will 'once more find himself in the minority'.

Comrade Martov, who represents a healthy element in our Party, has passed through all the stages of its development. The 'theory of stages' provoked his indignation precisely because he has always been so completely immersed in the stage at which our Party was at any given time that he could not distinguish it as one unit in a series, could not recognize it as merely one rung of the ladder. Once a champion of *kruzhkovshchina* [clandestine circles for worker education], later the author of the best pamphlets of 'so-called Economism', and still later a sharp and outspoken *Iskrovets*, he had already at the congress 'given me hopes' (p. 283) of 'the emergence of another trend in our Party'. And now he has already, to use his own expression, taken 'a new step'. Unfortunately, as the congress has shown, our Party does not yet understand the full importance of a programme grounded on principles, and Martov —who can, to paraphrase Reskin, be called the echo of the revolution—does not know where, in the programme which he himself signed, others find the views that he does not share.

Some of Comrade Martov's questions have already been answered in the present pamphlet. To the remainder I shall reply in connexion with the answers to my other opponents at the congress. However, one of his remarks may be analysed at this point. He said:

It is fanciful to imagine that the thesis concerning other strata of the working people has brought us nearer to the Socialist Revolutionaries. On the contrary, the latter have said that this thesis would have been acceptable to them if it spoke of 'the socialist viewpoint' rather than of 'the point of view of the proletariat'. The class character of the Party is expressed in the thesis clearly enough. The words 'working class' are used here only to avoid repetition of 'proletariat' in the same sentence.

I have been unable in this pamphlet to analyse in detail the last point of the programme, which is as unsatisfactory as the rest. However, since Martov refers to it, I shall at least briefly point out its shortcomings. The text of the programme reads:

[The Party] shows the rest of the labouring and exploited mass the hopelessness of its situation in capitalist society and the need for social revolution in the interest of its own liberation from oppression by capital.

The party of the working-class, the Social Democratic Party, invites into its ranks all strata of the labouring and exploited population, in so far as they adopt the point of view of the proletariat.[1]

To begin with, I shall examine individual expressions; then I shall attempt to analyse the whole idea.

'The rest of the labouring and exploited mass'—what does this mean? Which strata of the people belong to it? It may safely be said that this is the vast majority of citizens of every capitalist society. Bellamy has already painted this society as a huge chariot, carrying a tiny group of people and pulled by hundreds of millions, straining and falling by the wayside. Kautsky also says that in modern society the overwhelming majority must labour and suffer exploitation.

And so, all strata of society live under the yoke of capital, with the exception of the *haute bourgeoisie*—capital incarnate. All these strata have reason to struggle against capital, and indeed do so. With the exception of the big landowners, all these strata consist of labouring people. What, then, should be the attitude of the Social Democrats toward them?

The Gotha programme stated that all the strata of the people, except the proletariat, constitute a single reactionary mass. Marx, who sharply criticized the draft of the Gotha programme generally, felt that this assertion also was entirely wrong. 'This phrase is a direct quotation from Lassalle', he wrote in his letter to Liebknecht on 5 May 1875.* In this 'mass' counterposed to the proletariat, Marx singles out first and foremost the bourgeoisie. 'In the *Communist Manifesto*', says Marx, 'the bourgeoisie is seen as a revolutionary class, the bearer of big industry—as opposed to the feudal lords and the middle strata . . . These strata, therefore, do not constitute, together with the bourgeoisie, a single reactionary mass.'†

From the mass counterposed to the proletariat, Marx singles out the bourgeoisie as an unquestionably revolutionary class, and the feudalists as an unquestionably reactionary class. Then he goes on to analyse the 'middle strata', i.e., the 'labouring and exploited mass'. He finds that these masses also are not homogeneous. He notes the fact that these strata are oppressed by capital and that

---

[1] *Zaria*, no. 4, p. 5. See below Appendix II, p. 195.

* ['Zur Kritik des Sozialdemokratischen Parteiprogramms: Aus dem Nachlass von Karl Marx',] *Die Neue Zeit*, no. 18 (1890–1) [p. 568].

† *Ibid.*

they are fighting against the bourgeoisie. But he regards this struggle as 'conservative, more than that—reactionary'. However, there are elements within these strata that can be revolutionary. These are the elements that are about to become proletarian, the strata that are being proletarianized. And this is why Marx saw as deeply erroneous the judgment of the Gotha programme that all these strata 'constitute a single mass'.

Our programme commits the same error. It speaks about 'all strata of the labouring and exploited population' as a single mass. The only difference is that, while the Gotha programme saw 'this single mass' as opposed to the proletariat, the *Iskra* programme considers that it must be provided with sermons on the inevitability of the social revolution.

Furthermore, the Social Democratic Party is called 'the party of the working-class'. This term is used today in two senses. The Social Democrats use it to denote the proletariat; the Socialist Revolutionaries apply it to the proletariat plus the 'working peasantry' plus the intelligentsia. Of course, this is no reason for our giving up the term, which is widely current in our international literature. But we should use it only as a synonym for 'proletariat'. This is also Comrade Martov's view. He says that the term 'working-class' is used in the paragraph under discussion solely to avoid repetition of the term 'proletariat' in the same sentence. But we shall soon see that this is not so.

'The Social Democratic Party invites into its ranks all strata of the labouring and exploited population.' It invites them into its ranks under a certain condition. We shall examine this condition later. For the moment, let us suppose that it has been met. Such a supposition is certainly legitimate, for otherwise there would be no sense in including it in our programme.

And so, all strata of the labouring and exploited population have joined the ranks of our Party, having realized the 'hopelessness of [their] situation in capitalist society and the need for social revolution in the interest of [their] own liberation'.[1]

But this is all that the Socialist Revolutionaries demand. This is the basic, the starting point of their entire programme. All their tactics and plans stem from this one point—from the view that all the strata of the labouring and exploited population constitute a single class, the working-class, and can be led by one political party. To accept this point is to accept in principle the whole

---

[1] *Zaria*, no. 4, p. 5. See below, Appendix II, p. 195.

programme of the Socialist Revolutionaries. However, although he accepts this point, Comrade Martov declares that 'it is fanciful to imagine that the thesis concerning other strata of the working people has brought us nearer to the Socialist Revolutionaries'.

Yet we must remember that the programmes of political parties are not determined by the ideas of their leaders; on the contrary, leadership of a party comes into the hands of those people who answer the ideals of 'the strata of the population' that belong to the party. Suppose, then, that our Party were joined by all the strata of the working people. Even if they had sworn beforehand to accept the condition set by our programme, very soon one of two things would happen—either Comrade Martov would take yet another 'new step' and become a Socialist Revolutionary, or he would 'once more find himself in the minority' and soon afterwards be thrown out of the Party.

Today, the reconstituted *Iskra* has already become aware of the danger. The feuilleton in no. 62 [of *Iskra*][1] deplores the fact that the proclamations of 'the Moscow, Odessa, Nikolaev, and certain other highly influential organizations' (read 'and the Central Committee') are almost identical with those, for instance, of the Kiev Committee of the Socialist Revolutionary Party. But we opponents of *Iskra* had discovered this sad fact a year before the congress. For example, we noted this tendency in the proclamations of the 'Odessa Revolutionary Social Democrats', in which *Iskra* (see no. 30) found nothing objectionable. And this is why both Comrade Martov and the author of the feuilleton in no. 62 might have found our comments at the congress worth hearing— if they had not prevented us from stating them.

Iskra has conducted a long and sharp polemic with the Socialist Revolutionaries. It has declared that they are neither socialists nor revolutionaries. This, of course, is nonsense. They are both socialists and revolutionaries. And I am not saying this because I am in any way close to them. On the contrary, I am so far from them that I have no reason to make a mockery of them in order to distinguish myself from them. The *Iskrovtsy*, however—both those of the old *Iskra* and the present 'hard' *Iskrovtsy*—represent the trend in the Russian Social Democratic movement that is

[1] T., 'Nasha "voennaia" kampaniia', *Iskra*, no. 62 (15 March 1904), pp. 4–7. T. was here the pseudonym of Trotsky; for identification see Iu. Kamenev, *Russkaia politicheskaia literatura za granitsei*, vol. 1: *Sotsial'demokraticheskie izdaniia: Ukazatel' sotsial'demokraticheskoi literatury na russkom iazyke 1883– 1905 gg.* (Paris, 1913), 40.

closest to the Socialist Revolutionaries. This is why they find it necessary to make a mockery of the latter to the extent that even Comrade Martov fails to recognize kindred traits in the programmes of the *Iskrovtsy* and the Socialist Revolutionaries.*

The Socialist Revolutionary Party is unquestionably a socialist party, although it is not a party of scientific socialism. This is so because, and only because, it is not a proletarian party, but a party of all the exploited and labouring strata of the population. And this is why I 'discerned' non-Social Democratic tendencies in this point of the *Iskra* programme as well.

However, even Comrade Martov informs us that the Socialist Revolutionaries 'said that this thesis would have been acceptable to them if' it set a different condition for the admission of 'all strata' to our Party. Let us, then, examine this condition; let us see whether the Socialist Revolutionaries are indeed unable to accept it.

'The Social Democratic Party invites into its ranks all strata . . . in so far as they adopt the point of view of the proletariat.' Comrade Liber voiced some doubts regarding this condition:

Can entire strata of the non-proletarian population, *as such*, adopt the point of view of the proletariat? Never, it seems to me. Of course, in the fight for its minimum programme, the Social Democratic Party will be able to win over to its side the sympathies of other strata of the population as well, for they will see that this party is the most resolute champion of democracy. But the maximum programme, socialism,† can be and will be fought for only by the proletariat. And it is only individual members of other strata who can definitely come over to the point of view of the proletariat.[1]

Liber's argument was answered by Comrade Plekhanov. This answer is extremely characteristic of him:

Comrade Liber asks whether any social stratum as a whole can come over to the side of the proletariat. This seems to be an argument against the view expressed in our programme. But the programme does not touch upon this question. It says conditionally: We, the party of the proletariat, invite into our ranks all other strata of the labouring population, *in so far* [italics Plekhanov's] as they adopt our point of view. Comrade Liber feels that we do not express ourselves here with

* My views on the Socialist Revolutionaries are expressed in the leading article ['Sotsial'demokraticheskaia partiia i partiia sotsialistov-revoliutsionerov'] in *Krasnoe znamia*, no. 2 [December 1902, pp. 1–6].
† Of course, Comrade Liber has in mind the kind of socialism on which our programme is based—scientific socialism.
[1] *Protokoly*, p. 130.

sufficient exactness. But this is also what the *Communist Manifesto* says: All other strata become revolutionary only in so far as they come over to the point of view of the proletariat. Comrade Liber wants to be more orthodox than Marx himself. Individuals do this, but the Party as a whole has no need of it.[1]

Plekhanov's answer follows his usual pattern: (1) a slight alteration of the opponent's words, (2) an evasive formulation of the idea at issue, (3) a superficial reference to authority, and (4) ridicule.

Comrade Liber had never asked whether any stratum could come over *to the side* of the proletariat. Of course it can. Comrade Liber says so himself. But he asked whether any stratum can adopt the *point of view* of the proletariat. And that is quite a different question, to which Comrade Liber replied in the negative, and Comrade Plekhanov, evasively: We invite all strata into our ranks, and the rest is their own affair. If they come, well and good; if they don't, they've had their invitation. But this is no way to answer a question affecting the programme. And if 'individuals do this', the congress as a whole should never have sanctioned the statements of such individuals. The programme should invite only the strata which, according to our historico-philosophic views, can and inevitably will act together with us. The programme points only to those tasks and problems which will inevitably confront the Party. Its summons is not a genial invitation to all comers. A programme is not a proclamation and not a newspaper editorial; its purpose is not to agitate and summon but to state and proclaim. The superficiality of Plekhanov's reference to the *Manifesto* is simply astounding. Even from his inexact quotation, it follows only that 'all strata' become revolutionary in so far, etc. But the Social Democratic Party cannot invite into its ranks all strata, even if they are revolutionary. Being revolutionary is still not sufficient qualification for joining our Party. Therefore, Plekhanov's quotation by no means justifies the text of the programme. Besides, the expression in question, which Plekhanov himself underlines and which is supposedly 'what the *Manifesto* says' as well, is not to be found in the *Manifesto*, but only in Plekhanov's incorrect translation. In other words, Plekhanov was citing his own authority. The German text of the *Manifesto* reads as follows:

Die Mittelstände . . . sind nicht revolutionär, sondern konservativ. Noch mehr, sie sind reaktionär . . . Sind sie revolutionär, so sind sie es im

---

[1] *Ibid.* pp. 132–3.

Hinblick auf den ihnen bevorstehenden Übergang ins Proletariat . . . so verlassen sie ihren eigenen Standpunkt, um sich auf den des Proletariats zu stellen.[1]

Plekhanov's translation is not only inexact but ambiguous as well. 'They are reactionary. But they are revolutionary in so far as they come over to the point of view of the proletariat.' It turns out, then, that these strata are reactionary on the one hand and revolutionary on the other. The words 'in so far', which are not in the German text and which made their way from Plekhanov's translation into our programme, can be interpreted in one of two senses:

(1) The labouring and exploited population suffers from capitalism and fights against it. But the historic significance of this struggle is not the same for the whole mass. Its largest part is reactionary, for its struggle with the bourgeoisie retards the natural process of social development. But a certain portion of it, namely, the strata which are about to become a part of the proletariat, is capable of coming to understand the goal of the proletariat and of adopting the viewpoint of the proletariat. Therefore, we should 'invite' not the entire mass of labouring and exploited people but only a part of it, only those who will be capable of adopting the point of view of the proletariat. If this is taken to be the meaning of the expression 'in so far' as used in our programme, then we should not say that we invite all strata; we should say that we invite 'the strata which, etc.' Besides, we cannot invite even these strata into our ranks. The *Manifesto* considers that they are revolution-minded, but no more. Therefore we can call upon them to fight side by side with us but not in our ranks, where they would inevitably bring with them the prejudices of their transitional status.

(2) However, the text of the programme may also be interpreted differently.

The middle strata, generally speaking, are reactionary. But in some of their demands—specifically those which accord with the proletarian point of view—they are revolutionary. And in so far as they are revolutionary, they can join [our] ranks. For instance, the overthrow of the autocracy is an action desirable from the point of view of the proletariat. It is therefore a revolutionary action. And since it is desirable to all labouring and oppressed strata, they all can and should join our Party, but only in so far as it sets itself this goal. When the goal is achieved, these strata will leave our Party. For the time being, however, it is expedient

---

[1] Karl Marx and Friedrich Engels, *Werke* (Berlin), IV (1959), 472.

to use their help. This is a 'defence' of the *Iskra* programme that I
heard repeatedly from its adherents at the time that I was giving
lectures against the programme. I replied to them that the authors
of the programme would scarcely thank them for such a defence.
Iskra will begin to combat this idea when it filters into the proclamations of our committees. But then this struggle will entail
new dissensions, splits, and quarrels. The authors of such proclamations will point to our programme, will argue that it invites into
our ranks all strata . . . naturally, in so far as they come over 'to
the point of view of the proletariat'. But what is this 'point of
view'? And can it really frighten off the Socialist Revolutionaries?

When the Social Democrats wrote, with Plekhanov's pen, that
the intelligentsia should once and for all end its debates concerning
the best possible programme, because the proletariat had already
stated its programme, the Socialist Revolutionaries naturally
refused to accept this. Not only because the phrase is a paradox
but also because the correct idea implicit in it is alien to the
outlook of the Socialist Revolutionaries. This idea is that 'the
point of view of the proletariat' is created by the proletariat itself. But since [according to the old *Iskra*] this 'point of view' is not
something specific and definite, a product of the class movement
of the proletariat which we can either accept or reject; since, on
the contrary, it is developed by us and, to use Lenin's expression,
'introduced' into the proletariat 'from without', or—in Comrade
Gorin's even more apt description—is 'an imported teaching'
(*Protokoly*, p. 128), the Socialist Revolutionaries have nothing to
fear. They can agree in full to the formulation of this point in
the *Iskra* programme. Of course, they differ from the authors of the
programme over the point of view that the proletariat and all the
other labouring and exploited strata should have once they are in
our Party—or, more precisely, over the point of view that we
should prescribe for them. But this is a matter of our opinion. It
is our business, and not the business of those to whom we shall
bring our programme. And therefore it may be hoped that we
shall manage to agree on it, by argument and experiment.

Such an attitude on the part of the Socialist Revolutionaries
toward the 'point of view of the proletariat' is by no means my
own hypothetical construction. It was expressed in the *Vestnik
Russkoi Revoliutsii* [*Herald of the Russian Revolution*], no. 3:

We understand that when . . . the socialist revolution is regarded as
dependent on the will of the 'vast majority' of the nation . . . a wide gulf

opens between this viewpoint and that of the *Narodovol'tsy*. But when revolutionary Marxism recognizes the inevitability of intervention by a conscious minority at a given moment of the social evolution, the difference between such Marxism and the viewpoint of the *Narodnaia Volia* pales and disappears altogether . . . Let revolutionary Marxism give up the idea of making fine and fictitious distinctions between their views and those of the *Narodovol'tsy*. After all that we have heard from orthodox Social Democrats, there are no such distinctions, and there can be none . . . For both these parties, the working-class plays the part of a revolutionary weapon, in so far as socialist thought dislodges it from the rut of mere class struggle.[1]

The Socialist Revolutionaries want to unite in a single political party the conscious elements of three different strata of the 'labouring and exploited population'. The reason for this is that in Russia these strata have not yet become sufficiently distinct; the population has not yet become sufficiently differentiated. But this is also the reason why there are 'oscillations', deviations from the proletarian point of view, even among Russian Social Democrats. It makes possible the frequent shift of individuals and entire groups, including even workers' organizations, from one party to another. And this confusion of concepts had to be, and indeed was, reflected in the programme. When the 'unconscious historical process' finally differentiates these strata, it will create for each of them its own, separate ideology and will make such confusion impossible. If the congress had been a conscious vehicle of this process, it would at once have begun a particularly careful effort to eliminate from the Social Democratic programme the natural vestiges of the past. But this was exactly what the congress failed to do, for when it adopted without criticism the programme offered by *Iskra*, and particularly its paragraph concerning 'all strata', it sanctioned those very errors which *Iskra* is now compelled to combat. However, since *Iskra* still does not understand either the ideological or the practical foundations of these errors, it will inevitably have to wait for victory in this struggle until these errors are undermined by the unconscious historical processes. The waiting period entails painful dissensions inside the Party. The congress could have shortened this agonizing process if it had been equal to its tasks. The moral responsibility for the failure of the congress in this sphere falls upon its organizers, who set factional interests above the interests of the Party as

---

[1] 'Evoliutsiia russkoi sotsialisticheskoi mysli', *Vestnik russkoi revoliutsii* (Geneva), no. 3 (March 1903), pp. 10–11.

a whole and who kept out of the congress or silenced all the people who, by their criticism of the programme, could have helped the comrades to a correct evaluation of the Party's goals and tasks.

But if this is so, if we cannot gather into our ranks all those who work and are oppressed, does it follow that our Party is really a narrow class organization, concerned with the interests of the proletariat alone? By no means! On the contrary, our Party must take it upon itself to fight against everything reactionary, everything unjust, everything cruel and immoral in our society, and therefore it can and should fight for all who are wronged and oppressed. By doing so, it will win the sympathies and, in many cases, the support of all the labouring and exploited strata of the population. But in order to preserve its moral energies for this great task, it must remain a purely proletarian party in its composition, and, by that token, in its spirit and its programme. The error of *Iskra* as a Social Democratic group was precisely that, on the one hand, it 'sent detachments' everywhere and 'invited into its ranks' all the strata of the people—even going outside the labouring and exploited mass; while, on the other hand, it wanted to expel from our Party purely proletarian organizations that refused to adopt its point of view and did not support the programme which the *Iskra* group considered 'truly proletarian' and which, in the apt expression of the author of the feuilleton in no. 62, had been 'composed by the editors of *Iskra*'.[1]

But does not my insistence on another version of our programme constitute in itself a deviation from the programme of revolutionary Social Democracy? Do I not become an opportunist, Bernsteinian, etc., etc.? Anyone who takes the trouble to read the programmes of our Western European comrades will easily discover two facts: (1) in the current programmes which contain paragraphs about 'other strata', these paragraphs are worded as I proposed to word our programme; (2) in *none of the other programmes* does this paragraph express the idea contained in the *Iskra* programme.

Here are the texts of the Erfurt and Vienna programmes:

The Social Democratic Party of Germany is not fighting for new class privileges and advantages; it is fighting for the abolition of class rule and of classes themselves, for equality of rights and duties for every-

---

[1] *Iskra*, no. 62, p. 6. The verb used by Trotsky here was, in fact, not *sochinit'* (to compose), as remembered inaccurately by Akimov, but *izobresti* (to invent, discover, create).

body, regardless of sex and origin. Proceeding from this point of view, it wages a struggle in modern society not only against the exploitation and oppression of the workers but against every form of exploitation and enslavement, whether it is directed against a class, a party, a sex, or a race [Erfurt programme].[1]

The Social Democratic Labour Party in Austria . . . condemns and combats all limitations on the free expression of opinion, as well as all forms of tutelage by state or church. It strives to secure legal protection of the living standard of the labouring classes and seeks to win for the proletariat the greatest possible influence in all areas of social life [Vienna programme].[2]

The Iskra *Leaders in Debate*

Comrade Trotsky's 'arguments' were, if possible, even less substantial. Comrade Trotsky also began by expressing 'regret' that I had not 'tied up my broad, sweeping criticism to the draft programme'. This alone shows how elementary Comrade Trotsky considered the problem of criticism of the programme. He evidently expected me to deal with everything in ten minutes and, mistaking my introduction for the criticism proper, regretted that it was not tied to the draft programme.

As may be seen from the *Protokoly* (pp. 123, 124), my introduction was linked to the draft programme by several comments. In fact, there were four such comments, including a brief reference to the point concerning the conquest of political power by the proletariat. Unfortunately, Comrade Trotsky noticed only this latter point: 'There was only one point on which Comrade Akimov set himself up in entirely clear and fundamental opposition to the draft under discussion; this was the point concerning the dictatorship of the proletariat' (p. 132).

Comrade Trotsky then went on to recapitulate my views on dictatorship. I had said that 'the paragraph dealing with the conquest of political power is worded in such a way, as compared with all other Social Democratic programmes, that . . . the leading organization will necessarily have to relegate the class led by it into the background'. Or, as Comrade Trotsky summarized it, 'it shifts the centre of gravity . . . from the class to the party'. But since Comrade Trotsky 'knew' that I was an opportunist and Bernsteinian, he added—as though continuing his résumé of my idea —that I also criticized the draft for 'transferring the centre of

---

[1] *Erfurt*, p. 3.   [2] *Vienna*, p. 4.

gravity from the daily struggle to revolutionary dictatorship'. I
have never expressed such a view. After thus attributing to me
the desire to substitute reform for revolution, Comrade Trotsky
went on to a more or less convincing refutation of such social
reformism. What he said was correct,* but it had nothing to do
with my views, as may be seen from the present pamphlet. In
conclusion, Comrade Trotsky offered his own views concerning the
'dictatorship of the proletariat', with which I am in complete
agreement.[1] But this is exactly why I feel that our programme
provides a poor formulation of the idea regarding the conquest of
political power. 'He is frightened [said Trotsky] by the dictatorship
of the proletariat as a Jacobin act.' Yes, indeed. Let Comrade
Trotsky ask Comrade T., author of the feuilleton in no. 62. It
transpires that many people confuse the dictatorship of the proletariat with dictatorship over the proletariat. This is precisely
what I said at the congress, when I urged a clear and definite
formulation of the idea of the conquest of power—in accord with
all Western European programmes. I wanted our programme
to bring light and clarity into the thinking of those who confuse
these concepts, instead of merely befogging it, as it does now.†

---

* I am not touching here upon Trotsky's views on the Socialist Revolutionaries, whom he generally sees in a false light.

[1] Trotsky's words on this subject were: 'The dictatorship of the proletariat
frightens him [Akimov] as an act of Jacobinism. He forgets that this
dictatorship will be possible only when the Social Democratic Party and the
working-class—the dichotomy between which so disturbs him—are so
close to each other as to be almost one and the same. The dictatorship of the
proletariat will not be a conspiratorial "seizure of power" but the political
rule of the organized working-class, which will then constitute the majority
of the nation. In his rejection of the dictatorship, Comrade Akimov falls
into everyday social reformism' (*Protokoly*, p. 132).

† In a supplement to the recent issue of *Iskra* (no. 67), Comrade Martov says:
'Akimov incorrectly asserted that our programme approaches dictatorship
from the same point of view as the *Narodovol'tsy*—as a dictatorship of a
party rather than of a class. An answer to this charge may be found in
Trotsky's speech (*Protokoly*, p. 132). Since the Girondist Akimov made this
charge, new—Jacobin—Akimovs have appeared on the scene (namely in the
Urals), and have begun to speak in earnest about the dictatorship of a dictator over the party, and of the party over a class.'
  Both on the floor of the congress and in committee, I expressed anxiety
that the paragraph in the programme dealing with the conquest of political
power by the proletariat might be understood by many people in a sense
which neither Trotsky nor I would welcome. Trotsky's reply was that I was
unduly 'frightened'. Now the Urals comrades have demonstrated that
Trotsky's optimism was, unfortunately, unfounded and that my anxiety
was, regrettably, justified. Comrade Martov's reference to Trotsky's speech,
which supposedly demolished me, is therefore to no point whatever. Instead,

And how did the 'voice of the revolution', Comrade Lenin, refute my position?

As far as he was concerned, it was entirely unnecessary and undesirable to seize upon specific expressions and reply to them substantively. He did not think the congress could teach him anything. He wanted to teach the congress himself, in accordance with his notion of the rôle of a leader. And to this end he drew up or, as Comrade T. put it in *Iskra*, no. 62, 'composed' a programme —or, to be still more precise, had it composed. Discussion and debates could only have awakened doubts among the delegates and evoked criticism of his programme. Hence he simply adopted the attitude that all objections to the programme were, without any question, opportunist. That he realized how 'dangerous' discussion could be is shown by his careful efforts to keep all 'critics' away from the congress. But even when he had achieved his purpose, the danger was not wholly eliminated, and the bureau of the congress had to apply the policy of the 'mailed fist'. Today, *post factum*, as one reads in the minutes of the League congress about all the steps taken to assure an entirely tractable congress, one inevitably wonders: Against whom were these 'mailed fists'

Comrade Martov should have admitted that reality has *in this instance also* reproved the careless manner in which both he and his comrades dismissed the points made by the so-called Economists. I say 'in this instance also', because the same was true in regard to many other questions; and it would be well for the new *Iskra* to say straightforwardly that it considers erroneous the old *Iskra*'s position on the 'so-called Economists'.

Iskra has told the Odessa Committee that if the latter could not bring itself to acknowledge any merits in the new *Iskra*, it was free to reprint its articles without crediting the source. For my part, I also have no objection to the fact that every issue of the new *Iskra* repeats entire sentences and opinions from articles by Krichevskii and Martynov, and even *Schlagworte* from the literature of the so-called Economists. But I feel such action to be both improper and harmful to the cause when at the same time *Iskra* makes believe that it is the so-called Economists who have changed and not *Iskra* itself. I am certain, however, that our common friends 'among the hards' will not neglect to argue, on the basis of juxtapositions and quotations, that the 'so-called Economists' and the new *Iskrovtsy* are 'kindred souls'. This is perhaps the only meeting point between the so-called Economists and the 'hards'—*les extrêmes se touchent*!

As I was reading the final proofs of these pages, I received Cherevanin's newly published pamphlet. I should like to see this pamphlet read as widely as possible; it sums up excellently the most vital organizational problems of our Party. However, its author will probably be astonished to find in the document given above, bearing on the period of so-called Economism, the very principles he is now defending in the struggle with *Iskra*-ism. [Akimov is presumably referring here to the report of the Union to the Congress; see Appendix I, pp. 188–92.]

needed? After all, the enemies had already been barred, and those who had managed, despite every precaution, to get into the congress constituted a microscopic fraction of the delegate body and could easily have been curbed 'without bloodshed'.

Subsequent events showed that the 'mailed fists' were needed to guard against Lenin's own followers—and they proved inadequate to the task. But this became evident later when the congress went on to concrete problems* of organization and tactics. In programmatic questions and points of principle, the congress was easily kept within desirable bounds even without stern measures —by a mere wave of the conductor's baton.

And what cue was given by this baton in regard to the 'critics' of the draft programme? 'They have demonstrated graphically that the real point under discussion here is the episode of the fight against Economism. They have presented views that have already been described—and justifiably so—as opportunism. They have even gone so far as to "refute" the theory of pauperization and to dispute the dictatorship of the proletariat' (Lenin, *Protokoly*, p. 129).

At that time, as I have said earlier, the congress was still living up to Comrade Lenin's expectations, and it accepted even these words without 'criticism'. As regards Comrade Martynov, these reproaches were made solely because *à la guerre, comme à la guerre*. Comrade Martynov had not only never 'refuted' or 'disputed' the above tenets; he had, in fact, just declared, and indeed stressed, that he did not 'deny either the theory of pauperization or the dictatorship of the proletariat' (p. 127). As for me— whatever one may think of my views on the theory of pauperization and on dictatorship—I believe that no one could attribute to opportunism the amendments I urged in the programme, if only because my amendments were taken *in toto* from the Vienna and Erfurt programmes, in order to reassure those who were unable to distinguish on their own between opportunism and orthodoxy. Lenin unquestionably understood that his charges could not be substantiated, and he therefore took pains to put an end to all further discussion.

Another of Lenin's 'arguments' impresses me as particularly

* The delegates at the congress, as true *Iskrovtsy*, had the utmost contempt for people who 'thought concretely'. But the *Protokoly* of the congress show that only concrete, simple problems were within the grasp of the congress delegates, and even these problems remained unsolved by them.

outrageous: 'They have even gone as far as the *Erfüllungstheorie*, as Comrade A. called it. True, I do not know what it means . . .'[1] Now it is Comrade Lenin who 'does not know'. However, as with Martov and Trotsky, this does not prevent him from 'demolishing' what he does not know. 'Was Comrade A. referring, perhaps, to the *Aushöhlungstheorie*—the "theory of hollowing out" capitalism, i.e., one of the most popular stock ideas of Bernsteinian theory?'[2] Thus, for one theory Lenin substituted an altogether different one, which has nothing in cómmon with it. Not only that—in my speech, I argued *against* the former idea; he put it that I *defended* the latter. I had supposedly 'gone as far as' the most popular ideas of Bernsteinism.

The congress listened to this accusation as calmly as to the others.

Of course, Comrade Lenin also had to resort to ridicule. How could a debate on the programme be conducted without it? 'In his defence of the old principles of Economism, Comrade A. has even offered the incredibly original argument that the term "proletariat" never appears in our programme in the nominative case. And so, it turns out that the nominative case is the most honourable, and the genitive takes second place!'

Indeed, the cases are not equally 'honourable'. By a change of case, 'In the present dispute, Comrade Martov will defeat Comrade Lenin' becomes 'Comrade Martov will be defeated by Comrade Lenin'.

A mere change of case.

I pointed out at the congress that the draft programme makes a sharp distinction between the terms 'Social Democracy' and 'the proletariat'. The former always appears as the subject, the active element, and therefore it is everywhere spoken of in the nominative case; the latter is spoken of as the object of Social Democratic activity, as a passive medium, and it always appears in oblique cases.

As opposed to this, I support the view that Social Democracy is the politically conscious proletariat itself, or, more precisely, the conscious portion of the proletariat, which is itself acting as a party. Of course, there can be different views about this objection I have raised against the programme. But when a man who is certainly not ignorant asserts that my objection is 'an original argument concerning the relative place of honour to be accorded to grammatical cases' . . .! Once Lueger, the leader of the Vienna

---

[1] *Protokoly*, p. 131. [2] *Ibid.*

anti-Semites, declared that his party would adopt any decision he chose, that it would even elect a scarecrow as deputy if he, Lueger, advised it. Perhaps Comrade Lenin was testing the devotion of the congress to his person when he permitted himself such antics? In that event, he had reason to be pleased with the results of his experiments.

Finally, I shall go on to the arguments of the 'diplomat of the revolution', Comrade Plekhanov. Comrade Plekhanov's philosophy was formed during the period of the Gotha programme. This programme is generally regarded as a compromise between the various German Social Democratic factions of those days. But, as Mehring has pointed out, it was, in essence, an expression of views shared alike by Lassalleans and Eisenachists—views characteristic of a German Social Democratic movement which was still in the early stages of its development and crystallization. However, it was precisely these formulas of the emergent Social Democratic movement which could win the most ready response from the Russian socialists, who for their part had then hardly been prepared by the conditions of Russian life and the development of the Russian revolutionary movement to accept the principles of the international Social Democratic movement. In this respect, it is most interesting to examine the programme of the Group for the Emancipation of Labour, and to distinguish those features which were carry-overs from purely Russian revolutionary programmes; those which were common to both Russian and European movements of that period; and those which had been suggested to the authors by the more advanced movement in the West, were new to the Russian movement, and anticipated ideas not yet produced by Russian conditions.

Since then our Russian movement has joined the international proletarian movement and has developed and grown in complexity along with it. As it progressed, its ideas, its programme, changed as well. The Emancipation of Labour Group has already given up certain important postulates of its old programme, and this does it honour, proving that it has developed along with the movement; other ideas still remain to be abandoned.

Among these latter are, incidentally, the 'theory of pauperiza-tion' and that of 'dictatorship'. Comrade Plekhanov is their champion and defender. But he knows better than anyone else that there are few people in the ranks of the international Social Democratic movement who share his position in this respect. If a debate had arisen at the congress on the substance of these questions, Plekhanov would have been obliged to urge the congress to repudiate the generally accepted positions of the Social Democratic movement today. It was far simpler to eliminate these questions altogether.

However, Plekhanov found himself unable to leave one of my arguments without a 'reply', although this argument, properly speaking, was directed against Lenin rather than against him. I pointed out that the 'basic idea of *What Is to Be Done?*, which found expression in the draft programme, is entirely at variance with Plekhanov's statements in his commentaries'. I said therefore that 'I am convinced that Plekhanov disagrees with Lenin' (p. 123). As may be seen in the *Protokoly*, this seemed funny to the delegates.

Plekhanov has made two unforgivable and irreparable mistakes in his life. On two 'occasions he has 'consciously upheld and sanctioned by his silence grave deviations made by Russian Social Democratic thought in its anguished search for the right path. When 'economism'—devoted to the urgent tasks of the moment and caught up in the arduous struggle, in strenuous unceasing revolutionary work—minimized the importance of our political tasks and narrowed our programme, Plekhanov remained silent. When the pamphlet *On Agitation* was published, he was silent; he remained silent when it was reissued on his press. It was only six years later, when times had changed, that he said: 'I regret it deeply, but it is an unquestionable truth. This pamphlet was written by very serious and intelligent people, but it contains the roots of Economism.' When the staff was bent in the opposite direction, so that it still gave us no support, when Lenin's book distorted the fundamental principles of scientific socialism, he was silent. At the time of the publication of, and campaign for, the draft programme, which was clearly at variance with his own commentaries on the draft, he was silent about its faults and supported it.

I said all of this to him. As a comrade and a theoretician of Social Democratic thought, he was duty-bound to answer me, but he did not do so.

I asked him this question at his public lectures; he evaded answering it. I demonstrated the point in my own talks; he never came to them. Before our entire congress I challenged him to reply; he disposed of the challenge with a joke.

Here are his words (*Protokoly*, p. 133):

Napoleon had a hobby of divorcing his marshals from their wives. Some marshals yielded to him, even though they loved their wives. Comrade Akimov resembles Napoleon in this respect; he wants at any cost to divorce me from Lenin. But I shall show more character than Napoleon's marshals. I shall not divorce Lenin, and hope that he has no intention of divorcing me.

The congress laughed. And it *is* funny—with a single jest, the theoretician of the Russian Social Democratic movement disposed of the evidence that in their attitude to a crucial question, two leaders of our Party belonged to two different trends in international Social Democratic thought. But no matter! Now when *What Is to Be Done?* is living out its last days, we shall probably before long learn from Plekhanov that he was never in agreement with it.[1]

The *Protokoly* note that Comrade Lenin also laughed and shook his head to indicate his unwillingness to divorce. My poor Marshal Lenin! Did he have any premonitions at the time of how soon he would remain a grass widower? In his jest, too, Plekhanov was wrong. I did not resemble Napoleon even in his hobbies. I was not divorcing Lenin and Plekhanov; I merely predicted—and predicted correctly. And this lends me courage to make another prediction: Marshal Martov, be prepared! You, too, will soon need divorce papers, for you and Plekhanov also belong to different currents in Social Democracy.

Like all my other opponents at the congress, Plekhanov doubted that he understood me correctly. But of course this could not prevent him, too, from 'crushing' me.

'In Comrade Akimov's opinion,' says Comrade Plekhanov (p. 127), 'if I understood him correctly, the situation of the working-class in bourgeois society not only is not deteriorating absolutely but is not even deteriorating relatively.' I was sitting nearby, and it would have been quite simple for Plekhanov to ask me whether he had understood me correctly, especially since he was not certain that he had. But, of course, he did not ask me; I shouted (p. 127) that he did not understand me correctly. Despite my protest, he continued to argue that this view, which he had attributed to me—and which he now knew I did not hold—'must

---

[1] Shortly after Akimov had written these words, Plekhanov did publish just such an explanation in his 'Rabochii klass i sotsial'demokraticheskaia intelligentsiia', *Iskra*, nos. 70–1 (25 July and 1 Aug. 1904).

177

logically and inevitably lead to opportunism'. In addition, Plekhanov ascribed to me still another opinion which I have never expressed and which has nothing to do with me: 'Gradual improvements in the material conditions of existence of the working-class can lead to socialism.' After that, he solemnly went on to prove, by reflections on the nature of capitalism and references to French and German scholars of the past and present centuries, that Akimov's denial 'even of relative' pauperization 'puts him squarely under the banner of opportunism'. Concluding this solemn, learned speech, Plekhanov added: 'No, Comrade Akimov, we shall not go in this direction; we shall respond to the constant deterioration, both relative and *absolute*, in the proletariat's situation . . .' Thus, 'the most important of the burning questions of our time, which agitate the Social Democrats of the whole world, a question upon which all the others depend' (Plekhanov, *Zaria*, no. 4, p. 20), was bypassed. And the idea concerning the absolute worsening of the workers' situation was stated in passing, as something requiring no proof; yet it was just against this idea that I had argued.

'*Iskra*' on the Dictatorship of the Proletariat

But what is this? Such things, then, can happen in our Party! It is possible for Party leaders, in the presence of fifty delegates from the entire Russian Social Democratic movement, to deprive their opponents of the opportunity to reply and then to distort the latter's views, before the eyes of all, with a fantastic, incredible boldness, while no one, not a single comrade, is moved to rise in indignation, to interrupt them, to cry out that it is shameful!

One of my closest comrades and friends, to whom I had written about this, replied that although I was right to feel as I did about these facts, one should not attach so much importance to the actions of individuals. But for me these events were of enormous significance as a matter of principle; no other event has produced so strong an impression upon me throughout the twelve years of my revolutionary work. I have considered myself a member of a party whose activities were 'founded on truth and justice', as is proclaimed in the Statutes of the International. No matter how much falsehood and injustice I have encountered, it has always meant painful, bitter disappointment in individual persons, often persons I had once loved. But this time falsehood and injustice were perpetrated in the presence of fifty representatives of the

Social Democratic movement, and failed to arouse a single, even a single protest.

It would not be rational to explain all this by the individual traits of delegates who 'know not what they do'. It is essential to find the general principle at the basis of the actions of the delegates who knowingly perpetrated, as something proper and necessary, a thing that to me is shocking and inadmissible.

It seems to me that there is such a principle, and that it determined, in far greater measure than all other theoretical principles, the tactics of the old *Iskra*. This principle should be formulated, so that all members of our Party may take a definite stand toward it. At this point I merely wish to express my certainty that in time Russian socialists will take two sharply opposing, irreconcilable positions on this question, which will not only change the alignments within our Party but will actually lead to a regrouping into two separate parties.

The congress did not trouble to clarify this question, but a short statement from Comrade Posadovskii caused an incident which, I am sure, will not be forgotten.

Commenting on the amendment proposed in committee by Comrade Bruker, who urged the inclusion in the programme of a demand for proportional representation, Comrade Posadovskii said (pp. 168–9):

It seems to me that the statements made here for and against amendments are not a debate over details but the expression of a serious difference of opinion. It is clear that we do not agree on the following fundamental question: '*Should we subordinate our future policy to given basic democratic principles, recognizing them as of absolute value*, or *should all democratic principles be subordinated solely to the interests of our Party?*' I am resolutely in favour of the latter. There are no democratic principles that we should not subordinate to the *interests of our Party* [italics Posadovskii's].

Comrade Posadovskii was interrupted by exclamations: 'And inviolability of person?'

'Yes,' replied Comrade Posadovskii, 'inviolability of person too! As a revolutionary party, which is trying to reach its ultimate goal—social revolution—we should approach democratic principles solely from the point of view of the interests of our Party. If this or that demand is not in our interest, we shall not introduce it.'

Comrade Plekhanov immediately took the floor in support of Posadovskii:

I am completely in agreement with Comrade Posadovskii's words . . . If the success of the revolution should demand temporary curtailment of this or that democratic principle, it would be criminal to stop short of such curtailment. I would say, as my personal opinion, that even the principle of universal suffrage ought to be approached from the point of view of the basic principle of democracy I have indicated—*Salus populi suprema lex est*. The revolutionary proletariat can restrict the political rights of the upper classes as the upper classes once restricted its political rights.

The response to this speech was applause and hissing. Someone protested against the hissing. Comrade Egorov rose and said: 'If such speeches elicit applause, I am duty-bound to hiss.'[1]

Posadovskii formulated the controversial principle briefly and concisely. Plekhanov expressed his position on it still more concisely. He said: *Salus revolutiae* [sic] *suprema lex est*. This means: The end justifies the means.

But I think that the social revolution itself is only a means for destroying the Jesuitism of modern life.

That which some of us set out to destroy is regarded by others as their fundamental principle. All the other questions of the programme are mere details, as compared with this.

The motto of the 'hards' leads, by natural necessity and with logical consistency, to 'Nechaevism [*Nechaevshchina*]. Today, Comrade Martov is indignant about it. A pity he has only just come to see it; but, of course, better late than never. However, Comrade Martov ought to take the trouble to discover the facts and the principles at the root of this Nechaevism in our Party. It is much too superficial to explain it by the fact that Lenin is an obstinate blockhead. Lenin is a Blanquist, and nothing Blanquist is alien to him.

A Party of an Elite or the Party of the Proletariat

The 'Minority' declares that it supports all the principles of the programme but disagrees with the organizational principles of the programme's chief author. But what is a programme for if it does not determine even such basic, decisive events in the life of a party as the choice of the organizational principle? I recall the passionate words of Rosa Luxemburg: 'Our programme would be a sorry scrap of paper if it could not serve us in all eventualities and at every moment of our struggle—and serve us precisely

---

[1] *Protokoly*, p. 169.

because it can be implemented!' What conception of a programme can they have who declare agreement with all its points and then declare joint work impossible because of disagreement on organizational principles? Such a situation can occur only when one of the opposing sides does not understand the programme it has signed. In this case we must assume either that Lenin and Plekhanov do not understand the programme they have themselves drafted or that their opponents, who adopted it without discussion, do not understand it. Lenin's views on organization were known to everyone from his book *What Is to Be Done?* Plekhanov's views were known, if not from Plekhanov's whole past, then from his statement at the very opening of his commentaries on the draft programme:

'Today,' he wrote in the commentaries, 'none of our comrades doubts any longer that we must have a strong organization of the type that existed in Russia in the late 1870s and early 1880s. I mean organizations like *Land and Freedom* [*Zemlia i Volia*] and the *People's Will* [*Narodnaia Volia*].'[1] Plekhanov and Lenin agreed in their organizational principles, and these principles were but the logical outcome of their programme.

But Plekhanov disagrees with Lenin on one very important point of the programme,[2] and this brings him closer to the 'Minority'. This is why Plekhanov occupies an intermediate position on the organizational question. This is why he vacillates in his choice of a formulation for the first paragraph of the [organizational] statute, and does not see the sharp contradiction between the two formulations.

If there is, indeed, an absolute deterioration in the situation of the workers, if the workers find themselves under increasingly worse living conditions, if, as a result, they become less and less capable of conscious struggle, then we must of course create a party organization based not on broad strata of the proletarian masses but only on professional revolutionaries. And one fine day it will seize dictatorial power and suppress 'every social movement which directly or indirectly threatens' . . . the dictators. This is a perfectly correct conclusion, given the above premises.

There is no point in complaining over the absolutist bureaucratic organizational principle. Then, together with Lassalle, one

---

[1] *Zaria*, no. 4, p. 11.
[2] Akimov is presumably referring to Plekhanov's concentration on the vital importance of proletarian 'consciousness'.

must recognize that the organization has to be a mere hammer in the hands of one man. If the congress shared the fundamental theses of the programme, it had to look for this one man. It found him, and perhaps it was not mistaken. At any rate, it could not have selected anyone else. Let the comrades of the Minority, then, submit to the choice of the congress, as demanded by their duty as revolutionaries, and . . . let them be a hammer.

Instinctively, they sense that this is wrong, that it should not be so. And yet, instead of re-evaluating the premises underlying the conclusion, they declare the premises correct. They accept the programme and declare that it is not they who deviate from it, but Lenin who has deviated from the positions of *Iskra* and *Zaria.*

All this, of course, is incorrect. Lenin not only has not diverged from the views he has expressed since the very first issues of *Iskra* and *Zaria*, but has consistently continued to develop the positions which appeared even in his earliest pamphlets and in the first steps of his career.

The error lies not in Lenin's conclusions but in the programme adopted by the congress. The entire programme is wrong, beginning with its fundamental theses—*its own* theses, those which are characteristic of it and differ from the theses of other Social Democratic programmes—and ending with its characteristic modes of expression. For this document is remarkable for the completeness, order, and consistency of its basic erroneous idea.

But if—contrary to this idea—the situation of the proletariat in modern capitalist society is constantly improving, thanks to its unceasing molecular struggle; if it is arriving at better and better conditions for the development of its spiritual forces; if these forces render it, as a class, capable of becoming itself the creator of its ideology, as well as the fighter for it; if the proletariat itself, the vast majority of the people, must win political power—then, of course, we must say to the man with the hammer: Step aside! We shall open the doors wide. There are many who must join our Party in order that it may fulfil its great mission, for our Party is that entire section of the 'proletariat which fights under the Social Democratic banner under the leadership of its democratically organized revolutionary vanguard'!

APPENDIX I

REPORT OF THE DELEGATION OF THE UNION OF RUSSIAN SOCIAL DEMOCRATS TO THE SECOND CONGRESS OF THE RUSSIAN SOCIAL DEMOCRATIC LABOUR PARTY

From 1895 on, the Social Democratic movement in Russia began to shift from *kruzhkovshchina* to methods of mass agitation. This produced, among other things, a demand for agitational pamphlets for distribution among the worker masses. But there were few pamphlets available, and those only in extremely limited quantities. At that time the Union of Russian Social Democrats [Abroad] published only a few pamphlets a year and was unable to arrange adequate delivery of its publications to Russia.

Nobody was satisfied with the *Listok Rabotnika* [Worker Supplement] which was published abroad (there were eight issues from May 1896 to October 1898). Furthermore, its publication led to a clash between the GEL [Group for the Emancipation of Labour] and the majority of the 'young' comrades. As a result of these clashes, the 'youngsters' convened in November 1898, and decided to demand that the GEL allow them to publish independently the *Listok Rabotnika* and agitational pamphlets. If this right were not granted, they proposed to begin publication activities outside the Union. The 'youngsters' wanted the GEL to continue to edit the *Rabotnik* and also those pamphlets which it decided itself ought to be published. However, although it acceded to the changes demanded by the 'youngsters', the GEL refused to take any active part in the subsequent publications of the Union.

The 'youngsters' set themselves very modest tasks. According to their [new] statute, the Union's duties were: (1) to publish agitational literature and deliver it to Russia; (2) as their representative abroad, to carry out the instructions of the Party organizations in Russia; (3) to undertake other tasks that might arise, provided they were not in conflict with the Party's *Manifesto*.

The majority of the 'youngsters' had just arrived from Russia. They brought with them definite views, which they had developed while active in Russia, on the problem of clandestine literature. Therefore the Union's publications began to reflect the attitudes characteristic of our movement at that time.

The Union was reproached for bringing up the rear of the movement, for being 'with the majority', for descending to the level of the masses instead of leading them. These charges were entirely unfounded. The Union reflected the movement of that period just as our present congress reflects the movement of today. It was one section of a homogeneous Party and could have no characteristics other than those of the Party as a whole.

Later, as the Party developed and its component parts began to differentiate, the minority could and should have drawn attention to new and broader problems. These problems were: to work out methods for the political struggle of the proletariat, and to create a unified Party organization. It is generally assumed that at this time the Union was the conservative wing, the 'economist', the petty obstructionist *kustarnik*. I shall demonstrate below how erroneous this view is and explain how it came about. For the present, I return to 1898.

I have already pointed out that the Union was faced with the same general tasks as the Party as a whole. What specifically were these tasks?

The incredibly difficult living conditions of Russian workers in conjunction with the period of prosperity that followed the industrial depression of the 1880s prompted the workers to make frequent efforts to improve their position. 'The task Social Democrats set themselves was to enter into this working-class struggle, to provide it with proper organization, and to awaken the workers to a conscious attitude toward the struggle, its goals, its means, and the results that could be achieved' (Foreword to the first [Russian] edition of the *Erfurt Programme*, 1893).[1] 'To this end, the Social Democrats undertook themselves to stimulate a mass movement on the basis of economic needs.'[2] 'Constantly to mingle with the masses, to listen, to catch the pulse-beat of the crowd— this now became the aim of the agitator.'[3] But he wanted to be 'a step ahead of the masses'. He wanted to 'illuminate this struggle for the masses, to explain its significance from a more general

---

[1] See Foreword (dated July 1893), in Karl Kautsky, *Osnovnye polozheniia Erfurtskoi programmy* (Kolyma, 1894), p. 6. This introduction was republished by B. L. Eidel'man in *Proletarskaia revoliutsiia*, no. 10 (81) (1928), p. 150.

[2] *Ob agitatsii* (Geneva, 1897), p. 22. 　　　　[3] *Ibid.* p. 17.

point of view', without losing sight of 'the connexion between a given step and the ultimate goal'[1] (see *On Agitation*, 1895).

Such were the tasks which the Russian Social Democratic movement consciously set for itself and formulated at the time. It performed them with complete success. 'It also prepared the soil for political agitation.' 'The transformation of the political order is now only a question of time. One spark, and the stored-up fuel will explode'[2] (a prediction made in *On Agitation*). This is why it is utterly wrong to accuse those who consciously store up this inflammable material of forgetting our Party's political tasks.

The Union of Russian Social Democrats wanted to lend its energies to the work of our Party at that time. And, as one of the Party detachments, it did what it was able and had to do in its own sphere of action.

In the course of four years it put out seventy-two issues of agitational publications, totalling over two hundred thousand copies, or nearly sixteen million pages. It delivered to Russia 215 poods of literature, or an average of some 55 poods annually. And we must remember that the Union's work was done under incomparably worse conditions than those we face at present.

'Today one hates to die or grow old; today it is a joy to be alive',[3] said our chairman, opening the Congress. The Union worked when life was not 'a joy', when it was still necessary to build the road along which illegal literature could flow to the wide strata of the proletariat.

Especially important was the Union's work in organizing May Day demonstrations.

When the Union began its publication work, most comrades considered it impossible to organize public gatherings in Russia. In the May Day pamphlet of 1898, Plekhanov wrote that 'of course' demonstrations in Russia were then impossible,[4] that workers who came out to demonstrate would be shot down or, at best, imprisoned. Similarly, as late as August 1899, Aksel'rod still regarded street demonstrations as something fantastic. Refuting certain criticisms, he wrote: 'as though I had indeed even hinted to anyone that he might undertake organization of a terrorist conspiracy or *street demonstrations*'.[5]

---

[1] *Ibid.* p. 18.   [2] *Ibid.* p. 10.
[3] See Plekhanov's speech, in *Protokoly*, p. 19.
[4] G. V. Plekhanov, 'Nash svetlyi prazdnik', in *Rabotnik: Maiskii listok 1898 g.* (Geneva, 1898), p. 6.
[5] P. B. Aksel'rod, *Pis'mo v redaktsiiu 'Rabochego dela'* (Geneva, 1899), p. 10.

The Union came out in favour of organizing political demonstrations, particularly on May Day, as early as November 1898, at its first congress, and gave appropriate instructions to its editorial committee. Since then it has published a special May Day pamphlet or leaflet every year and has delivered all of these to Russia. The May Day campaign of 1901 was especially successful. The Union sent a representative to visit all the leading committees in order to draw up with them a list of general demands. It put out ten thousand pamphlets, ten thousand proclamations, and four thousand copies of *Listok Rabochego Dela* [*Supplement to the Workers' Cause*], no. 6, which was devoted entirely to the events of February and March 1901. Twenty-three people were sent to Russia to deliver these publications in time to all parts of the country, from Petersburg to Tiflis, from the area in which the Bund was active to the Urals. This required an expenditure of 8,000 francs. The entire work was carried out as planned, and not one of the twenty-three emissaries was arrested.

Beside this work, the Union set itself the goal of restoring the Party's central organization, broken up immediately after the First Congress. To the question of 'How to begin?' the Union answered: by calling a congress. The Union felt that a congress was the quickest way of ending the organizational and ideological division in our Party; for it was the view of the Union that the deviations of various Party organizations from the correct road were the inevitable result of the fact that the movement was still in its early stages, and that they were not evidence of an anti-revolutionary current within the Social Democratic movement. The truth of this interpretation, it seems to me, was amply borne out by the fact that none of the organizations that called themselves Social Democratic followed the authors of the 'Credo', which is now quite erroneously described as a reflection of the political ideas dominant at that time; nor did they follow any other anti-revolutionary trend. As for the Union, it was the first to publish the protest of the Russian Social Democrats against the 'Credo', adding its own outspoken words to theirs.

The Union sent its delegates to Russia several times in order to organize a congress. However, they came up against the inertia of our local organizations and even the fear that a reconstituted Central Committee of the Party might try to impose its own plan of operation in disregard of local conditions, which at that time were still not uniform throughout Russia. But the Union continued to agitate for a congress. And although it was unable to achieve immediate results, its work in this regard was certainly not in vain. This work hastened the moment when our committee, recognizing the importance of the congress and the need for it, energetically responded to the new call of the Organizational Committee. Moreover, the very existence of the Organizational Committee itself was the idea of the April conference, which was convened with the participation and at the initiative of the Union; and it was from resolutions adopted at this conference that the Organizational Committee acquired its formal sanction.

One of the Union's circular letters, addressed to all committees in November 1900, attests to the Union's views concerning the organization, programme, and tactics of our Party. This document has not yet been published, and I shall therefore include it here. Today we would not use some of the expressions found in it. We would also argue some of its theses differently and more sharply. But it must be remembered that the letter was written before the events of the spring of 1901. At any rate, it clearly shows how far the Union was from the *kustarnichestvo* and anti-political ideas ascribed to it. The agenda for the Second Congress outlined by the Union is indeed the same as that which will, from all appearances, be followed at this congress. Thus we see that the ideological unification of the Party, the formulation of a programme, was regarded by the Union as of the first importance.

There is no ground whatever for accusing the Union of failure to lead the movement. The Union never took this task upon itself and has always been clearly aware of the lack of an official organ to guide the movement. This is why it insisted from the very first on the publication, under the editorship of the GEL, of *Rabotnik*, which was to serve as a theoretical journal on the model of *Die Neue Zeit*. This is also the reason why later, in 1899, the Union proposed that the GEL should publish pamphlets in the name of the Union, but with full editorial control vested in the GEL. There was even an announcement concerning these publications. In it the Group for the Emancipation of Labour outlined the fundamental problems to be discussed in those publications of the Union which it was to edit, the basic ideas which it intended to advocate, and those which it felt should be attacked. The Union published this announcement in its own name. In so doing it endorsed the views of the GEL, or at any rate it recognized them as essentially correct and useful to the cause and undertook to disseminate these views.

The Union, incidentally, had always held that it had no disagreements in principle with the GEL, and it had repeatedly said so in print.

At present the situation is different. The Union does not share the views of *Iskra* and *Zaria* concerning the 'third period' in the history of the Russian Social Democratic movement; nor by any means can it accept all their other views.

The Union differed from *Iskra* and *Zaria* about what needed to be done in the 'fourth period', and it fought against certain of their policies and ideas which it has regarded and still regards as contrary to the interests of the revolutionary Social Democratic movement. This opposition was interpreted by the *Iskra* and *Zaria* camp, which is now dominant in the Russian Social Democratic movement, as a war against the principles of revolutionary Social Democracy as such. Nonetheless, the Union, in sending to the Second Congress two delegates who represent the two different poles of the Union's thought and whose task it is to defend its position in matters of principle, has resolved to submit unequivocally to the decisions of the congress in the interests of discipline and Party unity.

Circular Letter of the Union of Russian Social Democrats to the Committees of the Party [November 1900]

The Russian Social Democratic movement is facing new tasks and problems. During the last five years it has developed on the basis of a mass strike movement, and it has worked out methods of mass agitation which are suited to the struggle for improved economic conditions. The old debates of the early and mid-1890s concerning propaganda and agitation have been resolved by practical experience and are now forever a thing of the past.

But this same mass movement, which has inevitably brought the militant section of the workers face to face with the autocracy, has also brought the Social Democrats up against the problem of political agitation. This problem has been growing in urgency as the strike movement has drawn the masses of workers into the struggle and has brought them into conflict with the Tsarist régime. The raising of the political level of our movement may be seen everywhere, although not always in equal measure. On the whole, however, in making this advance we are only groping our way forward. The methods and forms of political agitation used by the Russian Social Democratic organizations still fall far short of the systems worked out by our Polish and Jewish comrades. In a certain sense it may be said that they are now in a transition period similar to that of the mid-1890s. Just as at that time a transition was being made from propaganda to agitation, so now a transition is in progress from predominantly economic agitation to political agitation. The fact that our movement is going through this transitional, and hence ill-defined, phase explains the dissatisfaction with established methods of action which has made itself felt in many recent developments.

Occasional deviations from the general Social Democratic programme—such as the 'Credo', on the one hand, and a noticeable resurgence of terrorist ideas on the other—unquestionably reflect a sense of dissatisfaction with the way in which our movement is facing its tactical problems. And, strange as it may seem at first glance, both the extreme 'economists' and the extreme 'politicians' stand essentially on the same ground. Consciously or unconsciously, both groups proceed from the same attitude toward the *political activity* of the working-class. The authors of the 'Credo' draw a line between the political struggle and the economic struggle of the working-class. And they leave political action to the liberal opposition in alliance with the Social Democrats and other members of the intelligentsia. The advocates of terrorism narrow down political struggle to conspiratorial activity, which of necessity must remain alien to the working masses. Consequently, both leave the working masses to one side in the active political struggle.

Both these extremes have been able to emerge solely because the Russian Social Democrats have not yet worked out well-defined methods for mass political struggle.

This is a problem which today demands urgent solution, and it is a problem which we can solve. The standstill in industry and the industrial crisis, now already beginning to make itself felt, have produced a lull in the strike movement which is freeing manpower that could be used in purely political agitation. It is now possible to exercise widespread political influence upon the masses, who have been prepared for this by the previous period, that of strike action. The lull can and should be utilized to work out the *general methods which the working-class should use in its political struggle.*

We have no desire to regiment the movement throughout Russia or to shackle the work of individual organizations with fetters of dogma. Even in Western Europe, in such a closely knit and homogeneous party as the German Social Democratic Party, tactical methods vary in accord with diverse local conditions. But if the Party is to attain unity and develop as it should, then all the various methods should serve not only the same large ultimate purpose, but also the same tactical purpose. For the Russian Social Democrats today, this tactical purpose is to draw the working masses as quickly as possible into the political struggle. And our organizations should direct all their various types of activity to this common goal.

The main obstacle to such unity of tactics among the Russian Social Democrats is their loose organization, the lack of a central organization and even of a central Party organ. Organizational unification is an urgent necessity, not only for purely practical or technical reasons, but also—still more important—in order to further that unified tactical planning on which the immediate future of our Party unquestionably depends. Threatened by the above-mentioned symptomatic deviations from the main Social Democratic stream, our Party is liable to lose its strength unless it can cope immediately with these pressing political tasks of today.

This is why it is essential to convene a Second Party Congress— the only body capable of putting an end to the lack of co-ordination which affects so adversely all the work of the Russian Social Democrats. We cannot delay the congress until the practical experience of the individual organizations eventually forces them to seek unification in order to solve their tactical and organizational problems.

It is the duty of the Social Democrats to hasten this process, which is often slow, and to utilize the elements of unity that already exist. Time does not wait. We must deny all opponents of the Social Democratic movement the opportunity to sow where they did not plough. The soil ploughed by the Social Democrats should be planted with Social Democratic seeds of political agitation.

The First Party Congress formulated our programme in general outline. The task of the Second Congress is to formulate in detail the programme which was envisaged in the *Manifesto*, but which has not yet been drafted. In combination with this, it must also define the general methods to be used by the working-class in its political struggle. The application of these methods will, of course, depend on the actual state of the movement and on the availability of manpower in individual areas. But the methods recommended should provide a general tactical guideline in the work of our organizations. To take an example: let us suppose that the congress expresses itself in favour of political demonstrations. It will by no means follow that all our organizations must immediately and under all circumstances hold such demonstrations. Nevertheless, the decision of the congress will render it the duty of all the organizations to exert efforts to make political demonstrations possible within the near future.

Further, the Second Congress will have to lay a firm foundation for the *unification of the Party organization*. To facilitate such unification, a Central Committee should be established whose chief function, in addition to the publication of a central journal, would be to provide regular assistance to individual organizations in terms of people, literature, and money. There is no need to expand on the importance of this function. Every active Social Democrat is well aware of the extent to which our movement suffers in a practical sense from the absence or weakness of ties between individual districts.

Finally, the *creation of a central Party journal* would assure the preservation of the tactical unity established by the Congress. It would also ensure that tactical problems be fully clarified. Such problems can be solved only if there is a lively exchange of ideas among those active in different areas, and only if the local organizations pool their experience.

The First Congress, which laid the foundations of the Party, made an important contribution to our movement. Unification, if only on a moral level, was a vital problem of the Russian Social Democratic movement as early as 1898. This can be seen from the fact that all the Social Democratic organizations thereafter called themselves 'Committee of the Russian Social Democratic Labour Party'—including those which did not participate in the congress and those which were formed later. Moreover, the name 'Party Committee' was by no means merely a label; it implied then, as it does today, a solidarity with the *Manifesto* and the organizational decisions of the First Congress. During the past two years this designation has become popular among *intelligenty* and among the workers, and it has acquired agitational importance. And, of course, no one would think of repudiating the valuable moral ties established by the First Congress.

The time has now come to take up the cause proclaimed by the First Congress and to transform a moral bond into close organiza-

tional links, which will strengthen our movement both quali-
tatively and quantitatively.

In view of the above, the undersigned organization proposes
to you, comrades, that it take upon itself the initiative in calling
the Second Congress of the Russian Social Democratic Labour
Party. Further, the undersigned organization suggests the following agenda for the Second Congress:

(1) The establishment of procedure for the congress (checking
credentials, drawing up agenda, the method for recording the
minutes, etc.).

(2) The reports from delegates on the state of the movement in
given districts.

(3) The drafting of a detailed Party programme.

(4) Party tactics: (*a*) economic and political struggle; (*b*) the
methods and forms of the economic struggle; (*c*) the methods and
forms to be taken by the political struggle of the working-class.

(5) The relationship to other parties.

(6) The Party organization: (*a*) district organizations and the
Central Committee; (*b*) a central journal, local journals, etc.

THE UNION OF RUSSIAN SOCIAL DEMOCRATS

APPENDIX II

DRAFT PROGRAMME
OF THE
RUSSIAN SOCIAL DEMOCRATIC LABOUR PARTY

(*prepared by the Editors of* Iskra *and* Zaria)[1]

The development of exchange has established such close links between all the peoples of the civilized world that the great liberation movement of the proletariat could not but become, and has in fact long since become, international.

As it considers its Party to be a unit of the world army of the proletariat, the Russian Social Democratic movement has pursued the same ultimate goal as the Social Democrats of all other countries.

This ultimate goal is determined by the character of bourgeois society and by the course of its development. The chief characteristic of this society is commodity production on the basis of capitalist productive relations. The most important and significant part of the means of production and of commodity distribution belongs to a class that is numerically small. Yet the vast majority of the population consists of proletarians and semi-proletarians, compelled by their economic position continually or periodically to sell their labour power, i.e., to hire themselves out to the capitalists, and by their labour to create the income of the upper classes of society.

The area dominated by capitalist productive relations constantly increases as steady technological advance gives greater economic weight to large enterprises and makes for the elimination of small independent producers, transforming some into proletarians, and narrowing the socio-economic functions of the others, who, in certain areas, are forced into more or less complete, more or less open, more or less oppressive dependence on capital.

This technological progress also enables the employers to use the labour of women and children on an ever-mounting scale in the

---

[1] The draft programme was first published in *Iskra*, no. 21 (1 June 1902). This translation was made from *Vtoroi s"ezd RSDRP: Protokoly* (Moscow, 1959), pp. 719–23.

production and distribution of commodities. On the other hand, it leads to a relative decline in the need for human labour. Hence, as the demand for labour power necessarily lags behind the supply, hired labour becomes increasingly dependent on capital, and the level of exploitation rises.

This situation within the bourgeois countries and the sharper competition between them in the world market make it more and more difficult to sell the goods which are produced in greater and greater quantity. Overproduction, which manifests itself in more or less acute industrial crises followed by more or less prolonged periods of industrial stagnation, is an inevitable result of the development of the productive forces in bourgeois society. The crises and the periods of industrial standstill, in their turn, encourage the growing ruin of petty producers and an even greater dependence of hired labour on capital. They hasten the relative or even absolute deterioration in the condition of the working-class.

Thus, in bourgeois society, advancing technology, which leads to an increase in labour productivity and social wealth, results in growing social inequality, a widening gulf between the haves and have-nots, and increasing insecurity, unemployment, and deprivations of every kind for ever wider sections of the labouring masses.

However, as all these contradictions inherent in bourgeois society grow and develop, so the labouring and exploited masses become increasingly dissatisfied with the existing order; the proletarians grow in number and in solidarity; and their struggle against their exploiters becomes ever sharper. At the same time the improvement of technology, which leads to a concentration of the means of production and of distribution and which socializes the labour process in capitalist enterprises, creates with mounting speed the material conditions for the replacement of capitalist by socialist productive relations, that is, for the social revolution which is the ultimate objective of the entire international Social Democratic movement, as the conscious spokesman of the class movement of the proletariat.

The social revolution of the proletariat will replace private by public ownership of the means of production and distribution and will introduce planned organization of the socio-productive process, in order to assure the welfare and the many-sided development of all members of society. It will thus abolish the class division of society and put an end to all exploitation, in whatever form, of one part of society by another.

194

A necessary condition for this social revolution is the dictatorship of the proletariat, that is, the conquest by the proletariat of such political power as will permit it to suppress all resistance put up by the exploiters.

The international Social Democratic movement, the task of which is to make the proletariat capable of fulfilling its great historic mission, organizes the proletariat into an independent political party which opposes all bourgeois parties, directs all phases of its class struggle, exposes the irreconcilable contradiction between the interests of the exploiters and those of the exploited, and teaches the proletariat to understand the historic significance and the necessary conditions for the coming social revolution. At the same time the Social Democrats show the rest of the labouring and exploited mass the hopelessness of its situation in capitalist society and the need for social revolution in the interest of its own liberation from oppression by capital. The Party of the working-class, the Social Democratic Party, invites into its ranks all strata of the labouring and exploited population, in so far as they adopt the point of view of the proletariat.

The Social Democrats of various countries work for the same ultimate goal, which is determined by the dominance of the capitalist mode of production throughout the civilized world. They are, however, compelled to seek immediate objectives which vary one from another, both because the capitalist mode of production is not everywhere equally developed and because its development in various countries takes place under different socio-political conditions.

In Russia, where capitalism has already become the dominant method of production, we still encounter at every step remnants of our old, pre-capitalist social order, which was based on the enserfment of the labouring masses to the landowners, the state, or the head of the state. These remnants act as a most powerful hindrance to economic progress; they do not permit the class struggle of the proletariat to develop fully; they encourage the state and the propertied classes to maintain and intensify the extremely barbarous forms of exploiting the many millions of peasants; and they keep the entire people in ignorance and deprived of rights.

The most important of these remnants of the past and the most powerful bulwark of all this barbarity is the Tsarist autocracy. By its very nature it is hostile to all social change, and it cannot be anything but the bitterest opponent of all the proletariat's strivings for liberation.

This is why the Russian Social Democratic Labour Party takes as its most immediate political task the overthrow of Tsarist absolutism and its replacement by a republic, based on a democratic constitution, which will guarantee the following:

(1) The sovereignty of the people, that is, the concentration of all the supreme power of the state in the hands of a legislative assembly composed of representatives of the people.

(2) Universal, equal, and direct suffrage in the elections both to the legislative assembly and to all local organs of self-government for every citizen who has reached the age of twenty; a secret ballet in the elections; the right of every voter to be elected to all representative assemblies; salaries for the people's representatives.

(3) The inviolability of the person and of the home of the citizen.

(4) Unlimited freedom of conscience, speech, press, assembly, strike, and association.

(5) Freedom of movement and occupation.

(6) The abolition of class privilege, and full equality before the law for all citizens irrespective of sex, religion, or race.

(7) The recognition of the right of self-determination of all nations within the state.

(8) The right of every citizen to prosecute any official without having to make prior complaint to the defendant's superiors.

(9) The replacement of the standing army by universal arming of the people.

(10) The separation of church from state and of the school from church.

(11) Free and compulsory education, both general and vocational, for all children of both sexes until the age of sixteen. The provision of food, clothing, and school supplies to needy children at state expense.

As a basic condition for the democratization of our state economy, the Russian Social Democratic Labour Party demands the *abolition of all indirect taxes and the establishment of a progressive tax on income and inheritance.*

In order to protect the working-class from physical and moral degeneration, as well as to develop its ability to engage in the struggle for liberation, the Party demands:

(1) The limitation of the workday to eight hours for all hired workers.

(2) The establishment by law of a weekly rest period of not less than thirty-six consecutive hours for hired workers of both sexes in all branches of the national economy.

(3) A total ban on overtime.

(4) A ban on night work (from 9 P.M. to 5 A.M.) in all branches of the national economy, with the exception of those which absolutely require it for technological reasons approved by the workers' organizations.

(5) A ban on the employment of children under sixteen years of age.

(6) A ban on women's work in those branches of industry where it is injurious to their health; the release of women from work for two to four weeks after childbirth.

(7) The establishment by law of the employer's civil liability for full or partial disability caused his workers whether through accident or harmful labour conditions; and the release of the worker from the obligation to prove that the employer was responsible for such disability.

(8) A prohibition of payment of wages in kind; the guarantee of weekly payment in all hiring contracts and payment during working hours.

(9) Government pensions for aged workers.

(10) An increase in the number of factory inspectors; the appointment of female inspectors in branches of industry where women's work predominates; the election by the workers of representatives who will be paid by the state and who will supervise the enforcement of the factory laws as well as supervising piece rates and penalties for rejected work.

(11) That the local institutions of self-government, together with the workers' elected representatives, supervise the sanitary condition of those dwellings which the employers allot to workers, the way in which these buildings are maintained, and the conditions under which they are rented. The purpose of this provision is to protect hired workers from interference by employers in their lives and activities as private individuals and citizens.

(12) The establishment of properly organized sanitary supervision in all enterprises employing hired labour, and of free medical aid for workers at the employer's expense.

(13) The extension of supervision by the factory inspectorate to all branches of the national economy and to all enterprises employing hired labour, including state-owned enterprises.

(14) The establishment of the criminal responsibility of employers for violation of laws protecting labour.

(15) The prohibition of monetary deductions from wages by the employers for any reason or purpose (fines, rejections, etc.).

(16) The establishment in all branches of the national economy of factory courts, composed equally of representatives of workers and employers.

(17) The obligatory establishment by local government of labour exchanges which will serve both local and newly arrived workers, which will cover all branches of industry, and which will include representatives of workers' organizations in their management.

With a view to eliminating the remnants of serfdom, which constitute a heavy burden on the peasants, and of advancing the free development of the class struggle in the village, the Party shall seek to bring about:

(1) The abolition of redemption payments and quit-rents, as well as the various obligations which are imposed on the peasantry today as a social estate overburdened with taxes.

(2) The abolition of collective responsibility and of all laws which restrict the peasant in the disposal of his land.

(3) The restitution to the people of the money taken from it in the form of redemption payments and quit-rents. For this purpose monastic lands and the feudal domains of the royal family [*udel'nye imeniia*] should be confiscated, and special taxes imposed on the lands of the nobility with great landholdings who have benefited from redemption loans. The sums thus obtained should be used to establish a special people's fund for the cultural needs and welfare of the village communities.

(4) The institution of peasant committees: (*a*) for the return to the village communities of lands which were taken from the peasants during the abolition of serfdom and which serve in the hands of the land-owners as an instrument for the enslavement of the peasants (the land involved should either be expropriated or, where it has changed hands, purchased by the state with money raised from the great estates of the land-owning nobility); (*b*) for the abolition of the remnants of serfdom surviving in the Urals, in Altai, the western areas, and other regions in the state.

(5) Empowerment of the courts to reduce excessively high rents and to annul agreements which reduce the peasants to a state of servitude.

In its efforts to attain its immediate political and economic objectives, the Russian Social Democratic Labour Party supports every opposition movement and revolutionary movement against the present social and political order in Russia. At the same time it resolutely rejects all those reformist schemes which in any way entail the expansion or consolidation of tutelage over the labouring classes by the police or officialdom.

For its own part, the Russian Social Democratic Labour Party is convinced that the political and social transformations outlined above can be accomplished fully, thoroughly, and enduringly only *by the overthrow of the autocracy* and the convocation of a *Constituent Assembly*, freely elected by all the people.

A SHORT HISTORY OF THE
SOCIAL DEMOCRATIC MOVEMENT
IN RUSSIA

BY VLADIMIR AKIMOV

This booklet appeared in two editions: *Materialy dlia kharakteristiki razvitiia Rossiiskoi Sotsialdemokraticheskoi Rabochei Partii* (Geneva, 1904) and *Ocherk razvitiia sotsialdemokratii v Rossii* (St Petersburg, 1905). It is the later edition which has been translated here; those few changes that were made for the second edition were of a stylistic nature alone. (The preface to the later edition added little to the original preface and has therefore been omitted here.)

Most of the footnotes are editorial and are keyed into the text by numerical indicators. Akimov's notes are keyed into the text by symbols.—*Ed.*

PREFACE TO THE FIRST EDITION

The spring of 1901 witnessed an event of enormous importance in the life of Russian society. Tens of thousands of people, men 'of every calling and condition', assembled in a number of cities, at a given place and a given time, to express their hostility to the autocratic government.

The so-called 'March events' did not occur suddenly and without warning. They were preceded during the winter by a number of outbursts which were touched off by utterly trivial incidents: an anniversary celebration by the editor of a certain newspaper which had been spreading reactionary ideas for a quarter of a century, the production of a play fomenting national hatreds by a journalist who had betrayed his liberal past, the expulsion from the university of two students guilty of a dishonourable action during a nocturnal drinking spree.

Such incidents had occurred repeatedly in the past. But it was only now that they produced a reaction. A hostile demonstration was held in Kharkov near the home of the editor, Iuzefovich, compelling him and his eminent guests to break off their celebration. At the Suvorin Theatre in Petersburg, the audience did not allow an anti-Semitic play, *The Smugglers*,[1] to continue to the end, and resisted the police when they tried to remove the noisiest protesters from the theatre. In Kiev, university students called a meeting to inquire into the reason for the expulsion of their colleagues. They found the action fully justified but at the same time passed a resolution that was sharply critical of the political régime which did not give the student body a chance to exert a moral influence upon its members, and which itself developed a repulsive type of student.

Several students were penalized by the government for their speeches at this meeting. Their comrades organized a sympathy demonstration and send-off at the railway station for the victims.

---

[1] *Kontrabandisty* or *Syn Izrail'ia* [*Son of Israel*], as it was first called, was written and produced by Aleksei Sergeevich Suvorin, the proprietor of *Novoe Vremia*, a major journal of the extreme right. The play was greeted by hostile demonstrations in St Petersburg and elsewhere. See, for instance, 'Pis'mo iz Peterburga', *Nakanune* (London), no. 24 (December 1900), p. 285; and P. Lepeshinskii, *Na povorote* (3rd ed. Moscow, 1935), p. 133.

In retaliation, 183 students were called-up into the army. The government hoped, and the revolutionaries feared, that this punishment would stifle the spirit of protest. Contrary to expectation, it stimulated further rebellion. A student movement sprang up throughout the country. The government replied with new persecutions. Twenty-eight students were called-up into the army in Petersburg, and three hundred more were registered for call-up in Moscow.

At that point an ex-student came to Petersburg and assassinated the Minister of Education.[1] It seemed probable that the shot fired by Karpovich would lead to others but that the mass movement would be affected adversely, that society would be frightened by such extreme methods. These expectations also proved incorrect. Nearly everybody was in favour of Karpovich's action, and the young people were positively jubilant. Far from subsiding, the mass movement rose to a new peak during the 'March days'.

The March events made a tremendous impression on all strata of our nation, and on the most diverse political circles. Some people were indignant with these 'disturbers of the peace' and perhaps fearful for their own safety. Others hoped enthusiastically that at long last the century-old dream of our country's best men had come true—that a new era had dawned, the era of political freedom, for which so many terrible and precious sacrifices had been made.

For the Social Democratic movement, too, the March days were a 'historic turning point'. The movement now entered into a new phase of development, most vividly expressed by the newspaper *Iskra*. This phase unquestionably marked progress and was distinguished from the preceding ones by two features: sharp emphasis on political tasks, and an effort to create a unified party organization. In my booklet I hope to show that these features were the product of a development that had been taking place for an entire decade within the Social Democratic movement.

In addition to these two positive features, which our movement should preserve, this phase was also marked by a negative feature, born of the general conditions of Russian life in which our Party had to formulate its political objectives. Swept along by the general upsurge of political radicalism in all sections of society, our comrades (hitherto totally absorbed in the economic struggle of the proletariat) now became as totally absorbed in the Party's

---

[1] The Minister of Education was Nikolai Pavlovich Bogolepov, who was shot by Karpovich on 14 February 1901.

most immediate political task—the overthrow of the autocracy. In consequence, this task was not approached correctly. In an effort to overcome the extremes of the preceding period in our Party's history, that of so-called Economism, we have ridiculed and rejected that which was sound, that which was really proletarian.

I shall try to present the events of our revolutionary history as aspects of the development of the Social Democratic Party in Russia. I feel that it is only from this point of view that we can properly understand and assess the past and the present, as well as the tasks facing us in the immediate future.

In so far as the elemental, spontaneous movement among the workers made the advanced strata of the Russian proletariat aware of their ever-growing concerns, so the methods employed by the Russian Social Democrats in the fight and in organization were transformed—for, in accordance with their principles, they sought merely to give conscious expression to this elemental movement.

At first the movement made only a little stir in the life of society, at the surface; it was not yet a mass movement. The conscious ideologists of the proletariat could do nothing but prepare themselves for the coming struggle and train individual workers in order to create cadres of politically conscious Social Democrats for the moment when the mass movement would need them. This was the period of individual education in small circles, the stage of *kruzhkovshchina*.

When the blind discontent of the masses with their material condition brought them into the movement, the Social Democrats rapidly changed their tactics and succeeded in becoming the leaders of the proletariat in its struggle. This was the stage of economism.

Later, as the struggle unfolded, the workers began to realize that they were deprived of those elementary civil rights that would have helped them to fight and win their battles for better economic conditions. Thus, in the course of its struggle, the proletariat advanced from an awareness of its material needs to an awareness of its legal interests. At this stage, which became known as so-called Economism, the Social Democrats were once again in the vanguard of the proletariat's fight for its rights in society.

By the beginning of 1901, the movement in various parts of Russia began to assume a homogeneous character. The struggle with the government for rights guaranteeing individual and social freedom brought the proletariat up against the necessity to fight the government, to fight for the right to participate in government, to wage political warfare. This was the stage of *Iskra*-ism.

I consider *Iskra*-ism to be only a stage in the development of our movement. I see the Party's future as a synthesis in which the political and organizational problems facing the Social Democratic movement in its *Iskra* stage will be solved by applying the principles prevailing in the preceding stage.

The materials I have succeeded in gathering are most limited and fragmentary. However, I believe they will prove useful to the comrades, since our literature is extremely scanty in this respect. I have presented these materials from the point of view of the 'theory of stages', a theory repeatedly reviled and ridiculed by *Iskra*.

It seems to me that three centres of the labour movement in Russia have been especially characteristic in their development: Vilna, Petersburg, and Kiev. All the stages of the movement's history are reflected with utmost clarity in the history of these centres. I have therefore devoted a separate chapter to each of these centres and have followed them individually through the various stages of their development: *kruzhkovshchina*, economism, and so-called Economism.

Each stage in the history of the Social Democratic movement was unquestionably a step forward. We may apply to our Party the words of a French historian of the great revolution: 'The chariot of history is moving steadily forward amidst a thousand obstacles. It knocks over anyone who tries to stop it. It topples the very man who only yesterday seemed to have so tight a hold on the reins but who fumbles today. It moves ever onward.'

As the most suitable keynote for my booklet, I shall take what Engels had to say, in the preface to his articles on Feuerbach, about the revolutionary significance of Hegelian dialectics:

Every stage is necessary at the time and under the conditions to which it owes its origin, and this is its justification. But it loses its significance and its justification under new conditions, which gradually develop within it. Dialectic philosophy itself is . . . but a simple reflection of this process in the thinking brain. This philosophy undoubtedly has a conservative aspect as well, for it justifies every given stage in the development of science or of social relations in the light of the conditions of a particular period, although this is as far as it goes. Its conservatism is relative, its revolutionary character absolute.[1]

[1] F. Engels, *Ludwig Feuerbach und der Ausgang der Klassischen Deutschen Philosophie* (Vienna and Berlin, 1927), p. 18 (first published in *Neue Zeit*, nos. 4–5 (1886)).

1. VILNA AND THE BUND

1

In 1885 a revolutionary circle was formed in Vilna. Although it consisted of young people, it adopted in full the old programme of the *Narodnaia Volia* [*People's Will*].[1] Basically, this programme meant action of two broad types: the propagation of socialist ideas among the masses by propaganda and by organizing artels, and direct terrorism against the absolutist régime.

Although the immediate efforts of this circle were not successful, it nevertheless trained a whole group of young people who subsequently rendered enormous services to the Social Democratic movement, not only in the western area, but throughout Russia. It conducted its propaganda among the local intelligentsia, primarily among students at the secondary educational institutions, in particular the Teachers Institute, and among the impecunious *yeshivah* students (*orembokhery*)—young men training to become rabbis.

The attempts to organize artels were unsuccessful. The largest-scale effort in this respect was the organization of women hosiery workers in the winter of 1885–6. But even this artel did not last more than three or four months.[2]

During 1886–7, Comrade Abramovich came occasionally to Vilna from Minsk. He had lived abroad for some time and then worked in Kiev. He brought with him Plekhanov's *Our Disagreements* and engaged in heated debates with the Vilna revolutionaries, advocating Social Democratic principles, which the Minsk circle was already trying to apply in its work. Among the members of the

---

[1] For first-hand accounts of this Vilna group (led by Anton Gnatovskii and Isaak Dembo), see, e.g., L. Aksel'rod-Ortodoks, 'Iz moikh vospominanii', *Katorga i ssylka* (Moscow), no. 2 (63) (1930), pp. 22–42; T. M. Kopel'zon, 'Evreiskoe rabochee dvizhenie kontsa 80-kh i nachala 90-kh godov', in S. Dimanshtein (ed.), *Revoliutsionnoe dvizhenie sredi Evreev* (Moscow, 1930), pp. 65–80; and C. Rappoport, 'The Life of a Revolutionary Emigré' (translation), *Yivo Annual* (New York), no. 6 (1951), pp. 206–36.

[2] The organizer of this artel was Lev Iogikhes. See A. Menes, 'Di yidishe arbeter-bavegung in Rusland fun onhaib 70-en biz sof 90-er yoren', in A. Cherikover, A. Menes, F. Kurski, and A. Rozin (eds.), *Di Yidishe sotsialistishe bavegung biz der grindung fun Bund: Historishe Shriften*, III (Vilna and Paris, 1939), 31–2.

latter circle at the time was also Gurvich, who had recently returned from penal exile, and his sister.[1]

The Vilna *Narodovol'tsy* were not, of course, won over by Abramovich, but their young comrades broke with their mentors and founded the first Social Democratic organization in Vilna. The circles they organized among the young men and women attending secondary schools and the Teachers Institute devoted themselves primarily to self-education. They read Pisarev, Mirtov [Lavrov], Mikhailov, Draper, and, finally, *Our Disagreements*. They studied Russian life and history: the Schism [*raskol*], the communes, the artels, and capitalism. In 1890 they went on to the study of Lassalle and Marx. The books they used were taken from the library of legal and illegal literature collected by the earlier *Narodovol'tsy* circle.

The new Social Democrats were faced with the problem of what direct revolutionary action they were to take. In essence the new political programme which had reached them through Abramovich, demanded that they awaken class consciousness among the workers and thus rouse wide strata of the proletariat to political battle.

To find and adapt methods of warfare and battle slogans which would be suitable to the broadest strata of the proletariat now became the central purpose of Social Democratic agitation and organization in the western area. Eight years later, in 1897, this goal of the revolutionary Social Democrats was attained with the creation of the Bund. But in the early years only the first steps had been taken in this direction. At that time it was not only futile to think of leading the working-class; it still remained to establish contact even with individual workers. The Social Democratic organization was neither the spokesman of the working-class nor closely linked to it as its vanguard; in fact, these two segments, which were destined to fuse, were still entirely separate and lacked all contact.

---

[1] Both Isaak Gurvich and his sister, Evgeniia, who were his comrades at that time, have described the rôle played by Emilii A. Abramovich in Minsk in the 1880s. Evgeniia writes, in agreement with Akimov's account, that 'if anybody could be called a Marxist as early as 1884–5, it was the late Dr Abramovich, who was already Marxist in the strict sense of the word' (E. A. Gurvich, 'Evreiskoe rabochee dvizhenie v Minske v 80-kh godakh', in Dimanshtein (ed.), *Revoliutsionnoe dvizhenie*, p. 48). Her brother, however, questions whether even Abramovich could, strictly speaking, be considered a Marxist until 1889 (I. A. Gurvich, 'Pervye evreiskie rabochie kruzhki', *Byloe*, no. 6 (1907), p. 76). See also N. A. Bukhbinder, 'Evreiskie revoliutsionnye kruzhki', *Evreiskaia letopis'*, no. 1 (1923).

1. *VILNA AND THE BUND*

The first task, naturally, was to seek contact, to establish purely personal links between individual Social Democrats and individual workers.

Among the Jewish workers at that time there was a longing to learn Russian. Revolutionaries began to offer their services, in teaching the workers reading, writing, and arithmetic. As reading material they gave their pupils Zobov's *Talks about Nature*, and they discussed botany and zoology with them. On better acquaintance, they read to their pupils such novels as *Two Brothers*, *No Way Out*, *Chronicle of the Village of Smurino*, *One Soldier in the Field is no Army*, *Emma*, *What is to be Done?* and Shchedrin's tales.[1] They also lent out these books for home reading. Finally, when the circle seemed sufficiently prepared, the teachers brought in Dickstein's *What do People Live by?*[2] After that came Marx's *Wage Labour and Capital*. Some twenty lessons were devoted to the latter, for it required endless commentaries. The course was concluded with Lassalle's *Workers' Programme*, as a parting word to the student who was now ready to become a teacher himself. In addition to the Russian books, there were also a few American publications in Yiddish.

The complaint has been made in Polish writings that the Jewish *intelligenty* of the period were Russifiers of the Polish territories.[3] 'We were not concerned with the national question at that time', I was told by P., one of the comrades, 'and therefore were not conscious Russifiers, although, of course, we did introduce

---

[1] *Dva brata* [*Two Brothers*] and *Bez iskhoda* [*No Way Out*] were both written by Konstantin Mikhailovich Staniukovich and serialized in the literary monthly *Delo*, January–October 1880, and February–October 1873, respectively. *Khronika sela Smurina* [*Chronicle of the Village of Smurino*] was written by Pavel Vladimirovich Zasodimskii-Vologdin and first published in *Otechestvennye zapiski*, August–December 1874. *Odin v pole ne voin* [*One Soldier in the Field is no Army*] was the title given to the Russian translation of Friedrich Spielhagen's *In Reih und Glied* (Berlin, 1866). *Emma* was first published in Russia in 1872 and was a translation of a part of Jean Baptiste Schweitzer's *Lucinde, oder Kapital und Arbeit* (Frankfurt, 1864). *Chto delat'?* [*What Is to Be Done?*] is the famous novel by Chernyshevskii, first published in the journal *Sovremennik*, March–May 1863.

[2] The brochure *Kto chem zhivet?* was written in Polish (*Kto z czego żyje?*) by Shimon Dickstein, who took the pseudonym Jan Młot. First published in Geneva, in 1881, it became the most popular of all the brochures for socialist propaganda among the workers and was constantly reproduced in Russian translation during the 1880s and 1890s.

[3] For example, see the organ of the Polish Socialist Party (PPS), *Przedświt* (London), no. 4 (1893), p. 23, and no. 9 (1894), pp. 26–8, where the Lithuanian Jewish socialists were attacked as Russifiers.

Russian culture. We used Russian literature to produce individual revolutionaries, both because there was no Yiddish literature and because we ourselves were strangers to the Jewish people. The Polish language was of no use to us because the people wanted to learn Russian, not Polish, and we made use of this desire in order to establish contacts.'

Such was the preparatory process in the development of the Social Democratic workers' movement in the western area (1885–92). The working-class played a purely passive rôle at that time. On the one hand, the worker's particular type of life had developed in him the characteristic psychology of the proletarian. On the other hand, the intellectual ideologists of the proletariat, the revolutionary Social Democrats, seized upon individual members of the milieu and trained them as future agitators. The group of *intelligenty* which received its revolutionary baptism from the *Narodovol'tsy*, and which later adopted Social Democratic principles, sought to rouse the working-class to political activity by propagating its ideas in workers' educational circles. This method proved ineffective; for the most part the working-class was not reached by propaganda.

2

The year 1892 may be regarded as the beginning of a mass labour movement in the western area. Its immediate cause was, as usual in such cases, a rather insignificant event.

To spite the Governing Board of the Crafts [*Remeslennaia Uprava*], the mayor of Vilna ordered placards posted throughout the city declaring that, according to the law promulgated by Catherine II, the workday in industrial establishments should be no longer than twelve hours. The workmen everywhere began to talk about shortening the workday to the legal limit and to discuss ways and means of making use of this forgotten law. Crushed by the incredibly long workday and by hopeless want—a want unequalled today even among Russian workers and reminiscent of Flerovskii's vivid and shocking descriptions of Russian working-class life in the 1860s and 1870s[1]—the unfortunate Jewish pariahs seemed suddenly to have come to life, to have realized that they all had common interests, that they could improve their frightful

---

[1] N. Flerovskii (pseud. of Vasilii Vasil'evich Bervii), *Polozhenie rabochego klassa v Rossii* (St Petersburg, 1869).

life by solidarity and mutual support. A spontaneous movement swept like a strong wind through the lower depths of Jewish society, through strata which had seemed immobile and incapable of comprehending, or guiding themselves by, any conscious idea. People to whom the Jewish community could not and did not wish to apply the term 'a respectable person' (*a balabatisher yid*) suddenly began to talk about their rights and even began to do something to protect them. The workers organized several small squads which made the rounds of the city at seven o'clock, demanding that the owners of workshops close for the day and threatening them with legal action. As yet the revolutionary Social Democrats had no connexion with this movement; they had gone no further than the organization of propaganda circles. They were not making any concrete proposals for the improvement of the workers' lives and had a sceptical attitude toward all plans for such improvement under the existing régime.

Just as in the first phase of the movement the Jewish Social Democrats sought to perform a great cultural service to their people and yet could say with Comrade P. that they were strangers to the Jewish people, so now they were actually strangers to the working-class. As a result, their fervent desire to lead the Jewish proletariat to its great tasks could not but remain ineffective. Inevitably, however, the conscious ideologists of the working-class came face to face with representatives of the unguided proletarian movement, and this had the most fortunate effects.

The workers who had been reached by earlier propaganda work decided to establish *kassy* [fund associations] for mutual aid and strike activity. Although the propagandists were opposed to all [workers'] associations, they nevertheless did not reject this plan because they hoped that even if the *kassy* failed in their primary purpose—mutual aid and industrial warfare—they would at least create a pool from which new members could be enlisted into the propaganda circles. This difference in the motives prompting the workers and the [Social Democratic] *intelligenty* to support and set up workers' *kassy* may be explained by the long history of the social groups to which these Social Democrats belonged.

The socio-political movement among the Jewish intelligentsia had begun long before the period described. As early as the 1840s, a progressive movement had emerged among the Jews. This development marked the awakening in Russia of Jewish national thought, which, as it seemed, had come to a halt, having fossilized the ancient commandments for two thousand years as something sacred, above criticism or analysis. There had been no attempt to advance. Under the influence of Russian and Polish democratic literature, stories and novels about Jewish life by Levanda, Bogrov, Osip Rabinovich, Abram Mapu, and others began to appear in the 1850s.[1] The 1860s even saw the appearance of a newspaper in Hebrew, urging a national renascence and combating the isolation of the Jews.[2] This was a kind of Jewish 'Westernism'. The activity of the *Chaikovtsy* circle in Russia was imitated among the Jewish intelligentsia.[3] It was only later, as it developed, that this cultural movement began to divide into the two branches we see today—the democratic, bourgeois-nationalistic movement, which chose Zionism as its platform, and the socialist movement, which merges with the movement of the Jewish proletariat.

But even in the 1880s, when the revolutionaries among the Jewish intelligentsia were wholly absorbed in the Russian liberation movement, even then cultural work in the western area—publication of books for the people and establishment of legal libraries and schools—seemed to unite the entire Jewish intelligentsia there in a common cause. The impecunious *yeshivah* students attracted the particular attention of the revolutionaries. This explains why, as the Social Democratic movement emerged, it was this group which produced so many adherents of the new trend—the trend which drew them toward the proletariat and

---

[1] L. O. Levanda and O. A. Rabinovich were leaders of the Jewish enlightenment movement in Russia and were among those who established the first Jewish newspaper in Russian, *Razsvet* [Dawn], published in Odessa in the years 1860–1. The best-known work of Grigorii Bogrov, another prominent Jew writing in Russian, was his autobiographical *Zapiski Evreia* [*Notes of a Jew*], published in serial form in the 1860s. Abraham Mapu, a popular novelist writing in Hebrew, published his most famous work, *Ahabat Tsion* [*Love of Zion*], in 1852.

[2] *Ha-Melits* [*The Advocate*], published in Odessa from 1860 by I. A. Gol'dbaum and A. O. Tsederbaum (Martov's grandfather).

[3] Revolutionary Populists of the early 1870s were frequently called *Chaikovtsy*, after Nikolai V. Chaikovskii, a well-known member of the St Petersburg group led by Mark Natanson. For its links with the Jewish socialist circles of the 1870s, particularly that of Liberman and Zundelevich in Vilna, see N. A. Bukhbinder, 'Iz istorii revoliutsionnoi propagandy sredi Evreev v Rossii v 70-kh gg.', in *Istoriko-revoliutsionnyi sbornik*, ed. V. I. Nevskii (Moscow, 1924–6), I, 37–66; B. Frumkin, 'Iz istorii revoliutsionnogo dvizheniia sredi Evreev v 70-kh godakh', *Evreiskaia starina*, no. 2 (1911), pp. 226–35; L. Deich, *Rol' Evreev v russkom revolutsionnom dvizhenii* (Berlin, 1923); A. Cherikover, 'Yiden-revoliutsioneren in Rusland in 60-er un 70-er yoren', in Cherikover and others (eds.), *Di yidishe sotsialistishe bavegung*, III, 60–172.

toward an active concern for the trade-union organizations popular with the workers.

The Jewish workers' movement was even older than that of the intelligentsia. Among the workers there had long existed fund associations [*kassy*] on which they drew for support in their struggle against the employers for improved labour conditions. These organizations may even date from the times when there were guilds in Poland and Germany which did not accept Jewish workers. At any rate, some of the customs of these fund associations are reminiscent of the guilds: the solemn initiation ritual, the annual guild holiday, the maintenance of deep secrecy concerning all of the society's affairs. A certain writer, well informed in this field, found some very old record books in Mogilev which had belonged to a mutual-aid organization that did not admit employers to membership.[1] In Zhitomir a friend of mine came across an old secret workers' organization which had managed to achieve considerable improvement in the living conditions of its members by dint of long and persistent struggle. Its history is cherished with reverence in tales and legends. When socialist propagandists came to them, they found these workers extremely hostile. In Łódź, the old trade organization *Akhdus* (*Solidarity*) enjoyed such an impressive reputation that its name became a common noun for organized workers and even for all class conscious workers generally.

These *kassy* first began to be established in connexion with synagogues. In every city there is one general synagogue for all the Jews, known by the ancient name—probably Hebrew and evidently borrowed from the Arabs—*Beis-Medres* (*Medres* means a higher ecclesiastical school among the Arabs and Moslems generally).[2] Along with this synagogue, however, there are also synagogues connected with individual trades. These are a combination of prayer house and school and are evidently of more recent origin, to judge from their German names: *shtibl* (small room) and *shul* (school). They serve the Jews of given trades, including in their membership both workmen and employers.[3]

[1] Sara Rabinowitsch, *Die Organisationen des jüdischen Proletariats in Russland* (Karlsruhe, 1903), particularly Part II, chap. 2, 'Die Chewra in Mohileff'.
[2] Akimov's etymology is erroneous. *Beis-Medres* is simply the Yiddish form of the Hebrew *Bet Ha-Midrash* (the root of *midrash* is *darash*, 'search' or 'investigate').
[3] Akimov exaggerates the frequency with which the *shul* or *shtibl* acted as the meeting place for the members of one profession rather than for a congregation of practising Jews in general.

But, unknown to the employers, the workmen belonging to these synagogues organized their own *kassy* to help their comrades who had suffered at the hands of their employers. Thus secret *kassy* were long familiar to the Jewish workers. And when it became necessary to form groups of workers for purposes of revolutionary socialist propaganda, both the more educated workers and the revolutionary *intelligenty* came by different roads to accept the need to support the workers' *kassy*.

In 1889 and 1890 these *kassy* expanded rapidly and their meetings became more and more lively. They took broader functions upon themselves and began to assume a militant character. The best of the *kassy*, those of the jewelry and footwear makers, succeeded in enrolling as members almost all the workers of their trades in Vilna. Supporting their comrades who had suffered losses for the common cause and threatening employers with strikes, they compelled the latter to make concessions.

However, the more the *kassy* became imbued with the spirit of a spontaneous labour movement, the weaker became the position of the 'propagandized' workers who represented the class conscious ideologists of the proletariat. And this is understandable. While the unpropagandized workers who voiced the spontaneous ambitions of the working-class argued at the meetings in terms of the immediate interests of the masses, the propagandized workers, the spokesmen of the class conscious ideological movement of revolutionary Social Democrats, valued the *kassy* only as a propaganda medium. Also, under the influence of their teachers, they attributed too little importance to the *kassy* as a means of improving the workers' living conditions.

Under such circumstances the 'man of the masses' could not follow the propagandized worker and, ignorant of his undeclared plans, could not even understand what exactly the latter was after. Of course, their constant defeats hurt the pride of the 'propagandized' workers, and they began to demand that their teachers appear at the *kassy* meetings themselves to defend their views. The mild propagandist of the far-off socialist order—the diligent teacher in a workers' circle—was brought and set before the crowd. The conscious revolutionary stood before the blind forces of revolution, which could neither guess nor understand his great and remote goals.

As he watched the movement emerging among the masses, which on the surface were so calm, and for the first time heard the sound of an elemental force, the conscious revolutionary, the ideologist of the proletariat, was compelled to admit that he had given the wrong advice to the 'propagandized' workers at the mass meetings. It was at this point that the words were spoken which later sped across Russia: 'We were wrong.'

'The Russian Social Democratic movement is on the wrong path', declared our Jewish comrades in the pamphlet *On Agitation*. 'It has locked itself up in educational circles. It should listen for the pulse-beat of the crowd and, finding it, should step ahead of the crowd and lead it. Social Democrats can and must lead the working masses because the proletariat's blind struggle inevitably leads it to the same goal, to the same ideal, which the revolutionary Social Democrats have consciously chosen.'[1]

But this required a change in the entire programme of action. The language of the Russian intelligentsia became useless. What the masses needed was Yiddish. Scholarly books and long novels were beyond the grasp of the masses—they needed pamphlets. The plans of the ideologist and political agitator had to be defended from the point of view of the immediate interests of the masses. It had to be recognized that side by side with the conspiratorial political organization of the revolutionaries there was room for a democratic economic organization of the workers.

Thus the second phase of the movement came into being. Progress in the economic development of the country created a spontaneous mass labour movement, a class struggle on the basis of economic interests. The revolutionary Social Democrats decided that they could attain their goal—to draw large sections of the proletariat into the class war—if they assumed leadership in the day-to-day, purely economic struggle of the workers. There sprang up a complex network of primitive fighting organizations in the form of workers' strike *kassy*, led by the organization of revolutionaries which remained hidden from the workers. The second phase embraces the period from 1892 to 1895.

3

Economic agitation was the living link between the revolutionary organization and the working-class, and yet the revolutionary organization was by no means identical with the organized

[1] A paraphrase of the central ideas of *On Agitation*; see particularly [A. Kremer], *Ob agitatsii* (Geneva, 1897), pp. 16–18.

proletariat. The workers were restless, not satisfied with what their ideologists and teachers were doing.

The propagandized workers, under the leadership of Abram, an engraver,[1] criticized the shift of the revolutionaries to agitation. They failed to understand the profound significance of this change of tactics. It seemed to them that by abandoning propaganda activity in workers' circles the *intelligenty* were giving up their cultural rôle, that they were seeking to exploit the unconscious elemental movement of the masses and regarded the workers as mere 'cannon fodder'. Indeed, the workers who belonged to the circles proved to be less democratic than the revolutionaries who were drawn from the intelligentsia. They felt superior to the masses and were irritated by the appearance of ignorant workers at the meetings. As a result entire trades, including the typesetters,* who until now had set the pace, withdrew from the movement.*

The development of the movement inevitably pushed the cultural-educational work of the revolutionaries into the background, and the 'opposition' was obliged to give way before the agitational activity of the Vilna Social Democrats. However, it must be admitted that this opposition came in protest against the one-sided concentration on agitation, against the tendency to cramp Social Democratic activity for the sake of being able to lead the broad masses of the proletariat.

However, dissatisfaction with the new tactics did not show itself merely in idealization of the previous period, that of *kruzhkovshchina*. These tactics were also criticized by the forerunners of the next phase in the history of the movement. They felt that economic struggle should not be the sole preoccupation of the Social Democrats and insisted that it was also necessary to make use of every possible occasion for 'political' agitation.

Just as one of the four speeches delivered on 1 May 1892—that of a woman worker—marked the opening of the second stage of Social Democratic history,[2] so 1 May 1895 must be regarded as a

---

[1] Abraham Gordon, who led the opposition to the Vilna Programme of 'agitation'. See L. Martov, *Zapiski Sotsialdemokrata*, I (Berlin, 1922), 230–5, 251–2; and Gordon's own account in *In friling fun Vilner yidisher arbeter-bavegung*, no. 1 (Vilna, 1926).

* It was not until 1896 that the typesetters' *kassa* was organized again, and not until 1899 that it became fully consolidated.

[2] This was a key speech delivered in Vilna on May Day, 1892, and later published in *Pervoe maia 1892 goda: Chetyre rechi evreiskikh rabochikh* (Geneva, 1893). The worker, Fania Reznik, called for more militant action in the workshops and factories: 'In order to overcome fragmentation and to further

new 'turning point', the beginning of the third stage of the Jewish labour movement. All the demands put forward by the Social Democrats on this day were purely economic. The red flag bore the single inscription: 'We fight for a ten-hour working day, for higher wages, for better treatment!' Out of four speeches, only one was 'political' in character. But it was just this speech that unexpectedly met the most enthusiastic response. On the following day, the same comrade's address to assembled agitators consolidated this new victory of Social Democracy.[1]

On 1 May 1896 we already see 'political' demands: 'We are fighting for freedom to strike, for freedom of assembly, freedom of speech, and of the press.' The orators' speeches were in line with these demands inscribed on the red banner. The next May Day there was an attempt in Vilna—the first by Social Democrats in Russia—to organize a demonstration.[2] The very fact of an open meeting was meant as a demonstrative protest against the suppression of the right to assemble.

It was the workers themselves who demanded the introduction of a 'political' element into the Social Democratic agitation. It was they who were determined to expose the wrongs of the political system, to bring out the people's lack of rights, to formulate the interests of the worker as citizen. But the revolutionary organization, which hoped to guide the labour movement toward Social Democratic ideals, was afraid that it would not be understood by the working masses, that it would lose its influence if it now raised *its own* demands for 'political' rights as the demands of the proletariat. Was the working-class already well enough educated

---

unity we must organize frequent meetings of the workers. All must strive to found *kassy* and try to make them expand. We must organize strikes. For strikes too we must have *kassy*' (p. 3). Akimov sees this speech as typical of the new policy introduced in Vilna in the years 1892–3. For identification of the speaker, see Y. Sh. Hertz and others (eds.), *Di geshichte fun Bund*, I (New York, 1960), p. 61.

[1] The speech of May Day, 1895, was delivered by Martov to a meeting of Social Democratic 'agitators', later published under the title *Povorotnyi punkt v istorii evreiskogo rabochego dvizheniia* (Geneva, 1900). Martov called for a movement with an appeal directed at the national and political as well as 'economic' grievances of the Jewish workers in Vilna. 'We must therefore recognize quite clearly that our goal, the goal of the Social Democrats working among the Jewish population, must be to found a special Jewish labour organization which will lead and educate the Jewish proletariat in its battle for economic, civil, and political liberty' (p. 19).

[2] For an account of this small-scale demonstration in one of Vilna's parks and of the celebration of May Day in general in Russia, see Akimov's 'Pervoe maia v Rossii', *Byloe*, nos. 10–12 (1906).

politically to appraise, to recognize its real interests? The leaders were not certain of this and hesitated to act.*

In August 1897 the first issue of the newspaper *Arbeter Shtime* [*Labour Voice*] appeared in Warsaw. It took the Jewish socialists in Warsaw by surprise, and they immediately sent inquiries to the Vilna comrades, asking where the newspaper came from and what their attitude to its publishers should be. It turned out that the paper was issued by a group of workers who had become tired of waiting for the revolutionary organization to meet their wishes†️ and undertook the publication of a 'political' journal on their own.

It would be unjust to accuse the revolutionary Social Democratic intelligentsia of bringing up the rear of the spontaneous workers' movement. With the first signs that the working-class had graduated to a point where it was capable of understanding the call to fight for wider interests, the intelligentsia immediately broadened its agitation, raised new demands, and so marched steadily at the head of the movement. But it would be still more unjust to assert that the working-class is itself incapable of reaching a broad and correct understanding of its class goals—of socialism. It cannot, of course, be said that the working-class as a whole is consciously moving toward socialist ideals. But the Jewish workers' movement developed rapidly and organically under the Social Democratic banner. Of its own accord it raised demands which brought it ever closer to the ideals of conscious socialists. It remained for the ideologists of the proletariat only to shorten the birth pangs of

---

* 'Let us not put forward a programme that might frighten off the struggling masses. Without deviating a single iota, let us be skilful. We want to rally all the forces of the proletariat. To do so, we must give our party the name "Workers" and not "Socialist"' (Volders). 'The term socialism frightens many workers, and therefore this term is a hindrance' (De-Paepe in *Compte-rendu du congrès de Parti ouvrier Belge de 1891*, p. 42). Whether these Belgian socialists were right or wrong, they certainly did not speak these words as trade-unionists. 'The socialist movement in America dates from the appearance of Bellamy's famous book *Looking Backward*. The author called his theory nationalism to avoid frightening the Americans by the then terrifying word "socialism"' (Muranov ['Pis'ma ob amerikanskom sotsializme'], in *Rabochee delo*, no. 10, Sect. II, p. 1).

† This, incidentally, was not the first attempt to publish material concerned with new and broader questions than those dealt with in proclamations. Bulletins were published in Vilna reporting facts about the life of Russian society. In Minsk, several issues of *Labour Sheet* appeared as early as the latter part of 1896. But evidently publications of this kind did not meet the requirements of the movement at that time. As soon as one of these experiments proved that a new situation had arisen, it won energetic support. [For a description of *Arbeter Bletel*, see Hertz and others (eds.), *Di geshichte*, I, 97.]

the new ideas by propaganda, by incitement, and by leadership in the mass struggle. In the picture *The Marseillaise*, a strong and inspired female allegorical figure leads the masses. Some people in the crowd she leads outrun her and instinctively anticipate the next step she is about to take along the path which she has consciously chosen.[1] Just so, individual workers, having absorbed the ideals of their teachers, outdistanced them in their impatience to transform their dreams into reality.

During the previous stage of the movement, that of economic agitation (1892–5), as during the first stage, that of the circles, the tactics of the revolutionaries rendered enormous service to the movement but did not quite achieve their purpose. They did not win for the conscious minority, the ideologists of the working-class, the position of spokesmen for the spontaneous proletarian movement. What new features were introduced by that [third] stage [beginning in 1895] which is under discussion here?

The workers were no longer satisfied either with the programme or with the organization created for them by the revolutionaries. The programme which the Social Democrats offered at this time to the workers did not criticize all aspects of the existing society and did not defend all the interests of which the labouring masses were already becoming aware. The Jewish workers were strongly indignant at their lack of national and civil rights. They felt the need for the right to strike and the right of assembly, for freedom of speech and inviolability of person. These were called political rights, and the revolutionaries now had to formulate the new and broader demands of the masses and lead the struggle for these interests. They understood their obligations and took over the publication of the political newspaper *Arbeter Shtime*.

The old conspiratorial form of revolutionary organization was also at odds with the mass character of the workers' movement. The organization rested on the secret *kassy* which were controlled by their own representatives meeting in joint councils [*skhodki*] with *intelligenty*. The council meetings were political in character; general questions were discussed, books were taken from and returned to the clandestine library, circles were assigned to propagandists, and illegal literature was brought for distribution to the various associations. However, although they were regarded

---

[1] Almost certainly *La Marseillaise*, a well-known drawing made by Gustave Doré in Paris during the Franco-Prussian War. Two thousand copies were reproduced for May Day propaganda in 1900 by the Union of Russian Democrats Abroad.

as representatives of the *kassy*, the workers who attended these meetings were not elected but were chosen 'from above' as the 'best people'.

The members of the *kassy* realized that the movement was directed by some inner circle, unknown to them. This elicited the desire to learn about it, to get into it, and to influence policy making at this higher level. The masses turned out to be sufficiently well prepared to intervene in the running of their own affairs. Moreover, the scope of these affairs had become so sizable that they could no longer be managed by a group of revolutionaries in secrecy from the masses.

This led to the establishment of a central, and elected, workers' *kassa*. Its function was to help strikers with men and money, to lead strikes, to publish proclamations, and to maintain contacts with other cities in order to prevent the import of strike-breakers.

But just as the organization of the propagandists was kept secret from the 'men of the masses'—the general members of the *kassy*—so was the [inner] circle of the *intelligenty*, the soul of revolutionary activity in the western area, kept secret from the select workers who met with these *intelligenty* at the councils [*skhodki*]. As early as 1895 the Social Democratic organizations began to spread through many cities, and Vilna became the natural centre of their activity, thanks to the personal contacts of the Vilna circle and thanks to the fact that Vilna was the distribution point for illegal literature, most of it hectographed. Although some workers also belonged to this inner circle, they were, again, drawn in 'from above', unknown to their comrades in the councils. This conspiratorial organization remained in existence later as well.

Such were the characteristics of the third phase of the movement, which lasted from 1895 to 1897. Several years of organized economic warfare had gradually impressed upon large sections of the working-class the necessity for civil rights—for individual and civil freedom. At first the revolutionaries regarded examples of this awareness as isolated, accidental phenomena. Reluctant to endanger their ties with the wide masses of the proletariat, for some time they did not venture beyond purely economic agitation. However, under pressure from the growing aspirations of the masses, they raised the demand for civil rights, without touching upon the question of whether these were attainable under Tsarism. The movement had by now expanded so greatly that the old conspiratorial organization had to yield to a broadly based democratic organization. But since the labour movement had not yet adopted all the goals of the revolutionaries—for it had not yet developed sufficiently to undertake political tasks—the revolutionary organization remained separate from the workers' organization.

4

When the Social Democratic movement first emerged, its imposing strength was not immediately recognized by its friends, the Russian socialists, nor by its enemy, the government. The movement in the western area escaped the close attention of the government for a particularly long time. There were two reasons for this. First, the movement originated there earlier than in Russia proper. And, second, the segregation of the Jewish people and the hostility of the oppressed nationality toward the Russian government made it difficult for the Ministry of the Interior to follow the changes that were taking place in the psychology of the Jewish proletariat.

However, when the revolutionaries at the head of the labour movement began to demand civil rights for the working-class and resorted to a new method of war—demonstrations—the events in the western area took on so blatant a political significance that the government had to intervene. But since nothing can stop the development of an elemental class movement, the intervention of the police—of governmental power—could only serve to give the movement, which until then had been merely economic and social, a political character. It could only awaken political consciousness in the workers.

So far even those rights demanded by the revolutionaries and workers under the heading of political rights did not touch upon the question of state power. Regardless of whether the autocratic government could or could not grant the citizens freedom of speech, of assembly, of strike and organization, the proclamations, the speeches of revolutionary orators, and even the banners demanded such rights. Although of enormous political significance, these demands were not in themselves political, since they were not demands that the new social forces enter the government.

Individual theoreticians could decide for themselves whether or not the autocracy could grant the citizens freedom of speech, assembly, strikes, and organization. But the masses are convinced only by the logic of events. It therefore seemed essential, if the

219

workers' movement was to become political in character, that the government prove to the workers by its actions that they could not hope for reforms and must prepare for revolution, for the conquest of political power, and, above all, for the overthrow of absolutism.

Just as Oedipus in his very eagerness to escape his doom met disaster, so the Russian government, prompted by fate, hastened throughout its entire Empire to make its own fears become realities. It forced the labour movement into politics. As if afraid that the happenings at one end of the vast country would not convince the politically backward people at the other, the government made haste, in Yaroslavl and Ekaterinoslav, in Kiev and Vilna, to mobilize its political power for the suppression of civil rights or even of the merely 'economic' movement. And it did so despite the fact that these movements were still peaceful.

The arrests of 1897 in the western area were no longer just local or accidental. A new colonel of the *gendarmerie*, Vasil'ev, was appointed in Vilna. When he declared that it was already too late to stop the movement, Zubatov, an official of outstanding ability in the field, was dispatched to Vilna to study the situation.

The government's anxiety was aroused by the course which the movement was now taking. After the first demonstration of the year 1897, this new method of presenting demands was used with increasing frequency and success. In 1897 the Vilna workers gathered in the city park at a designated time and sat silently on the benches or walked in formation along the avenues. After that, demonstrations became a familiar occurrence in the western area. They became bolder and were organized in response to such important events as the call-up of army recruits, deportation of political prisoners, or funerals of comrades.

May Day proclamations began to voice the demand for a constitution. On 1 May 1899, the red flag was raised at the demonstration. The marchers sang the 'Marseillaise', and their cries of 'Down with the autocracy!' were met by the crowd with excited and loud hurrahs. It was not just that constitutional demands were now openly made in proclamations and that anti-government declarations were well received by the crowds; the fact was that the masses had had enough of police oppression, and that the demonstrations began to assume a violent character.

In the beginning of May 1900 a crowd, indignant over the arrests of several comrades in Novyi Gorod near Vilna, attacked the police station where prisoners were kept and attempted to liberate them. After this attempt failed, an ambush was organized; when the prisoners were led out, the lookouts gave a signal to the crowd to come out of hiding and attack the convoy. The police used their sabres and wounded two workers. In reply, there were shots from the crowd. The prisoners were freed and their temporary prison, the police station, was reduced to a shambles.

The workers' movement became political. It grew and expanded under the Social Democratic flag and should therefore be regarded as Social Democratic in the sense in which every elemental mass movement is called by the name of the basic doctrine of its leaders, the motto on its banner. Thus the organized proletariat had now become identified with the organization of the revolutionary Social Democrats.

The General Jewish Workers Union of Lithuania and Poland— the Bund—founded in the autumn of 1897, carried out this historical task. The fourth stage in the development of the Jewish labour movement, organized political warfare, now began.

5

'The organized Jewish proletariat (the Bund), which constitutes a strong organized force and which ably leads the socialist struggle of the Jewish proletariat in Russia, impatiently awaited the results of the Second Party Congress', states *Vestnik Bunda* [*Bund Courier*], no. 3. The word 'Bund' is here identified with 'the organized Jewish proletariat'. As we have said above, this was indeed the historical mission of the Bund. But, of course, it did not attain this goal all at once.

For fifteen years Lithuania and Poland have seen the development of a Jewish Social Democratic movement which in its forms and activities has always had a great deal in common with the movement in the rest of Russia, but which has always anticipated that movement by several years. The state of the Jewish workers' movement at a given moment is of great interest to Russian workers. It is significant both because of the lessons to be learned from the experience of our Jewish comrades who work under the same political conditions as we do and also, to some extent, as a model of the Russian labour movement as it is bound to develop in the near future.

The activities of the Jewish Social Democrats are quite

accurately reflected in *Poslednie Izvestie* [*Latest News*], published weekly by the Bund Committee Abroad. During the past one and a half or two years the character of these activities has changed considerably, as can clearly be seen from the reports in *Poslednie Izvestiia*. Formerly these reports bore the imprint of purely local work. Today this work gives the impression of an enthusiastic response to the appeals and declarations of the central committee of the Bund. I say 'gives the impression', for in reality the situation is quite the reverse—the central committee of the Bund is but the spokesman and representative of the Jewish proletariat.

One is struck by the great number of meetings attended by tens and sometimes hundreds of workers in various parts of the Bund's area of activity. In these meetings all the major developments in Russian politics and society, as well as the internal life of the Bund, are discussed. In 1904 some 70,000 workers attended these meetings. Thus the conscious Jewish proletariat is gradually being transformed into a unified collective organism, with a mass of pulsing centres and a single heart; it begins to respond as an entity, as a class.

That the Jewish proletariat has thus developed a complete form of class life is the more striking since the Bund's system of organization remains concealed and unobserved.

I should like my attempt to formulate the basic principles of the Bund's organization to prompt further study of this question. I say this because it seems to me that until now no attempt has been made to write the history of the Bund with emphasis on its evolution. There has been no attempt to abstract the general features from the specific and thus to clarify the general organizational principles and lines of the Bund's development. The raw facts of its history were laid out quite fully in the report to the Congress of the Socialist International in Paris, published by the Union of Russian Social Democrats. Rather detailed material was also published in *Zhizn'* [*Life*], a journal published abroad. Information on recent years is contained in the Bund pamphlets *The Fourth Congress, The Fifth Congress, The Work of the Bund for the Past Two Years*, and *The Report of the Bund Delegation at the Second Party Congress*.[1] But these publications do not contain any over-all idea; nor, it seems to me, are the Bund comrades aware of any such idea.

---

[1] For the publications referred to, see Bibliography under Bund, and G. Ia., 'Bund', *Zhizn'* (London) no. 2 (May 1902). G. Ia. was almost certainly a pseudonym used by Gleb Iakovlevich Mutnikovich.

1. *VILNA AND THE BUND*

Unfortunately, I do not know Yiddish and have never worked or lived among Jews. For several years I have sought to question comrades who worked at different times in various places in the western area about their work. I wrote down their accounts, compared them, and tried to draw conclusions, which I again verified and tested. It seems to me that in this way I have succeeded in becoming acquainted with the true course of the Bund's development. However, the Bund comrades have not only failed to help me to draw general conclusions from the facts but have regarded my very efforts to do so as futile and naïve.

I regard this as an unquestionable shortcoming of the Bund; the Jewish proletariat lacks theoreticians. At the Second Congress of the Party, the Bund delegation did not even try to contribute to working out the programme, which it accepted as submissively as did the rest of the delegates. Although it instinctively sensed that its own organizational principles were in sharp contradiction to those of *Iskra*, it proved incapable of formulating its opposition to *Iskra* in clearly defined terms. The Bund delegation thus showed itself unable to crown the Bund's historical services to the Party and to assume the leadership of the Party's purely proletarian wing. The Jewish proletarian movement is moving along the highway in exactly the right direction. Yet, lacking theoreticians, it is powerless to point the way to others. It moves forward itself, but it does not lead.

The highest organ of the Bund is its congress, which, according to established custom, must be convened at least once every two years. So far congresses have been held more frequently—five times in six years (1897–1903). A congress is convened by the central committee either on its own initiative or on demand of two-thirds of the committees. Its 'customary law' does not provide for the fact that the failure of a portion of the delegates to arrive could render a congress 'unconstitutional'. 'The reason for this', I was told by comrades, 'is that it is quite impossible for any significant number of delegates to be absent from the congress. The signal to come is not given unless preparatory work has made it possible for all delegates to come. Only a last-minute arrest can prevent a delegate from attending.'

The congress elects by secret ballot three members to the central committee, one of whom is openly designated after the election as the representative of the central committee. The three elected members co-opt as many additional comrades to the committee as they find necessary. The central committee directs the work of the local committees in accordance with the resolutions of the congresses. It issues proclamations to all Jewish workers in its own name: it is the duty of the local committee to distribute these proclamations. It publishes the central journal of the Bund, which thus completely loses the function of a free forum, essential in the quest for truth, and becomes a powerful instrument with which the central committee can give force to its own decisions. Local committees enjoy full autonomy within their districts, where they guide themselves by the instructions of the congresses.*

Thus the general character of these two institutions of the Bund —the central committee and the local committees—and their relationship to each other can be sketched as follows: (1) The central committee of the Bund has emerged as an institution which uses all the methods developed [by parties] throughout the world to influence the life of the party it leads. (2) The local committees are autonomous organizations, which conduct independently all party work in their districts. (3) The relationship between the central committee and the local committee is that of mutual co-operation, in which neither can dominate the other.

And this sketch actually corresponds to reality.

(1) The central committee of the Bund is invested with enormous powers. According to the Bund's statute, the central committee is empowered to expel any member of a local committee at its own discretion, as well as to appoint another member. The local committees must submit regular reports on their activities and plans to the central committee. The members of the central committee may visit at any time, and gain access to, all the organizations of the local committee. Such arrangements permit the central

---

* After listening to these lines one of the comrades from the Bund's central committee said to me: 'Your mind tends to think bureaucratically! Your basic error is that you want to formulate phenomena which do not fit any formula. Of course, what you have written here is as obvious as that you and I walk on two feet. But your formulation presupposes that the influence of the central committee on local committees is limited, and there is no such limitation in practice within the Bund. Living reality cannot be fitted into graphs and columns.' I do not agree with this comrade. It seems to me that there is no phenomenon in the world that cannot be described in more or less precise formulas. The difficulty of the task should not make us abandon the attempt. The general principles of the Bund's organization not only can but must be formulated so that what is sound in its development can be given conscious support and what is outworn can be eliminated.

committee to familiarize itself with—and to exert a real influence upon—the work of the local committees. It formulates the Bund's general goals, which the local committee in its own actions must advance and cannot oppose. The central committee's proclamations, addressed to the broadest circles of the Bund members, enable it to exercise a direct influence upon the masses. Its control of the central journal gives it a powerful instrument with which to influence the thinking of the local leaders. In comparison with the various central institutions of Social Democratic parties abroad, the powers of the central committee of the Bund are very great indeed.

(2) The local committees may issue any local publications they please without special permission. The resolutions adopted by the local committee require no confirmation whatsoever. The local committee draws up the statutes of its organization independently and decides for itself how to set about its work. In reality, of course, local organizations have developed along similar lines, but such uniformity is not obligatory. The local committee co-opts its new members independently. If it finds that the central committee has assigned to it a new member in order to impose upon it an unwelcome policy, the local committee may bring in another member with acceptable views and thus frustrate the central committee's plan. The central committee has no authority to dissolve local committees, and has never done so.

(3) Whenever a conflict develops between the central committee and one of the local committees, it must—in so far as the work of the local committee is the work of the party itself—be settled by mutual concessions, similar to those between the upper and lower chambers of parliament. In general party affairs, however, the central committee acts independently, through those channels envisaged by the statute; in such cases, the local committees are mere executors of its will.

When I questioned the Bund comrades, they could not give any examples of a clash between the central committee and a local committee in which the latter was compelled to submit to the former. In Belostok, for instance, a proclamation was prepared by the Belostok committee during the textile workers' strike. The proclamation was strongly disapproved by the central committee, which refused to print it on its press. Nevertheless the Belostok committee issued it. The central committee declared that it would criticize the proclamation sharply in *Arbeter Shtime*. So far I as know, it did not do so.

On another occasion the Łódź committee sent one of the issues of *Frehets-glok* to the central committee for printing. The latter found it extremely unsatisfactory and suggested revisions, particularly of the editorial article. The Łódź committee refused and sent the issue abroad to be printed. In this case, too, the central committee did not deem it proper to use its authority to compel the local committee to yield. Interestingly, the committee abroad also found the editorial highly unsatisfactory and revised it, although it had no right to do so. However, the Łódź committee did not protest its action.

'Generally speaking,' a comrade of the central committee of the Bund told me,

the central committee 'recommends' and 'suggests' its views to the local committee. Juridically, it is not empowered to issue orders but, in fact, it is listened to. I am not even sure whether one can say that the central committee does not interfere in the affairs of the local committees. I know of a case when the central committee, having examined the record of a certain local committee, resolved that a number of reforms were needed in the city in question. The central committee suggested them to the local committee, and they were all carried out.

Although the local committees have the right to begin publication of their own journals without consulting the central committee, they do not embark on so important an undertaking without its approval. At one time a great many local committees launched their own journals. The central committee was opposed to this and felt that the number of these journals should be reduced. It achieved its aim; today there are no local journals, but none of them was compelled to close. Most characteristic is the fact that the question of 'rights' is never raised in the relations between the central committee and the local committees. *Of course, no commands can possibly be given by the central committee.* The latter has the power to introduce new members to a local committee, but if the local committee should oppose the central committee's candidate, the central committee would *obviously* not press such a new member upon the local committee. We know that the local committee can only work harmoniously when there is mutual respect among all its members. It is a fundamental principle for us that the movement be run on a basis of mutual trust and moral influence.

It seems to me that these latter words themselves constitute a formula which expresses the actual situation, and which can become the norm in organizational relations.

I shall now attempt to sketch in general outline the apparatus through which the Bund acts locally.

1. *VILNA AND THE BUND*

The Bund has fourteen local committees: in Warsaw, Łódź, Belostok, Grodno, Vilna, Dvinsk, Kovno, Vitebsk, Minsk, Gomel, Mogilev, Berdichev, Zhitomir, and Riga. The regional trade-union of the brush workers, like that of the tanning workers, also has the status of a committee. In places where the Jewish labour movement is not yet sufficiently developed or has not struck deep roots, the Bund organizations are not called committees and do not enjoy the latter's powers. Such organizations exist in Pinsk, Sedlice, Petrokov, Płock, Brest-Litovsk, Vilkomir, Priluki, Rezhitsa, Kiev, Odessa, Bobruisk, and innumerable townships.

In the cities where a committee exists, the following organizations are formed: (1) trade councils [*fakhovye skhodki*]; (2) revolutionary groups; (3) propagandist councils; (4) councils for the *intelligenty* [*intelligentskie skhodki*]; (5) discussion groups for the *intelligenty*; and (6) agitators' councils.

(1) Trade councils are designed to conduct the work of the Bund in a given trade. Their membership varies from five to ten persons, and there are usually several councils of this kind in a city, sometimes as many as ten. Their members are designated 'from above'. Similarly, the representative of the council who acts as the liaison with the committee is not elected by the group but is appointed by the agitators' council. Meetings are held regularly. The group discusses and studies all the problems relating to its trade (such as arbitration, apprenticeship, conditions at the factories). The council is informed by the committee about proposed demonstrations, and through it the committee calls workers to mass meetings. The members of the trade council seek out new people for propaganda circles, distribute literature, and collect money. Meetings of the trade council are attended by a representative of the agitators' council and by a propagandist, its 'leader', who must possess not only an education but also much experience and sound practical sense. A single trade council may be active in several minor and related trades. Some 2,000 workers evidently participate in the Bund's trade councils; they also belong to other organizations, but it seems to me that the trade groups must be regarded as the basic units of the entire organizational network. They developed historically out of the strike *kassy* of the early 1890s and gradually became Social Democratic organizations active among workers of a given trade. They are the syndicates of the future and sooner or later will have to be given the right to co-opt new members and to elect their delegates to the agitators'

councils. The Bund estimates that there are approximately 30,000 workers who are grouped around the trade councils and who thus come under its influence.

(2) The revolutionary groups are made up of the most advanced workers, and they act as discussion circles which deal with various questions related to ideology and the programme. Their membership is usually more than fifteen, sometimes as many as thirty. The activities of the group are guided by a representative of the committee; its members are designated by the agitators' council. There may be several of these groups in a given city, and their composition is fairly fluid. This type of organization was declared desirable by the Fifth Conference of the Bund, which, then in its 'break-up period', was adopting policies corresponding to those of *Iskra*-ism in the Russian movement.[1] It was seeking to remodel its own structure, which hitherto had rested on the 'economic' organizations of the workers, on the *kassy*. In order to overshadow the old 'trade-union' labour organization, an inter-trade council of 'conscious Social Democrats' was established. However, the proletarian character of the Jewish movement was already so far advanced that the newly formed organizations did not destroy the trade councils but acted as a highly important adjunct to them. Like the self-education circles, these groups are made up of workers who are at about the same level of development. The worker who progresses from group to group thus goes through a course of study, an entire school, as it were.

(3) The propagandist council discusses problems connected with the conduct of propaganda work. It consists of propagandists, hence mainly of *intelligenty*. There is one such council in every city, which usually has more than eight members, most often about twelve. This group decides on the programme and system of study in the circles, prepares lectures on specific problems, and trains and assigns propagandists to the circles. The trade councils prepare lists of persons recommended for membership in the self-education circles and assess the progress they have already made.

---

[1] By 'break-up period' Akimov means primarily the period from summer, 1902, to summer, 1903. At that time the Bund, under the influence alike of mounting political indignation among Lithuanian Jewry, of a prolonged economic crisis, and of pressure from *Iskra*, attempted to reorganize, making a strict separation of the political section from the workers' trade organizations. This new policy, which was embodied in a resolution of the Bund's Fifth Conference in August 1902, was explained in an article in *Arbeter Shtime*, no. 28, published (together with the resolution of the Fifth Conference) as *Nasha blizhaishaia organizatsionnaia zadacha* (London, 1903).

The propagandist council assigns these persons to its various circles.

(4) The council for the *intelligenty* is in charge of work among the intelligentsia. In some of the larger cities it is of enormous importance. Its meetings are attended by a committee member. The council engages in propaganda among the student youth, distributes literature, collects money, and organizes groups to do conspiratorial work for the committee.

(5) The discussion groups for the *intelligenty* assist people who are anxious to train for work in one branch of the movement or another, to study certain general questions, and to advance their own education.

(6) The agitators' council co-ordinates the work of all the organizations active among workers. It evolved from the central council of representatives from the trade *kassy* but it was modified by the idea that the organizations should be made up solely of professional revolutionaries. As a model for what the supreme local organization should be, therefore, it is still not fully developed. Until recently these councils were rather large, with memberships of some thirty or forty persons, sometimes even more. According to the comrades I have spoken to during the past two years—since the Fifth Conference—these groups have shown a tendency to concentrate and limit their membership; if they should do so, they would cease to express the attitudes of wide strata of the Bund. As a result of this trend the committees, in dealing with particularly important questions, are forced to call together meetings of agitators which are more comprehensive than the agitators' councils. The actual situation is beginning to come into conflict with the formal organizational structure and thus reveals the errors of the 'break-up period'.

This occurred, for example, when the resolutions about the Bund's resignation from the Party had to be drawn up. *Poslednie Izvestiia* reported a large number of meetings of agitators in various cities, usually attended by forty, fifty, or even sixty persons.* The agitators' council should be familiar with developments in all the trade councils—the cells of the Bund. Formerly, it enjoyed such a position because it was composed of representatives of the trade *kassy*; today, new members are brought into the council by co-option, and the council seeks to concentrate within itself the best revolutionary forces. Such a method is less likely to achieve the

* A total of more than 2,500 people have taken part in these meetings.

desired goal than election by the trade councils. New members are accepted by a simple majority of votes, that is, democratically. The agitators' council elects the local committee. Sometimes the council, voting by secret ballot, elects three committee members directly; one of the three is designated the committee's representative. His name is given to the council, and the committee maintains its contacts with the council through him. At other times, the council elects a special commission which in turn appoints the committee. In this case, too, the identity of one member of the committee is revealed to the entire council. The last time that a local Bund organization became a committee occurred in Riga in the winter of 1902–3. The committee there was not appointed by the central committee but was elected by the local organization. There were cases, as in Dvinsk and Gomel, when a committee that was disapproved by the council was forced to disband and to be replaced by another. There were absolutely no protests.

Thus the right of the local agitators' groups to elect their committee is incontrovertibly established. But the agitators' councils rarely make use of this right because the committee is elected for an indefinite term, and as its individual members are arrested it is replenished by co-option.* As long as the work of the Bund proceeds along familiar lines, this fact does not cause any difficulty. As life becomes more complex and as forces of innovation emerge within the Bund, it will make itself felt. It is essential to make the committee open to new forces, and this requires that members of the committee be elected for specific terms.

The relationship between the council and the committee is not defined by any precise rules. But the fact that the committee can exercise its influence upon the masses only through the agitators' council and conducts its business with the council through a comrade elected by the latter does, it seems to me, ensure in practice that the committee is quite dependent on the council. The committee is therefore something like a responsible ministry of the agitators' council.

* Note to the second edition. In the summer of this year (1905) I visited Łódź, Warsaw, and Grodno, and found that the electoral rights of the agitators' councils have lapsed completely.

2. PETERSBURG

1

One day in the early 1890s I was in the Caucasus, riding down a narrow mountain path along the coast. Around me rose giant oaks, cedars, and cypresses, covering the mountain slopes with trackless forest. My friend met me near his country home. He was taking in logs brought to him from across the sea in feluccas.

'Do you mean to say', I asked him, 'that, living in this virgin forest, you still need timber brought in?' 'But of course', my Caucasian friend replied. 'These logs were bought a hundred versts from here. If I wished to take them from my own forest, they would be very expensive. It is too difficult and takes too long to break a path through these thickly overgrown mountain sides.'

It occurred to me that this was indeed similar to the conditions under which we were labouring to 'build' our Social Democratic movement in Petersburg. We knew that the only force capable of realizing our ideals was the proletariat. We lived in a city where more than 100,000 proletarians lived and worked. And yet what incredible difficulties we had to overcome merely to meet with workers, to talk to them, make friends with them, tell them about our ideals, and inspire them to join us in the struggle for the common cause![1]

Wishing to establish contact with workers, one of my friends began to frequent daily a dirty little tavern in an outlying workers' district. He would sit there for hours, scanning the faces of the visitors, striking up acquaintances with workers, trying to become a familiar tavern habitué and thus enter into their circle of interests and gain acceptance as an insider. Another comrade spent many summer nights in the fields outside the city, where he met many unemployed—hungry and weary men who never suspected that

---

[1] Ol'minskii (Aleksandrov) believed that Akimov exaggerated the difficulty of making contact with the workers in St Petersburg. Akimov's description, he wrote, was therefore 'rather odd' (M. S. Aleksandrov, '"Gruppa Narodovol'tsev" (1891–1894 gg.)', in *Byloe*, no. 11 (1906), p. 9 n.). In practice, the situation changed rapidly, often from month to month. Even Shelgunov, a leading socialist worker of the period, found it no easy task to re-establish contact with the revolutionary circles in the capital following a series of arrests in 1892; see 'Vospominaniia V. A. Shelgunova', in *Ot gruppy Blagoeva k 'Soiuzu bor'by'* (*1886–1894 gg.*) (Rostov, 1921), p. 55.

231

the chance companion of their poor shelter in abandoned brick sheds was a student and a socialist propagandist. Such were our ways of meeting with workers.

The first Social Democratic group in Petersburg was formed in 1885. In January the first issue of the 'newspaper of the Russian Social Democrats', *Rabochii* [*Worker*] appeared. The second issue appeared in July of the same year, including, among other material, articles by Plekhanov and Aksel'rod.[1] Although it adopted Social Democratic principles, however, the circle was unable to effect an immediate change in the tactics of the Russian socialists, and, to a considerable extent, it retained the old propaganda methods. Its tactics were not those of the new proletarian socialism then just emerging but rather those of the preceding period in Russian socialist history, that of the *Narodnaia Volia* at its peak. And this is precisely why these tactics seem to us today to have been more varied and multifaceted than the subsequent steps of the Russian Social Democrats.

The *Rabochii* group conducted propaganda among cadets and soldiers, attempted to establish contacts with peasants, advocated terror, and regarded the workers merely as the most revolutionary material with which to work. It was therefore quite willing to transfer its workers' circles to propagandists of the *Narodnaia Volia*. The Social Democratic movement still had to re-examine all the theoretical postulates of socialism, to 're-evaluate all values', before it could create its own tactics and find its own way to solve the problems facing the socialists of the 1880s. It is only today that the question of propaganda among the troops and the peasantry has presented itself to the Social Democrats, and that the opportunity for such work has become a reality; it is only now that it has become essential to use arms in the struggle. But at the time the attempt to implement such plans was simply a survival from the past.

The Social Democrats recognized the necessity to ground their political viewpoint on firm foundations, and so they devoted most of their energies to study and to debates with socialists of the old school. A typical representative of the new trend in socialist

---

[1] This group, led by Dmitri Nikolaevich Blagoev and Vasilii Grigor'evich Kharitonov, was active from the winter of 1883 to 1887 and called itself the Party of Russian Social Democrats (*Partiia Russkikh Sotsial-demokratov*). It was able to bring out the only two numbers of the journal *Rabochii*. For the article of Plekhanov published in *Rabochii*, no. 2, see G. V. Plekhanov, *Sochineniia*, II, 363–72.

thought was N. V. Vodovozov (who has died so prematurely). We know how warmly he was treated by the sensitive writer V. G. Korolenko, who opposed his views; we know how attentively this 'new man' was observed by Shelgunov during the last years of the latter's life, and how he was loved by the comrades who shared his convictions.*

The students became more and more involved in debates about socialist theory. Meeting in secret, like conspirators, young students —men and women—argued sharply and passionately all through the night about the significance of the economic factor in history, the destiny of the peasant commune, the rôle of the peasantry and the proletariat. Chirikov's story *The Invalids*[1] reflected some of the nervous mood created by these debates in the ranks of Russian revolutionaries. And it seems to me that Makovskii's famous painting *A Party*,[2] which depicts a scene from the Populist period, gives us a glimpse into the life of the youth of the early 1890s and into the change-over in socialist thought from the *Narodnaia Volia* to Social Democracy.

The *Rabochii* group was arrested on 27 January 1886. The list of those arrested included V. Kharitonov, a university student who later died of tuberculosis in penal exile,[3] Butkov, Teselkin, Prince Kugushev, the Kataev brothers, and Artaumov, an engineering student of the Technology Institute. Their press on Ropshchen-skaia Street was also seized.†

---

* See the reminiscences about him in *Novoe Slovo*. [Vodovozov was a law student in St Petersburg University in the early 1890s. He became known for his articles defending Marxist thought in leading Russian journals. He died on 25 May 1896, and articles about him appeared in *Novoe slovo* (1897), no. 9, pp. 215–24, and no. 10, sect. II, pp. 56–62.]

[1] Evgenii Chirikov, 'Invalidy', in *Razskazy* (4th ed.; St Petersburg, 1903), II, 1–103.

[2] The well-known work painted in 1897 by the Moscow artist Vladimir Egorovich Makovskii.

[3] Kharitonov did not die in Siberia, as Akimov thought, but survived until after the October Revolution. He published memoirs in *Proletarskaia revoliutsiia*, no. 8 (79) (1928).

† In the appendix to Thun, Kol'tsov reports the following about Petersburg: 'In 1884 it was already possible to organize a Social Democratic group, which immediately began its activities. By 1885 this group had worked out its programme and launched into practical work—propaganda of our Social Democratic views among workers and the intelligentsia, primarily in student circles and even in "society". At that time the group consisted of 15 or 16 men and girl students, one engineer-architect, one journalist, and two old members of *Chernyi Peredel*, who lived in hiding from the police (*nelegal'nye*).' [D. Kol'tsov, 'Konets "Narodnoi Voli" i nachalo Sotsial-demokratii', in A. Tun (Thun), *Istoriia revoliutsionnykh dvizhenii v Rossii* (Geneva, 1903), p. 247.]

The Sisyphean labour of forming new circles among workers had to be begun anew. It was undertaken by a circle of students of the Technology Institute, led by Brusnev. This circle still had much in common with the *Rabochii* group. Although its members considered themselves Social Democrats, their methods of propaganda were essentially those of socialists who devoted themselves to cultural–educational work [*Sotsialisty-kul'turniki*]. The tactics of the *Narodnaia Volia* had already been abandoned, but Social Democratic tactics had not yet been worked out. The idea of direct warfare was given up, and preparatory work—the dissemination of ideas—was begun.[1] Brusnev and his comrades hoped to expand their activities and established contacts with many cities in Russia; in April 1892, however, they too were arrested.

The events of 1891—the famine, followed by an epidemic of cholera—heightened social unrest in Russia. The Social Democratic theories were by no means dictated by the logic of these events. But the national disaster awakened all the vital energies of the nation and compelled people to seek one definite answer or another to the question of what was to be done. Naturally everyone began to do what he considered imperative. All opinions were aired, both those carried over from the past and those only just emerging. A battle of ideas began, and those which best met the needs of the historic moment—the Social Democratic—emerged victorious.

In 1891 a new *Narodnaia Volia* group was formed in Petersburg. It was headed by Mikhail Stepanovich Aleksandrov, and its excellent proclamations were written by Astyrev. The group began by reissuing the old programme of the *Narodnaia Volia* with some slight changes which reduced its sharply terrorist orientation. It also published the first, and somewhat later the second, number of *Letuchii Listok* [*Express Review*] and several small publications. The group had its own press. In addition, it

---

[1] Akimov's description of the methods employed by the so-called Brusnev group as essentially educational (or 'cultural') has often been criticized by those who consider the group to have been fully revolutionary; see, for instance, V. V. Sviatlovskii, in *Byloe*, no. 19 (1922), p. 151. The programme of the group was reproduced in *Ot gruppy Blagoeva*, pp. 87–8. For descriptions of the Brusnev group, see M. I. Brusnev, 'Vosniknovenie pervykh sotsial-demokraticheskikh organizatsii (Vospominaniia)', *Proletarskaia revoliutsiia*, no. 8 (14) (1923), pp. 17–32; V. S. Golubev, 'Stranichka iz istorii rabochego dvizheniia (pamiati N. V. Shelgunova)', *Byloe*, no. 12 (1906), pp. 105–21; and R. A. Kazakevich, *Sotsial-demokraticheskie organizatsii Peterburga* (Leningrad, 1960).

organized a number of propaganda circles among students and workers in Petersburg and its environs.[1]

At approximately the same time the *Partiia Narodnogo Prava* [People's Rights Party] was formed.[2] This party felt that all the controversial questions of Russian revolutionary thought should take second place and should yield to the 'most urgent problem of our time'—the overthrow of the autocracy. In order to solve this problem all the revolutionaries, regardless of their particular allegiances, should unite. This group was headed by the old socialist Mark Andreevich Natanson. It organized a press in Smolensk. Both these groups sustained heavy losses during the arrests of April 1894.

The Social Democrats also continued their work. After the arrest of Brusnev and his friends, workers' circles were once again organized by their comrades at the Technology Institute. Theirs was a closed group, concerned purely with propaganda, and its educational circles resembled a clandestine school.[3] The *Narodovol'-tsy* complained that now they too had to teach the workers' circles physics and natural history. 'Of course,' one of them said to me, 'the workers are much more interested in hearing stories about flowers than engaging in revolutionary work. But there is nothing we can do about it. The Social Democrats have set the fashion, and we have to reckon with this if we are not to lose our influence among the workers.'

Indeed, the tactics of the Social Democrats were simply to educate a number of workers who, grouped in circles, would become conscious Marxists and enjoy influence among their fellows. A worker's speech on 1 May 1891 vividly summarized this approach. Our comrade said:

At this time the only thing we can do is devote ourselves to the education and organization of workers—a task that, I hope, we shall carry

---

[1] Aleksandrov denied that he was the leader of this group established in the winter of 1891–2: 'To play a dominant rôle in the eyes of the police is by no means to do the same in reality' ('"Gruppa Narodovol'tsev" (1891–1894 gg.)', *Byloe*, no. 11 (1906), p. 25). The four numbers of the paper published by the group, *Letuchii Listok*, are reproduced in full in P. F. Kudelli, *Narodovol'tsy na pereput'i: Delo Lakhtinskoi tipografii* (Leningrad, 1925), pp. 49–165.

[2] Founded in 1893 as an underground organization advocating an alliance of all anti-Tsarist forces to fight for a constitutional régime. Its leaders were, for the most part, veterans of the revolutionary Populist movement of the 1870s, including Osip Aptekman, Mark Natanson, and Nikolai Tiutchev.

[3] The leading organizer in the years 1892–4 of what Akimov here terms the 'clandestine school' was S. I. Radchenko. (See the articles on S. I. Radchenko by G. B. Krasin and I. I. Radchenko, in *Staryi bol'shevik*, no. 2 (1933).)

through regardless of the threats and obstacles raised by our government. In order to make our efforts bear fruit, we must do our best to educate ourselves and others intellectually and morally; we must work at this as energetically as possible, so that the people around us will regard us as intelligent, honest and courageous men, have greater trust in us, and take us as an example for themselves and others.*

Thus personal influence was at that time regarded as the only means of spreading Social Democratic ideas. The plan of action of the first Social Democrats was to gather together small groups of promising people and give them a systematic education in Social Democratic ideas. The handful of early Social Democrats was like a grain of sand among the millions of the country's population and the many hundreds of thousands of proletarians. What else could they have chosen as their symbol if not the spark [*iskra*], which glows in the dark and from which will spring the flame! Such was the psychology implanted in its best representatives in the period of *kruzhkovshchina*. And it is interesting to see this psychology preserved over the years to this day, when (although there are cadres which no longer require a spark) wide strata of the proletariat are still shrouded in darkness. It is interesting also to see how there has emerged a new type of leader for the proletarian masses, a leader with a different psychology, and how a conflict has developed between the old and the new outlook in the ranks of the Social Democratic movement.

During the period of *kruzhkovshchina* there was as yet no such conflict of viewpoints. At that time it was necessary to break a path through the undergrowth to the oaks and cedars which will go into the making of our temple. This was how we, the *intelligenty*,

* See *Four Speeches Delivered by Workers in St Petersburg* [*Pervoe maia 1891 goda: Chetyre rechi rabochikh proiznesennye na tainom sobranii v Peterburge* (Geneva, 1892), p. 12. This speech was delivered by N. D. Bogdanov (see Vilenskii-Sibiriakov and others (eds.), *Deiateli revoliutsionnogo dvizheniia*, v, 386)]. It is interesting to compare these speeches with the *Four Speeches by Jewish Workers* delivered a year later, on 1 May 1892, in Vilna. In Petersburg, the workers' speeches still reflect the period of *kruzhkovshchina*. The Vilna speeches already express readiness for economic struggle. The following words of a woman worker [Fania Reznik] are as typical of the Vilna speeches as the passage quoted above was typical of the Petersburg speeches. She said: 'We must fight against our enemies. But, of course, every individual must take account of his capacity; he must not undertake what he is not able to carry out. We know very well that we cannot change everything all at once. We must therefore fight for the time being against our closest enemies, whom we encounter every day—our employers.' [*Pervoe maia 1892 goda: Chetyre rechi evreiskikh rabochikh*, pp. 2–3.]

subjectively saw the situation. But the objective effect of our approach was that when the elemental mass movement sprang up of itself, a number of enlightened and educated workers were already prepared. A subjective re-evaluation of the significance of our work was, perhaps, psychologically inevitable, for its price was so very high. Long, painstaking, and dangerous effort was required to obtain these first results which, although essential, were of too little immediate importance.

2

In distant Kolyma, a revolutionary poet poured out his sorrow because he felt that no one listened to his call, no one answered his song:

> I sing in darkness, in the dead of night . . .
> Who hears my voice? What living soul is near?
> In vain my eyes search in the gloom! . . .
> I raise my arms high . . .
> Who sees me? Answer! . . .
>
> I sing in darkness . . . .[1]

We, too, heard no answering echo! What could be done to make the proletariat respond to the battle cry? From time to time the government locked up the propagandists in prison. Their pupils stubbornly and fearlessly continued their work, but they remained just as alone as their teachers. The circles did not achieve their purpose. What was the word that would fire the spirit of the proletariat and unleash the elemental power of the labour movement? It was for this we searched.

In the summer of 1894 [I was told by Comrade Ch.], while an apprentice mechanic, I travelled as an assistant machinist on a locomotive. I became closely acquainted with several railway workers who seemed pleasant and quite intelligent men. I had long conversations with them, and waited for a convenient moment to shift our talk to political topics. A suitable occasion presented itself before long. The governor of Nizhni Novgorod, Baranov, had announced that he would order anyone flogged who spread alarming rumours among the people (about cholera, as I remember). It seemed to me that Baranov might act on his word, and I

---

[1] The poet was V. G. (Natan Mendelevich) Bogoraz, who wrote under the pseudonym Tan. He was arrested as a member of a *Narodnaia Volia* group in December 1886 and sent to Kolyma (Iakutsk Oblast) in 1889. For the poem 'V mrake ia poiu' [I Sing in Darkness] see V. G. Tan, *Stikhotvoreniia* (St Petersburg, 1910), p. 9.

was utterly infuriated by the thought of how helpless the Russian citizen is in the face of such violent threats. I spoke about it to my new acquaintances. So long as I spoke about the Russian's lack of rights, the arbitrary rule of the authorities, they all agreed with me. But when I mentioned Baranov's threat as an example, they roared with laughter. Dumbfounded, I asked why they laughed.

'What do you think? You'll say something in a tavern, and they'll lay you out and let you have it ! . . . Simple enough ! . . . They'll let you have it ! What can you do with them? They're the masters!'

On another occasion Comrade Iu. told me about her visit to a working woman, a maker of silk stockings.

She was still young, but ill and exhausted, with red-rimmed eyes. I began to question her about her life. The major portion of her income came from Princess San-Donato, for whom she knitted fine evening stockings. The stockings were very expensive, and every pair took a long time. Often they were needed in a hurry, and the knitter sat night after night over the fine loops of silk, ruining her eyes. But the princess wore a pair only once and then discarded it or gave it to her maid. The contrast between poverty and wasteful luxury was striking, and I began to speak heatedly to the young woman about the injustice of social relations. But the unfortunate stocking maker suddenly exclaimed with admiration: 'Ah, if you knew how beautiful she is! How rich and graceful! And what manners she has! And what are we? Should we have stockings made for us? Why, every time I help her on with one of my stockings, I can't tear my eyes away from her pretty little feet.'

As I have said, at that time conscious Social Democrats had contacts not with the labouring masses, but with individual workers. The Social Democrats tried to rouse some response by drawing the workers' attention to the glaring injustice of the existing order. But even the most outrageous facts did not bring the workers to protest. The propagandists were in despair over this attitude of the average worker, untouched by propaganda, toward the world around him. And the advanced workers treated him with outright contempt. A worker who delivered a magnificent speech on 1 May 1891 said to one of my friends later, when in penal exile: 'Leaflets are a waste of time. What can you explain in a single leaflet? The worker should be given a book, not a leaflet. He must be taught. He must be drawn into a circle!'

But the workers who continued revolutionary work after 1894 were dissatisfied with the circles too. 'In the winter of 1894', writes Comrade Peterburzhets, 'the work of organizing workers' circles and of educating individuals continued. But there were already signs of disappointment. Something was lacking' (p. 12). 'Some of the conscious and advanced workers who called themselves Social Democrats were beginning to criticize *kruzhkovshchina.*' 'No, they said, the success of the cause must be sought in the labour movement. And in order to create a conscious labour movement, there must be leaders specially trained for the task. The working-class propagandist and organizer must have an exact knowledge of all the circumstances of his working life' (p. 6).[1]

At the same time there was deep, unspoken ferment among the labouring masses, a growing but still unrecognized discontent which expressed itself here and there in individual flare-ups, in scattered, unorganized protests—disorders at Semiannikov's, at the Port shipyard, at Voronin's. Under these conditions the manuscript of the pamphlet *On Agitation* came to Petersburg from Vilna.

'Anyone whose activity does not further the growth of class consciousness and revolutionary demands among the proletariat', read the pamphlet,

cannot call himself a Social Democrat. Yet these aims can only be achieved by rousing a mass movement on the basis of material discontent; and every step in this direction will facilitate the subsequent development of the movement. The obstacles which hinder even educational work and which seem—and for the small revolutionary circles really are—insuperable will fall one by one. In view of all this, we feel that it is necessary for the Social Democratic circles to make a change in their work . . . (p. 23), to take up constant agitation among factory workers on the basis of existing daily needs and demands. The struggle stirred up by such agitation will train the workers to defend their interests. It will give them courage, make them aware of their strength and the necessity for unity, and eventually will bring them face to face with the most vital questions. On the basis of this class struggle, which will take on an increasingly conscious character, it will be possible to agitate for political change in favour of the working-class. The subsequent programme of the Social Democratic movement is self-evident (p. 16). Anger, constant dissatisfaction, constant striving for improvements in one's position and an unceasing fight for such improvements, together with a broad understanding of victories already won—such is the goal toward which the agitator should lead the masses (p. 22).

The necessary note had been struck. The period of 'economic' agitation was launched in Petersburg. And the agitators who had raised no echo when they indicted the existing political and social order found that not only the workers with whom they were in

[1] Peterburzhets, *Ocherk peterburgskogo rabochego dvizhenia 90-kh godov* (London, 1902).

direct contact but also the wide strata of the working-class to which they had no direct access responded uniformly and boldly to their call to 'economic' warfare. Thus we see here a repetition of the pattern of developments observed earlier in Vilna.

'I came to Petersburg', I was told by Comrade K., 'in January 1895, soon after the publication of the first leaflet [*proklamatsiia*] about the strike at Semiannikov's.* Everybody waited with impatience and excitement to see its results. Agitation by means of leaflets was a new method, and it was difficult to foresee what the experiment would lead to.'

The experiment proved very successful. In the meantime ferment among the workers was growing. At Shrovetide a strike broke out in the Port shipyard. It was followed by a strike at Voronin's cotton mill. In the autumn there was unrest at Thornton's.

'The past month' (November 1895) 'was full of major developments in our life', we read in the proclamation of the Union of Struggle.

Three times in one month Petersburg workers rose against oppression by the employers, three times they tried to win better living conditions by an active fight. The first to rise were the textile workers at the Thornton factory. Everybody knows how difficult life has been in recent times for textile workers, who have been ruined and pauperized as a

---

* 'A leaflet for agitation was rapidly prepared. It took the form of a slim pamphlet which described the conditions at Semiannikov's plant. Read at a meeting of several workers, it was hectographed and distributed at the factory, although not very successfully. Though as yet only tried out in an isolated incident, the new method of the Social Democrats attracted the workers' attention' (Peterburzhets, p. 14). [N. K. Krupskaia recalled that Lenin had written a leaflet for distribution to the workers of the Semiannikov plant after they had rioted on 23 December 1894 (*Vospominaniia o Lenine* (Moscow, 1933), pp. 19–20). A fragment—all that had survived—from what might have been Lenin's leaflet was first published by B. I. Nikolaevskii in *Letopisi marksizma*, no. 3 (1927), pp. 64–6. However, the authorship of this fragment is in dispute. A number of historians ascribe it to Lenin: see V. G. Sorin, *Pervye shagi Lenina po sozdaniiu partii* (Moscow, 1934), pp. 44–7; G. Tikhomirnov, 'Pervye agitatsionnye listki Lenina', *Proletarskaia revoliutsiia*, no. 8 (1937), p. 128 n.; and R. Pipes, *Social Democracy and the St Petersburg Labour Movement, 1885–1897* (Cambridge, 1963), pp. 66–7 n. But in general, Soviet historians have supported G. M. Krzhizhanovskii, who claimed authorship in *Letopisi marksizma*, no. 4 (1927), p. 140. See, for instance, S. N. Valk and I. Tovstukhi (eds.), *Listovki Peterburgskogo 'Soiuza bor'by za osvobozhdenie rabochego klassa': 1895–1897 gg.* (Moscow, 1934), p. 134 n.; N. Paialin, 'V. I. Lenin i rabochie Semiannikovskogo zavoda v 90-e gody', *Krasnaia letopis'*, no. 1 (58) (1934), p. 53 n.; and F. M. Suslova, 'Peterburgskie stachki 1895–1896 godov i ikh vliianie na razvitie massovogo rabochego dvizheniia', in *Istoriia rabochego klassa Leningrada*, II (Leningrad, 1963) 54 n.]

result of the sharp drop in wages. The long simmering discontent finally flared up, and the workers rose in protest against a new wage reduction. Almost simultaneously there were disorders at the Laferm Tobacco Factory. Here, too, the employers had long tried the patience of the women workers, resorting to downright swindles in order to squeeze a few more pennies from their starvation wages . . . Patience finally came to an end, and the women workers put fear in the hearts of the Laferm company, wrecking the factory and beating up the hated overseer. The third incident occurred at the Machine-Made Shoe Factory. This wealthiest of companies, not content with legal robbery and oppression, did not hesitate to use flagrantly illegal means of exploiting its workers. Forty workers in one of the shops struck, demanding abolition of excessive penalization for defective products. Since their stoppage halted work at the entire factory, the employers yielded after a three-day strike.[*]

'The first to rise were the textile workers at the Thornton factory.' And the Union of Struggle immediately applied its new tactics.

After a large number of meetings over a period of several months [writes Comrade Peterburzhets], and after heated debate between spokesmen of a workers' group of the Nevskii Gate district and representatives of an *intelligenty* group, it was decided to initiate the new tactics of mass agitation based on the daily, urgent needs of the workers of this or that factory. The plan was that printed leaflets distributed in the factories would describe the conditions in a given factory and state the workers' demands for specific changes. Leaflets summing up the situation and stating the demands of the Thornton workers were scattered in the factory workshops and buildings, and produced a tremendous impression on the workers (p. 19).

Along with the Union of Struggle, a group of 'youngsters' was also active in Petersburg at the time.[1] This group grew up separately not because it differed ideologically from the older group but solely as a result of the conditions under which it had to

---

[*] The proclamation evidently belongs to December 1895. It is undated. It is addressed 'To All Petersburg Workers' and signed 'Union of the Struggle for the Emancipation of the Working Class'. This was the name of the Petersburg Social Democratic group at that time. [According to Valk, this leaflet was published on 18 December 1895 (Valk and Tovstukhi (eds.), *Listovki*, pp. 16–17). M. A. Sil'vin ascribed the authorship to G. M. Krzhizhanovskii: *ibid.* p. 137 n.]

[1] The group of the so-called 'youngsters' or 'roosters' (*petukhi*) was led by I. V. Chernyshev. Among its members were M. M. Shat, E. G. Bogatyrev, E. I. Muromov, and the police agent (and dentist) N. N. Mikhailov. (See *Sbornik materialov i statei* (Moscow, 1921), I, 137–49.)

work. The workers' circles were few, and it was not easy to increase their number. Hence even the veteran members of the first group were not all occupied. Some of them had to wait their turn. Yet there were already quite a number of Social Democratic students eager to engage in revolutionary activity. Since the 'veterans' did not provide them with such work, they sought it on their own. 'In the autumn of 1894 I happened to meet a certain worker', one of the 'youngsters' told me, 'and began to visit other workers with him. I attempted to organize a circle, but without success—none of the workers came more than three times to our discussions.'

The efforts of the 'youngsters' bore fruit only in the summer of 1895, when the workers' circles began to turn to them in the absence of the 'veterans' away on vacation.[1] Soon both groups, the 'old' and the 'young', met in the workers' circles. The 'veterans' always followed established rules and procedures. The 'youngsters', on the contrary, sought by purely experimental means to evolve new tactics which would permit them to become the workers' spokesmen and leaders. This was why the 'veterans' disapproved of the leaflets of the 'youngsters'.*

In the summer of 1895 the 'youngsters' responded to the strike at the Port shipyard by issuing a proclamation to all Petersburg workers, which opened with the words: 'Workers! There is a strike on Galernyi Island.' It went on to develop the idea that all workers should take up collections to help the comrades at the Port, for victory on Galernyi Island would be a victory for the working-class. It pointed out that the workers had to organize in order to fight the capitalists. Describing the difficult conditions of the workers and the fact that the employers were organized, the proclamation concluded: 'We shall reply to the unions of the employers with unions of our own.'

The manuscript was submitted for duplication on the mimeograph of the 'veterans', but the latter disapproved of it: 'This leaflet', they said, 'could have come from *Vorwärts* and is not applicable to Russian conditions. Leaflets should deal with concrete events and working conditions, and there is still no point in speaking of unions in Russia.'† Nevertheless the youngsters

---

[1] V. A. Shelgunov, one of the leading worker Social Democrats, later recorded the fact that in mid-1895 he had introduced members of the 'young' group to workers in the Nevskii Gate area of St Petersburg (*Ot gruppy Blagoeva*, p. 57).
* The proclamations of this group appeared unsigned.
† I do not have the original of this leaflet but wrote down the above quotations from the words of its author, Comrade M. [G. Tikhomirnov suggests in

printed their leaflet on a hectograph, after copying it by hand. It enjoyed great success, although only seventy copies were printed.

Another leaflet, given out to the workers at the Shpalernaia factory,* did speak only about local matters, but it also stated that 'our manufacturer serves as a graphic example of the capitalists' attitude toward workers'. Further, it said: 'We must begin by raising demands that can be won. We must test our strength. A strike will not bring about the golden age, but it will strengthen our sense of solidarity and unite us all the more closely for the struggle with the enemy.' This leaflet was also criticized by the 'veterans': 'You pour buckets of cold water on the hopes of the workers while calling upon them to strike.'

There were also disagreements concerning organizational questions. In November 1895 the youngsters organized a circle of patternmakers. Patternmakers are the most advanced element among the workers. Besides, they all know each other and are scattered over all the mechanized factories. Hence with their aid it was possible to establish contacts with all factories. The 'veterans', however, criticized such a workers' organization as bourgeois.

Gradually the youngsters came to accept the tactics of purely economic agitation, and their proclamations in November 1895 to the workers of the Putilov plant were purely economic. It now seemed possible for both groups to unite. Such a unification was prevented by the Union's mistrust of one of the 'youngsters', N. N. Mikhailov, who did, in fact, turn out to be an *agent provocateur*.

I shall deal in greater detail with the groups of 1895 both because there is a scarcity of data on them in our literature and because this period in which economism originated and grew is quite mistakenly represented by Lenin in his book *What Is to Be Done?* as diametrically opposed to economism.

Economism was marked by two characteristic features: (1) Proclamations urged war on the capitalists but said nothing of war against the government. Workers were called upon to fight employers *despite* the government's support of the latter; (2) *Parallel* with the conspiratorial organization of the revolution-

---

Proletarskaia revoliutsiia, no. 8 (1937), p. 129 n. that the leaflet here ascribed to the summer of 1895 was in fact published in February. There is almost no evidence available, but it is possible that Akimov is in fact referring here to the leaflet of February 1895, described in *Letuchie listki*, no. 23 (15) (3 Aug. 1895)—the newsletter of the Fund of the Free Russian Press.]

* This leaflet was in the archives of the Union [Abroad].

aries emerged workers' organizations devoted entirely to 'economic' issues. The former feature is clearly seen in the work of both groups in 1895; the latter is just barely discernible.

About this definition Comrade T.[1] wrote to me:

What a strange distinction you make between a conspiratorial and a purely economic organization! What do you mean by a workers' organization which is purely economic and, by implication, non-conspiratorial? I would say that there has never been any such organization. Some of us wanted to substitute for the central organization of the Union, which was composed solely of *intelligenty*, an organization composed solely of workers. But I insist that in practice we had neither a purely conspiratorial organization of the Union nor a purely economic one conducted openly by the workers. The workers' organizations have been forced by the political conditions under which we live to be secret and therefore conspiratorial; moreover, they did not deal with 'economics' alone, for in most cases the money of the workers' *kassy* was spent both on political literature and to aid comrades arrested for political reasons.

It is true that at this time no such distinction was made, and it appeared as if there was a struggle between the workers and the *intelligenty* for a place in the Union. But such an explanation of the intraparty struggle in 1895 is as superficial as Comrade Lenin's interpretation of the present fight as a fight for places in the Central Committee and the central journal. If people fight for places, it is not because, or at any rate not only because, they would like to possess them. The contestants assume that they will conduct the work differently when they are at the helm. Underlying the conflict of individuals we must see the conflict of principles. This is the first point. Second, although the workers' *kassy* and the Union of Struggle were both clandestine, it is nevertheless essential to distinguish the one from the other, for each had its own goals and its own methods. The *kassy* had a single objective—industrial warfare. They helped comrades who had suffered in *this* war, and bought forbidden books for propaganda in *this* war. From the government's point of view, all these were political crimes, and indeed these activities were of great significance for the cause of political freedom and socialism. But the participants in the *kassy* were unaware of this significance, although some of them sensed it vaguely. On the whole, they regarded their secret organizations merely as weapons in the

---

[1] Comrade T., judging from his letter, probably was K. M. Takhtarev.

economic struggle of the working-class. This was how their proclamations explained their fight.*

The Union of Struggle had its own, broader goal, and it saw the workers' economic struggle merely as a means. In creating and supporting the workers' *kassy*, the Union had in mind not their direct results but their rôle in developing the proletariat's class war. But the Union did not state its goal—the overthrow of the existing order—either in leaflets or at the meetings of the *kassy*. This lent the Union of Struggle the character of a conspiratorial organization which sought to base itself on the labouring masses.† And it distinguished the Union from the organizations of the masses, the *kassy*.

This growing complexity in the revolutionary organizations, this crystallization of Social Democratic groups, was not only a typical aspect of the economist stage but was also the factor that determined its second characteristic—the fact that the leaflets said nothing about politics.

Comrade Plekhanov and later Comrade Lenin held that economism originated in 1897. The Union of Struggle of 1895 is

---

* See 'What Is a Socialist?' ['Chto takoe sotsialist?']: 'Socialists are those who strive for the liberation of the oppressed from the yoke of the capitalist bosses.' See also Lenin's 'To the Tsarist Government' ['Tsarskomu pravitel'-stvu'], which contains this line: 'To be a socialist is to support the workers in their struggle against capital.' Comrade Trotsky says in his *Our Political Tasks*, p. 22, that 'while the theoreticians and publicists of "Economism" have ruthlessly cut away the socialist banner, the group of *Zaria* and *Iskra* is utterly innocent of this sin against the holy spirit'. Comrade Trotsky merely forgot to add that 'the theoreticians and publicists of "Economism"' and the members of 'the group of *Zaria* and *Iskra*' are one and the same people at different stages of their development. He probably forgot this because he himself is one of these people, the author of the ultra-economic report from Nikolaev on the one hand and an *Iskra* contributor on the other. [The author of the leaflet 'Chto takoe sotsialist i politicheskii prestupnik?' was the worker I. V. Babushkin; see Valk and Tovstukhi (eds.), *Listovki*, pp. 20–1. For Lenin's 'Tsarskomu pravitel'stvu', see *ibid.* pp. 99–106, or Lenin, *Sochineniia* (2nd ed.; Moscow, 1927–32), I, 455–8. The works of Trotsky referred to are *Nashi politicheskie zadachi* (Geneva, 1904) and his report on Nikolaev in *Iz rabochego dvizheniia v Odesse i Nikolaeve* (Geneva, 1900). In the latter pamphlet, published by the Union Abroad, the report on Odessa was written by Iu. M. Steklov. (See Iu. Kamenev, *Russkaia politicheskaia literatura zagranitsei*, I (Paris, 1913), 10 n.)]

† See Lenin, [*Chto delat'? Nabolevshie voprosy nashego dvizheniia* (Stuttgart, 1902)], p. 81: 'Today the Russian revolutionary, basing himself on the spontaneously awakening class, can at last—at last!—draw himself up to his full height and unfold his whole epic strength.' See also his *One Step Forward* [*Shag vpered, dva shaga nazad: Krizis v nashei Partii* (Geneva, 1904)], p. 140: 'A Jacobin, indissolubly linked to the organization of the proletariat—such is the *revolutionary Social Democrat*.'

taken by Lenin as a model from which the Economists should
learn. Yet it was just the activity of the Union of Struggle in 1895
which laid the foundations of economism. However, the year
1897, as we shall see later, saw the end of the economist stage.

In Schippel's pamphlet *Trade-Unions*, Comrade Kol'tsov makes
the following comment on page ix, 'for readers of the twenty-first
century': 'During the summer of 1901 A.D., the appellation
"Economist" (in quotation marks) was given not to those who
engaged in the study of economic science but to those who asserted
that the workers should eschew all except economic aims.'[1]

This comment distorts historical truth for the sake of polemics.
In Russia there were never any Social Democrats who denied that
the political struggle was essential. Even the most extreme organ
of so-called Economism, *Rabochaia Mysl'* [*Labour Thought*], never
rejected the political struggle of the working-class as a matter of
principle. References are usually made to the famous 'Credo'.
The author of the 'Credo' was an extreme politician,[2] who maintained that the working-class was not capable of overthrowing the
autocracy and therefore urged the socialists to look elsewhere, to
look to the intelligentsia, for support in its struggle against the
autocracy. However, this 'Credo', for which only two individuals
were responsible, met with no response from any Social Democratic group. Besides, it was not merely that the 'Credo' did not
advocate Economist theories. It was actually antithetical to the
ideas of the Economists, who urged that Social Democrats devote
themselves wholly and exclusively to the cause of labour, and who
felt that the proletarian struggle was all-important.*

[1] D. Kol'tsov, Foreword, p. ix n., in M. Shippel' (Schippel), *Professional'nye
soiuzy rabochikh* (Geneva, 1901).

[2] On the 'Credo', see above, p. 35.

* Since *Iskra* has completely distorted the historical appraisal of the 'Credo',
it might be useful to sum up its history at this point. Several private individuals (I believe there were four of them) met accidentally at the editorial
office of a Petersburg magazine. In conversation, a certain N. [Kuskova]
expressed the ideas which I cited above. The others present felt that the
ideas were erroneous, but asked the speaker to formulate them in writing,
which [s]he did. One of our party comrades [Lenin] who saw the manuscript
gave it the impressive name of 'Credo' and sent it to his acquaintances.
Seventeen of these met and sharply criticized this 'Credo', then sent their
criticism to the Union of Russian Social Democrats Abroad for publication.
Rabochee Delo published this critical protest and added its own criticism.
The author of the 'Credo' never belonged to any Social Democratic organization active in Russia. [S]he is a former member of *Narodnoe Pravo*. At
one time, it is true, [s]he belonged to the *old* Union Abroad and hence was
accepted into the Social Democratic organization by the Group for the

2. PETERSBURG

If, however, the appellation 'economist' is to be applied to Social Democrats who believed, for tactical reasons, that for a period of time the political tasks of the proletariat should not be mentioned in *leaflets*, then the first economists, and indeed the only real economists, were none other than the members of the Union of Struggle of 1895—the subsequent founders of *Iskra* and sharp critics of Economism.

And though the future members of the *Iskra* group were themselves at that time the theoreticians and practitioners of economism the Group for the Emancipation of Labour, which considered their activities unsatisfactory, did not venture to point out their errors in the press. On the contrary, it publicly approved them. In the conclusion to the pamphlet *The Tenth Anniversary of the Morozov Strike*, V. I. Zasulich wrote:

The Union of Struggle for the Emancipation of the Working Class was founded in the autumn of 1895, and by winter the labour question already confronted the government in all its force. By early summer of 1896, the whole world was speaking about the Russian workers' movement. But what did this Union of Struggle do in the beginning? It took down from the words of the workers all the details of the employers' malpractices, all their malicious tricks and deceptions in connexion with the accounts, deductions, spoilage, stretching the workday beyond all limits, and so on. All this information was printed in leaflets which were distributed among the workers, urging them to defend themselves against such malpractices, which were condemned, however reluctantly, even by the State Council itself.[1]

Thus V. I. Zasulich saw that the Union of Struggle confined itself to merely economic agitation. However, in its report to the London Congress of the International in 1896,[2] the Russian delega-

Emancipation of Labour. However, [s]he had no connexion whatsoever with the young Union and was not even present at the congress at which this Union was founded. Consequently, only prejudiced critics of 'Economism' could hold it responsible for the 'Credo'.

[Leading participants in these events have left accounts of what happened both in St Petersburg and in Siberian exile: E. D. Kuskova in her review of F. Dan's *Iz istorii rabochego dvizheniia i sotsial-demokratii*, in *Byloe*, no. 10 (1906), pp. 324–6 n.; Elizarova's letter in Lenin, *Sochineniia* (2nd ed.), II, 637–8; Lepeshinskii, *Na povorote*, pp. 117–19; M. A. Sil'vin, 'K biografii V. I. Lenina (iz vospominanii)', *Proletarskaia revoliutsiia*, no. 7 (30) (1924), p. 79; Martov, *Zapiski*, pp. 408–10. Unless otherwise indicated, all citations of Lenin, *Sochineniia*, are to the 2nd ed.].

[1] V. I. Zasulich, *Desiatiletie Morozovskoi stachki* (Geneva, 1897), p. 35.

[2] *Doklad predstavlennyi delegatsieiu russkikh sotsial-demokratov Mezhdunarodnomu rabochemu sotsialisticheskomu kongressu v Londone v 1896 godu* (Geneva, 1896).

tion stated that 'the Union of Struggle missed no opportunity to discredit the Tsarist government in the eyes of the worker' (p. 10). As I shall show with quotations from its leaflets, this was not so, and the writers of the report embellished the facts. This was a lapse on their part, but it proves that they, too, were dissatisfied with the facts. Yet they did not say this openly, evidently 'out of diplomatic considerations'.

I shall demonstrate later that *Rabochaia Mysl'* followed a path broader than that taken by the Union of Struggle in 1895. For the moment I shall merely say that none of the leaflets of the Union of Struggle in 1895 dealt with political issues.

A leaflet to the Thornton workers, issued on 10 November, says nothing about the government, or even about the 'authorities'.[1] Another leaflet of November 1895, 'To All Petersburg Workers', speaks about 'the authorities, in the person of the factory inspector', and discusses the action of the 'government', which sent a battalion of soldiers to the Thornton factory. 'General von Wahl permitted himself to abuse the women workers.'[2] A leaflet distributed at the Lebedev factory says that 'the government' helped the employers keep the workers in subjection.[3] These leaflets were issued by the 'veterans'. In a leaflet distributed by the 'youngsters' at the Machine-Made Shoe Factory, we read that 'the government is hand-in-glove with the bosses'. These are all the political allusions to be found in the proclamations of the period. But neither the 'veterans' nor the 'youngsters' pointed out that the workers would, at any rate in the future, have to fight *against the government too*. In response to the arrests of 8 and 9 December, the Union of Struggle issued a leaflet expressing a clearly economist position. This leaflet[4] is cited by Peterburzhets on page 22.

Of great interest, too, is another leaflet issued by the Union of Struggle. According to the custom followed by both groups at that time, it is undated. If I am not mistaken, it was written by a worker and issued on 1 January 1896. Its title is 'What is a Socialist and a Political Criminal?' It might be thought that such a leaflet could hardly fail to take a political stand, and yet it is typically 'economic'. 'We are robbed by our employer,' it states, 'whose side is taken by the government. The socialists are people who

[1] This leaflet was written by Lenin. See Valk and Tovstukhi (eds.), *Listovki*, pp. 6–12. [2] *Ibid.* pp. 17–18.
[3] *Ibid.* p. 22. (The author of this leaflet was Ia. M. Liakhovskii.)
[4] Issued on 15 December 1895, and written by Martov (*ibid.* pp. 14–16). It was reproduced in full by Peterburzhets in his *Ocherk*.

strive for the liberation of the oppressed from the yoke of the capitalist bosses. And they are branded political criminals because they go against the aims of our barbarous government, which defends the interests of the factory owners.'[1] Fight the employers despite the fact that they are helped by the government—such is the slogan of economism!

In order to prove that the Union's activity was political in character, Lenin in *What Is to Be Done?* cites the headings of the articles in the first number of the Union of Struggle's journal for 1895, which was never published. 'Some future *Russian Historical Journal* may unearth the manuscript of this journal in thirty years from the archives of the Police Department',[2] he adds. Indeed, until then the character of these articles cannot be properly judged; the titles say nothing about the content, for the Union of Struggle of 1895 found it necessary to explain even such terms as 'socialist' and 'political criminal' without pointing out the political tasks of the Russian proletariat. The fact remains, at any rate, that in the publications which the Union managed to issue, it did not touch upon the political tasks of the working-class.

On the night of 8–9 December, members of both groups were arrested. The arrests continued throughout December, January 1896, and part of February. The Union of Struggle suffered most severely, since many of its members were arrested at the very beginning. The arrests of the 'youngsters' were spread over a longer period, and those whose arrests came later had managed to turn over the work to new recruits. Therefore, after January 1896 the revolutionary work fell mostly upon the shoulders of the 'youngsters' who had contacts at the Aleksandrovsk plant, Pal''s, Semiannikov's, the Warsaw [Line] workshop, the Volynkovskii factory, Koenig's, the All-Russian Rubber Plant, the Machine-Made Shoe Factory, the Putilov plant, at Bert's on the Priazhka River, the Baltic and Port shipyards, and at the Shpalernaia factory. In short, the 'youngsters' had far more contacts with workers than did the Union. So the Union made an effort to reach an agreement. The problem was discussed by two delegates from each group. The Union argued that the leaflets of the 'youngsters' were weak and demanded that their publication be placed in its hands, especially since it commanded adequate technical facilities

---

[1] Valk and Tovstukhi (eds.), *Listovki*, pp. 20–1.
[2] Lenin, *Chto delat'?*, p. 21.

for this work. The 'youngsters' refused. For their part, they demanded that in the event of an agreement the organization should be given a new name. This demand was rejected by the Union, which insisted that its name was already well known and popular. No agreement was reached at that time.

Two months later the force of events compelled all Social Democrats active in Petersburg to work together, to unite. And in the autumn they came forward as a single organization, adopting the name of the Union of Struggle. In addition to these two groups, there were still others active in 1896: a very influential group, which had originated among the workers of the Nevskii plant, and an organization formed in connexion with a Sunday school. Both these organizations also joined the Union of Struggle.[1]

I shall not describe the events of the summer of 1896 and January 1897. They are briefly but adequately described by Peterburzhets. They revealed a highly skilful application of the tactical and organizational principles which had already crystallized in 1895. I shall merely note that the rejoinder of the Union[2] to the letter circulated by the Minister of Finance, Witte, on 15 June 1895, was devoted to purely economic matters. Nevertheless, the Union had just issued an appeal to 'society' which was political in character, which explained the political importance of the workers' battle, and which invited 'society' to help in this battle.[3] Later, in November, the Union received a proclamation written by Lenin in prison, 'To the Tsarist Government'. It was published, and is a remarkably interesting document. It speaks in great detail and very critically about the government, proving that the

[1] The influential group centred in the Nevskii (Semiannikov) plant was probably that which had been led by I. V. Babushkin in the years 1894–5. Although Babushkin was arrested in January 1896, underground work was successfully taken up in the Nevskii Gate area by M. Z. Ginsburg and A. A. Davidovich, whose group entered the Union of Struggle in the autumn of 1896. The other group mentioned was presumably the one formed around the Smolensk Workers Evening and Sunday School. Among the teachers who joined forces with the Union of Struggle were N. Baranskaia, L. Knipovich, N. Krupskaia, A. Iakubova, and Z. Nevzorova. (On these groups, see V. Katin-Iartsev, 'Teni proshlogo', *Byloe*, no. 25 (1924), pp. 114–15; Krupskaia, *Vospominaniia o Lenine*, pp. 14 and 17–19; and B. I. Gorev, *Iz partiinogo proshlogo: Vospominaniia, 1895–1905* (Leningrad, 1924), p. 33.)

[2] This is the leaflet issued by the Union,' To the Workers of St Petersburg' on 27 June 1896 (Valk and Tovstukhi (eds.), *Listovki*, pp. 77–8). It was a reply to Witte's appeal to the workers for order, which is reproduced in Lenin, *Sochineniia*, I, 481–2.

[3] The appeal *To Russian Society* was issued on 10 June 1896, and was written by A. N. Potresov (Valk and Tovstukhi (eds.), *Listovki*, pp. 65–7).

government always takes the side of the capitalists against the workers. But it fails to discuss political tasks, and certainly does not mention the overthrow of the government. Moreover, it does not even say that the workers have to, or will have to, fight against the government too. On the contrary, the author describes the rôle played by the economic struggle and shows that for the workers to take part is itself to fight against the government—'as the government itself has shown by taking action against the workers. And this is what the socialists have stated in their leaflets.' From the leaflets referred to by the author of this proclamation it may also be seen that the socialists did not call the workers to fight against the government. They merely pointed out that the support provided the employers by the government was an obstacle to labour in its industrial war. All this was stated also in *Rabochaia Mysl'*, but more was said, as I shall show later.

As may be seen from the above, what in my view was the first characteristic of this stage of economism—the fact that leaflets confined themselves to the fight for labour's economic interests—was a remarkably constant feature of the Social Democratic publications from 1895 to 1897. Let us now examine the second feature of this stage—the emergence of labour organizations devoted to the economic needs of the workers. In Petersburg, as in the western area, the workers' organizations (created by the organization of revolutionaries) took up only a part of what the Social Democrats had to do. Consequently, side by side with, but independent of, the workers' organizations, the revolutionaries had to have their own conspiratorial organizations.

The emergence of workers' organizations prompted Peterburzhets to describe the entire period 1896–7 as 'the period of organization'. But the workers' attempts of 1896 to create an organization were only the first steps. From documents published by Peterburzhets we see that the dreams of the 'organizers' were confined to Petersburg and to industrial warfare. This was exactly what had happened in the western area during the analogous period of the movement's development there.

The workers' organizational demands were highly characteristic of this stage in the movement. The workers did not demand that they be given full control of the work of the Social Democratic organization, as they did in Petersburg in 1901 and elsewhere at the corresponding stage of development. On the contrary, they knew of the existence of a central organization of revolutionaries and yet willingly left the central functions to this organization. They felt, however, that the organizations in immediate control of economic warfare should be built according to democratic principles.*

'The Union itself', writes Peterburzhets,

debated whether or not to admit workers to the central organization. The debates on the improvement of the Union's organizational work and on the admission of workers to active participation culminated in the decision, late in February 1897, to admit two workers[1] to the central group of the Union. They were to represent the agitators' group or, as this group was still called, the Workers Committee. But before the central group of the Union in its reconstructed form could hold a general meeting, a wave of arrests in March 1897 carried off all those who advocated worker participation in the inner organization of the Union. After that, everything returned to the old pattern. The Union was temporarily weakened; worker participation in its central group became impossible for the time being, and was achieved only at a later date.[2]

In discussing the events of 1896 in Petersburg, it is necessary to mention the 'group of [Express] Review, no. 4' [gruppa 4-go 'Listka']. On 13 July the press of the Narodovol'tsy at Lakhta was seized.[3] The work of this press demonstrates how, in the 1890s, the Social Democratic movement swept along with it all the active and revolutionary elements of the Russian socialist movement.

The press, which survived the arrests of 19 April 1894, had earlier belonged to the group of Narodovol'tsy led by M. S. Aleksandrov. It was turned over to the newly organized Narodnaia Volia group by Dr Feit, who was at that time in charge of the talks begun before the police raid of 19 April, dealing with the unification of

---

* See the interesting documents published by Peterburzhets in his booklet [Ocherk], pp. 65 ff., and the material on Moscow in Rabotnik, nos. 3–4 [Sect. II, pp. 33–60, 94–9].

[1] A. M. Solov'ev and Karl Sak (Katin-Iartsev, in Byloe, no. 25 (1924), p. 117).

[2] Peterburzhets, Ocherk, p. 72. For accounts of the debate in February 1897 between the innovators and conservatives in the Union, particularly between Apolinaria Iakubova and Lenin, see Martov, Zapiski, pp. 316–17; Gorev, Iz partiinogo proshlogo, pp. 37–8; and A. I. Elizarova, 'Vladimir Il'ich v tiurme (dekabr' 1895–fevral' 1897)', Proletarskaia revoliutsiia, no. 3 (26) (1924), p. 120.

[3] The Group of Narodovol'tsy maintained its press during 1895 near the Kriukov Canal in St Petersburg, but early in 1896 it was taken to Lakhta, a nearby village. It was seized by the police on 24 June 1896. Lenin's pamphlet Ob"iasnenie zakona o shtrafakh [On the Law concerning Fines] was printed on this press. See Kudelli, Narodovol'tsy na pereput'i, pp. 5–30.

the *Narodnaia Volia* and People's Rights [*Narodnoe Pravo*] groups. The *Express Review* issued by the new group was marked no. 3, as a continuation of the first two. However, the [older] *Narodovol'tsy* were troubled by the new stand which it adopted. The series of pamphlets which the new group now published differed sharply from the publications of its predecessor and was Social Democratic in character. With these pamphlets, the group rendered an inestimable service to the labour movement.

Finally, in the spring of 1896, the fourth number of *Express Review* appeared, edited by Belevskii.[1] It made a tremendous impression throughout Russia, and throughout Siberia all the way to Iakutsk. It was obviously tending toward Social Democratic principles. After its publication the Kiev group of the *Narodnaia Volia* broke off relations with the 'group of [*Express*] *Review*, no. 4', as the Petersburg group of *Narodovol'tsy* began to be called. In Petersburg some *Narodovol'tsy* published a protest against *Express Review*, no. 4, but this protest was actually self-defeating and simply bore witness both in its content and its appearance to the bankruptcy of the old ideas. Illegibly handwritten on a sheet of paper folded into eight and copied on a hectograph, it was fighting the *Express Review*, which, from the technical point of view, was excellently produced. Although indignant at the new ideas proclaimed under the banner of the *Narodnaia Volia*, this protest did not attempt to make any improvements in the old programme, which had been condemned by life itself. As far as I can remember, this was the last publication of the *Narodnaia Volia*.

Swept along with the movement, which in 1896 was in full flow, the 'group of [*Express*] *Review*, no. 4' issued a printed proclamation to the workers, and it proved a sensational success. The workers laughed at the handwritten declarations of the Governor, saying: '*Our* proclamations are printed'.

The group urged that a congress of Social Democratic organizations in Russia be called immediately and a party formed. It offered to put its press at the disposal of this new party. The plan was frustrated by arrests. Eight comrades were sentenced to two years' solitary confinement, to be followed by eight years of penal exile. Several dozen others were sent to Siberia for varying terms. All of them were betrayed by the provocateur M. I. Gurovich.

---

[1] Aleksandr S. Belevskii was the leading ideologist of the Group of *Narodovol'-tsy* in the year 1895 when he negotiated a working agreement with Lenin for co-operation between their respective organizations. At a later date, then called Belorussov, he became a Kadet. (See Martov, *Zapiski*, pp. 273–4.)

In the summer of 1896 the Union of Struggle also sustained heavy losses. Later, after the January strikes of 1897, it was once more broken up by the police on 21 March.[1] At this time the police also seized the press on Sergievskaia Street, which had just been assembled and was meant to serve the Union. During the summer everything was at a standstill.

3

The lull that came in the summer of 1897 was, of course, only superficial. Below the surface men continued stubbornly to think out plans for the new period of the Social Democratic movement in St Petersburg. In this new phase the labour movement itself raised demands for civil rights and began to require democratic procedures within its own organization. However, the formal leadership of the Union, weakened by repeated arrests, consisted not of the comrades who had led the struggle of 1896 and early 1897, but of the 'veterans', members of the Union of Struggle of 1895. At that time they had themselves chosen the path of economic agitation; but now the proletarian movement, which they had formerly tried to unleash, forced them to adopt slogans which they were bound to find unsatisfactory. The 'veterans' refused to reckon with the new demands of the labour movement.[2] The new tasks and problems, therefore, inevitably called forth new organizations. Several small groups appeared, which began to work independently; they justified themselves with the argument that participation in the Union only made work more difficult. The Union lost almost all its contacts among the workers.

The Petersburg movement had expanded in breadth and depth so rapidly that the various elements affected by propaganda were bound to take different paths. In order to work with the broad strata of the proletariat which had only just been drawn into the movement, it was essential to agitate on the basis of daily economic interests. This was done with great success by *Rabochaia Mysl'*, whose sole aim was to reflect the thinking of wide strata of workers.

---

[1] Among those arrested on 21 March were N. E. Bauman, V. N. Katin-Iartsev, and Akimov himself. See *Rabotnik* (Geneva), nos. 3–4, 1897, sec. II, p. 177.

[2] The dominant figure among the small group of 'veterans' left at liberty in the years 1897–1900 was S. I. Radchenko. Of this period his brother has written: 'On his own admission, this was the most difficult period of his life when he worked alone and all his efforts were directed merely to preserving conspiratorial ties with other cities and with those abroad' (I. I. Radchenko, in *Staryi bol'shevik*, no. 2 (5) (1933), p. 183).

But to the smaller section of the proletariat which for many years had been well trained in the school of active war, more ambitious aims presented themselves. Their needs also had to be met, and this was undertaken by the group of *Rabochee Znamia* [Labour Banner].

If the Union of Struggle had been strong enough and had understood its tasks in the autumn of 1897, it 'would have taken into account the different levels attained by the various strata of the proletariat'. But there was no complete unity in the Union of Struggle, even among the 'youngsters'. It was unable to concentrate in its hands the work at all levels. Thus the two strata at each extreme of the working-class found the right spokesman for their own needs.

This, however, did not mean the emergence of an 'economic trend'. On the contrary, as I shall show, it meant that the proletarian movement which hitherto had been homogeneous was now putting out more comprehensive sociopolitical branches. The break between one phase of the movement and the next may be set at the arrests of 21 March 1897, and I shall now try to sketch the subsequent organizational developments.

As early as the summer of that year we saw the formation of the workers' group *Rabochaia Mysl'*. In October it published the first issue of its newspaper. In the autumn, too, the Group of Technology Students was formed by people who had left the Union.[1] This group, which later took the name *Rabochee Znamia*, established contact with the Group of Revolutionary Workers, which, centred in Belostok, was opposed to the Bund. It was at about this time that the Group of Revolutionary Workers issued the pamphlet, *The Tasks of a Workers Party* (reissued in 1903 by Comrade Kuklin), and published the story *The Spy*. The spring of 1898 saw the publication of *The Battle Cry*, a reprint from *Rabochee Znamia*, no. 1. In June the journal itself appeared.[2] Both

---

[1] This group was dominated by a number of revolutionaries who had previously studied in Kharkov either at the University or at the Technology Institute: I. M. Romm, Kh. Kh. Lur'e, I. Shilenger, and D. Gershanovich. This group ceased to exist after the large number of arrests carried out on 26 July 1898. (S. N. Valk, 'Peterburgskaia gruppa *Rabochego znameni*', in *Istoriko-revoliutsionnyi sbornik*, I, 127–8 and p. 147 n. 9; and his 'K dokumental'noi istorii "Rabochego znameni"', *Krasnaia letopis'*, nos. 2–3 (1922), p. 336.)

[2] The Group of Revolutionary Workers (*Gruppa Rabochikh Revoliutsionerov*) in Belostok was led by M. V. Lur'e. It was linked not only to the *Rabochee Znamia* group in St Petersburg but also to groups in Grodno and Kiev. It was

the *Rabochaia Mysl'* and the *Rabochee Znamia* groups tried to join forces with the St Petersburg Union, but their attempts failed because the 'veteran' members of the Union did not understand the new organizational problems and refused to tolerate the views expressed by *Rabochaia Mysl'* on the one hand and *Rabochee Znamia* on the other. Nevertheless, also at loggerheads with these 'veterans' were quite a number of newer members within the Union, who soon took over all its work. Thus three independent groups came to the fore in Petersburg in the autumn of 1897, and the political lull of 1897 did not continue into 1898.

At this time the most important work was conducted by the 'youngsters' in the Union. They were divided into two groups, which I shall call 'A' and 'B', and which were both at odds with the 'veterans'. Group A had its contacts chiefly at the Aleksandrovsk works, at Pal''s, and generally along the Shlissel'burg Road. Group B had contacts in Kolpino, at the Port shipyard, at the Ekaterinhof, Samsoniev, and Guk mills. Both groups issued leaflets in the name of the Union.

On 19 April, the May Day leaflets 'A Dream of May Day Eve' and 'The Strike of Lies', published by the Union Abroad, were spread throughout Petersburg, wherever the organization had contacts. A strike was called for 1 May at the Port shipyard on Galernyi Island. The workers assembled at the shipyard, but left work an hour or two later. There were violent words with the management; the workers themselves blew the shipyard whistle, streamed out into the street, and marched off toward the New Admiralty yard, to call out more workers there. The New Admiralty looked like a fortress under siege—the drawbridge was lifted, the gates were shut, and the port authorities stood at the gate. As a result, the strikers failed to halt work there. After some talk with the authorities, the crowd went home. Several days later

opposed to the reliance of the leading Social Democrats in St Petersburg, Vilna, and Kiev on 'economic' action. See B. L. Eidel'man, 'K istorii vozniknoveniia Rossiiskoi sots.-dem. rabochei partii', *Proletarskaia revoliutsiia*, no. 1 (1921), pp. 35–6; D. L. Gershanovich, 'Vospominaniia o gruppe "Rabochego znameni": O Moisee Vladimiroviche Lur'e', in *K dvadtsatipiatiletiiu Pervogo s"ezda partii 1898–1923* (Moscow, 1923), pp. 170–2; V. Akimov, 'Stroiteli budushchego', *Obrazovanie*, no. 4 (1907), p. 115; and S. Gel'man, 'Pervaia podpol'naia tipografiia gruppy *Rabochee Znamia*', *Katorga i ssylka*, no. 6 (27) (1926), pp. 46–52.

The publications of the Belostok group referred to here are: *Zadachi russkoi rabochei partii*, *Shpion (kartinka iz zhizni)*, and *Boevoi klich rabochego klassa*. All were first published by Lur'e's group in Belostok and republished abroad in the years 1899–1900.

two workers were dismissed and arrested, and the workers of some of the workshops were fined for absence on 1 May. On payday the Union distributed a large leaflet, almost a pamphlet, about the dismissal of the two workers and the working conditions at the Port shipyard generally. It dealt in detail with the complicated and confusing wage system which tended to reduce the workers' earnings, with the system of calculating overtime work, and with the frightful exploitation at the government plants.

The leaflet opened with the words: 'They say that it is easy to fish in muddy waters!' It declared that the workers' troubles were due to their failure to understand clearly who their enemies were; it explained the contradiction of interests between the proletariat and the bourgeoisie, and said that the latter depended on the strength of 'spies, soldiers, and gendarmes'. Despite this, it continued, the proletariat must wage its fight with the bosses.* The leaflet unleashed a real furore. A strike was ready to break out, but the management forestalled it by abolishing the fines and by openly initiating an inquiry into the abuses exposed in the leaflet.

At Guk's mill a leaflet also provoked the strike which had long been prepared by the workers' unrest.† The workers went to the office and won their chief demand. The strike was originally to be called immediately after the leaflet had appeared, but large numbers of police and gendarmes appeared as soon as it was distributed. 'With the leaflet in our hands', says one of the workers, 'we did not venture to continue the agitation and kept quiet.' Two days later the police were withdrawn, and the workers went to the office. They gained the introduction of a minimum wage. I believe that this was the only instance when textile workers presented a minimum-wage demand. A week later, using the same method, they won all the other demands contained in the leaflet.

---

* 'We, the workers, fraternally extend our hands to one another in the sight of all and say to you: "We are marching against you." . . . You hide like cowards behind the backs of spies, soldiers, and gendarmes—your loyal servants . . . Look around you: the sea of workers is surging everywhere, its waves are rising ever higher . . . An end will come to your kingdom—a kingdom of evil, darkness, poverty and violence . . . We also shall make merry, our day will come! Let us speak out! We demand: (1) the reinstatement of our dismissed comrades; (2) revocation of the fines for 1 May. . .' A number of other economic demands followed. (Written down from the words of Comrade L.)

† See *Listok rabotnika*, nos. 9–10 [pp. 20–1], for a description of the struggle of the Guk factory workers for a holiday on 2 February.

In Kolpino a proclamation was issued in connexion with the steep lowering of wage rates.* The machines in Kolpino work for the Port. The Port Commander, Verkhovskii, had long been hated by the workers, and the reduction in wage rates was the last straw. Their patience was at an end, and a strike began on 1 May. Groups of workers walked along the streets, singing revolutionary songs. Cossacks were brought in, and several clashes followed. Some four hundred persons were arrested; forty-six of these were sent to Petersburg to the House of Preliminary Detention.

Two leaflets were distributed at the Aleksandrovsk plant. The workers decided to come to work on 1 May, and then to walk out in a body. However, the gates were locked, and the yard teemed with police and gendarmes. Proclamations were also distributed in other places. There was ferment at Pal''s about holidays, and unrest at Voronin's,† the Gas Works, the Bone Products plant, and Gol'darbeiter's.‡

Such was the work conducted for the Union by its young members in Group B and Group A. By now *Rabochaia Mysl'* also had contacts at the Putilov plant, at the Obukhovskii plant, and in Kolpino. But most of its energies were concentrated on the newspaper, the third number of which was in preparation. The *Rabochee Znamia* group concentrated all its energies on its publications. In the spring it published its May Day proclamation, well written and printed. It suddenly became known that a Party Congress had taken place (in March 1898). A *Manifesto* appeared, and the Party published its May Day proclamation. The only group represented at the Congress was that of the 'veterans'. In other words, all the active groups had been ignored by the organizers of the Congress.[1]

The formal unification of the Party did not affect the factional relations in Petersburg. The effort to unite all groups was made not by the agents of the Congress, but by the youngsters. Despite the serious losses resulting from the arrests of 11–12 March, the groups succeeded in reaching an agreement, and joint work was planned for the autumn. The proposed agreement meant, broadly

---

* April 1898. See *Listok rabotnika*, nos. 9–10 [p. 19].

† On this women's rebellion [*babii bunt*], see *Listok rabotnika*, no. 7 [p. 6].

‡ I.e., Gol'darbeiter's textile factory. See *Listok rabotnika*, nos. 9–10, p. 21 and the leaflet of 21 January 1897.

[1] The sole delegate from St Petersburg to the First Party Congress was S. I. Radchenko. He was selected at a meeting of the inner core of the Union of Struggle by I. A. Sammer, L. N. Radchenko (née Baranskaia), and N. K. Krupskaia. (See Krupskaia, *Vospominaniia o Lenine*, p. 25.)

speaking, that agitation would be devoted to economic struggle while propaganda publications would raise political demands.

During the summer work continued and contacts were extended, but no proclamations were published. The only publication to appear was the third issue of *Rabochaia Mysl'*. New arrests took place on 29 July. The greatest losses were suffered by *Rabochee Znamia*. Moreover, its press in Belostok was seized. The arrests involved the Bund as well, and the illegal transport route to Petersburg had to be abandoned. *Rabochaia Mysl'* also suffered. The Petersburg Union lost the people who had held its various constituent elements together.

In the autumn, forces had to be gathered afresh. Group A gradually established closer relations with *Rabochee Znamia*. Group B established contacts with *Rabochaia Mysl'* and worked parallel with it.[1] But even at this time these two sides were so close to each other that Group A and Group B formally remained in one organization, the Union, and there were new talks about the unification of all groups. The existing disagreements were recognized, but it seemed possible to satisfy both factions within a single organization not by way of compromise but by a division of functions. It was proposed to publish two organs: *Rabochaia Mysl'*, for wide circles of workers, and *Rabochee Znamia*, with a pronounced political character, for the advanced strata. The central organization was to be composed of two members from the Union (actually Group B), two from *Rabochee Znamia* and Group A, two from *Rabochaia Mysl'*, and one from the veterans.

Thus the Union, as represented by its younger members, again came forward as the champion of the idea of democratic unification. The proposition worked out at this time (October 1898) by the Union Abroad—that we must 'take into account the different levels attained by the various strata of the proletariat'—described a situation which was well understood in Petersburg too. It was this situation which inspired the unification efforts and policies of the young Union.

The 'veterans' were determined to retain the right to make policy untrammelled and to control the affairs of the Union. The

[1] In the autumn of 1898 a leading member of what Akimov here calls 'Group A' was S. V. Andropov. He was also among those who later in the year refounded the *Rabochee Znamia* organization which had been destroyed by the arrests of July. Among those in Group B was N. N. Lokhov. (See Andropov's introduction to Nogin's letters, in *Proletarskaia revoliutsiia*, nos. 8–9 (31–2) (1924), pp. 325–6.)

'youngsters', groups A and B, in their struggle against the 'veterans' demanded 'democratic principles of organization' (this was the term they used), responsibility of the central group to all the members of the organization, controls, and the electoral principle. They argued that all active members who had direct contacts with the workers' groups and who therefore, in a sense, were representative of the labour movement, should participate in the central group. They also proposed that with the growth of the movement workers be brought into the central group. Among the workers the struggle went on throughout the autumn and ended in a victory of the youngsters.[1]

Rabochee Znamia at this time attained its greatest influence, thanks particularly to its ties with Group A. The circles at the Pal' and Maxwell cotton mills, the Putilov plant, and the Obukhovskii steel mill were under its influence. It was also instrumental in the strike organized at Maxwell's.

Leaflets (of Group A) were distributed at Pal''s. Other leaflets (of Group B) were spread at Gol'dberg's iron foundry, at Chesher's, and at Voronin's. The plan for the unification of all groups was fully worked out at a meeting on 10 December.[2] In the negotiations the Union (Group B) favoured the complete merger of all groups into a single organization—the Union of Struggle, which had now also become the Petersburg Committee of the Party. *Rabochee Znamia* and *Rabochaia Mysl'* wanted a federal union which would leave its constituent elements with full autonomy. The Union regarded the proposed agreement as the internal reform of a joint enterprise and as a step forward for the various organizations involved. It felt, therefore, that under these conditions the independent existence of *Rabochaia Mysl'* and *Rabochee Znamia* would be superfluous. The work done by *Rabochaia Mysl'*, the newspaper of the Petersburg workers, as well as the work done by *Rabochee Znamia*, were but the necessary and essential functions of a single local organization. On the other hand, the existence of independent organizations (*Rabochaia Mysl'* and *Rabochee Znamia*) would inevitably compel them both to engage in diverse local activities. Thus there would be three mutually exclusive and competing groups in Petersburg and an intensification of ideological and tactical

---

[1] The disagreements in the autumn of 1898 between the newcomers and the veterans, S. I. Radchenko and Nonna Feliksovna Ustinovich, have been described by Andropov (*Proletarskaia revoliutsiia*, nos. 8–9 (31–2) (1924), p. 326).

[2] This agreement of December 1898 was described by Peterburzhets (*Ocherk*, pp. 76–7).

disputes. On a number of questions there were disagreements, but these disagreements could and should exist side by side within one and the same organization. It was only with such an approach to unification and democratic organizational principles that the Union would seek to unite *Rabochaia Mysl'* and *Rabochee Znamia.*

Despite the fact that on the night of 14–15 December a new police raid wiped out *Rabochee Znamia,* an agreement was reached by the remaining organizations at the end of December. *Rabochaia Mysl'* became the organ of the Committee and was joined by many *intelligenty.* An outline was drawn up for an article on the Maxwell mill, but the editorial in *Rabochaia Mysl',* no. 5, which was written abroad, had nothing in common with the outline. The editorial was greatly disliked, and the issue was not distributed for an entire month, despite the fact that it had been delivered to Petersburg.

After the agreement *Rabochaia Mysl'* ceased to exist in Petersburg as an independent group. New members drawn to *Rabochaia Mysl'* joined the Union directly. The Union of Struggle (the Petersburg Committee of the Party) thus became the only organization in the capital which united all the remaining groups (*Rabochee Znamia* had been destroyed before it could join) and all the available Social Democratic forces. It was also joined by a number of propagandists who until now had worked alone [*odinochki*] and who had firm ties among the workers. Moreover, the influx of funds increased.

Newly united by the agreement of December 1898, the Union of Struggle (the Petersburg Committee of the Party) began in January to work out its plans for the coming May Day campaign. It was decided to publish long questionnaires for agitators and two short ones specifically for the steel and textile workers. The information thus collected was to serve as the basis for a series of leaflets to be issued before May to various factories. In April two general leaflets were to be published for the engineering and textile workers. And, finally, there was to be a general proclamation for 1 May summing up the results of the year's work, bringing together the appeals made in the specialized leaflets, and calling for a general strike on 1 May. The questionnaires were published abroad in the form of small booklets; two special leaflets were printed in Russia. A number of proclamations were printed and distributed at Thornton's, the Volynkovskii factory, Chesher's, Samsoniev's, the Aleksandrovsk works, and other factories. But a large number of arrests followed.

The entire Group X[1] was wiped out in the beginning of March. On 20 March, a part of Group B was rounded up. On 16 April the group at the Technology Institute was arrested.[2] On 19 April several members of *Rabochaia Mysl'* were seized while transporting a load of illegal literature. The general leaflets were not issued at all, and the demands that were to be raised in them were published in the May Day proclamation.[3] The proclamation, incidentally, was quite different from the one planned. According to the initial plan the proclamation was to speak about the international significance of the 1 May holiday, the political goals of the Social Democratic movement, and the eight-hour working day. Only in order to encourage an immediate general strike was it also to raise the demand for a law guaranteeing the ten-hour workday.*

The comrades evidently had in mind two previous experiments in producing May Day leaflets. In 1896 'many workers said that if it had not been for the May Day leaflet there would have been no May strikes . . . This view is exaggerated, but it is typical' (Peterburzhets, p. 26). In 1898 the Party's May Day leaflet, excellently produced and containing very good demands, had no effect, but the May Day leaflets of the Union of Struggle distributed at Guk's,

[1] Group X may possibly be the agitators' group of the St Petersburg Union. Among those arrested on the night of 9–10 March 1899 were N. L. Barabanshchikov and A. G. Bezrukova, both members of this group (*Rabochee delo*, no. 1 (1899), p. 149).

[2] This group included M. N. Gorbachev, Sergei Kirpichnikov, Vladimir Noskov, and Vasilii Fominich. (*Rabochee delo*, nos. 2–3 (1899), sect. II, p. 96.)

[3] The May Day proclamation (1899) of the St Petersburg Union was reproduced in V. P. Ivanshin's article, 'Maiskii prazdnik v Rossii v 1899 g.', *Rabochee delo*, nos. 2–3, sect. I, pp. 15–16.

* The first issue of *Zaria* called the demand for a ten-hour workday in the Petersburg proclamation 'a betrayal of international Social Democracy'. The charge was too serious to be used so lightly in party literature against one of the party committees. Moreover, Plekhanov, Aksel'rod, and Zasulich, who were closely participating in the publication of *Zaria*, should have remembered that they had done exactly the same only a year earlier: the May Day leaflet of 1898, published under the editorship of the Group for the Emancipation of Labour, contained a demand, printed in the largest type, for this very ten-hour day. The Bund at the analogous stage of development, in 1895, had also raised the demand for a ten-hour workday in its 1 May proclamations. [In his article, 'Pervoi maia v Rossii', *Byloe*, no. 10 (1906), pp. 178–9, Akimov quotes in full the Group for the Emancipation of Labour's demand for a ten-hour day made in one of its May Day proclamations. But there he gives the date of the proclamation as 1897, not 1898. In the proclamation published by the Group for May Day, 1898, Plekhanov in fact called for an eight-hour day (G. Plekhanov, 'Nash svetlyi prazdnik', *Rabotnik: Maiskii listok 1898 g.* (Geneva, 1898), p. 6.]

the Port shipyard, and Kolpino provoked unrest.* The pre-May campaign of 1899 was excellently planned, and it was not through any fault of the comrades that it was not carried out.

At the height of these events the Group for the Self-Emancipation of the Working Class was formed in March. It was wiped out several months later by the mass arrests which followed when the authorities discovered that one of their new prisoners had in his possession a list of the workers implicated. This group formulated its basic position in a proclamation issued in April 1899. 'The Union, which is made up of *intelligenty*, has really most touching intentions. But it keeps out of its organization precisely those whose interests it undertakes to "defend" . . . The workers must at last take their own cause into their own hands.'

We are not throwing political struggle overboard, for we remember all too clearly that political freedom is one of the conditions for the triumph of the working-class. But we do not want political agitation to hang in mid-air; we want it to be linked with the immediate, realistic needs of the working-class, to answer the pressing demands of the moment. Politics are the superstructure which rests on the social relations of production, and political agitation should be the superstructure which serves the economic struggle; politics must grow out of this struggle and follow it. Propaganda is a different matter. Here our political ideals can and should be developed to their full scale.[1]

It would be difficult in a few lines to improve on this document's brief summary of the character and tactics of the entire third period: organization along democratic lines and proclamations which demanded no more than civil rights.

In the pre-publication announcement of *Iskra*, it was said that the emergence of the Group for Self-Emancipation proved that the

---

* It is most interesting to compare these documents. They reflect with utmost clarity the contradiction between the two trends which then were already in conflict in our Party, and which still stand opposed to each other. I regret that considerations of space prevent their inclusion *in toto*.

[1] This proclamation first published, together with a highly critical introduction by E. Serebriakov, in the journal *Nakanune: Sotsial'no-revoliutsionnoe obozrenie* (London), no. 7 (July, 1899), pp. 78–80, was reproduced by E. Mikhailova as an appendix to her article 'Iz kommentariev k *Chto delat'?*, gruppa samoosvobozhdeniia rabochego klassa', *Krasnaia letopis'*, 1 (12) (1925), pp. 243–4. According to her, among the leading members of the Group for the Self-Emancipation of the Working Class were K. A. Popov, V. A. Kozhevnikov, and Vera Davidovna Gurari. Another member mentioned by V. O. Tsederbaum was V. A. Gutovskii (Evgenii Maevskii). (See V. O. Levitskii, *Za chetvert' veka*, vol. I, part 1: *Revoliutsionnaia podgotovka 1892–1901 gg.* (Moscow, 1926), p. 103 n.)

ideas of the 'Credo' had been influential.[1] As the above quotation shows, the Group for Self-Emancipation had nothing in common with the 'Credo'. To be exact, it expressed diametrically opposite views. The fact that *Iskra* could confuse these two viewpoints shows graphically how poorly it understood the events then taking place and how it confused all thinking about the Party's historical development. Today only the publicists of the 'new *Iskra*' raise as something novel the slogan of the Petersburg workers of 1899, 'Down with self-appointed representatives!' ['*Doloi zamestitel' stvo*'].

As I have said, the arrests of the spring of 1899 greatly weakened all organizations. In the autumn the leading rôle in agitation among workers was assumed by the Group of Twenty.[2] A number of people, unwilling to be bound by the traditions of the old groups, proposed to publish their own organ. In their views, they considered themselves more akin to the *Rabochee Znamia* Group than to any other. This group managed to gather together people with good contacts and to unify fourteen workers' circles. It issued two proclamations and, in January 1900, *Rabochii Listok* [*Labour News Sheet*].[3] The first blow was struck at this group on 4 October, when eleven comrades were arrested. In early spring unrest among the students absorbed all the energies of the group; the arrests of 13 March and 29 April 1900 brought the work to a total standstill.

Such was the complicated course followed by the factional disputes during the third stage of the movement in Petersburg. I shall try to summarize it briefly. At the beginning of the third stage—so-called Economism—the work was conducted chiefly by the Union, but at the same time *Rabochaia Mysl'* and *Rabochee*

---

[1] In the editorial pronouncement, 'Ot redaktsii', attached to *Iskra*, no. 1 (as in Lenin's *Chto delat'?*, p. 32), the Group for Self-Emancipation was denounced as guilty of extreme 'Economism'.

[2] According to the accounts of E. Broido (Gordon), Levitskii, and M. Logacheva-Piletskaia, who had all belonged to revolutionary circles in St Petersburg in the years 1899–1900, the following were among the leading members of the Group of Twenty: N. I. Iordanskii, P. E. Shchegolev, I. I. Ladyzhenskii, S. N. Saltykov, Boris Savinkov, and Mar'ia Vil'iamovna Kistiakovskaia (née Berenshtam). Marta Furman, a member of the *Rabochee Znamia* group in St Petersburg, told the police after her arrest that during the winter of 1900–1 she had conducted unsuccessful negotiations with Sergei Dmitrievich L'vov for unification with the Group of Twenty. Levitskii, *Za chetvert' veka*, p. 103 n.; Logacheva-Piletskaia, in *Byloe*, no. 3 (31) (1925), pp. 95–6; E. Broido (Gordon), in *Letopis' revoliutsii* (Berlin, 1923), i, 127. Marta Furman is quoted by Valk in *Istoriko-revoliutsionnyi sbornik*, i, 154.

[3] First used for the publication of the Group of Twenty in January 1900, the title was taken over later in the year by the St Petersburg Workers Organization for its own paper.

2. *PETERSBURG*

Znamia also developed and gained strength. The spirit of the time made itself felt in the Union too. The younger members of the Union were not united in their views: Group A inclined toward *Rabochee Znamia*, and Group B toward *Rabochaia Mysl'*. Group C —the 'veterans'—was displeased with everything and lost touch with active work.* At the end of this period, in the spring of 1899, the Union succeeded in unifying the entire work in Petersburg, but numerous arrests once again nullified this achievement.

Having outlined the main developments in the history of the organizations in Petersburg, I shall now discuss the tactics of the Petersburg comrades from 1897 to 1900.

It became apparent that a new period had begun when the Union felt driven to raise demands in its leaflets for civil rights—freedom to strike, freedom of assembly, free speech and press, and inviolability of person. The Union had no time for demands that could not be backed up by power. It was futile to raise 'demands' that clearly could not be realized. Such demands are mere wishes. Of course, it said, we must make propaganda for our aspirations; but only those aspirations which can be backed up by sufficient forces and means should be raised as demands. Agitation is a call to war. Leaflets raise demands and guide the war. Hence, in our publications we must make propaganda for universal, equal, and secret electoral rights; but it would be futile and misplaced to set forth this aim in a leaflet as a demand when it is known beforehand that the workers will do nothing to defend this demand, and when the organization itself does not explain how this wish is to be achieved. Such was the attitude of the Union.

Inevitably, the question occurs: can civil rights be attained under an autocratic régime?

We knew very well [I was told by a comrade from Group B] that they were not attainable given the autocracy. But we felt that these demands would logically, organically, lead the workers to a demand for broader political rights. This was a consciously chosen method to provide the masses with a practical political education. It is absurd to think that we reconciled ourselves to absolutism at the time, and merely demanded concessions from it. It was clear to everyone that this was only an agitational device which would lead to the overthrow of the autocracy.

* Lenin's view that 'the original policy of the Union of Struggle was dominant in Petersburg, at any rate until 1898', is entirely unfounded and erroneous. [The group labelled 'C' by Akimov was that small nucleus surrounding S. I. Radchenko in the years 1897–1900.]

265

In this, however, the Union differed from *Rabochee Znamia*, which found it possible and necessary to give first place to the call for the overthrow of absolutism, to issue leaflets of a sharply political character, and to publish a political newspaper.

But then an event occurred that was subsequently widely discussed in our press and that still remains unexplained. The organized workers at Maxwell's prepared a leaflet and turned it over to the agitators for printing. The Maxwell factory was one of those in which the *Rabochee Znamia* group was active. The leaflets were issued in the name of the Union of Struggle. Hence the leaflet of 13 December was to have been published by Group A of the 'young' members of the Union. This group was sharply political in character; it was not satisfied with the Union, and still less with *Rabochaia Mysl'*. Moreover, Group A had in practice gone over to *Rabochee Znamia*, whose very *raison d'être* was the fact that it emphasized the need for political action.[1] How could it have happened, then, that this group *deleted* from the workers' leaflet the demand for the right to strike and assemble?

And yet it was obvious that the workers had included these demands deliberately and were annoyed when they were left out of the leaflet. When a factory inspector came to them on 15 December and asked what they wanted, voices from the crowd replied that they wanted the things demanded in the leaflets and also freedom to strike and assemble. This occurred during that memorable strike which ended with the 'battle for justice'.*

This incident has usually been cited to show 'the lengths to which the Economists sometimes go'. But the important thing about it is precisely that it involved people who were *not* Economists and who sought for an occasion to act differently from the Economists. I can explain it to myself only by the supposition that *Rabochee Znamia* considered itself too political to raise 'immediate' and 'partial' political demands—in other words, to raise demands for civil rights under the autocratic régime.

---

[1] The *Rabochee Znamia* group at the end of 1898 was led by the following revolutionaries, many of whom had previously been members of what Akimov calls 'Group A' of the St Petersburg Union: S. V. Andropov, M. B. Smirnov, V. P. Nogin, Lidiia Osipovna Kantsel' (née Tsederbaum), Ol'ga Appolonovna Zvezdochetova, and S. O. Tsederbaum (Ezhov). See Valk, in *Krasnaia letopis'*, nos. 2–3 (1922), p. 337; and Levitskii, *Za chetvert' veka*, pp. 102–10.

* This was how a worker described the events of 14 December. His story was published by Peterburzhets on page 108 of his booklet. [A summary of] the leaflet referred to may be found in *Rabochee delo*, no. 1 [p. 79].

Only this supposition can explain the fact that those who in theory placed extreme emphasis on politics proved, over a long period in their practical work, to be politically more moderate than the so-called Economists. It was still impossible to urge in *proclamations* the overthrow of the autocracy as an immediate goal. This was felt by everyone. At the same time, to raise demands for 'partial' political rights was regarded by the 'politicians' as a compromise. Subsequent events demonstrated that the tactics of the so-called Economists were correct, for they led to their objective—the struggle against the existing political order. The fact cited above shows, too, that only these tactics were possible, for those of their opponents led *in reality* to political inaction.

The *Rabochee Znamia* group never had any firm or substantial ties with workers and could act only while a third group (beside the Union) existed in Petersburg—first the Group of Technology Students, then Group A, then the Group of Twenty, and finally the Socialist Group.[1] Given the practical programme of *Rabochee Znamia*, which consisted, properly speaking, only of 'training conscious agitators in the propaganda circles', it was impossible then, and will always remain impossible, to create a firm organization. *Rabochee Znamia* had its adherents chiefly among the intelligentsia; it was supported also by the Polish Socialist Party— the PPS. The viewpoint represented by *Rabochee Znamia* has been replaced or, to be more precise, is being continued by *Iskra*-ism. And just as *Rabochee Znamia* was alien and unconnected with the workers' movement in Petersburg, so *Iskra*-ism has withdrawn from the workers' movement in Russia, has opened a gap between the Social Democrats and the working-class.

When the Party had passed beyond the stage of so-called Economism this period was subjected to a myopic critique. The stress then laid on strikes [*stachkizm*] was not recognized as a tremendously significant expression of purely proletarian, albeit primitive, warfare. As for the political significance of the events I have described, at the time, they were judged at their true worth

[1] This argument of Akimov was severely criticized by Valk, who saw it as an example of the former's tendency to exaggerate the isolation of the extreme 'political' wing of the Social Democratic movement from the workers. Valk was convinced that in the years 1897–8 the Group of Technology Students was, in fact, identical with the *Rabochee Znamia* group. (Valk, in *Istoriko-revoliutsionnyi sbornik*, I, 147 n.)

even by our enemy—the government—and even by people who favoured only 'politics'.

In the journal *Nashe Vremia* [*Our Time*], published by the People's Rights society [*Narodnoe Pravo*], which was concerned solely with the political struggle, we read the following about the strikes of 1897 and early 1898:

The facts are all of a kind, even monotonous. To some readers they may seem altogether uninteresting; the same thing over and over again: reductions in piece rates, impositions and abuses, demands for penny increases, strikes . . . and, as a result, either penny concessions to the workers, or defeat and a sullen return to work under the old conditions . . . Indeed —the same, grey, 'undramatic' events! Grey and undramatic, like our entire life, like everything we do. Yet . . . the most humdrum, the greyest strike, however dull its story may seem, is an event of enormous, of vital significance to all its participants, and not to the participants alone. Whoever was in Petersburg in the summer of 1897, whoever saw and heard what was happening and what was being said in the streets of our capital during the general strike of the textile workers, will probably agree with us. Those alert, excited faces, that heightened tone in the conversations of people accustomed to silent labour . . . Everyone speaking loudly, asserting that they would not yield until they won. And you felt that within the most ordinary, most average member of this crowd a man had awakened. Amidst the total and age-old silence, you heard a single protesting voice, the voice of the worker. His speech was still incoherent, still primitive, still expressed only immediate needs and 'crude' material interests. But it was the speech of men, not slaves! The cause of freedom had been born and was growing. And the effect of such events on other social groups could also be observed in the streets. The most modest, the most humdrum strike is a great event as an element of the future.*

Agitation through leaflets, as we have seen, was continued by the Union and Group B in exactly the same spirit as before. But in other spheres work was taking on a new form different from that of the Union when run by the veterans. The 'youngsters', the so-called Economists, now set themselves up in opposition to the 'veterans'. They differed in their approach to the working-class, the various strata of workers, the workers' needs, and the workers' independent activities. They disagreed about the organizations emerging among the workers, the party structure (to be built from 'above' or from 'below'), the principle of democratic organization, the programme, propaganda, and agitation. They also differed in

* 'Russkoe rabochee dvizhenie v 1897 godu i v nachale 1898 goda', *Nashe vremia*, no. 2 (1898), pp. 34–6 (published by *Narodnoe Pravo*).

their attitude toward the intelligentsia, toward liberal society (toward Aksel'rod's pamphlets, the ultimate conclusion from which has only just recently been drawn by *Iskra*-ism in the 'Letter to the Party Organizations'), toward the economic and the political struggle. The disagreements on all these questions made themselves felt and were understood; unfortunately, they did not find their way into print at the time. The conflict between the Union Abroad and the Group for the Emancipation of Labour (the 'veterans' of the colony abroad) was often reminiscent, even in detail, of the conflict between the groupings in Petersburg. But it was only at the very end that even the Union Abroad took a stand on principle and developed the ideas which were sensed in the air in Petersburg from 1898 to 1900.

The agitational tactics of the so-called Economist period were twice brilliantly vindicated by history. First, they permitted the Social Democrats to lead the proletarian masses in their class struggle. Even the opponents of these tactics admitted that they 'revolutionized the moods and the minds of the proletariat' (Aksel'rod). Second, the opposite tactics, followed by *Iskra*-ism, weakened the ties between the proletariat and the Social Democratic movement and culminated in total fiasco.* Nevertheless, the foes of so-called Economism assert that such ties had been created at the price of bringing Social Democracy down to the level of the masses, at the price of deserting the principles of revolutionary Social Democracy. This is profoundly untrue. While the agitation of the Union of Struggle transformed 'the moods and

---

* Comrade Aksel'rod states that 'during the period of so-called Economism, our movement struck deep roots in the proletariat, revolutionized the moods and the minds of considerable circles within it and stimulated their revolutionary activity' (*Iskra*, no. 55). He says further in the same article: 'Thus the result of the party struggle between revolutionary Social Democrats (*Iskra*) and the parochialists [*kustarnichestvo*] has been the triumph of bureaucratic centralism in the party organization. In short, the ideological crust is revolutionary Social Democratic, but the real content, in essence and principle, scarcely transcends the framework of bourgeois revolutionism.' Having become convinced, during the fourth period, that the paper on which *Iskra* is printed will bear anything, Aksel'rod comes to the following conclusion: 'The major facts have thus graphically and clearly vindicated the criticism of the theory and practice of so-called Economism, which was initiated by the publications of the Group for the Emancipation of Labour and was continued by *Iskra*.' I can only add to this that Comrade Aksel'rod does not cite these 'major' facts or indeed any other facts, contenting himself with a discourse on what 'could have' happened. [See P. Aksel'rod, 'Ob"edinenie rossiiskoi sotsial'demokratii i eia zadachi', *Iskra*, no. 55 (15 December 1903), pp. 2–5.]

the minds of the proletariat', its propaganda brought to the
proletariat a knowledge of scientific socialism. And in this
respect the period of 1898–9 unquestionably witnessed a step
forward.

The oldest Petersburg programme for systematic propaganda I
have been able to discover belongs to 1896. It is entitled *A Study
Programme for the Petersburg Workers' Circles* and contains
seventeen lectures. The last of these lectures is a conclusion, and
the last but one deals with the history of the socialist movement
in Western Europe. In the footnote below I quote the outline for
the fifteenth lecture.* It leaves no doubt that its writers were
socialists and regarded the political struggle as one of the means of
achieving their objectives. Consequently, there is no suggestion
here that our principles were being lowered to the level of mass
understanding. On the contrary, the propagandists raised the
workers in the circles to the level where they clearly understood
Social Democratic principles.

This applies in still greater measure to the period from 1897 to
1900. In order to improve its propaganda work, the Union, in the
autumn of 1898, undertook to prepare *A Programme for Self-
Education*, which, like the 'Questions' in agitation, would systematize and unify all propaganda work. The experience of the preceding years showed that the longer and more detailed the
programme for courses of study and lectures, the less they
achieved. The lecture form generally did not satisfy the workers.
Police conditions in Petersburg permit only small groups to gather
periodically; besides, the composition of the groups is always
changing. A revolutionary's period of activity is too short; the
arrest of a propagandist removes his skill and experience from the
scene, and the continuity of the propaganda work is broken.

In preparing *A Programme for Self-Education*, the Union sought

---

* Fifteenth lecture. The workers' movement and the tactics to be used by both
agricultural and industrial workers for better living conditions (strikes,
unions, funds, arbitration courts, boycott, May Day celebrations). The
importance of the various strata of the proletariat for the class struggle. The
attitude of Russian law toward the workers' struggle for their existence.

Self-awareness—the idea of the working-class and self-emancipation;
universal suffrage and political struggle, the significance of parliament for
the proletariat. The importance of legislation in safeguarding concessions
already gained by the workers. The policy to subject all the means of
production, distribution, and exchange to democratic control, and the idea
of socialization of the means of production.

The attitude of our régime toward the self-awareness and self-emancipation
of the workers, and the attitude of the workers to the existing order.

to make propaganda a collective undertaking, to have the pro-gramme embody accumulated personal experience and elaborate on it. Moreover, aware of the fact that as the movement grew it was constantly outstripping the influx of educated manpower and that the influence of the propagandist was confined to small circles, the Union wanted the workers to run their own propaganda activity. With the aid of this programme, the Union hoped to help the workers educate themselves without making them wait for the propagandist to answer every question. In this way it expected to give the more educated workers an opportunity to exert a system-atic influence on those less advanced. In turn, this would enable the propagandists to put their energies to another urgent task: the organization of *ad hoc* lectures and discussions on current events and on special problems of propaganda and tactics. It was not until several years later that the Petersburg comrades managed to make this plan a reality: in 1901 the Workers Organization [*Rabochaia Organizatsiia*] published a series of propagandist pamphlets, *Problems of Russian Life* and *Letters about How Things Work and Don't Work*, which represented the first attempt to conduct a systematic propaganda course by the printed word.[1]

The character of *A Programme for Self-Education* was deter-mined above all by the need to train conscious Social Democrats. It was decided not to depart far from the present day, not to begin with problems of the universe, Darwin's theory, or primitive culture, as had been the custom earlier, but to start with a general vivid description of the classes and social groups in modern society and its fundamental contradictions. The question, 'What Do People Live By?' was posed at the outset. The answer was given first in the most general terms, in descriptions of modern exploita-tion of the working people and in a statement of the socialist ideal. After that, other problems were raised: the origin of the capitalist system, the economic evolution and social differentiation of Europe, the changes of political forms since the Great Revolution, social and political movements in Europe, the economic condition of Russia and its political system, the revolutionary movement

[1] The brochures *Voprosy russkoi zhizni* and *Pis'ma pro nashi poriadki i neporiadki* were composed by a specialized 'literary group' which amal-gamated with the St Petersburg Union of Struggle (the Workers Organiza-tion) in the spring of 1901. Among its members were V. P. Krasnukha, M. L. Kheisin, Lidiia Vasil'evna Shcheglova, and E. O. Konevaia. See L. Shcheglo, 'Rabochaia Mysl'', *Katorga i ssylka*, nos. 4–5 (101–2) (1933), pp. 80–2; and Logacheva-Piletskaia, in *Byloe*, no. 3 (31) (1925), p. 98.

in Russia, the international Social Democratic movement, the Social Democratic programme. A detailed study of the Erfurt programme with the aid of Kautsky's book was suggested as a summing up of this short course in self-education.

The text of the programme was in the form of a conspectus. On each topic there were footnotes referring to legal and illegal publications, which were listed in order from easy to difficult and divided into three sections. By taking the first part, one obtained a bibliography and an explanatory text for workers with little cultural background; the second part was suitable for intermediate groups; and the third part was for the more advanced. Such bibliographies combined with the *Programme for Self-Education* made it possible to bring the entire Social Democratic programme to all strata of the working-class. All that was required was to vary the difficulty of the course. Since the available literature, legal and illegal, was inadequate, a series of small pamphlets was planned on various propaganda questions. The Union tried to recruit comrades in exile and abroad to write these pamphlets and to elaborate the programme. It also sought the aid of writers outside the revolutionary underground for the publication of legal pamphlets. The plans were extensive, perhaps even too extensive. But at any rate, they certainly did not reveal that indifference to theory which has been so shamelessly attributed to so-called Economism by Social Democrats who forget their origins.

A special group was formed to draw up and develop the programme, including several persons who were not members of the Union but who were well equipped by their talents and experience to lend assistance. The Union appealed for assistance to several committees. The upsurge of the student movement and the mass arrests in the spring interrupted this work. It has not yet been completed.

And so these were the practical objectives which the young Union of 1898–9 set itself: (1) to unify all Social Democratic groups and forces of Petersburg into a single organization—The Union of Struggle (The Petersburg Committee of the Party)— which would be based on a division of functions and on a democratic organization; (2) to strengthen and systematize agitation (the 'Questions' and a series of leaflets); (3) to intensify and systematize propaganda ('A Programme for Self-Education' and a series of pamphlets); (4) a journal for the working masses—

2. *PETERSBURG*

Rabochaia Mysl'; (5) a journal for advanced workers—*Rabochee Znamia*; (6) the May Day general strike in St Petersburg.

I shall now give a brief description of the *Rabochaia Mysl'* group —brief, because we already have the specialized work of Comrade Peterburzhets on this question. The peculiar and characteristic trait of the *Rabochaia Mysl'* group was that it strove consciously to make its newspaper mirror exactly the ideas of the Petersburg workers. '*Rabochaia Mysl'* will reflect the workers' life in its true light. It will help to awaken in them an interest in their surroundings, to express their needs, and to overwhelm our tyrannical system [*oprichina*] with contempt and ridicule.'[1] These were the concluding words of the leading article in the first number, which set forth the objectives of the editors.

For decades the Russian socialists sought to make the workers think for themselves. And gradually the mind of the worker came to life. From the days of Khalturin, the workers' thoughts tried to break out, to shape themselves in words, to manifest themselves in a workers' newspaper. For a long, long time they failed, crushed as it were in the vice of the autocratic political régime. At last, on the peripheries of Russia, in Vilna and Petersburg, the workers managed in the same year to create their own newspapers,[2] *Arbeter Shtime* and *Rabochaia Mysl'*. The Jewish *intelligenty*— Social Democrats—caught the voice of the workers, supported it, made it loud, strong and glorious. But it was actually the orthodox wing of the 'revolutionary' Social Democrats that ridiculed and condemned the thinking of the Petersburg worker. True, his ideas were untutored, clumsy, unsubtle! Nevertheless, it is a matter for rejoicing that there were Social Democrats, *Economists*, in Petersburg who supported and served those workers who thought for themselves! For this they should be forgiven all the errors that were forced upon them on this difficult road.*

[1] Quoted from *Rabochaia mysl'*, no. 1, in Peterburzhets, *Ocherk*, p. 85.
[2] For descriptions of how the workers in Kolpino came together with those at the Obukhovskii plant to produce *Rabochaia mysl'*, see Ia. A. Andreev, '1897–1898 gg. v Kolpine', *Proletarskaia revoliutsiia*, no. 2 (14) (1923), pp. 77–83.
* Several years later the Voronezh workers wrote a letter to the [Social Democratic] committees about the question of organizing the Second Congress. *Iskra* ridiculed the letter as 'illiterate'. 'Yes, it is true that we had no time to learn enough grammar', replied the Voronezh workers to this criticism. [For these letters from Voronezh, see *Vtoroi s"ezd RSDRP: Protokoly* (Moscow, 1959), pp. 729–32 and 738–41.]

The so-called Economists are accused of 'lowering socialism to the level of the mass mind' by creating a newspaper which merely expressed the thinking of the workers, instead of introducing the workers to new ideas. 'Perhaps it is a mistake', says Peterburzhets at the end of his pamphlet, 'to conduct a workers' newspaper along these lines. But this is an altogether different question, which we shall perhaps discuss elsewhere at some other time.' It seems to me that there can be only one answer to this question: such newspapers are not enough for the Social Democratic movement, but they are enormously important and necessary, for the thinking of the workers can develop only on the condition (though not the sole condition) that the workers have an opportunity to formulate their ideas.* Indeed, is it only the working-class which needs such a newspaper?

The first issue of the radical-democratic newspaper *Osvobozhdenie* [*Liberation*] carried an editorial which contained the following lines:

To give literary expression to ideas which have already formed and matured—such is our aim. We would be quite content if we had nothing more to do than simply record the political ideas which had been freely formulated in Russia; if, here abroad, we could just print the words of liberty emerging from Russia, and act as mere typesetters and printers.[1]

Iskra (no. 23) cites these words of *Osvobozhdenie* as evidence that the editor of the latter 'is too moderate, too non-revolutionary even to urge forward the liberal democrats'. *Iskra* finds in this a con-

---

* People are constantly attributing to me the view that the Social Democratic movement at every stage of its development is merely a reflection of the moods and views of the working-class at a particular historical moment. I have never said this. I hope that my subsequent works will show that I attribute a far greater creative significance to ideas than do my factional opponents. But even the formula employed by my organization, the Union Abroad, to express its attitude toward theory acknowledges its prime importance: 'Social Democrats can only be effective if they guide themselves not only by the general principles of scientific socialism, but also by the general political conditions and the degree of development of the labour movement' ('Instructions for the Editorial Committee' ['Instruktsii dlia redaktsii'], *Rabochee delo*, 1901). [(A. S. Martynov), *Dva s"ezda: Tretii ocherednoi s"ezd Soiuza i 'ob"edinitel'nyi' s"ezd* (Geneva, 1901), p. 15.] Thus we consider that the first condition for effective Social Democratic action is to be guided by the principles of scientific socialism. But our opponents have been doctrinaire about the doctrine by which we wish to guide ourselves. They have become entangled in contradictions, between doctrines and reality, and we therefore consider it essential to stress that Social Democrats as men of action must reckon with the realities of the time.

[1] 'Ot redaktora', *Osvobozhdenie*, no. 1 (18 June 1902), p. 6.

firmation of the idea that 'every bourgeoisie is a stern "master" to the political and literary spokesmen of its class, to its "ideologists"—a master who seeks to turn the ideologists into mere "recorders", mere coolies at its own service.'[1] By its ironic quotation marks, *Iskra* is saying: what kind of 'ideologists' are these, after all, when they are merely 'recorders' and 'coolies'?

Nevertheless, not all the 'orthodox' Social Democrats responded in this way to Struve's statement. Here is what Comrade Riazanov, whom Plekhanov characterized as an 'orthodox pedant', wrote about it:

We hail you, Mr P. Struve! We shall certainly have no criticism of you if you merely record the uncensored political thinking of the bourgeoisie. We, too, should like simply to record the uncensored political thought of the working-class. We are proud to be the spokesmen for the interests of the working-class, proud to formulate as best we can its political ideas, which must be ours as well. We always reply with contempt when various 'important' people accuse us of being coolies in the service of the proletariat. And we can only rejoice that our bourgeoisie has found a man who openly and directly declares that he is the servant of the 'moderate fathers'.*

Still, the *Iskra* editors—or at least half of them—should have remembered that they too had a different view on this question when *Rabotnik* began publication in 1896:

We address our modest publication to the new, working-class Russia, which is our joy, our pride. We shall devote it entirely to the interests of the working-class. We shall not impose our views upon the workers who read our publication. We do not assume the rôle of leaders. We only want to be as useful as we can to those dispossessed but energetic and courageous labourers who are fighting in our distant and unhappy homeland for their economic and political freedom. The pages of our publication will be open to all workers who wish to discuss their problems and to express their aspirations. But we are firmly convinced that the more clearly our readers come to understand the tasks that await them and the significance of their own situation, the more resolutely they will rally to the Social Democratic banner (*Rabotnik*, no. 1, 1896, p. xiv).

The Group for the Emancipation of Labour not only stated its readiness 'not to impose its views', but even refused the 'rôle of leaders'! That was going too far! And so, the fact that *Rabochaia Mysl'* strove merely to mirror the workers' thinking cannot in itself be branded as an error of the so-called Economists.

[1] 'Programma russkikh liberalov', *Iskra*, no. 23 (1 Aug. 1902), p. 1.
* N. Riazanov, *Materialy* [*dlia vyrabotki partiinoi programmy*], II [*Proekt programmy 'Iskry' i zadachi russkikh sotsial'demokratov* (Geneva, 1903)], 127.

Let us see now whether and how the *political* thought of the Petersburg workers was reflected in *Rabochaia Mysl'*. In a separate supplement to no. 7 of *Rabochaia Mysl'* (September 1899) the theoretician of *Rabochaia Mysl'*, an *intelligent*, offers the following definition of the concept of 'political warfare': 'We consider it political warfare when the workers fight for the common good, for labour legislation to improve the position—be it material or legal —of all the workers.' And so *Rabochaia Mysl'* designates as political those rights which are guaranteed by law for an entire group of citizens. But this is true of all rights, and therefore it is not a specific characteristic of political rights. Thus the definition given by *Rabochaia Mysl'* is obviously wrong. It contains no hint of the fact that political warfare is a struggle for power, or for the right to share power. But the necessity to fight for civil rights— the rights of personal and social freedom—was included in this definition, and was mentioned by *Rabochaia Mysl'* from its very first issue. And this, as I have said before, is characteristic of the stage we are now examining. I shall cite in support of my assertion several passages from *Rabochaia Mysl'* which deal with the fight against the government.

Rabochaia Mysl', no. 1: We see before us the dark wall of the monarchic régime, which prevents the light from reaching us. We know all the discomfort of living in the dark . . . The wall of the present régime is strong, and the arbitrary rule of Tsarism is invincible—but it is invincible only if attacked by scattered forces which are so small that they easily fall victim to arbitrary power. The situation will be quite different when against the lawless rule of the capitalists and the government is launched a united power—the power wielded by the working-class when it knows its own strength. Its just demands must be fulfilled.[1]

No. 2: The government openly and without shame takes the side of the capitalists. With the aid of the police and the army, with arms in hand, it tries to force the workers back under their intolerable yoke. Thus we must fight two enemies: the factory owners, and the government which defends them.[2]

No. 3: The government and the employers have united to fight against the workers. Through the joint efforts of the police, the troops, and the clergy they are able to suppress the workers' demands. It is clear that in order to repulse this hostile alliance we must form a union of the working-class.[3]

No. 7: The strikes of 1896 are in a sense a transition from the former fragmentary struggle of the workers to political warfare. . .[4] Down

---

[1] Quoted in Peterburzhets, *Ocherk*, pp. 84–5. [2] *Ibid.* pp. 88–9.
[3] *Ibid.* p. 89. [4] *Rabochaia mysl'*, no. 7 (July 1899), p. 1.

with despotism! Long live 1 May! Long live international Social Democracy![1]

No. 8: Let us abandon reliance on the government! Let us accustom ourselves to the idea that we must fight the government and the capitalists.[2]

A comparison of these quotations with passages from the proclamations of 1895 shows that, narrow as it was in its political objectives, *Rabochaia Mysl'* took a step forward. It was an advance on the previous stage reached by the movement—that stage which Lenin presents as the golden age of the Russian Social Democratic movement. *Rabochaia Mysl'* broadened the workers' circle of interests from the economic, to which the proclamations of 1895 were confined, to the socio-legal. There is no doubt that the founders of the Union of Struggle of 1895 were *subjectively* more conscious and advanced politically than the founders of *Rabochaia Mysl'*. It is all the more interesting and significant, therefore, that *objectively*, in what they wrote, they placed more emphasis than *Rabochaia Mysl'* on economic concerns.

And so, the objective significance of *Rabochaia Mysl'* was that during the period of so-called Economism it served a special purpose—it fulfilled *one* of the tasks of Social Democracy. It was successful in its attempt to let the workers formulate their own line of thought.*

4

It was with a heavy heart that comrades left for Petersburg in the autumn of 1900. Everything was crushed. Everything had to be started again. But how? Was it best to re-establish one of the former organizations, broaden its programme, and seek to unify the Petersburg comrades? Or perhaps it would be better to give up the old names which, because of the ideas associated with them, might interfere with unification, and found a new organization? But would this new organization be just one more among all the others? Would it not simply increase that fragmentation of effort which it was intended to eliminate? All these difficult questions vanished of themselves as soon as work was begun.

---

[1] 'Pis'mo k tovarishcham', *Rabochaia mysl'*, no. 7, p. 2.
[2] 'S"ezd rabochikh', *Rabochaia mysl'*, no. 8 (February 1900), p. 1.
* See 'A Worker's Reply to *Iskra*' ['Otvet rabochego *Iskre*'], *Rabochee delo*, nos. 11–12, and also the article by Comrade B.-V. ['Peterburgskoe dvizhenie'], 'The Movement in Petersburg', *Rabochee delo*, no. 6. [B.-V. was the pseudonym of Boris Savinkov. See Kamenev, *Russkaia politicheskaia literatura*, p. 32.]

Not everything had been destroyed, as it turned out; the circles created by the Union had not collapsed after the massive arrests, but had actually expanded rapidly during the summer and now formed an entire organization of many hundreds of workers. When the agitators who had returned to Petersburg came to them and began to present their plans for an organization and a programme, they were told that an organization and programme already existed. There was a Workers Committee.

This unexpected declaration made a great impression on the *intelligenty*. Some were offended by the cold and somewhat slighting reply of the workers to their self-sacrificing teachers of the recent past. Others saw in it a cause for real enthusiasm. 'At last', they said, 'the intelligentsia will take up its proper position —a subordinate position—in the workers' movement.' The Union published the programme of the Workers Committee. This first attempt of the workers in Petersburg to formulate their principles in a programme is far from perfect. But it is important to note that the political tasks awaiting the workers' movement are stated here for the first time. In the autumn of 1900 the Union, which was joined by the Workers Committee, was strong, and its strength at the same time marked the triumph of two principles: organization, and a new enthusiasm for political action. Even *Rabochaia Mysl'*, no. 9, declared that the overthrow of the autocracy was the workers' most important task.

In the programme of the Workers Committee, published in *Rabochaia Mysl'*, no. 11, but drafted earlier, in the autumn of 1900, we read among other things that 'the ultimate goal of the workers' movement is the political and economic emancipation of the working-class, which can be attained only by the Social Democratic movement of the broad labouring masses'. 'The Union supports this struggle (in defence of the workers' vital daily interests) in every possible way. It strives to transform every unorganized movement into an organized, conscious battle against capitalist exploitation and the Tsarist government.' 'The Union goes hand in hand with all the Social Democratic groups and considers their unification a matter of prime importance.' 'The unity of the enemy—the government—means that we must consider temporary alliances with other revolutionary factions in specific cases.'[1]

But the Union continued to be 'cautious'. In *Rabochii Listok*

[1] 'Programma S. Peterburgskogo Soiuza bor'by za osvobozhdenie rabochego klassa', *Rabochaia mysl'*, no. 11 (April 1901), p. 2.

2. PETERSBURG

[*Labour News Sheet*], no. 5, also issued in December 1900, workers are called upon to prepare for the struggle. 'Our fate is sad, our sufferings heavy; much injustice is done us, and our demands should not be petty.' In reality, however, the demands were quite petty; they were purely economic, and only the last—the vaguest —was broader: 'the right to assemble in order to discuss our needs, freedom of organization, and strikes'.[1]

This disparity between the Committee's agitation and its political programme annoyed those comrades who were more advanced politically.[2] They grouped themselves around the remnants of the Group of Twenty, called themselves the Socialist Group,[3] and published a proclamation in which they clearly stated their disagreements with the Union. The Socialist Group presented its programme in the first publication issued by the Social Democratic Library.* Although fewer workers' organiza-

---

[1] 'Chto zhe nam delat', tovarishchi?', *Rabochii listok*, no. 5 (December 1900), p. 1. *Rabochii listok* was the official news sheet of the Committee of the Workers Organization which in 1900 became the central executive of the St Petersburg Union of Struggle for the Emancipation of the Working-Class: Committee of the RSDLP. For accounts of how it was published, see Logacheva-Piletskaia, in *Byloe*, no. 3 (31) (1925), pp. 97–8, and N. Ustinovich, 'Pervaia tipografiia Peterburgskogo Soiuza bor'by za osvobozhdenie rabochego klassa v 1900 g.', *Krasnaia letopis'*, no. 2 (11) (1924).

[2] For a description of the tensions and divisions within the St Petersburg Union during 1900, see K. Semenov, 'Pervyi god Peterburgskoi "Rabochei Organizatsii"', *Minuvshie gody*, no. 12 (1908), pp. 265–94.

[3] According to V. O. Tsederbaum, among the leading members were P. Rutenberg, Aleksandr and Boris Savinkov, Sofiia M. Zaretskaia, D. Zaitsev, V. A. Slepian, and Lidiia Kantsel (née Tsederbaum). From the time of its foundation in the spring of 1900, the Socialist Group was closely linked to a group in Vilna, led by Eva L'vovna Broido (née Gordon) and M. I. Broido, which ran an illegal publishing organization known as the Social Democratic Workers Library. The Library published the leaflets of the Socialist Group. See Levitskii, *Za chetvert' veka*, pp. 135–6, and E. Broido (Gordon), in *Letopis' revoliutsii*, i, 126–32.

* Editorial statement, *Social Democratic Workers Library* ['Ot redaktsii', *Sotsialdemokraticheskaia Rabochaia Biblioteka*], no. 1 (1900), p. 25: 'In order to attain both our immediate aims (a considerable improvement in the material and spiritual condition of the labouring masses) and our ultimate goals (the triumph of a new, socialist order) it is essential that the working-class be organized as a *political* party, i.e., a party which sets out to prepare the masses for the conquest of political power.

'To prepare the labouring masses for the great day of their liberation, to educate them by means of politico-economic warfare to such an extent that they will be able to exploit their coming victory—such is the present goal of the labour movement in Western Europe. The tasks of the Russian movement are both broader and more complex. The workers' movement in Russia is beginning in a period when despotism is still in full sway. In the West, a bourgeois revolution was possible; in our country it is not. The

279

tions had been linked to the Group of Twenty than were attached to the Union, they too gained in strength during the summer of 1900; by autumn they were in full fighting condition, and the work progressed rapidly. The [Socialist] Group declared in a proclamation that it had

deliberately refrained from joining the Committee, since it found that the latter's official organ *Rabochaia Mysl'*, on the one hand, tended to sympathize with the moderate wing of the German Social Democratic Party and almost ignored the local and immediate conditions of Russian life, while on the other hand it lacked confidence in the ability of the working masses to gain political self-awareness (*To Society*, January 1901).[1]

At the same time that *Rabochii Listok*, no. 5, and *Rabochaia Mysl'*, no. 11, appeared, the Socialist Group issued a proclamation (December 1900) which declared that 'apart from a few of our more gifted and politically conscious comrades, the workers until recently had only a very vague understanding of the necessity to fight for political freedom, but as time went on the workers began to understand that the struggle must be waged not only with capitalists, and not only for economic interests.'[2] They began to understand that without 'political freedom, that is, the right to participate in the government of the state through elected representatives, without the right to associate and assemble, without freedom of speech, press, and conscience, and without inviolability of person, the workers could not radically improve their position'.[3] The Socialist Group—or Labour Organization, as it was called—therefore expressed its desire to 'co-operate with this ever-

Russian bourgeoisie is perfectly content for the time being. The absolutist government has allied with it. The workers' movement alone courageously fights its way ahead. It cannot develop successfully and broadly until the workers win political freedom for themselves. If in the West political freedom was achieved by the bourgeois revolution, in our country it can be won only by a proletarian revolution. Russian workers must make an intensive effort to develop their political thinking. The economic struggle and organization of the masses must go on, but it must be injected with the living spirit of the political fight.' [This policy statement of the Library was written by M. I. Broido and favourably received by *Iskra*. (See E. Broido, in *Letopis'* revoliutsii, I, 131, and 'Iz partii', *Iskra*, no. 2 (February 1901), p. 6.)]

[1] Quoted in Boris Olenin, 'Po povodu poslednikh peterburgskikh proklamatsii', *Nakanune: Sotsial'no-revoliutsionnoe obozrenie*, nos. 26–7 (February–March 1901), p. 315. The proclamations of the winter, 1900–1, which Akimov here assigns to the Socialist Group alone were, in fact, issued jointly with the *Rabochee Znamia* Group. The two organizations amalgamated at that time.

[2] *Ibid.*   [3] *Ibid.* p. 316.

growing consciousness among the workers. It is convinced that the working-class is already so strong that in the near future it will begin to fight openly for its political rights.'[1]

We see, then, that in December the Union was still speaking with caution about the struggle against the government. On the other hand, the Socialist Group also felt is necessary to be cautious; the 'changes in the moods of the working-class' were said in its proclamation to be of 'recent' origin, while the struggle for political rights, after all, was not to begin until the future, albeit the near future.

All these developments took place in December 1900. The beginning of the new year 1901 was, therefore, exactly the right moment to hope for the shift of the labour movement in Petersburg to political warfare. And indeed the war did begin during the 'March days'. A unified organization was needed to direct this struggle, and, as we have seen, such an organization was already being prepared by events.

During the previous—the third—period (1897–1900), four groups successively held the leading rôle in Petersburg: the Union of Struggle, *Rabochaia Mysl'*, *Rabochee Znamia*, and the Group of Twenty. And if the second period (1894–7) was marked by the tendency of the Social Democratic forces to unite into a single Union of Struggle, the third period, on the contrary, was marked by organizational fragmentation. The second period was clear and simple; it can be encompassed at a glance. The third presents a mosaic of small facts, a network of individual episodes, which I have tried to depict. But memory does not preserve their full diversity, and it is difficult for the mind to grasp their interrelation. This is why the second period seems so bright and the third so confused and tangled; one wishes the new period to resemble the second, rather than the third.

And yet the third period was one of progress rather than regression, compared with the second. Of course, it would have been best if a single organization had been sufficiently strong, stable, and competent at the time to meet the multiple demands of the advanced and complex workers' movement in Petersburg. But the constant arrests annually robbed the movement of dozens of people and gave the young political leaders no chance to gain experience, to develop a many-sided approach, to answer the needs both of the most ill-prepared strata and of those already growing

---

[1] *Ibid.* p. 314.

familiar with the idea of revolution. These different tasks were fulfilled by separate groups. It remained only for these groups to realize that they were performing separate tasks of one Social Democratic movement and to show the desire to unite. This was demanded by the very logic of events. It had been bequeathed to the new period by the past.

But in no case could, or should, the ideas of the different Petersburg organizations performing different Social Democratic functions have disappeared. Unification therefore could have taken place only on the basis of democratic organizational principles, which would have given each group a chance to maintain its own position. These organizational principles, upheld during the third period by the Union of Struggle, were advanced and upheld in the new stage of the movement by the Workers Organization. However, it was defeated by the new *Iskra* faction.

Why?

The development of the labour movement under the banner of Social Democracy has made the workers feel all the more keenly the need for political rights. And since these rights are essentially incompatible with the autocratic régime, the overthrow of the autocracy has become for the labouring masses the immediate, concrete objective of their battle. The overthrow of absolutism has always been the objective of the Russian Social Democratic programme. This goal is the logical outcome of the entire course of Russian history. Moreover, it was bequeathed by the early revolutionaries. Now it has passed from the realm of Social Democratic propaganda into the realm of direct revolutionary warfare.*

By this time Social Democrats everywhere in Russia had set as their next objective that task which could be performed only by the united effort of the entire Russian proletariat—the overthrow of the autocracy. Thus special influence was now acquired by the *Iskra* group, which had seized upon objectives brought to the fore by the third period and as its slogan had taken the unification of the Party and the battle against the autocracy.

Although the workers' movement in Russia was now advanced enough to enable the Social Democrats to place this aim on the agenda, it was still not sufficiently developed to give the correct proletarian answer to the problem and to avoid lapsing into radicalism. The organizational principles and tactics of *Iskra* were over-simplified and conspiratorial. They were all right for the

* *Instruktsii dlia redaktsii 'Rabochego dela'* (September 1901). [Martynov, *Dva s"ezda*, p. 16.]

average Social Democratic *intelligent* group in Russia but could not answer the needs of the far advanced workers' movement in such centres as Petersburg or Ekaterinoslav, or of the Jewish proletariat in Poland and Lithuania. Therefore a long struggle ensued between the policies of *Iskra* and those of such purely proletarian organizations as the Bund, the Petersburg Workers Organization, the 'old' Ekaterinoslav Organization, and their ideological spokesman—the Union Abroad. The Bund, as the strongest proletarian organization, succeeded in maintaining its position, although it had to break with the Party to do so. At the fifth stage of our Party's development, when the Russian movement will rise to the level attained by the Jewish workers' movement, the just demands of the Bund will be met by our Party. The Petersburg Workers Organization, which was not yet as advanced or as strong as the Bund, proved unable to hold its own in this struggle. As a result of the historical conditions under which *Iskra* appeared (and which I described in the Preface) it was able to win over, with a very few exceptions, the entire Social Democratic intelligentsia. The advanced Petersburg workers' movement was left without *intelligenty*. The workers' organizations in Kiev, Ekaterinoslav, and other cities were destroyed in a similar manner. And finally their spokesman, the Union of Russian Social Democrats Abroad, like a superstructure with its foundation removed, inevitably collapsed.

I shall not venture at this moment to describe the full drama of the struggle between *Iskra*'s 'organization of professional revolutionaries' and the Workers Organization in Petersburg. The events are still too recent, the documents involved still too little known. It is still too difficult to divest oneself of the subjective bitterness and chagrin evoked by these conflicts in our Party in Petersburg. But it is possible and necessary even now to point out the fact, an unfortunate fact for the Social Democratic movement, that not enough *intelligenty* were found in Petersburg to take on the leadership of its proletarian movement. Day after day the *intelligenty* who had assisted the Workers Organization abandoned it. They lacked sufficient grit, courage, and political consciousness to stand firm on the summit to which they had been raised by the highly developed proletarian movement of Petersburg. The 'run of the mill' Social Democratic *intelligenty* could not withstand the overall trend of the intelligentsia at this stage of the Social Democratic movement in Russia. Some yielded to the influence of radicalism, which was so evident in *Iskra*; others for the sake of Party unity consciously abandoned the fight for internal democratic principles.*

The Petersburg proletariat remained without the support of the intelligentsia. There are no longer any proclamations, leaflets, or newspapers to express its moods, its mind, its will! Its spirit once again works within, hidden from the eye, uncontrolled! What does the proletariat conceal within its depths? This mighty force which is building up unnoticeably and constantly in the proletariat will result in an explosion unexpected by enemy and friend alike. But how? And when?

* 'Russian Social Democracy' (of the *Iskra* period!—V.A.) 'is the product of the revolutionary movement of the intelligentsia, which sought support among the masses in the name of socialism, in order—objectively speaking—to fulfil the task of the revolutionary bourgeoisie': P. Aksel'rod, ['K voprosu ob istochnike i znachenii nashikh organizatsionnykh raznoglasii',] *Iskra*, [25 June 1904, pp. 2–3]. 'We would have had' (if the *Iskra* plan had been victorious—V.A.) 'a revolutionary political organization of the democratic bourgeoisie, leading the labouring masses of Russia as a fighting army. And to crown its evil irony, history might have given us at the head of this bourgeois-revolutionary organization' (i.e., the *Iskra* organization—V.A.) 'not simply a Social Democrat, but the most honest-to-goodness orthodox Marxist (orthodox in his origins)': Aksel'rod, ['Ob''edinenie rossiiskoi sotsial'demokratii i eia zadachi', part 2,] *Iskra*, no. 57, p. 4, cols. 2–3 [pp. 2–4].

3. KIEV

1

Under the impact of Western European literature, Social Democratic ideas appeared almost simultaneously among socialists in different parts of Russia. 'Marx discovered the internal causes of the historical progress of mankind; it remained only to examine Russian social relations from his point of view', wrote Plekhanov in a note in *L. Feuerbach* (p. 79). 'And this was done by Social Democrats, who often arrived at the same views on Russian life quite independently of one another.'[1] Indeed, even in the late 1880s and early 1890s we find small circles of people who wished to adopt the Marxist point of view—in Petersburg, Dorpat, Riga, Vilna, Minsk, Moscow, Nizhni Novgorod, Kazan, and Odessa. Later the movement was carried by various people to Kharkov, Kiev, Saratov, Ufa, Ekaterinoslav, Elizavetgrad, and Samara; and finally it spread throughout Russia.

In 1888 Dr Abramovich came to Kiev from Minsk and went to work as a locksmith in the railway workshops in order to establish contacts with workers.[2] Together with Sokolov, a recent arrival from penal exile, and four Minsk workers, he soon was able to organize some thirty workers, mostly locksmiths working in railway shops and typesetters. He also founded a clandestine library. The arrests of August 1889 destroyed this first Social Democratic organization in Kiev. In this same period a Ukrainian organization existed in Kiev which advocated the theories of Dragomanov. It exerted great influence on students and educated many future Social Democrats.[3] There was also a group of Polish

[1] F. Engels, *Liudvig Feuerbakh: Perevod s nemetskogo G. Plekhanova* (Geneva, 1892).

[2] On his rôle in founding the first Marxist workers' circle in Kiev, see I. N. Moshinskii, *Na putiakh k 1-mu s"ezdu R.S.-D.R.P.: 90-tye gody v Kievskom podpol'e* (Moscow, 1928), pp. 110–12; N. A. Bukhbinder, in *Krasnaia letopis'*, no. 7 (1923), pp. 263–74; V. Manilov, in *Letopis' revoliutsii* (Kharkov), no. 3 (1923), pp. 128–30, and L. Fedorchenko, in *Katorga i ssylka*, no. 6 (27) (1926), pp. 21–2.

[3] Dragomanov's disciples in Kiev were grouped around the elderly teacher and radical politician N. V. Kovalevskii. The leaders of the younger generation were B. A. Kistiakovskii, K. I. Arabazhin, E. V. Degen, and P. L. Tuchapskii. See Moshinskii, *Na putiakh*, pp. 31–7, and P. L. Tuchapskii, *Iz perezhitogo: Devianostye gody* (Odessa, 1923), pp. 13–47.

socialists, which subsequently produced many local Social Democratic leaders.[1] We must also note here the existence of Fokin's
infamous Organization of Radicals (*Organizatsiia Radikalov*),
since the young people misled by it included several future Social
Democrats.[2]

As early as 1891 a small group of people who called themselves
Social Democrats came together from these various sources. This
group had to start from scratch in establishing contacts with
workers. In order to train comrades for the work, it founded
several student circles. Everything was done in a highly conspiratorial manner. As a result, the group escaped the numerous
arrests of the early 1890s and by a direct line of descent led to all
the later Social Democratic organizations in Kiev.[3] By 1894 its
propaganda and organizational work had become systematic, but
it preserved all the typical features of *kruzhkovshchina*. Even in
1895, when the spoken word could no longer satisfy the demand for
propagandists and when it became essential to distribute clandestine literature on a wide scale, the old system of closed-circle
propaganda was retained. In the summer of 1895, when several
Vilna comrades visited Kiev, the Kiev people heatedly opposed
agitation. They argued that it was impracticable under conspiratorial conditions.[4]

The work in the circles followed the same pattern as in Petersburg and Vilna, and thus there is no need to dwell on it in detail
here.

2

However, in Kiev, too, life encouraged those same ideas which it
itself had prompted in the more advanced centres of the labour
movement. A number of strikes which took place in 1896 enabled

---

[1] A reference to those Polish socialists who in 1892 founded the Union of
Polish Socialist Youth (*Związek Polskiej Młodzieży Socjalistycznej*). Leading
members of this group were I. N. Peresvet-Soltan, V. M. Bogutskii, and
Liudvig Levkovich. See P. Polonskii, 'Na zare sotsial-demokraticheskogo
dvizheniia v Kieve', in *Katorga i ssylka*, no. 3 (40) (1928), pp. 13–15, and
Moshinskii, *Na putiakh*, pp. 46–7.

[2] On the group of Dr Mikhail Dmitrievich Fokin, which was active in Kiev
from 1885 to 1892, see Moshinskii, *Na putiakh*, pp. 8–29.

[3] The 'Russian' group of revolutionary Marxists active in Kiev during the
1890s had as its earliest members I. I. Chorba, I. M. Liakhovskii, D. K.
Lavrent'ev, S. K. Merzhvinskii, and B. L. Eidel'man. See B. L. Eidel'man, in
Proletarskaia revoliutsiia, no. 1 (1921), p. 65 n.

[4] Martov too has recalled that the advocates of the Vilna agitation programme
were at first sceptically received in Kiev: *Zapiski*, p. 250.

—indeed, compelled—the comrades in Kiev to adopt the new tactics of the Petersburg movement. The unrest among the workers of the railway shops in the autumn of 1894 is usually described as the first 'strike' in Kiev, although in actual fact the strike was forestalled by concessions from the management. In January 1895 the management was compelled to make further concessions. This period witnessed the appearance of the first *Letter to Comrades*, which dealt with only the economic needs of the local workers. Next, there was ferment at the Graf machine-building plant. We know of six clashes in industry prior to February 1896. Only one led to a short strike.

At the same time the movement of the handicraft proletariat grew up, principally among Jewish workers. The campaign opened with a strike of 150 tailors in November 1895, and even earlier with a strike of twenty-five paper hangers. These were followed by an unsuccessful strike of twenty-five shoemakers. A second *Letter to Comrades* was issued in February 1896, in connexion with the strike at the Kravets Tailoring Shop.[1] This *Letter* also confined itself to economic matters. In March the police interfered for the first time in the strike of nineteen tailors at Liudmer's factory. Two workers were arrested. These were the first of the police victims in the emerging labour movement. By 20 June the number had risen to eleven, and by the end of the year, to thirty. Immediately after the Liudmer strike, there was a third, brilliantly written *Letter to Comrades* explaining the close ties between the government and the capitalists.[2] However, it did not say that it was essential to begin the fight against the government but merely that the struggle would be carried on *despite* the government's use of force (see this *Letter* in *Listok Rabotnika*, no. 1).

The spring saw the arrest of five workers from a Kiev tram-car shop, one from the locomotive works, one printer, two tailors, and several *intelligenty*, including Iuvenalii Mel'nikov, who had

---

[1] For this leaflet—*Pis'mo k Kievskim rabochim*—see N. V. Bugaev and V. Z. Sergiuk (eds.), *Listovki revoliutsionnykh sotsialdemokraticheskikh organizatsii Ukrainy 1896–1904* (Kiev, 1963), pp. 22–3. It was written by N. A. Vigdorchik, the most able and prolific writer for the clandestine press of the Kiev Marxists, 1896–8. (See B. L. Eidel'man, 'Literatory Kievskogo sotsial-demokraticheskogo podpol'ia do 1-go s"ezda', *Katorga i ssylka*, no. 2 (51) (1929), pp. 36–7).

For Vigdorchik's *Letter* written in response to the Liudmer strike (*Pis'mo k Kievskim rabochim po povodu stachki v masterskoi Liudmera*), see *Listok rabotnika*, no. 1 (November 1896), pp. 20–4, or Bugaev and Sergiuk (eds.), *Listovki*, pp. 24–8.

rendered enormously important services to the movement and who later died of tuberculosis in penal exile. But arrests could no longer halt the work, which continued to develop in scope and character.

All this shows clearly that the emphasis of the work was shifting from the confined educational circle to agitation based on economic interests. This was why the Petersburg strikes in the summer of 1896 made so strong an impression in Kiev and acted as the final sanction for the new tactics, for the second phase in the development of the Kiev movement.

It is significant that the workers in the Kiev circles responded with the same hostility to innovations as did those in Vilna and Petersburg. 'One day', relates Comrade E., a participant in the activities of 1896–7,[1]

I went to see a woman worker and found her in tears. I asked what troubled her, and she said that some of her friends, former members of a workers' circle, had visited her and ridiculed her for presuming to preach without undergoing circle training herself: 'They seem to have turned you into a half-baked Social Democratic agitator, haven't they? You ought to do some studying yourself before you teach!'

It must be said, however, that the transition to the new tactics aroused misgivings and doubt everywhere in the movement. In October 1895 a huge strike of textile workers took place in Ivanovo-Voznesensk:

Unfortunately [we read in the Ivanovo-Voznesensk report] the local Social Democratic organization, many members of which had been arrested shortly before, had not yet recovered sufficiently to participate on a large scale in the strike (p. 14). It was heatedly debated whether or not to play a part in the strike. In the end, in view of the weakness of the organization, it was decided to refrain from taking part in the strike. As for issuing leaflets, it was feared at the time that this might lead to another attack on the Workers Union, which was still weak.[2]

Another passage in the same report tells us, on the contrary, that the organization was functioning excellently at the time and that the decision to refrain from participation in the strike had been prompted by considerations of principle (p. 23). The 'weakness' of the organization was evidently purely relative. On page 13 of the report we read that by this time 'the workers had become more

---

[1] *Odna uchastnitsa raboty 96–97 godov.* Comrade E. was probably Evgeniia Samoilovna Etinger. She was an active participant in the agitation campaign in Kiev from 1896 to 1897, when she went abroad.

[2] *Rabochee dvizhenie v Ivanovo-Voznesenskom raione* (Geneva, 1900), p. 23.

animated, the number of participants was growing constantly, the meetings were lively and well attended'.[1]

In Kharkov 'the successes of Social Democratic *propaganda* were negligible. It was only among the artisans and the printing workers that it made more substantial progress. The few young workers who had been drawn into the movement did not deny the value of agitation in theory, but felt that it was still premature in Kharkov.'*

Somewhat surprising in this context is the assertion that in Odessa 'the idea began to emerge in the workers' circles as early as the end of 1893 that it was necessary to change over from circle propaganda to mass agitation. There were even plans, enthusiastically supported by the workers, for a general strike of sailors, stokers, and mechanics' (p. 7).[2] However, these ideas were evidently confined to particular individuals. Hence the arrests of 28 January 1894 (Nakhamkes, Kopeliush, and others) disrupted the work. The movement in Odessa, it seems, did not enter the period of mass agitation until the beginning of 1899. This supposition is corroborated by another passage in the report (p. 15): 'That period (1892–3) was not agitational but propagandist. Agitation was just beginning to be considered, and only by the most farsighted.'

Until now I have been giving examples of how timid and wary

---

[1] In referring to the report from Ivanovo-Voznesensk, Akimov has apparently jumbled together two entirely separate episodes. Some of the passages which he quotes here describe the strike of December–January 1897–98, and not, as he implies, that of September–October 1895.

* See the report on the movement in Kharkov [(B. L. Feinberg), *Rabochee dvizhenie v Khar'kove* (Geneva, 1900), pp. 3–4]. All the reports quoted here and published by the Union of Russian Social Democrats Abroad had been sent to the Union as material for the report to the Paris Congress of the International [in 1900]. The Union made a special effort to encourage the Party committees to play a highly active rôle in the Congress. In the early spring of 1900 Comrade G[rishin], a member of the Union, was sent to Russia for this purpose, although the time was admittedly inconvenient and dangerous for such a journey. The Union insisted that the committees send their own representatives as delegates to the Congress and that they dispatch their reports beforehand for printing. It is highly characteristic that the committees were not enlisted for the Amsterdam Congress [in 1904]. On the contrary, the Council decided that it would itself represent the Party at the Congress. No *Iskra* committee—whether Bolshevik or Menshevik—sent delegates, reports, or credentials. Only the anti-*Iskra* Voronezh Committee sent both a delegate and credentials. However, the delegation did not confirm this delegate; its conduct on that occasion was both illegal and unworthy. This is not the place to prove the point, but if the delegation finds my assertion incorrect, it may demand that I supply evidence.

[2] [Steklov], 'Rabochee dvizhenie v Odesse', in *Iz rabochego dvizheniia v Odesse i Nikolaeve.*

comrades were in making the transition to campaign methods which they treated as something new, even though they were already well entrenched in other centres of the movement. It is even more interesting, however, to observe the different levels attained by various strata in one and the same city. Some were far advanced politically and others were in need of elementary lessons. Minsk is one of the cities where the movement developed earliest. A Bund committee, as well as the local journal *Minsker Arbeter* [*Minsk Worker*], has been in existence there for a long time. However, the non-Jewish workers have remained almost untouched by the movement until quite recently. The Kiev newspaper *Vpered* [*Forward*], no. 10, in July 1900, carried a report from Minsk:

Leaflets issued by the Minsk Committee of the Russian Social Democratic Labour Party and printed on a hectograph were distributed on 16 April. These leaflets explained to the workers that 1 May was a holiday to celebrate the battle for their *economic* betterment. They appealed to all 'shopworkers and labourers' to unite in order to win a better life for themselves. No political demands were raised in the leaflet, since the non-Jewish workers in Minsk had as yet not been adequately prepared for this. These were the first leaflets in Russian to be issued in our city.

The most characteristic report, however, came from Nikolaev in 1900. By this time the workers' movement in Nikolaev was at a stage approximating that of Kiev in late 1896, Moscow in early 1896, Ivanovo-Voznesensk in late 1895, and Vilna in late 1893. In other words, it was in transition from propaganda to agitation based on those petty daily needs and demands which could be grasped even by the worker who completely lacked political education. But the author of the Nikolaev report, who was evidently wholly absorbed in local work and unfamiliar with the development of the movement in more advanced centres, drew general theoretical conclusions from the local methods. He spoke of the harm involved in the workers' organizing themselves, and even in their concentrating their resources in a strike fund. He considered it impossible to speak to the worker except in connexion with his 'daily interests'.[1] However, this preaching of political moderation is sincere and naïve, and can be explained not only by the youth of the writer but also by the youth of the movement itself in Nikolaev.

[1] [Trotskii], 'Rabochee dvizhenie v Nikolaeve', in *Iz rabochego dvizheniia v Odesse i Nikolaeve*, p. 24.

At this time, as I shall show later, the comrades representative of the 'third period' were already heatedly advocating the organizational unification of the party and the development of methods with which to wage mass political warfare. But the comrades who were still at an earlier level of development could not regard their own tactics as simply a stage in the movement's development, as a stage which was bound to give way to the broader tasks confronting the party. These comrades, who adhered to the tactics of the 'third period' in an instinctive and blind fashion, not only did not respond to the appeal for unification and for political warfare but did not even hear this appeal. It is not enough to have ears to hear. But when the progress of the movement raised them to a new level, they were able to hear the appeal and even respond to it. Then it seemed to them that it was the *Iskra* group that uttered the new words. The fact that they joined *Iskra* meant a great step forward *for them*. They were unable to by-pass the stage of *Iskra*-ism, the 'fourth period'. They could not move directly to the stage when the organizational and political problems of the Party would be solved on the basis of the proletarian approach which characterized the 'third period'. This fact simply shows how each stage of the movement completely absorbed even so-called intellectuals.

The movement developed in stages; indeed, it could not develop otherwise. Conscious Social Democrats, who, thanks to their individual political education, had a sufficiently broad outlook, *should* have taken this into account and led the movement along this path. If they had done so, the transition from one stage to the next would have been rapid and painless. If I should now find myself in Turkey, where there is no Social Democratic movement, I would not join the 'Young Turks', who are waging a political struggle. I would begin to organize workers' 'circles'. And after I had trained at least several dozen Turkish comrades, I would begin to persuade them to go over to mass agitation based on the economic interests of the working-class. After this the 'Young Turks' would show the same energy as the Russian Zemstvo groups today, and we would join forces to get rid of Abdul Hamid.

Let us, however, return to Kiev.

With the change of tactics in Kiev, as in Petersburg and in Vilna, it was necessary to change the organization as well. Side by side with the organization of revolutionaries, it was necessary to create a democratic organization of workers. In addition to the

Social Democratic group discussed above and known as 'Russian', there was at this time in Kiev a 'Polish' Social Democratic group, which also had wide contacts with workers.[1] As early as the autumn of 1896 negotiations began for the merging of these groups. The first meeting was held in the woods. It was attended by five *intelligenty* and about ten workers, but it led to nothing because the 'Russian' group favoured agitation, while the 'Polish', which was by then no longer confined to Poles, advocated workers' circles. The 'Russian' group then took the name *Rabochee Delo** and began to publish a newspaper, *Vpered*. The first number, which appeared in January 1897 (dated 8 December 1896), was hectographed. By the time the second—which came out soon afterwards—was issued, a mimeograph was used. Leaflets, which had begun to appear at the end of 1896, were now issued systematically. In 1897 6,500 leaflets were distributed in factories and plants.

The success of the new tactics convinced their opponents, and in May the long-awaited unification of the Social Democratic groups in Kiev finally took place.[2] The statute of the new organization was highly typical of this stage in the movement's history. The members of both groups were regarded as members of the new organization, but they met separately for reasons of secrecy. They informed each other of decisions taken. The controlling body was an administrative or executive committee, which consisted of five members. Four were elected by the two groups, two from each;[3] I do not know how the fifth was chosen, but it was probably by co-option. Side by side with the committee, but entirely separate

---

[1] On the contacts established by the Polish Social Democratic group with the workers in Kiev's railway workshops, see A. Krovatskii, 'Moi vospominaniia', in *K dvadtsatipiatiletiiu*, pp. 79–83.

* It may be of interest to note here that the slogan 'Workers' Cause' was raised quite independently by Social Democratic organizations of the 'third period' in Petersburg, in Kiev, and later abroad. The 'fourth period' sought to divest itself of the 'purely workers'' cause even in the titles of its publications.

[2] On the long drawn-out negotiations of 1896–7 between the three socialist groups—the 'Russian' Social Democrats, the 'Polish' Social Democrats, and the PPS—see Tuchapskii, *Iz perezhitogo*, pp. 57–8; Eidel'man, in *Proletarskaia revoliutsiia*, no. 1 (1921), pp. 33–4, and Polonskii, in *Katorga i ssylka*, no. 3 (40) (1928), pp. 16–20.

[3] According to Polonskii's account, the representatives of the Russian group in the executive committee of the Kiev Union at the end of 1897 were P. L. Tuchapskii and L. V. Tesler; those of the Polish group, V. M. Bogutskii and A. D. Rabchevskii. See Polonskii, in *Katorga i ssylka*, no. 3 (40) (1928), p. 20.

from it, was the Workers Committee. It was organized democratically and consisted of elected representatives of the workers'
circles. It invited to its meetings both a representative of the
Social Democratic committee and a representative of the Socialist
Revolutionaries, although the latter for some reason refused to
attend. Thus, the Workers Committee and the new Kiev Union
of Struggle for the Emancipation of the Working Class were
completely independent organizations. The proclamations were
issued in the name of the Workers Committee, which jealously
guarded this prerogative; they bore, however, the Union's stamp,
or an indication that they were published by the Union.

The effect of unification was highly beneficial, and during the
summer of 1897 the comrades in Kiev worked with great enthusiasm. A series of lectures was held on the history of the revolutionary movement in Russia and abroad. The lectures were delivered
in the woods and were attended by sixty to eighty people.[1] They
made a profound impression on the listeners, who remember
them to this day. Illegal publications were now in great demand
and were requested from other cities too—from Ekaterinoslav,
Nikolaev, and Rostov. The Union established a literary group
which wrote leaflets and later, in July, began publication of
Rabochaia Gazeta [*Workers Gazette*].

The year 1897 marked the end of the second period of the movement's development in Kiev, the period of economic agitation,
when agitation—'calls to action' and leaflets—raised purely
economic demands. It would be a mistake to assume that no anti-
government activity took place at this time. On the contrary:
the masses of the working-class were consciously, deliberately, and
systematically being trained for the class—the political—struggle.
The comrades in Kiev seized every opportunity to explain to the
workers the true nature of the autocracy, to rouse hatred against
it, and to awaken in the workers the sense of their own dignity and
class consciousness. How nearsighted are those who permit themselves today, when the economists' agitation has proved its
effectiveness, to ridicule the slow, painstaking, and therefore
'tedious' work of the early days! The persevering workers in the
revolutionary cause were aware of the tediously petty character
of their activities. 'And so, little by little, the Kiev workers are
learning to fight their oppressors', says one leaflet of November

[1] These lectures were delivered by Tuchapskii. See Eidel'man in *Proletarskaia
revoliutsiia*, no. 1 (1921), p. 38.

1896, commenting on the strike of eleven workers in the struggle for a thirteen-hour day! And how clearly these words express painful awareness of the slowness of the work and literally heroic patience. 'This will be a small victory,' the leaflet continues, 'but in the first stages of our struggle we value small victories too. The first step is always difficult.' Of course these comrades had no inkling that several years later Narcissus Dullwit would come upon the scene and begin to mock their words.

A number of leaflets were issued in connexion with the special 'economic' demands at Graf's (November 1896), the strike in the workshops of the Dnepr Steamboat Company (January 1897, addressed to all Kiev workers),[1] the strikes at the Egiz Tobacco Factory (May 1897), the Shimanskii plant (29 April 1897), the Kimaer Furniture Factory (May 1897), the Dutois Corset Factory (May 1897), and the Krimaer Locksmith Shop (20 July 1897). Leaflets were also addressed to the women workers at the cigarette factory (5 July 1897), to the Gretter and Krivanek machine-building plant (May 1897), the workers on the municipal railway (3 November 1897), the Dnepr machine-building plant (December 1897), the Zarambskii machine-building plant (December 1897),[2] and probably many others which I do not have to hand.

This indicates how broad a range of activity the new tactics permitted the Social Democrats to develop. But there were other leaflets in addition to those issued in response to specific material grievances. On one occasion a foreman struck a worker in the railway workshops. An excellent leaflet was issued on 28 August dealing with this incident.[3] A foreman ordered a music-making worker to leave the lunch counter in a club; when he refused, the foreman beat him up. A leaflet was issued on 9 July urging the

---

[1] A leaflet to the workers of Kiev about a strike at the Dnepr Steamboat Company was issued in February 1896. (An account of this strike was published in *Rabotnik*, nos. 3–4 (1897), sect. II, p. 56. For the leaflet, see Bugaev and Sergiuk (eds.), *Listovki*, pp. 20–1). Akimov, like V. I. Nevskii in his *Ocherki po istorii Rossiiskoi Kommunisticheskoi Partii*, 2nd ed., I (Leningrad, 1925), 512, probably assumed that this strike took place in the January of 1897 rather than in that of 1896.

[2] The leaflets issued at the Egiz, the Shimanskii, the Gretter and Krivanek, and the Dutois factories were all republished by Eidel'man, in *Katorga i ssylka*, no. 2 (51) (1929), pp. 46–56. For the first three of these leaflets, see Bugaev and Sergiuk (eds.), *Listovki*, pp. 33–46.

This leaflet—'K rabochim kievskikh zheleznodorozhnykh masterskikh'— was republished by Eidel'man in *Katorga i ssylka*, no. 2 (51) (1929), pp. 47–8. See also Bugaev and Sergiuk (eds.), *Listovki*, pp. 43–5.

workers to defend their dignity and describing the baseness of the foreman's action. It is written passionately and effectively.[1]

It is still more erroneous to assume that the economists did not touch upon the question of the government. On the contrary, they wrote plainly that the government was the enemy of the workers. But all the leaflets of this period gave the idea that it was essential to fight against the capitalists even though they had the support of the government, while nothing was said about war against the government as such.

A May Day proclamation ended with the general statement: 'Long live 1 May—the world-wide holiday of the workers! Long live the struggle for happiness and freedom!'[2] Five hundred and thirty workers at the railway workshops celebrated 1 May by refusing to work on this day. The proclamation issued in this connexion stated: 'All workers are brothers. All have the same enemies and oppressors: the factory owners and their defenders.' 'Both the railway and the police authorities proved powerless against the railway workers.' 'Let us then prepare ourselves and our less conscious comrades for the May Day holiday.'[3] Similarly, the letter about the law of 2 June 1897, published in two editions (the second on 1 November 1897), was also distinguished by these two features: it was openly and sharply hostile to the government, but it did not even hint at the need to fight for the establishment of another, constitutional or republican, form of government.

And so the same minister who only a year ago would not even consider the idea of concessions to the workers is now setting up a commission to draft a law! And the Emperor! It was he who in 1895 proclaimed his 'royal thanks' to the soldiers who shot at workers during the strike in Yaroslavl . . . And now this same Nicholas II who thanked the soldiers for spilling the workers' blood is decreeing a law which limits the working day!

The pamphlet goes on to explain that all this is the result of the fact that the textile workers in St Petersburg waged a united and

---

[1] 'Pis'mo k rabochim kievskikh zheleznodorozhnykh masterskikh', in Eidel'man's article, *Katorga i ssylka*, no. 2 (51) (1929), pp. 49–51 and Bugaev and Sergiuk (eds.), *Listovki*, pp. 40–2.

[2] For this proclamation of May Day, 1897, see Bugaev and Sergiuk (eds.), *Listovki*, pp. 30–3. It was extensively quoted in *Rabochaia gazeta*, no. 1 (August, 1897).

[3] For this proclamation—'Pis'mo k vsem kievskim rabochim'—of 19 May 1897, see Bugaev and Sergiuk (eds.), *Listovki*, pp. 37–8.

courageous battle against their employers, and urges the workers in Kiev to do the same.[1]

But apart from these agitational publications of the Kiev Union for this period, we have another highly interesting document, which sets forth the principles underlying the tactics I have described. This is the *Letter to Class Conscious Workers*, issued on the occasion of Vetrova's death.[2] On 17 March, a Thursday, the Kiev Socialist Revolutionaries called the workers to a demonstration to be held on the following Sunday. 'Workers of Kiev!' their leaflet urged,

Join us in honouring the memory of a friend of the workers' cause . . . The Russian government exiles thousands of socialists to Siberia and buries them alive in its prisons, yet the just cause of the socialists is growing. Kiev workers! The Russian land is still crushed by the shameful yoke of Tsarist lawlessness. Let us fight for justice and freedom. Down with the despot! Down with the shameful yoke of the Tsarist government!*

Thus a demonstration was called in Kiev, and the Social Democrats were compelled to take a definite stand on it. But even now they did not venture to speak to all workers on this subject; instead, they addressed themselves in their proclamation of 20 March to the 'class conscious workers', that is, only to those workers who had been through the socialist propaganda circles. Here is what they wrote:

The tragic fate of Maria Vetrova, who committed suicide as a result of inhuman treatment at the hands of Russian gendarmes, has, of course,

---

[1] See [N. A. Vigdorchik], 'Novaia pobeda russkogo rabochego dvizheniia: po povodu zakona ob ogranichenii rabochego dnia na fabrikakh i zavodakh', in *K dvadtsatipiatiletiiu*, p. 311. The copy reproduced in this latter source was to have been published in March 1898 (*ibid.* p. 26) and is worded slightly differently from the edition here quoted by Akimov.

[2] On the demonstration held in Kiev in March 1897, as a protest against Maria Fedoseevna Vetrova's suicide in prison, see Moshinskii, *Na putiakh*, p. 87.

* This was not a fortuitous leaflet. The Socialist Revolutionaries talked in the same way on earlier occasions—in connexion with the anniversary of 1 March, and later in connexion with their unsuccessful demonstration. Thus, at the time when the economist leaflets of the Social Democrats began to appear, there were also political leaflets, both in Kiev and in Petersburg. But they were not issued by the Social Democrats. Moreover, the total failure of the organizations which issued these leaflets demonstrated clearly the impossibility of conducting agitation on the basis of purely political issues. Equally, the *political* character so soon assumed by the workers' movement in Russia under the leadership of the 'Economist' Social Democrats demonstrates how rational the methods of the latter actually were.

moved you all and has called down your curses upon the Tsarist government, which has imposed the yoke of slavery on the Russian people.
The yoke of Tsarist despotism lies especially heavy on us, the workers.
As we are deprived of the right to organize unions and meetings and of
the right of free speech, it becomes extraordinarily difficult for us to
wage the struggle with our immediate enemy—the capitalist class. This
is why the working-class will never achieve final victory without first
crushing the forces of the Tsarist government. But how can we crush
them? Will we come any nearer to victory by taking part in the proposed
demonstration? We are convinced that we shall not, that, indeed, we
shall move still further away from it . . . Let the workers themselves
begin to feel and realize that the government hinders their struggle.
Then they will become conscious adherents of political warfare. Let
them go through the necessary school of economic war, and then call
them to the political fight.[1]

'But today, when they have not yet undergone this schooling,' an
unsuccessful demonstration could repel them from the movement.
And even if it were to succeed it would make no impression,
because the workers would not see the cause as their own.

Were the Kiev comrades right in principle? I believe they were.
And, in fact, one of the extreme opponents of the Economists,
Plekhanov, said in 1901 (*Zaria*, no. 1): 'What I insist upon
absolutely is only the necessity for political warfare. The methods
employed have always been for me only a question of effectiveness and expediency.'[2] The same thing was said by the economists
of 1897: 'The working-class will never achieve final victory without
first crushing the forces of the Tsarist government.' 'The workers
must be made into conscious adherents of political warfare.' And
then the economists asked (as Plekhanov, too, advised them in
retrospect to ask): Will a demonstration serve this end? And they
answered: No, it will not.

But perhaps in their answer they misjudged what would be
most expedient? Even if this were so, their mistakes would not
have stemmed from mistaken principle. It would not mean that
the comrades in Kiev at that time were to be numbered as a special
faction of the Social Democratic movement. It would simply have
been a practical error. It must be said, however, that it was
generally held at the time that demonstrations were still impossible.

[1] This leaflet of 23 March 1897—'Pis'mo k Kievskim soznatel'nym rabochim'
—was republished by V. I. Nevskii in *Proletarskaia revoliutsiia*, no. 1 (1921),
pp. 108–10, as an appendix to his article 'K voprosu o pervom s"ezde
Rossiiskoi sotsial-demokraticheskoi partii'.

[2] G. V. Plekhanov, 'Eshche raz sotsializm i politicheskaia bor'ba', *Zaria*,
no. 1 (1901), p. 21.

Plekhanov also stated this opinion, both in his article and in the
May Day leaflet of 1898, as did Aksel'rod in his *Letter to the
Editors of 'Rabochee Delo'* in December 1899.*

In the chapter on Petersburg I showed that at the corresponding
stage of the movement's history there, the members of the *Iskra*
group had also been typical economists. The account of the activity of the Kiev economists shows that the future founders of
Iskra were ultra-economists even among the Russian economists.
Du glaubst schieben, und du bist geschoben! You think you create
events, but events have created you!

3

After publishing the first number of *Rabochaia Gazeta*, the Kiev
Social Democratic group sent a delegate[1] abroad to request the
help of the Group for the Emancipation of Labour and to discuss
its views with the Group. According to the Report of the Kiev
Committee to the Second Congress of the Party, 'the delegate,
who delivered a report of his journey, noted that the members of
the Union of Russian Social Democrats (the old Union) did not
attribute much significance to the experiment: they barely
glanced through the issue. . . Nevertheless, the delegate was promised assistance. However, the two articles they sent for the second
number were found by the editors to be too moderate and were not
published in the newspaper.'†

* In my report to the Second Congress I quoted these lines of Plekhanov
and Aksel'rod. [See above, Appendix I, p. 185; G. V. Plekhanov, 'Nash
svetlyi prazdnik', in *Rabotnik: Maiskii listok 1898 g.* (Geneva, 1898), p. 6,
and P. B. Aksel'rod, *Pis'mo v redaktsiiu 'Rabochego dela'* (Geneva, 1899),
p. 10.]

1 Probably P. L. Tuchapskii, who has described his meeting at this time with
Plekhanov and Aksel'rod in his *Iz perezhitogo*, p. 65.

† In *What Is to Be Done?* Lenin speaks of two letters by Aksel'rod, subsequently published as a pamphlet, *The Tasks and Tactics of the Russian
Social Democrats* [*K voprosu o sovremennykh zadachakh i taktike russkikh
sotsial'demokratov* (Geneva, 1898)]. This is wrong. Of the letters included in
it, only one was meant for *Rabochaia Gazeta*. It deals specifically with the
party's political tasks. I do not know which articles the Report is talking
about. I trust the Report because it was obviously written by a very well
informed person; and although the author was extremely biased, his bias
was in favour of the Group for the Emancipation of Labour, rather than the
Kiev movement. Besides, this incident is quite an old story in the practice
of the Group for the Emancipation of Labour. [The view advanced by the
Report from Kiev to the Second Party Congress and accepted by Akimov
was erroneous; the material sent by the Group for the Emancipation of
Labour was not rejected because of its 'moderation'. Plekhanov's letter,

Thus the Group for the Emancipation of Labour proved at the time to be more cautious than the economists and felt it necessary to move at a still 'slower pace'. How can this strange fact be explained? Only by the fact that by the time of the publication of the second number of *Rabochaia Gazeta* the Kiev movement had entered the next stage of its development, while the Group for the Emancipation of Labour, having decided to assist the Kiev comrades, evidently reckoned on the former attitude, of which it disapproved, and tempered its articles to the 'spirit of the time'.

Of course, many people will not agree with me when I call the period in Kiev up to 1898 one of economism. It is commonly asserted that 1898 was only the beginning of economism. I shall prove later how mistaken this is as it pertains to Kiev, as I have already shown in relation to Petersburg. At this stage, however, I must point out that the Group for the Emancipation of Labour saw economism in the Russian movement considerably before 1898. Plekhanov says with full justice in the first issue of *Zaria* that the principles of economism were already laid down in the pamphlet *On Agitation*. 'The logic of this pamphlet', he writes, 'is clear and unequivocal: purely economic agitation is not merely possible but actually obligatory for two entire "phases" of our labour movement. And until these "phases" are over, the dedication of our Party to purely economic action is not only possible but altogether legitimate and highly desirable' (from the point of view of the pamphlet *On Agitation*) (*Zaria*, no. 1, p. 11). Yet the pamphlet *On Agitation* had appeared in Vilna early in 1894. It was according to the logic of this pamphlet that our comrades began agitation on economic grounds in Petersburg in 1895 and in Kiev in 1896. As early as 1897 P. B. Aksel'rod was able to declare in the preface to the edition of the pamphlet published abroad that 'the ideas of its authors have already been put into practice'. And, of course, the practical realization of the 'logic of this pamphlet' is economism. This was the view of the Group for the Emancipation of

in fact, called upon the Marxists in Russia to lay greater stress on political demands in their agitation. For the letter, see *K dvadtsatipiatiletiiu*, pp. 287–9; for the subsequent reply from Kiev asking Plekhanov to accept alterations in his letter, see *Krasnyi arkhiv*, no. 6 (19) (1926), p. 208. Aksel'rod's article was apparently accepted without reservation for publication but was seized by the police in March 1898, with other material meant for *Rabochaia gazeta*, no. 3. See B. N[ikolaev]skii, 'Pis'mo G. V. Plekhanova v redaktsiiu *Rabochei gazety*', *K dvadtsatipiatiletiiu*, pp. 284–7.]

Labour at that time. Here is what Comrade B.[1] said to me about this:

In the autumn of 1896 I came from Switzerland to Kiev. The Group for the Emancipation of Labour had no contacts in Kiev, and P. B. Aksel'rod merely generally sent his greetings to the comrades in Kiev, informed them of the publications about to be issued, and promised to help by publishing their pamphlets. He indicated, however, that his Group would under no circumstances publish vulgarized literature for wide circles of workers.

I came to Kiev to Comrade N.,[2] who invited his friends. They were very interested in the views of the comrades abroad. I transmitted Aksel'rod's last words, which puzzled them: they could not make sense of the hostility shown by the Group for the Emancipation of Labour toward the comrades in Russia. The Group for the Emancipation of Labour had told me that there were Social Democrats in Russia who had no time for political warfare; the Group was very critical of the Petersburg Union. I wanted to know whether there were indeed such Social Democrats. N. replied that they did not oppose 'politics', but considered that political action was dependent on the possibilities for agitation. I do not remember his exact explanations, but they fully satisfied me—and I was a fervent advocate of politics.

I was the go-between who handled the correspondence between Kiev and the Group for the Emancipation of Labour concerning the publication of pamphlets. However, the negotiations came to nothing. We wanted the Group to publish our pamphlets without editorial changes, and in our name. The Group for the Emancipation of Labour would not agree to these terms.

Similarly, a Petersburg comrade, E.M., told me that the Group for the Emancipation of Labour was completely out of sympathy with the work of the Union of Struggle in 1895. It not only refused to publish the manuscripts submitted to it, but it ridiculed them.

This was why, having decided after all to help the Kiev comrades, the Group for the Emancipation of Labour wrote the most moderate articles at a time when the Kiev comrades had taken a step forward, a step toward politics. This step was the recognition that it was now possible to call upon the workers to fight the government as such, as in itself an enemy of the working-class. However—and this is a typical feature of the new stage—the call

[1] Almost certainly L. V. Tesler, who carried letters back and forth between Kiev and Switzerland. On his rôle, see M. B-ov, 'Otvet *Rabochei gazety* (1898 g.) G. V. Plekhanovu', *Krasnyi arkhiv*, no. 6 (19) (1926) pp. 207–9.
[2] Probably Nikolai Abramovich Vigdorchik. In 'Pervyi s"ezd R.S.D.R. partii', *Minuvshye gody* (1908), no. 2, Akimov called Vigdorchik 'N.' For this identification, see Eidel'man in *Proletarskaia revoliutsiia*, no. 1 (1921), p. 80.

was to fight against the injustices committed by the government rather than against the government itself. This, too, shows complete parallelism with the activity in Petersburg.

A proclamation dated 26 November 1897 marked the transition of the movement to the new stage. It was lengthy—four large, closely typed pages—and summed up the results of the year's work. These were its conclusions:

> The struggle of the Russian workers was at first directed solely against the employers. It was a purely economic struggle. But the government wasted no time in letting the workers know that it was at the service of the capitalists and was the enemy of the workers. It challenged the workers, and they have no choice but to take up the challenge. In trying to win concessions from the capitalists, the workers will at the same time fight all those tricks and lawless acts of the government and police which help the factory owners rob and oppress the workers. Every strike, every workers' meeting, every union will be a weapon in the war not only against the capitalists but also against the government, which, to please the capitalists, harries the workers' unions and strikes. In addition to the struggle against the employers—economic warfare— the workers must also take up the struggle against the government— political warfare.[1]

The new tasks of the workers' movement clearly demanded new tactics, new methods of struggle, new organization. We must now examine how the comrades in Kiev gradually accomplished this during 1898, 1899, and the first half of 1900, at which point the movement entered a new stage.

To begin with, the tone of the leaflets had to change. This occurred immediately. But it took comrades time to work out a new type of leaflet which would be as effective in the direct leadership of the political battle as the previous type had been in the leadership of the economic battle. The events in Huta-Bankowa (in Dombrowa), where troops shot at striking workers, provided an occasion for the 'political' leaflet of 19 December 1897. The leaflet speaks in extremely vague terms about the 'downfall of the government', but it fails entirely to say what kind of government we should have in its stead, or what precisely the workers could do to hasten its downfall. However, these were the first experiments, and therefore of the utmost interest. Hence, I shall cite several excerpts from this long leaflet:

[1] 'Pis'mo k vsem Kievskim rabochim', in *Listok rabotnika*, no. 6 (February 1898), pp. 11–12, and Bugaev and Sergiuk (eds.), *Listovki*, p. 50.

Letter to all Kiev workers. Comrades! Every class conscious worker knows that the capitalists and the government are bound in a close and friendly alliance. In order to maintain good relations with the factory owners, the government stops at nothing, does not hesitate to adopt the most inhuman methods against the workers, is not even afraid of spilling the workers' blood to please the insatiable factory owners. Every worker has heard about the shooting down of workers in Zhirardov, Łódź, and Yaroslavl by troops acting on orders of the government. He knows about the new campaign of the Tsar's soldiers against the workers in the small town of Dombrowa. The government hopes to quench the flame of indignation with workers' blood. It hopes that the thunder of guns will drown out the battle cry against oppression and injustice.

But the workers know how to sacrifice their lives, and not only when they have to settle accounts with a thieving manager. They have enough courage to declare life-and-death war on those who are always supporting the capitalists in their lawlessness and plunder, those who are trying by prison, torture, and bullets to close the workers' road to happiness and freedom. . .

When the hundreds of thousands and millions of workers living in Russia unite as one man in the fight against exploitation and oppression, the fate of the government itself will also be decided. Through the forest of guns and bayonets, the workers will drive a wide road to a society in which there is no looting, no injustice, and no lies. . . And the cruel government will not escape the stern judgment of the labouring and dispossessed people. Let this government, which is stained with blood and injustice, perish soon. Let liberation from the yoke of Tsarist officials and from the violence of its valiant troops come soon![1]

The tone of this December leaflet was by no means fortuitous. The leading article in *Rabochaia Gazeta*, no. 2 (December 1897), also speaks of 'political' warfare. The editorial committee of *Rabochaia Gazeta* was at this time actively preparing for the congress of Social Democratic groups, which it had initiated. It had sent invitations to all organizations with which it had contacts. Most of them responded to the call. A manifesto and a programme were to be drawn up before the Congress, which would discuss and ratify them. However, the police had set up surveillance which interfered with the work, and the Congress was therefore held earlier than originally planned. Immediately afterwards there was a massive police attack on Social Democratic organizations throughout Russia. Some 500 people were arrested. One hundred and seventy-six comrades were arrested in Kiev. But the movement

---

[1] 'Pis'mo k vsem rabochim', in *Listok rabotnika*, no. 5 (January 1898), pp. 13–17; in 'Materialy i dokumenty', *Letopis' revoliutsii* (Kharkov), no. 3 (1923), pp. 71–3, and in Bugaev and Sergiuk (eds.), *Listovki*, pp. 51–3.

had already become so strong that even this lesson could not halt it, as was shown only a month later by the May Day leaflets scattered throughout the entire city. Nevertheless, the work lagged that summer, and the organization could not be properly re-established until autumn.

What changes, then, were made or at least initiated in the structure of the organization? It seems to me there were two, similar to those observed at the corresponding stage both in Vilna and in Petersburg: centralization and democratization. The authors of the Kiev Report to the Second Party Congress characterize the organizational relationships of this time as follows:

The relationship between the groups of the *intelligenty* and the workers was re-evaluated, and the opinion of the workers' circles was accepted as authoritative (1899–1900). In the autumn of 1899 there were rumours that the *intelligenty* were seeking closer relations with workers in order to further their own secret interests. To counter these rumours, serious attention had to be paid to the 'intermediate' elements and the organization had to be built on ultra 'democratic' principles.

The authors of the Report regard this as a shortcoming of the period. But I regard it as progress; in my view, the shortcomings lay in the fact that there was still too little centralism and too little democracy. The committee consisted, as formerly, of two parts: a committee of *intelligenty*, or simply the Committee, and a Workers Committee. This in itself reflected these two shortcomings. On the other hand, each section of the organization developed its own character, and each was equally necessary for a genuinely Social Democratic organization. The Workers Committee was composed of two sections: one for factory workers, the other for craft workers. The cells of the organization were the workers' circles. Every circle recognized as part of the general organization elected a representative, and every week there was a meeting for all the representatives within a given shop, factory, plant, or group of plants. They elected their 'leader', who became a member of the Workers Committee.

No workers belonged to the Committee. As early as February 1898, Comrade N. proposed that some workers be brought into the Committee. This proposal was rejected for the sake of conspiracy by a majority, with two dissenting votes (N. and B.). What an astonishing parallel to Petersburg!

Isolated though it was from the proletariat, the Committee of *intelligenty* continued to develop. 'The group of *intelligenty* was beginning to reorganize according to the principle of the division of labour', states the Report. In the autumn of 1898 the Committee consisted of ten persons. Connected with it, however, was a 'circle of propagandists', which enjoyed no powers but was active in the workers' circles. This in itself made clashes between the Committee and the voiceless executors of its will inevitable, and indeed such clashes began before long. 'In the spring of 1899', we read in the Report, 'disagreements arose between the Committee and the propagandists about the giving and receiving of commands. The propagandists demanded that the Committee provide a detailed explanation of each assignment.' However modest and legitimate these demands, they were not met by the Committee.* The massive arrests of April once more put a stop to the work for a long time. It resulted in an almost complete change in the composition of both the Committee and the propagandists' circle. However, the organizational problem, which was still not solved, continued to vex the comrades, to cause conflict and dissension, and to interfere with the work. The Committee was obliged to make a number of small concessions, but this was not enough. 'The question of the relationship between the propagandists and the Committee was raised again in the autumn of 1900.' 'Disagreements continued, and a state of armed neutrality followed.'

At this point the Committee took a step that went far beyond proper bounds, so far as we can judge from the Report. This could only convince the propagandists still further of the need to protect all those active in the cause from the arbitrary rule of those who wielded the 'conductor's baton'. To the authors of the Report, however, the Committee's action seemed 'the height of political wisdom'. 'Anxious to be rid of the ballast,' they write, 'the Committee instructed its representative, who attended the meetings of the propagandists' group, to announce that it was breaking with the group. He was then to organize all who genuinely wanted to work [i.e., those who were obedient!—V.A.] into a new group.' How easy it is to solve the problem of conflicting points of view when there is no democratic organization!

However, after a new series of arrests in March, the Committee

---

* The 'genuine', 'revolutionary', and 'orthodox' Social Democrats behaved in exactly the same way both in St Petersburg (as I demonstrated above) and abroad (as I shall show below). Thus each particular dispute over some matter of organization merely reflects the general divisions of opinion about organization which exist within our Party.

was radically reorganized and adopted democratic procedures for the section of the *intelligenty* as well.

The Committee now based its work on the principle of division of labour and constituted itself into several groups: an editorial group, a technical group, and two groups for agitation and organization. All questions of principle were decided in common at general meetings held not more than once a month. In the interim periods the direction of the work was vested in an Executive Committee of three persons, elected for a period of six months. The decisions of the Executive Committee were binding for all members and could be revoked only by a general meeting.*

This was how the organization developed. How did the methods of war change? In order to present demands to the government, the old method of protest—strikes—was obviously not enough. But until militant methods were found which would frighten the government as much as strikes frightened the capitalists, every 'demand' was bound to remain a mere impotent declaration of wishes. And such impotent demands could have no place in the calls to battle —the agitational leaflets.

As late as 1899 [Comrade Nazar'ev wrote to me] I still encountered Social Democrats who argued against the inclusion of demands for freedom of speech, press, assembly and organization in leaflets. 'To whom would the workers present these demands?' they asked. The

* Report of the Kiev Committee to the Second Congress [*Otchet Kievskogo Komiteta vtoromu s"ezdu*]. It is regrettable that neither the commission elected by the Second Congress for the publication of its protocols nor the editors of the Party journal considered it their duty to publish the committee reports submitted to the Second Congress. No one, of course, felt more strongly than the present author the full tendentiousness of these reports. They had obviously been composed according to plan, under instructions from the Organizational Committee, and were strongly imbued with the *Iskra* spirit. They were clearly meant to illustrate the liquidation of the third period and the triumph of *Iskra*. As I remember, none of them even mentioned the Union of Russian Social Democrats, as if the committees had not distributed approximately *eight million* pages of the Union's publications! As if they had not expressed their complete sympathy with it at one time! Nevertheless, the reports collected a good deal of highly valuable and instructive material. This inattention to facts and reality, I must stress again, is not due to negligence but is a characteristic feature of the doctrinaire approach of the 'orthodox'. [The only extant part of the Report of the Kiev Committee was the fragment eventually published in 1930 (together with an explanatory note by B. I. Nikolaevskii) in N. Angarskii (ed.), *Doklady sots.-demokraticheskikh komitetov vtoromu s"ezdu RSDRP* (Moscow–Leningrad, 1930), pp. 228–36. This fragment was republished in *Vtoroi s"ezd RSDRP: Protokoly* (Moscow, 1959), pp. 644–8. The first section of the Report, which Akimov here quotes extensively, has been lost and was never published in full.]

employers? They would only laugh and declare that they were quite prepared to satisfy them, but it was not their business—it was the business of the government. Or should they be presented to the government? . . . How, when, in what manner? And how could these demands be backed? They did not know. . .

As we have seen, in the summer of 1897 demonstrations were considered entirely impossible. But as the movement developed, this view began to change.*

In the beginning of 1899, after long discussion, the Kiev Committee resolved that demonstrations were desirable and highly useful. This was especially true, it felt, of May Day demonstrations. But when the question was raised as a practical one in April, the Committee was obliged to admit that 'the ground was not prepared and the available manpower had been depleted by the arrests of 13 April 1899'. The Committee slowly began to prepare the ground, to build up its forces. Sharp hostility to the government marked its publications of this time, chiefly the pages of *Vpered*.[1] Number 3 of the paper appeared in 1898. Numbers 4 and 5 were issued in January and March 1899. Number 6, dated April, describes the demonstrations in the Kingdom of Poland and draws the following conclusions: 'And so, workers' demonstrations are possible in Russia as well. Let us hope, then, that next year's May Day will be celebrated by Russian workers not in small circles but with a peaceful mass demonstration.' Number 7 did not come out until September, by which time the press on which it was printed had been seized. In this issue there is yet another article in support of demonstrations. Leaflets were spread throughout the

---

* 'The Economists argued against the "mad idea" of political demonstrations' (Trotsky, *Our Political Tasks* [*Nashi politicheskie zadachi*], p. 49). This is entirely incorrect. I have already referred to the Vilna demonstrations, organized by the so-called Economists. Now I shall cite facts which typify the attitude of the so-called Economists in Kiev to demonstrations. I have pointed out earlier that the arguments mentioned by Comrade Trotsky were precisely those of the extreme 'politicians'—Plekhanov and Aksel'rod. The truth of the matter is that at a certain stage of the movement's development it was indeed impossible to organize demonstrations, and this was recognized by all comrades regardless of their general viewpoint. But when demonstrations became possible, their organization was undertaken first of all by the so-called Economists. Will Comrade Trotsky, therefore, attempt to substantiate his theory with facts, now that I have disproved it here with facts?

[1] On *Vpered*, see B. L. Eidel'man, 'Kievskaia rabochaia gazeta *Vpered*, i: 1897 g.', *Proletarskaia revoliutsiia*, no. 6 (65) (June 1927), pp. 249–71, where he gave the history of the journal and republished nos. 1 and 3; and 'ii: 1897–1898 g.', *Proletarskaia revoliutsiia*, no. 12 (71), 1927, for no. 2 of *Vpered*.

city on 1 May 1899. They were thrown in through windows, pasted up, and scattered in the streets. There were 10,000 copies, excellently printed, with red headings. They called upon the workers to strike and demanded an eight-hour workday.

As I have said, it proved impossible to call a demonstration. But there were meetings, of which two were discovered by the police. Eighty workers were arrested, and a red banner was seized at one of the meetings.

A year later the idea of a demonstration had become so popular that the Governor General, Dragomirov, found it necessary during a bakers' strike to issue a proclamation warning that he would take the most stern and energetic steps if the workers decided to organize a demonstration. Of course, it was not these threats that prevented a demonstration: the elemental revolutionary cause had not yet attained the power to take up the movement of the bakers like a whirlwind and make it a movement of the people. As for the class conscious workers, already prepared by propaganda and agitation, they were crushed and scattered by a series of mass arrests—on 12 March, at the end of March, and at the end of April, as well as by a number of extraordinary military and police measures. Thus, in 1900, too, it proved impossible to organize a demonstration. On 1 May the Committee merely spread leaflets on red paper and called a meeting, which over a hundred people attended.

I have now examined the changes brought about by the new stage of the movement, so-called Economism, in the character of the leaflets, in the nature of the organization, and in the type of tactics. The special characteristics of this stage of the movement were reflected even more clearly than those of the preceding stage in the statements of theory worked out by the Kiev comrades. I have in mind a certain *Profession de foi* of the Kiev Committee. Since this document is not well known,[1] I shall cite here its most important section:

Although it regards the struggle for the political rights of the proletariat as the immediate general task of the labour movement in Russia, the Kiev Committee does not consider it possible at this moment to appeal to the labouring masses with a call to political action. In other words, it feels that it is impossible today to conduct political agitation, since the

---

[1] Drawn up by the Kiev Committee late in 1898 or early in 1899, it was first publicized by Lenin and his comrades, who reproduced it together with Lenin's critique. See *Leninskii sbornik*, ed. L. Kamenev (Moscow, 1924–5), VII, 16–18.

mass of Russian workers is not yet ready for political warfare. Hence, agitation can be used to influence the masses only in the following ways:

(1) To assist and further the proletariat's economic struggle. This is why the Committee utilizes every conflict between workers and employers, every malpractice of any importance committed by the employers, to speak to the workers in appeals and leaflets. The Committee explains their position to the workers, urges them to protest, leads strikes, formulates their demands, points out how best to achieve these demands, and in all these ways develops the self-awareness of the working-class.

(2) To educate the masses politically on the basis of day-to-day economic battles. So far as each particular case permits, the Committee uses every outbreak of economic warfare to show up the political position of the working-class, to introduce the masses gradually to the idea of political liberty, and to arouse awareness of the need for political rights.

For the political education of the labouring masses, the Committee considers the publication of a local workers' newspaper to be of great importance. It tries to make this newspaper accessible to the widest possible strata of workers, to encourage the workers to participate by submitting correspondence, and so to teach them to regard the paper as their own. Although it gives priority to economic agitation and to the political education of the working masses, the Committee does not consider it possible to give up its educational activity in the workers' circles, which it sees as a means of creating a contingent of conscious worker-agitators, to broaden its contacts among the workers, and to spread literature. The Committee does not consider it possible at this time to call the broad working masses in Kiev to political action. But it regards as desirable the organization of limited demonstrations, the sole aim of which would be agitation (not influence upon the government) and which would be based on ideas readily understood by the broad masses.

This *Profession de foi* was published only a year and a half later, not by its authors, but by its opponents; not to give it favourable publicity, but to criticize it.* As a statement of theory, the *Profession de foi* was certainly open to criticism in many respects, but it was totally misunderstood by the person who published it. This misunderstanding, it seems to me, stems from his failure to take into account the conditions of time and place under which this document appeared, and from the fact that he evaluated it not as a historian, but as a polemicist.

* By all indications, this critique was penned by Lenin. [Akimov's deduction here was correct, and Lenin's analysis of the *Profession de foi* has been published in the last three editions of *Sochineniia*: e.g., 5th ed. (Moscow, 1958–65), iv, 310–21.]

The very first phrase of the *Profession de foi* [writes its critic] produces extreme bewilderment. . . One is driven to ask oneself: Can its authors be Social Democrats? 'The mass of Russian workers is not yet ready for political warfare.' If this is true, it is tantamount to a death sentence for the entire Social Democratic movement, for it means that the mass of Russian workers is not yet ready for Social Democracy. Indeed, there has never been anywhere in the world, nor is there today, a Social Democratic movement that is not indivisibly and indissolubly bound up with political warfare. A Social Democratic party without political warfare is a river without water, a crying contradiction, a return to the utopian socialism of our grandfathers, who disdained 'politics', or to anarchism, or to trade-unionism.[1]

To interpret the 'first phrase' in this way indicates a failure to understand it. It is not merely that the authors did not disdain 'politics'. From the very first sentence they actually declared that they regarded 'politics' as 'the immediate general task of the labour movement in Russia'. Whether they approached this task correctly or not is another question. The fact that they stated it and indeed considered it urgent sharply distinguishes them from the grandfathers of socialism, from the anarchists, and from the trade-unionists.

'If this is true, . . . it means that the mass of Russian workers is not yet ready for Social Democracy.' Quite correct. And so it was at the time: the mass labour movement at that point was not yet Social Democratic. But the critic is entirely wrong in asserting that this is 'tantamount to a death sentence for the entire Social Democratic movement'. On the contrary! The mass movement had not yet become Social Democratic, but there were already many Social Democrats. Moreover, the mass movement had already passed the first phases of its development; it did so under the guidance of the Social Democrats and was on the verge of becoming 'ready for Social Democracy'. But the movement was ripening precisely because those who were already Social Democrats attempted to influence the mass movement, to 'educate the masses'. This was the task undertaken by the comrades in Kiev at that period.

Were they successful in their choice of method? The critic considers that they were not, and that this led them to 'crying contradictions'.

How, indeed, can anyone speak about the 'political education' of workers if he considers it impossible to conduct political agitation and

[1] *Leninskii sbornik*, VII, 7; Lenin, *Sochineniia*, 5th ed., IV, 311.

to wage political warfare? Is it still necessary among Social Democrats to prove that there can be no political education except by political warfare and political action? Does anyone suppose that the labouring masses can be educated politically by study and books without political activity and political war?[1]

Again, the critic here is arguing outside time and place. Of course, ultimately the masses can be educated politically only when they are working and fighting for political goals. But the pioneers of the Social Democratic movement could, and had to, content themselves for a long time with 'study and books' in order to propagate their ideas. This is one point. The second point is that the authors by no means considered it necessary at that time to confine their activities to 'study and books'. Another method they felt suitable for educating the masses politically was the 'limited' demonstration. However, the authors' views in this respect were also misunderstood by their critic.

'Strangely,' he writes, 'and at the same time very characteristically for the entire *Profession de foi*, the Committee, without considering it possible to call the broad labouring masses to political action at the present moment, nevertheless advocates the organization of limited demonstrations. These, it says, are to be held with the sole aim of agitation, not in order to influence the government, and are to be based on ideas readily understood by the broad masses. Socialists are thus telling the workers not to bring pressure to bear on the government! Can you go any further?'[2]

This is an outright distortion of the idea of the authors. Although it recognizes political warfare as the next task of the labour movement, the *Profession de foi* considers the working masses not yet ready for this task. It therefore tries to find means which would enable the advance guard of the proletariat—the Social Democrats—to educate the masses for this political war. One such means, in its view, is to call the workers to demonstrate for specific (limited) political rights: freedom of speech, press, assembly, organization, and so on. In proposing this, the authors state that they do not believe these demands could lead to the winning of such rights under the existing political order ('the aim . . . is not influence upon the government'). But they assume that in fighting for these rights the proletariat will come to recognize that to achieve them the autocracy must first be overthrown.

[1] *Leninskii sbornik*, VII, 8; Lenin, *Sochineniia*, 5th ed., IV, 312.
[2] *Leninskii sbornik*, VII, 12; Lenin, *Sochineniia*, 5th ed., IV, 316–17.

These, then, were the views that characterized not only the work of our comrades in Kiev at that time but also that entire stage in the movement's history. I cannot help being reminded at this point of the words used by a comrade from Petersburg to describe the methods used in this stage: 'It was a consciously chosen method to educate the masses politically.'

4

Our comrades kept a close watch on the surroundings in which they had to work; they were careful to follow the moods of the masses, waiting for an opportunity to take the next step. The opportunity came before long. By the end of 1899, and especially in the beginning of 1900, the workers were in a tense, agitated state, which culminated in April in the strike of some thousand bakery workers who had the support of another thousand workers.[1] 'In February and March', we read in the Report,

the Committee discussed in passing whether to revise its tactics. In April this question was raised officially. . . The Committee resolved by a majority, with one dissenting vote, that it was necessary to change over to broad political agitation. One of the best methods of arousing the masses, it decided, was to organize protest demonstrations against the most arbitrary acts of the autocracy. The same meeting voted to revise the *Profession de foi*.

Consequently, by the time it came out, the criticism of the *Profession* 'was already of merely historical significance'. It was, in short, out of date and, as I tried to show above, also profoundly erroneous and superficial.

In *Vpered*, no. 10, dated December 1900, the need for political action is stated sharply and clearly. The paper no longer put forward demands for specific rights, which were intended merely for agitation. It now called for a fight against the entire political system, a fight for participation in power. 'Our immediate goal', it said, 'is the overthrow of the criminal absolutist order and the conquest of the political rights of freedom.' 'Side by side with the demand for a radical reconstruction of the entire social order, the red banner of the Russian Social Democratic movement bears the words bequeathed to us by the heroes of 14 December [1825]:

[1] The large-scale strike of bakery workers in Kiev in April–May 1900 was described in *Listok 'Rabochego dela'*, no. 1 (June 1900), pp. 6–7.

'For political liberty! For the rights of the people! Down with the autocracy!'

Thus the study of the Kiev movement also shows that two factors developed inextricably in our movement: its political character, and its organization. By the beginning of 1901, during the February and March days, the logic of events demanded the beginning of organized political warfare, and that war began.

4. THE CONFLICTING ORGANIZATIONAL PRINCIPLES

The Roots of Disagreement

Highly deplorable developments are taking place in our Party today. People who see themselves as disciples of the great concept of scientific socialism, as teachers of a philosophy which in its breadth and profundity should succeed the universal theories of Plato, St Augustine, Giordano Bruno, and Rousseau—these people lack respect and understanding for others as for themselves. They engage in petty, abusive quarrels. They reduce their great cause to the level of a factional squabble.

And this is happening at a decisive historical moment. Our country is undergoing the most severe ordeals. All the moral energies of society are strained to the utmost. All citizens—revolutionaries and socialists in particular—are called upon by the very course of events to act firmly and without hesitation in their duty to their homeland and to mankind. Yet at this moment many people are asking a question which must be painful for a Social Democrat: if the Russian Social Democratic movement cannot understand and solve the problems of our time at the very moment when the social energies of our country have been unleashed, can it act generally as the progressive champion of eternal and universal ideas?

I am deeply convinced that it can. When its composition changes, when it becomes truly proletarian, the Social Democratic Party will tell its teachers 'what is to be done' and 'what is not to be done'. 'Bad shepherds! What did you do with our name? Why did you degrade and dishonour it, making it hateful to so many of our brothers? Why, speaking in the name of the proletariat, did you hinder the proletariat from learning to use its own voice, its own will?' Such will be the words of the proletariat when it begins to speak. And then our Party will be reborn after dangerous battles without, after grave dissensions within. But when that time comes, the Social Democratic movement will not be able to reconcile itself to the slogans, the formulae, and the programme which had been produced by its anti-proletarian wing. The Russian Social Democratic movement will re-evaluate the very principles of its philosophy and will make substantial additions to them. With these additions scientific socialism will make another advance, dictated both by our Russian life and by that of the international Social Democratic movement.

If this is so, then our next historic task will be to organize the vanguard of the proletariat—the Social Democratic movement— so that it will be able to speak for and lead the entire Russian working-class in the fight for its needs. This is why the disagreements and strife within the Party have centred around organizational principles. In my last work,[1] I tried to describe the ideological disagreements which, albeit not recognized by the disputants themselves, nevertheless drove them to adopt their conflicting attitudes toward the organizational question. It seems to me that the materials I have gathered together in the earlier chapters of the present booklet allow us to observe these disagreements and this struggle *in statu nascendi*, as it were, at the moment that they emerged. I have examined these disagreements from the viewpoint of theory in my last booklet and from the viewpoint of history in the present one.

Comrade Lenin explained our disagreements by the fact that our Party is divided between the *intelligenty* and the proletarians. Comrade Galerka attributed them to the division into an organization abroad and an organization in Russia.[2] Comrade Martov ascribed them to the fact that the movement had become psychologically accustomed to the era of the confined educational circle [*kruzhkovshchina*] and was unable to adapt itself immediately to the new conditions under which the Party now had to function. But after all these explanations, one is compelled to agree with the view that 'the points at issue have not been clarified. This is the central fact in the present disorder—an incredible, but indubitable fact' (Comrade Galerka).

How true this is. All the explanations cited here are accepted by both sides. But each claims that it is proletarian; each insists that it answers the requirements of those active in Russia and that it is advancing the cause of Party centralization; and each accuses its factional opponents of prejudices typical of intellectuals, émigrés, and *kruzhkovshchina*. Every attempt to clarify the disagreements is a hypothesis. And that hypothesis which can

---

[1] *K voprosu o rabotakh vtorogo s"ezda Rossiiskoi Sotsial-Demokraticheskoi Rabochei Partii* (Geneva, 1904).

[2] See [M. S. Aleksandrov and A. Bogdanov] (Galerka and Riadavoi), *Nashi nedorazumeniia* (Geneva, 1904).

explain the stand taken by both sides on all the points at issue will win the right to recognition and show the way out of the miserable state in which our Party finds itself today. A number of pamphlets and articles published during the past year—by Lenin, Martov, Panin, Trotsky, Galerka, Aksel'rod, Plekhanov, Riadovoi and Riazanov—attempted to do this. And as for me, I too have a point of view to defend. It may be summed up as follows: 'In so far as the elemental, spontaneous movement among the workers made the advanced strata of the Russian proletariat aware of their ever-growing concerns, so the methods employed by the Russian Social Democrats in the fight and in organization were transformed.'

This is the basic idea of the present book—an idea which I advanced in the introduction and which I hope I have demonstrated in the preceding chapters. But the Social Democratic movement expanded in breadth as well as depth and caught up ever new strata of the proletariat. The advanced strata of the proletariat were becoming ready for the higher forms of warfare. But those strata which had only just been drawn in were passing through stages long outlived by the more advanced. The workers' movement as a whole is therefore a complex organism. And the complex class struggle waged by the proletariat requires the simultaneous use of extremely diverse types of action and forms of organization. At the same time, all of these strata produce their own leaders and theoreticians; hence, different groupings form within the Party, each with its own ideas about tactics and organization. The leaders of each grouping see themselves subjectively as the true spokesmen for the interests of the entire proletariat, the champions of the true interests of the entire Social Democratic movement. Consequently, they fight every other grouping in order to win hegemony for their own tactics. This, in my view, explains the disagreements in our Party today.

To prove this idea, I shall try first to summarize the organizational principles of the two most divergent trends within the Russian Social Democratic movement: the policy of the old *Iskra*, and the 'democratism' of the third period, of *Rabochee Delo*. I shall show, on the basis of the materials collected above, how each of these two groupings was related to the stage associated with it in the development of the Social Democratic movement. I shall also attempt to analyse the tactical and organizational principles of the new *Iskra*. Only when I have done this shall I be able, in concluding my book, to return to the idea formulated here about the nature of our disagreements and suggest how they might be eliminated.

The Old 'Iskra': Lenin

We are faced with the question of what kind of organization our Party needs. But what is the Party? Our literature offers two answers to this question, both equally definite and clearly formulated and representative of two different positions in our Party. One answer was given by Lenin; the other, in the publications of the Union of Russian Social Democrats.

From Lenin's point of view, the party is the organization; the members of the party are members of the organization.* This organization is complex; it consists of many 'cells', combined in such a way as to produce a complicated system of collaboration— a single 'complex' of organizations.† The boundaries of the party, therefore, as seen by Lenin, are absolutely defined: 'This, approximately, is how I see the matter: (1) an organization of revolutionaries; (2) an organization of workers, as broad and diversified as possible. . . These two categories constitute the party' (Lenin, *One Step Forward* [*Shag vpered*], p. 46).

Between this party and the working-class, which lives a blind, unthinking life and 'should act under the leadership of the workers' party only in wartime, in a period of civil war' (*ibid.* p. 41), there are intermediate forces: 'First, workers' organizations which are affiliated with the party; second, workers' organizations which do not belong to the party but are in fact subject to its control and leadership; third, unorganized sections of the working-class, which . . . partially submit to the leadership of the Social Democrats' (*ibid.* p. 46).

'We are the party of a class, and therefore the entire class must act under the leadership of our party', says Lenin (*ibid.* p. 41). To make it possible for such a closed organization to direct the actions of an entire class, Lenin proposed to build it according to conspiratorial principles: every member and every cell in the organization would follow the 'conductor's baton' in the hand of the party leadership.

Lenin has repeatedly expressed his views on party organization.

---

* According to the first paragraph of the [Organizational] Statute as proposed by Lenin. [See *Vtoroi s"ezd RSDRP: Protokoly* (Moscow, 1959), p. 262 n.]
† See Lenin's *One Step Forward, Two Steps Back* [*Shag vpered*], p. 39 and n.

4. CONFLICTING ORGANIZATIONAL PRINCIPLES

I believe that he discussed this for the first time in his booklet, *The Tasks of the Russian Social Democrats*, in 1897. Today, *post factum*, it is easy to discern in this booklet the seeds of that purely conspiratorial idea of party organization which Lenin later came to advocate. However, when the booklet first appeared, urging the Social Democratic movement to create a firm revolutionary organization, it was well received by everybody. Aksel'rod, in his introduction to it, announced that he fully shared its ideas. For its part, the editorial committee of the Union of Russian Social Democrats, in the review in *Rabochee Delo*, no. 1, 'noted with pleasure' that 'in essence, the booklet says exactly the same as the editorial programme of *Rabochee Delo*.'*

Thus this booklet, *The Tasks*, written by the leader of today's Bolsheviks, was at that juncture fully acceptable to Aksel'rod, the theoretician of today's Mensheviks, and equally to the editors of *Rabochee Delo*, which spoke for a specific grouping, the so-called Economists. Clearly, it is to this statement of the tasks facing the

---

* [*Rabochee delo*, no. 1 (April 1899), p. 142.] This review sparked off the factional polemic which, unfortunately, is still being waged with ever greater intensity in our Party press. 'The booklet is especially valuable', wrote the editors of *Rabochee Delo*, 'in that it acquaints us at first hand with the actual state of our movement, with its living programme. In this respect, we cannot agree with Comrade Aksel'rod, who tends in his introduction to suggest that on the whole "our movement is still only aspiring to that stage of development which has already been fully attained by the tactical ideas of the author". It must be said, however, that Aksel'rod bases his opinion solely on "the statements of younger comrades who have recently come abroad". We do not know which "young" comrades Aksel'rod has in mind. For our part, we have reason to assert that the younger Russian Social Democrats, who gained experience and worked in the mass movement, share both in theory and in actual practice the viewpoint of the author' (*Rabochee delo*, no. 1, pp. 141–2).

In his *Letter to the editors of 'Rabochee Delo'* [*Pis'mo v redaktsiiu 'Rabochego dela'* (Geneva, 1899)] Aksel'rod argued against these lines, and said, among other things, that [Lenin] 'the author of *The Tasks*, was not describing the actual work of the Russian Social Democrats but was merely presenting the programme of action which necessarily follows from Social Democratic thought'. The editors of *Rabochee Delo* published a *Reply* to Plekhanov's *Vademecum* and Aksel'rod's *Letter* [*Otvet redaktsii 'Rabochego dela' na 'Pis'mo' P. Aksel'roda i 'Vademecum' G. Plekhanova* (Geneva, 1900)], proving in Lenin's 'own words', with 'a number of quotations from [Lenin's] booklet', that Aksel'rod was wrong. This *Reply* remained unanswered. Lenin later declared, without showing proof, that Aksel'rod and not the editors of *Rabochee Delo* had been right in the interpretation of his booklet. He did not take the trouble to refute the arguments of *Rabochee Delo*. This tendency to make unsubstantiated assertions is highly typical of this author, as I have shown on many occasions and will show many times in the future. The readers of Lenin's pamphlets must always be on guard against his unproved statements.

Social Democrats that we can trace back our disagreements: all of us were still in agreement with the ideas formulated by *The Tasks*; but as these ideas unfolded, we diverged. Let us turn, then, to this booklet.

In his *The Tasks* Lenin quotes the following lines from P. L. Lavrov's letter in no. 4 of *Letuchii Listok*, published by the Group of *Narodovol'tsy*:* 'Can there be a strong workers party under our absolutist system unless there is a revolutionary party to oppose that system?' Is it possible to 'organize a Russian workers party under absolutist rule without simultaneously organizing a revolutionary party to fight this rule'?

Lenin comments on P. L. Lavrov's questions:

We fail to understand these distinctions, which are of such cardinal importance to P. L. Lavrov. What is this? 'No workers party unless there is a revolutionary party to oppose absolutism'? But isn't the workers party itself a revolutionary party? Does it not oppose absolutism? This strange idea is explained in the following passage of Lavrov's article.

And Lenin again quotes from Lavrov's letter:

The 'organization' of the Russian workers party must be created under the absolutist system with all its charms. If the Social Democrats were able to create such an organization without at the same time organizing a political *conspiracy* against absolutism—a *conspiracy* with all its inevitable characteristics—then, of course, their political programme would be the proper programme for Russian socialists. It would mean the emancipation of the workers by the workers themselves. But this is extremely doubtful, if not impossible. [The italics throughout are Lenin's.]

Lenin goes on with his criticism of Lavrov's views:

So that's the gist of it! To a *Narodovolets*, the concept of political warfare is identical with that of political *conspiracy*. It must be admitted that P. L. Lavrov has indeed succeeded with utmost clarity in showing the basic difference *between the tactics of political warfare* [italics mine—V.A.] employed by the *Narodovol'tsy* and those employed by the Social Democrats. The traditions of Blanquism, of conspiratorial methods, are enormously powerful among the *Narodovol'tsy*—so powerful that they cannot imagine political warfare in any form but that of a political conspiracy. However, the Social Democrats are not guilty of such a narrow view; they do not believe in conspiracies. They have always

---

* This interesting letter has now been republished by Comrade Kuklin as no. 53 in his publication series [For the letter—'O programmnykh voprosakh'—see P. Kudelli, *Narodovol'tsy...*, pp. 155–9.]

thought, and think today, that this struggle should be waged not by conspirators but *by a revolutionary party based on the workers' movement* [italics mine—V.A.]. They believe that the struggle against the autocracy should be waged not by organizing plots but by educating the proletariat, by disciplining it, by political agitation among the workers.[1]

Lenin's *The Tasks* has since been issued in a second edition, and it has been announced that a third is in preparation. Is there any point in this? The booklet still expresses views shared by us all and still formulates correctly the tactical principles which distinguish us, the Social Democrats, from socialists of other schools. But it is no longer adequate for us. It speaks in terms which are too general and therefore too difficult to analyse. It contains theses which, as they have evolved, have proved open to too many different interpretations.

Of particular importance for the problem under discussion, it seems to me, are the following statements which I have already quoted from Lenin: 'Lavrov has shown the difference between the tactics of political warfare employed by the *Narodovol'tsy* and those employed by the Social Democrats'; 'The Social Democrats think that the political struggle should be waged by a revolutionary party based on the workers' movement'. These theses conceal within themselves the roots of our present disagreements. Indeed, they can be interpreted in two different ways.

The first interpretation is that, in the form taken by its organization, the Social Democratic party is a party much like the *Narodnaia Volia*, but that it differs from the latter in its tactics and methods of action. It does not use its own forces for a frontal attack on the government but mobilizes the working-class against it. The second interpretation is that the Social Democrats see political warfare as an advanced form of the labour movement. Moreover, at this advanced stage, the labour movement and the Social Democratic party will be united in action, doing the same work.

The first view, it seems to me, was held by Lenin; the second, by the Union of Russian Social Democrats. Today's Mensheviks have already divorced themselves from the first view but have not yet adopted the second. I shall now have to demonstrate all this, for, I must repeat, although both these conceptions of the Social Democratic party are inherent in Lenin's booklet, neither is clearly expressed in it.

[1] [Lenin,] *Zadachi russkikh sotsial'demokratov* (Geneva, 1898), pp. 20–1.

Rejecting conspiratorial tactics, Lenin retained a conspiratorial view of the structure a revolutionary organization should have. This exactly matched the state of the socialist organizations in that transition period when the *Narodnaia Volia* was giving way to Social Democracy and when the author of *The Tasks* was actually crystallizing his ideas. The materials I have collected in this book show that the Social Democratic organizations of the economist period were conspiratorial. The tactics of the socialists had already changed by that time, but the organizational structure had not yet been adapted to the new tactics. It was possible for this to be so only because the work undertaken by the socialists of the new school, the Social Democrats, was itself rudimentary. As the work became more complex, the organization changed. And today in the most advanced sector of Social Democracy, the Bund, the structure of the organization is suited in substantial measure to the new tactics of war.

By the time he came to write his articles for the first issues of *Iskra*, and later his book *What Is to Be Done?* Lenin had defined his views on organization with far greater clarity. Now the Union of Russian Social Democrats and its adherents could no longer consider themselves in agreement with the author of *The Tasks*. Two groupings crystallized within the Social Democratic movement. Let us, then, examine the theses of *What Is to Be Done?*—carried further than those of *The Tasks* but still not fully developed.

(1) 'The economic struggle against the employers and the government does not in the least demand—and therefore cannot produce —an all-Russian centralized organization that will merge *all types of political opposition*, protest, and indignation into one general assault. It does not demand an organization made up of professional revolutionaries and led by the real political leaders of *"the entire people"*' (p. 75; italics mine—V.A.).

The Social Democratic organization is here required to speak in the name of 'all types of political opposition' and to follow the leaders of 'the entire people'. Such a demand in itself implies that the proletariat is only one of the forces to be led by the Social Democratic organization. And it sees the Social Democratic organization merely as an independent associate of the proletarian movement. This view, as I have already shown, simply reflected the actual situation at the time when the Social Democratic organizations in Vilna, Petersburg, and Kiev were first emerging.

(2) 'So frequent were the arrests, so many the losses, so total the uprootings of local groups that the labouring masses were losing literally all their leaders. The movement developed in a fantastically piecemeal way, and it was absolutely impossible to establish any continuity and connectivity in the work' (p. 77).

If the first quotation imposed on the Social Democratic organization tasks which did not properly belong to it as a proletarian party, the second denied that the proletarian movement had any influence on how Social Democratic organizations develop or on what they do. It turns out that there was *absolutely no* continuity in the work of Social Democratic organizations. The author explains this fact by the arrests, which had produced too rapid a turnover in the membership of the Social Democratic organizations. It is entirely true that the composition of the Social Democratic organizations changed with amazing frequency. Many of them lasted for six months in all, and many for less. But this makes it all the more astonishing that the work had both continuity and connectivity, a fact which I hope has been demonstrated by the materials collected in this book. Tactics and organizational structure developed with such logic that one can easily discern certain underlying laws. If the author of *What Is to Be Done?* deniest his, it merely shows that his views were formed at the very first stage in the development of the proletarian movement. But of course, once formed, these views demanded that if nothing else would suffice then the revolutionaries would have to devote all their energies to the preservation of organizational continuity. And this was the conclusion drawn by the author himself:

(3) 'Our primary and most imperative practical task is to create an organization of revolutionaries which can maintain the energy, stability, and continuity of the political struggle' (p. 79).

The creation of a stable and firm Party organization was indeed the next urgent task facing the Social Democratic movement, and in so far as *Iskra* advocated this idea it was—though unaware of the fact—merely voicing a need brought to the fore by history. The spark of organized political struggle was carried forward by the winds of the third period. If *Iskra*, Lenin's organ, failed to win the support of the so-called Economist section of our movement, it was not because it set itself this task, but because of the way in which it did so. Neither Lenin nor the rest of the *Iskra* group understood this, however. They accused their opponents of *kustarnichestvo*, *khvostizm*, Economism, and so on. Later, when I analyse the

organizational views of this other section of the movement, I shall
show how incorrect these accusations were.* For the moment, I
shall merely note—in following the evolution of Lenin's views—
that 'the organization of professional revolutionaries' was transformed from a means by which the proletarian movement could
find expression into a self-sufficient end in itself. This will become
even clearer from the subsequent quotations.

(4) 'With what matchless, truly Narcissistic superciliousness these
sages [*Rabochee Delo*] lectured Plekhanov on the fact that the
workers' circles were "generally incapable of coping with political
tasks in the real sense of the word, incapable of an effective and
successful *practical* battle in support of political demands"'
(*Reply of the Editors of 'Rabochee Delo' [Otvet redaktsii 'Rabochego
dela'*], p. 24).
There are circles and circles, gentlemen! Of course, for a circle of backward-looking provincials [*kustari*] political tasks are a closed book. But
a circle made up of leaders like Alekseev, Myshkin, Khalturin and Zheliabov, can handle political tasks in the most real and practical sense of
the word. They can do so just because—and to the extent that—their
passionate teaching meets with a response from the masses which are
awakening of their own accord, to the extent that their own seething
energy is caught up and supported by the energy of the revolutionary
class (p. 80).

Here, expressed with real clarity, is the idea that the 'circles',
the Social Democratic organizations, have an autonomous rôle to

---

* *Iskra's* methods of 'ideological' struggle with opponents remained the same:
no polemical excesses were shunned if they discredited the 'critic'. A fair
example of this is provided by Lenin's argument in his *One Step Forward*
(p. 47 and n.) concerning the problem under discussion here. He writes:
'Akimov frankly explained that "their very purpose" (Plekhanov's,
Martov's, and mine—namely, the creation of a leading organization of
revolutionaries) is regarded by him as unrealizable and harmful. Like
Comrade Martynov, he defends the Economists' idea that an organization
of revolutionaries is unnecessary. Comrade Martynov wants to make his
listeners *forget* that those against whom I have fought did not see any need
for *an organization of revolutionaries*, just as Comrade Akimov does not see
it today.' I now publicly demand that Comrade Lenin tell me what right he
has to use and publish these words! Surely he must know that I have never
said, either orally or in print, that I consider unnecessary an organization of
revolutionaries? That, on the contrary, I have myself been a member for
ten years of various organizations of revolutionaries? Doesn't Comrade
Lenin know that for ten years I have been, to use his terminology, a professional revolutionary, and as such have always belonged to organizations
of revolutionaries?
(Note to Second Edition: Comrade Lenin did not deem it his duty to
reply to me. I do not know what methods Comrade Lenin recognizes for the
protection of individuals against slander in our milieu, if a public challenge
to reply is insufficient for him.)

play. A *direct* attack by the Social Democratic organizations on the autocracy is impossible. This was precisely what the editors of *Rabochee Delo* said. They sought other methods of political warfare and opted for leadership of the mass struggle of the proletariat. Although he ridicules this idea, Lenin, without realizing it, adopts it *in toto* himself, and he assigns the difficult task of the political reconstruction of Russia to the 'energy of the revolutionary class'.

But if Lenin's ridicule of *Rabochee Delo* stems from his failure to understand his opponent, it nevertheless vividly reflects one idea characteristic of Lenin, which really distinguishes him sharply from *Rabochee Delo*. He does not see the movement and activity of the 'revolutionary class' as spontaneous, as creative, as capable of forming the organs, the organizations, it requires. On the contrary, he sees them as the 'response' to, the echo of, the seething activity of the organization of revolutionaries. Comrade Nadezhdin has called his newspaper *The Echo [Otkliki]* of the proletarian movement. Lenin regards the proletarian movement itself as an 'echo' of the seething activity of the professional revolutionaries. He called his organ *Iskra [The Spark]*, from which the flame of popular rebellion is to be kindled. In describing the work of the first Social Democratic organizations in Petersburg, I showed how such a psychology was formed. It was there and at that time that Lenin received his political education. Let us see, then, how he distinguishes more and more between the Social Democratic movement and the workers' movement as two independent social phenomena.

(5) 'Today the Russian revolutionary, who is guided by a genuinely revolutionary theory, and *bases himself* [italics mine—V.A.] on a genuinely revolutionary class which is awakening spontaneously, can at last—at last!—straighten out to his full height and throw his whole giant strength into action' (p. 81).

We have thus approached the problem of the relationship between the organization of professional revolutionaries and the unadulterated labour movement (p. 83). I assert that the more we *narrow* the membership of our organization to include only those who are professionally engaged in revolutionary work . . . the larger will be the number of people both of the working-class and of *other classes* [italics mine—V.A.; cf. paragraph 1] who will have the opportunity to take part in the movement and to work in it actively (p. 94).

We objected and, of course, will always object to reducing the political struggle to the level of a conspiracy. But naturally this does not mean that we deny the necessity for a strong revolutionary organization

(p. 103). In its structure, a strong revolutionary organization in an autocratic country may be described as a conspiratorial organization, for the translation of the French word *conspiration* is the Russian 'conspiracy' [*zagovor*]. It would therefore be naïve in the extreme to be afraid of the charge that we Social Democrats want to create a conspiratorial organization (pp. 103–4).

It seems to me that all these quotations from *What Is to Be Done?* clearly delineate two tactical principles held by Lenin: (1) in its *functions*, the Social Democratic organization repudiates conspiratorial methods of warfare and is designed to produce a 'response' from, to win the 'support' of, the masses; (2) in its *structure*, this organization should be conspiratorial. This contradiction between the functional and structural aspects of the Social Democratic organization reflects the fundamental contradiction inherent in Lenin's views. It shows that in his ideas he stands midway between the party of socialist conspiracy, the *Narodnaia Volia*, and the party of proletarian socialism, the Social Democratic party. Such is his position, whether viewed from the theoretical angle (as in my last book) or from the historical angle (as in this one).

What Is to Be Done? appeared in March 1902, and, unfortunately for the cause, met no opposition. Some failed to realize the extent to which this book was superficial, erroneous, and dedicated to purely polemic ends. Others, aware of this, nevertheless gave ground, too weak to take up this new challenge from the *Iskra* group. Still others, like Plekhanov by his own admission, were silent for reasons of diplomacy. Lenin saw himself as the victor, and in his *Letter to a Comrade* [*Pis'mo k tovarishchu*], written in September, dotted the i's in his organizational plans. This letter became the point of departure for criticism of Lenin's plans even among those who had formerly agreed with him. However, this criticism came not at the time of its appearance but much later, after an entire year, and after the split at the Congress.

When he published this letter in January 1904, Lenin asked, quite correctly: 'But really, doesn't everyone see that our Party's Organizational Statute contains within itself those very organizational plans we have always had?'[1] Let us see, then, what these plans were.

[1] N. Lenin, *Pis'mo k tovarishchu o nashikh organizatsionnykh zadachakh* (Geneva, 1904), p. 4. The worker for whom Lenin wrote his *Letter* was the St Petersburg Social Democrat A. A. Shneierson. See Lenin, *Sochineniia*, v, 411 n.

4. CONFLICTING ORGANIZATIONAL PRINCIPLES

'The entire local movement, all local Social Democratic work, is directed by a committee' (p. 17). This committee consists solely of professional revolutionaries, 'fully conscious Social Democrats who devote themselves entirely to Social Democratic work' (p. 7). The composition and rôle of the local committee are discussed only in the closing paragraphs of Lenin's letter. At the beginning of the letter he merely indicates that the committee controls the local party organization, and he then proceeds to analyse the other sections of the local organization. He starts out by summarizing the views of the comrade to whose letter he is replying:

'After the committee, you name the following institutions subordinate to it: (1) discussion groups; (2) district circles; (3) circles for the propagandists attached to each district circle; (4) factory circles; and (5) councils [skhodki] made up of representatives from the factory circles.'[1]

In answer, Lenin observes: 'I agree with you that all other institutions should be subordinate to the committee, but it seems to me that in certain details I do not entirely agree with you.'[2] It will become clear from the following pages that Lenin might have put it more correctly if he had said the reverse: 'I am fully in agreement with one detail of your plan, the detail that absolutely everybody will accept. But as for all the rest, particularly the most important points, I entirely disagree with you.' And if this does actually turn out to be what Lenin means, then we shall have to grant that there is no less finesse in the phrasing he uses for his friends than there is in the polemical graces intended for his 'enemies'.

(1) 'As for the discussion groups, I think that there is no need for such an institution. The best revolutionaries should all be in the committee or in special organizations. Why have a special institution for discussions?'[3]

In describing the Bund's system of organization, I showed the important place held in it by discussion groups, and the Petersburg worker to whom Lenin is replying evidently recognizes this importance.* But to Lenin, all party organizations except the central

[1] Lenin, *Pis'mo k tovarishchu*, pp. 8–9. [2] *Ibid.* p. 9. [3] *Ibid.*
* This comrade [Shneierson] was under the influence of *Iskra*, and from the very beginning of his Party career he fought against the Petersburg Workers Organization. Though he fought against it, he imperceptibly fell under its influence. This transition was reflected in the letter we are analysing here. Later, immediately after the Congress, this comrade evidently realized how mistaken he had been to regard himself as a follower of Lenin, as an *Iskra* man. He was one of the first to go over to the Minority [Mensheviks].

ones are mere agencies, mere organs serving special functions. He ridicules the 'committees of the old type made up of throngs of people, in which everyone deals with everything, where they never divide up the work between them and thus waste great energy in noisy bustle and confusion'. He also mocks the 'workers' circles, busy —like the committee—with interminable conferences "about everything" [ironic quotation marks Lenin's], elections, and the drafting of statutes' (p. 21).

Lenin feels that when it comes to deliberating on and judging policies, there must also be a division of labour: some may deliberate, while others must obey without argument. Later I shall cite a passage from page 22, where he says this literally. However, he is also clear enough on the question of discussion groups: 'Everybody active in the movement and all the circles should have the right [how generous!—V.A.] to make their resolutions, wishes, and questions known to their local committee as well as to the central journal and the Central Committee. If we guarantee this right, then we shall be able to have full consultation among all party workers [!!—V.A.] without creating such unwieldy and non-conspiratorial institutions as discussion groups.'[1]

This is the first 'detail' about which 'it seems' to Lenin that he disagrees with his correspondent. Of course, if a circle makes its questions known to the Central Committee, then 'we shall be able to have full consultation among all party workers'!

(2) 'As for district groups, I entirely agree with you that one of their most important tasks is to organize correctly the distribution of literature' (p. 10).

Here, Lenin is evidently 'entirely in agreement'. But he immediately tones down this idea: 'I feel that the district groups should act primarily as *go-betweens* [underlined by Lenin] between the committees and the factories.' Then follows another qualification: 'go-betweens and even, primarily, *transmitters*' [italics Lenin's]. 'If we assure regular contacts between the special district group of deliverymen . . .' Now it is deliverymen! The men responsible for distributing illegal literature were first transformed into go-betweens, then into transmitters, and finally into deliverymen! 'If we assure regular contacts between the special district group of deliverymen and all the factories in the district, this will be of enormous importance.' But perhaps Lenin at least agrees with the author of the letter that the 'delivery' of leaflets should be only

---

[1] Lenin, *Pis'mo k tovarishchu*, pp. 9–10.

one of the tasks of the district organization? Not at all! 'In my view, the district group should not be called upon to do anything more than act as go-between and transmitter. Or, to put it more precisely, its functions should only be broadened with the utmost caution. Otherwise nothing but harm would be done to the secrecy and effectiveness of its work' (p. 11).

(3) 'I shall now go on to the question of the circles for propagandists', Lenin continues. 'It is hardly possible and hardly desirable to organize one for each district.' 'Propaganda should be conducted along uniform lines by the entire committee.' 'The committee should assign several of its members to organize a group of propagandists. This group, recruiting the help of the district groups, should conduct propaganda throughout the area under the committee's jurisdiction. This group may form subgroups, but only with the approval of the committee' (p. 12).

Thus, according to Lenin's plan, the groups of 'propagandists' are transformed into groups which are to disseminate by word of mouth the views of the committee or, rather, as we shall see later, the views of the party's central institutions; the district organizations likewise are to do no more than deliver the printed declarations of the higher authorities. In the plan of the Petersburg comrade, however, the district organization was to be a separate body [*kollegiia*], carrying on all the work in the district—naturally, under the direction of the committee. Similarly, the propagandists' group was also to be a separate body with the full responsibility for propaganda work in its own district. The propagandists could safely be expected to work in one and the same spirit because they would all consciously and independently advocate Social Democratic ideas, all follow the Party's programme, and all adhere to the decisions of the Congresses. Lenin's plan would deprive these groups of all independence and initiative; they would be nothing but 'deliverymen'. Both they and the district organizations would be subject to the idea that 'independence should be allowed only in the technical organization of transmission and distribution' (p. 12). Under such conditions, all its 'dissenting' elements would have to remain outside the party.

(4) 'And now for the factory circles', Lenin goes on. 'Every factory should be our fortress. The factory circle should consist of a very small number of *revolutionaries*, who receive instructions and assignments *directly from the committee*'[1] (italics Lenin's). 'All

---

[1] *Ibid.* pp. 14–15.

members of the factory committee must regard themselves as agents of their local committee and must obey all its decisions. The committee will decide which of these agents should act as its liaison and how he should carry out his liaison work.'[1] 'It may be pointed out here that at times it may be necessary or more convenient for the local committee to appoint a single agent to act in place of a factory committee' (p. 16).

In this manner Lenin hopes to transform 'every factory into our fortress'. Here we see the now familiar evolution of thought from the plan of the Petersburg comrade to Lenin's plan: (*a*) the factory circle; (*b*) the circle of a small number of revolutionaries; (*c*) the circle of agents, who must obey; (*d*) a single agent, appointed by the committee. And so we have one more fortress—almost as impregnable as Port Arthur!

(5) In connexion with the fifth point in his correspondent's plan, Lenin comments laconically: 'I am not only against the discussion groups, but also against the council of representatives' (p. 10). Indeed, 'it seems' that 'in certain details' Lenin does 'not entirely agree' with the Petersburg comrade!

And so all the party organizations at the local level have turned out to be mere agents of the local committee, which directs 'the entire local movement, all local Social Democratic work'. But this creates the danger of the local committee itself beginning to discuss or act on its own and hence of its straying from the true path. Hastening to avert this danger, Lenin turns the local committees themselves into agents of 'the party's central institutions'.

'We have now arrived', writes Lenin on page 20, 'at a most important principle for the entire organization and work of the party.' '*The centre will be powerless* unless we ensure that responsibility to it is *decentralized to the maximum extent* and that it is fully informed about every wheel, however large or small, of the party machine.'[2] In this machine, therefore, the local committees are the transmission levers which make it possible to set the entire machine, with all its wheels, into motion at once. Lenin dismisses independent activity by the committees as 'noisy bustle and confusion'. According to him, it only 'screens the work of the party from the centre's view'. 'It will be impossible to build a strong fighting party if local committees of the old type continue to *screen off* direct practical work from the party centre' (p. 21).

Lenin goes on, in brief but highly characteristic and vivid terms,

---

[1] Lenin, *Pis'mo k tovarishchu*, p. 15.   [2] *Ibid.* p. 21.

4. *CONFLICTING ORGANIZATIONAL PRINCIPLES*

to formulate his view of the local committees as transmission gear which the 'centre' could and should install, transfer, or discard at will: 'So that the centre can not only advise, persuade, and debate (as it has done until now), but truly conduct the orchestra, it must know precisely who plays which violin, and who needs to be transferred where and how in order to correct the dissonance' (p. 22).

This is what the authors of our Party's [Organizational] Statute meant by the point which states that the Central Committee *organizes* the committees.

But the Central Committee? How can its stability and orthodoxy be assured? 'If by chance it should turn out that in the Central Committee there was somebody incompetent and yet possessed of enormous power, this could only be counteracted by measures of "comradely pressure", beginning with resolutions and ending with the overthrow of this authority which had proved so incapable.'[1] Here Comrade Lenin stops. He does not specify who can exert such a salutary influence upon the centre of the party or how it can be done. However, in his appendix to the *Letter*, he publishes a letter from another comrade, addressed to Lenin from ———. Comrade Lenin evidently thinks that this letter can teach us a thing or two, and indeed it is most instructive. The author of the letter has thoroughly absorbed Lenin's views on the party. To him it is nothing but a machine in the hands of the leaders: 'If the leaders are ortho- dox, the party's position is also orthodox; if they are opportunists, the party is too!'[2] And what kind of party organization will assure its orthodoxy? The comrade from ——— feels that this can best be done by placing the centre, the Central Committee, under the direction of the central journal. This central journal, he explains, will be organized abroad, and therefore its editorial board will 'have a longer life'; in other words, its membership will not change.

But what if the central journal should nevertheless become corrupted? 'Can it then be granted ideological leadership?' Of course not! 'No, it would then be our duty to divest the central journal of the right to lead, and our duty to transfer this right to another institution. And if this should not be done for any reason whatsoever, whether for party discipline or anything else, then we should all deserve to be called traitors to the workers' Social Democratic movement.'[3]

All this bears so clear a stamp of a purely conspiratorial view of party organization that any further comment is superfluous.

[1] *Ibid.* p. 13.   [2] *Ibid.* p. 29.   [3] *Ibid.* p. 30.

The New 'Iskra': The Mensheviks

The Second Congress of our Party began under conditions that were extremely favourable to that section for which Lenin spoke on matters of organization and tactics. Several pamphlets (mine, Comrade Riazanov's, and the pamphlet of the Bund delegation) have already shown that the *Iskra*-ist Organizational Committee had artificially excluded from the Congress many of its factional opponents and had just as artificially increased the influence of organizations which it saw as reliable supporters. This fact has as yet not been refuted by anyone. Everything therefore suggested that the organizational plan of the *Iskra* group, as set forth in no. 4 of its journal, would be carried through in full.

True, from the very first meetings it became clear that the delegates were not all of one mood. But since no one understood the ideological basis of this disunity, it seemed to be due to a clash of personalities. Besides, whenever the Congress had to make a decision about the factional opponents of *Iskra*, its supporters, who were in the majority, voted with complete unanimity.

The Union of Russian Social Democrats was closed down. The real interests of the Party did not demand this. We all agreed that all the organizations abroad should be united into one.* The only question at issue was whether the Union should be *combined* with the League or disbanded, leaving only the League in existence. The Second Congress had to be a triumph for *Iskra*, and therefore the Union, representative of another point of view, was disbanded. The League, which was the spokesman for *Iskra*, was left, 'despite its having done so little', as Lenin put it at the League's congress.[1] The Union's delegates—Martynov and I—were powerless to prevent this unfortunate precedent and could only protest against it. As a form of protest, we refused to take further part in the

---

* That is to say, we did agree then. But when Martov's followers turned out to be in the minority after the Congress, they began to act as a group without the slightest hesitation. In his *Our Political Tasks* Comrade Trotsky discourses on discipline (p. 71) exactly like the Leninist from ———— . Similarly, Lenin's adherents, who had argued with such unchallengeable conviction that no newspaper should be tolerated except *Iskra*, and no organization should exist abroad except the League, formed their own organization and began their own newspaper as soon as *Iskra* and the League ceased to be a tool in their hands. But, of course, these people say that they hate unprincipled opportunists.

[1] See *Protokoly 2-go ocherednogo s''ezda Zagranichnoi ligi russkoi revoliutsionnoi sots.-demokratii*, ed. I. Lesenko and F. Dan (Geneva, 1904), p. 95.

voting. The victorious grouping refused to put up even with this protest, and demanded unquestioning submission. We were presented with a clear-cut choice: either retract our protest or leave the Congress. We had to choose the latter. With this resistance to the disastrous tactics of *Iskra*, the Union, as represented by us, fulfilled its last duty to its followers, even though this resistance could no longer have any direct results.

The Bund's turn came next. It was presented with the same alternative, but even more sharply. It was either to sign its own death-warrant without a word of protest or leave the Party. Its delegates took the same action as the delegates of the Union. They had been empowered to act in this way by their organization, and so their departure meant in fact that the Bund had left the Party.

After the Congress was over, the Central Committee began to reorganize the League. Of course, it did not intend to close down the League as it had the Union. But essentially this was an example of the same tactics—to treat Party organizations as mere agencies of the Central Committee. Like the Union and the Bund before it, the League, which had now become the organization of the Mensheviks, resisted this principle. The League was strong enough to oppose the policies of the Central Committee within the Party. Battle was joined, and the Central Committee was compelled to give up its former policies—those of the old *Iskra*, which were preserved by the Bolsheviks. The Bolsheviks were forced out of the Party's central institutions. The new *Iskra* and the new Central Committee set out, as Aksel'rod put it, on a 'new road'.

The *Iskra* group first divided over the organizational question during the debate about the first paragraph of the Statute, when the Congress had to choose between the formulas of Lenin and Martov. Defending his formula, Martov delivered a speech in an extreme *Iskra*-ist spirit. His argument in favour of granting comrades who were not members of the Party organization the right to call themselves Party members was based precisely on the fact that the organization had to be narrowly exclusive. It was precisely because Martov, too, advocated a Party organization built on conspiratorial principles that he did not want all Party members admitted into the organization. And he saw the title of 'Party member' merely as a designation that would allow many Party members to be kept outside the organization and at the same time to be duly honoured.

Thus it seemed that the argument was merely about methods of attaining the common goal—to fence off the organization of professional revolutionaries from those whom it had to influence. But in reality Martov made a mistake from the point of view of *Iskra*'s principles: the 'Party members' would, of course, never be content merely with an 'honorary title' and would wish to have a voice in what the Party organization was doing. More than that, they would want to make this organization speak and act in accordance with their own will, the will of the Party. Under such conditions, the organization would inevitably cease to be conspiratorial and become democratic. Lenin realized this and did not like the prospect. Martov did not realize it but was instinctively aware that the framework of a conspiratorial organization was too narrow for the Party. Still, merely by admitting that the Party included those outside the framework of the conspiratorial organization, he was unconsciously breaking this framework. He was betraying his organizational principles. Subsequently, he was bound to go forward along this road. And this road led away from *Iskra*'s organizational principles and toward those of the Union— from a conspiratorial to a democratic organization.

This move of the 'soft' *Iskra*-ists toward the so-called Economists in organizational and tactical questions is recognized by everyone except the 'softs' themselves. Yet even they are ready to admit that 'we can learn a good deal from the Economists'.

Even at the Congress, the Union's delegates supported the Mensheviks and voted for Martov's formulation. Today all the members of the former Union regard the tactics of the 'softs' as more correct, and as a concession to their own viewpoint. When it disbanded, the Petersburg Workers Organization declared itself at one with the Mensheviks. The Voronezh Committee twice declared its satisfaction with the reversal in *Iskra*'s tactical views.

On the other hand, Lenin and his associates, the 'hard' *Iskra*-ists, also discern the views of the old Union in those of the new *Iskra*. In his booklet *One Step Forward* Lenin mentions my name on virtually every page to show that the 'softs' are repeating my 'errors'.* Thus empirically, as it were, we may take my statement

---

* Similarly, people outside our Party and equally remote both from the Majority and Minority, recognize that the 'softs' 'are developing the views of the Economists—but, unfortunately, carry them to the point of absurdity' (*The Liberation*). [See 'Bibliograficheskii listok Osvobozhdeniia', *Osvobozhdenie*, no. 57 (2 October 1904), cover, p. 2.]

on the position of the Mensheviks as established. It only remains for me to prove this by an analysis of Menshevik ideas, in so far as they have been formulated in polemical writings.

It must be noted, however, that the more the Mensheviks adopt the views which they had so recently and so violently condemned, the more categorically and, of necessity, the more arbitrarily, they attribute fantastic theories to the opponents of the old *Iskra*. The Mensheviks, then, duly condemn these theories, hoping to dissociate themselves from the so-called Economists.

I shall permit myself here to say a few words about myself, since I am today the target for attacks upon that grouping to which I belong. Both the Bolsheviks and the Mensheviks have repeated too many times—without ever having demonstrated the fact—that I represent the opportunist strand of the Social Democratic movement. It may be seen from my speeches at the Congress that I have nothing in common with opportunism, and that I am not in agreement with that line of thought. But now a Comrade Rostovets, whom I do not know, remarks in his letter to *Iskra*: 'Not one of the delegates defended opportunism. We usually regard Akimov as such a supporter. It seems to me, however, that when the smoke of the cannonade raised at the Congress blows away, everyone will agree that even Akimov played the rôle of the ghost of opportunism at the Congress, rather than its actual spokesman.' The editors of *Iskra* appended the following note to these words: 'We cannot agree with this opinion. Comrade Akimov's ideas about the programme bear the clear stamp of opportunism' (Supplement to nos. 73–4).[1]

My attitude toward the programme found expression at the Congress in that I introduced twenty-two amendments to one section of the programme alone [the section dealing with theory]. This fact may prove one of two things: either that I am an opportunist and do not agree with the Social Democratic programme, or else that the programme drawn up by *Iskra* and adopted by the Congress deviates in many points from the programme of the international Social Democratic movement.

All the twenty-two amendments which I suggested to the programme adopted by the Second Congress were taken *entirely* and *solely* from the following sources: the Vienna programme of the Austrian Social Democratic party, the Erfurt programme of

---

[1] S. Rostovets, 'Pora! (Pis'mo k tovarishcham)', *Otdel'noe prilozhenie k no. 73–74 'Iskry'*, p. 6.

our German comrades, the programme of the Guesdist French Labour Party, and the Statute of the International. How, then, could my amendments have expressed opportunistic ideas? This would be too difficult to prove, and *Iskra* therefore preferred to dismiss them with a single sweeping sentence. And yet gradually it is itself being forced to adopt the amendments to the programme which I proposed. Thus my main amendment, which was defended at the Congress by Comrade Martynov too, and which was introduced on behalf of the entire Union, has been adopted *in toto* by the new *Iskra*. I am referring to the question of the socialist consciousness of the proletariat. Everyone can see that Plekhanov, in his articles in *Iskra*, nos. 70 and 71,[1] merely repeated—often word for word—the arguments developed by Martynov in his speech at the Congress. However, he failed to mention that by so doing he was accepting the amendment to the programme which he had himself rejected at the Congress. The same thing is done by the author of the ideological leading article in *Sotsial-Demokrat*, no. 1, who in it also accepts my amendment on the question of 'dictatorship', as well as several others which are less important.[2]

Apart from the articles already mentioned, the questions involved in the programme have not been discussed since the Second Congress either in *Iskra* itself or in any other of the publications of its editorial committee. Thus the fact that the Party has adopted a programme passed entirely unremarked, and this confirms that its adoption was a formality. *Iskra* is silent about my criticism of the programme because it can no longer defend the existing Party programme but does not yet wish to criticize it openly.

So much for the questions raised by the programme. However, in questions of organization and tactics the new *Iskra* has come somewhat further. It is already criticizing the period of *Iskra*-ism, but it has made only the first timid steps toward formulating principles which are new to it.* This is so because it is groping its

---

[1] G. V. Plekhanov, 'Rabochii klass i sotsial'demokraticheskaia intelligentsiia', *Iskra*, nos. 70 and 71 (July and August 1904).

[2] 'Klass protiv klassa', *Sotsial-demokrat: Rabochaia gazeta*, no. 1 (1 October 1904), pp. 1–5. This unsigned article is attributed to Martov (Kamenev, *Russkaia politicheskaia literatura*, p. 44).

* 'Aksel'rod's feuilletons in *Iskra*, nos. 55 and 57, mark the beginning of a new era in our movement' (Trotsky, *Our Political Tasks*, p. 25). 'In his excellent feuilletons, Aksel'rod demonstrates a correct theory' (Rabochii, *Rabochie i intelligenty* [*v nashikh organizatsiiakh* (Geneva, 1904)], p. 31).

way forward from the concrete and specific to the general. It does not admit the errors of the old *Iskra* in its attitude toward the so-called Economists, and it does not accept the principles of the Union as its starting point. Rather, it continues to distort and hence to misunderstand these principles because it fears that spectre which it itself created in its war against the Union. Hence its hesitant steps, its half-hearted resolutions, its inconsistent actions. Although it had adopted in theory the Union's democratic attitude toward organization, the new *Iskra* has retained the general concepts of the old *Iskra*. This has given rise in practice to an irreconcilable contradiction, which must completely paralyse the work of its organization. Meantime, its organizational opponents—the Bolsheviks—have evidently taken up the task of the day and are having their revenge by also setting out on a 'new road', to use the expression of Comrade 'Galerka'.

I have already said that competent and multifarious authorities have established the fact that the new *Iskra* has adopted an intermediate position between the old *Iskra* and the Union on organizational and tactical issues. This halfway position has naturally found expression in print too, and as an example I shall analyse the feuilletons of Comrade Aksel'rod.

Aksel'rod's articles in *Iskra*, nos. 55, 57 and 68, represent without question and by general consensus the Mensheviks' most serious attempt to examine from their side the state of our Party.* The crude errors and distortions, the muddled conclusions, the baseless assertions, the prevarications which mark these articles must therefore be considered all the more characteristic. Aksel'rod formulates the mission of the Mensheviks as follows: 'What should be done—and how—to help transform the Russian Social Democratic movement at least partially from a hobbledehoy, politically speaking, into a true proletarian party? To find a way to solve this problem—that is the mission of the Mensheviks' (no. 68).[1] These words are printed in italics and appear at the very end of Aksel'rod's article. He evidently regards them as a summary of all that went before. But this summary is empty and meaningless, for it does not answer the question to which the articles are

---

* Note to 2nd edition: Since that time the Mensheviks have made considerable strides forward.

[1] P. B. Aksel'rod, 'K voprosu ob istochnike i znachenii nashikh organizatsionnykh raznoglasii', *Iskra*, no. 68 (June 1904), p. 3.

devoted. What issues divide the factions in our Party? Aksel'rod's vague formula can be endorsed by everyone.

The two wings of the Russian Social Democratic movement are at loggerheads because they cannot decide what the Party is. Let us see how Aksel'rod solves this question. 'The Party's principal distinguishing mark is that the Party organization in its work is close to—is bound directly to—broad strata of the people or classes, for it fights together with them for their interests' (no. 68).[1] Again a most inept formulation. Lenin also seeks to give our Party this shape. Therefore Aksel'rod's formula does nothing to clarify the disagreements between the Bolsheviks and the Mensheviks. Aksel'rod does not indicate the nature of the differences between the Bolsheviks and the Mensheviks with regard to the Party's tasks and objectives. No wonder, then, that he says: 'Our disagreements with Lenin's followers (in Russia, but not abroad) are in large measure due to misunderstandings' (no. 68, p. 2, col. 1). 'And this is what makes our situation so monstrous— the fact that on the basis of trifling incidents a bureaucratic-Bonapartist régime could spring up and gain predominance in our Party' (no. 68, p. 2, col. 3). But to attribute the present split in our Party to 'trifling incidents' is worse than irrational. It is also irrational to pretend that the split in the Party is due merely to the fight with Lenin's group abroad and not to the fact that two opposing trends have crystallized. The disagreements between the Mensheviks and Lenin's followers in Russia are due to misunderstandings and trifles, but the disagreements with Lenin himself are neither trifles nor misunderstandings. This is a polemical stratagem that harms the Mensheviks themselves most of all.

No! The grouping of which Lenin is the leader has emerged and developed thanks to definite historical conditions, which I have attempted to analyse in this book. And thanks to the same conditions, it will continue to exist in our Party for a long time, even after the fall of the autocracy, just as the Blanquist group of Vaillant still persists in France, if only as a survival of the past. It came into being historically as one of the stages in the development of our Party. It is persisting, and will persist, for new members of the Party will go through this same stage even when the Party itself has outlived it.

And so neither in his summary of the Party's tasks nor in his definition of the Party's principal characteristics has Aksel'rod

[1] *Iskra*, no. 68 (June 1904), p. 2 n.

4. *CONFLICTING ORGANIZATIONAL PRINCIPLES*

succeeded in defining the disagreements within our Party. Let us now examine the argument of the articles themselves in order to fill the gaps which mark his conclusions. I shall attempt to present in Aksel'rod's own words his view of how our Party has developed.

During the period of so-called Economism, our movement struck deep roots in the proletariat, revolutionized the moods and even the consciousness of important sections of the proletariat, and inspired them to more revolutionary activity [no. 55, p. 2, col. 2].[1] But the great majority of comrades moved away from the initial, strictly Marxist, basis of our Party, as laid down in Plekhanov's works. They did so, not only unawares in their practical work, but also consciously in their ideas [no. 57, p. 2, col. 2].[2] The socio-political implications of the practical methods employed by so-called Economism were formulated by the authors of the 'Credo'; it cleared the way for the subjection of the masses to the bourgeois democrats [no. 55, p. 5, col. 1]. Then came that impetuous turn by the opportunist elements toward politics, which revealed the same readiness to sacrifice the fundamental interests of the proletarian movement to the mood of the moment [no. 55, p. 3, col. 3].

But revolutionary Social Democrats sharply opposed these policies and their exponents. They took their stand on such undeniable facts as the enormous growth of the mass movement and the close ties, practical and ideological, which had developed between it and our Party during the period of Economism [no. 55, p. 3, col. 2]. Even the most near-sighted of the *praktiki* were forced to see the most glaring shortcomings of the period just ending, and to recognize the need for unity in the programme and organization of the Social Democratic movement [no. 55, p. 2, col. 3]. 'Down with the anarchy in our organization. Long live the unification of all Social Democratic forces into one single, strictly centralized organization!' This cry united the majority of our Party members. Today this slogan has become a fact: the Second Congress gave reality to the desire of most of our comrades for unification [*ibid.*].

But many factors impeded the evolution of an organizational structure suited to the historical tasks and needs of our Party, and our comrades were overcome with a sense of impotence. It was to this psychological state that Lenin owes the success he enjoys among a wide circle of our comrades [no. 68].[3] The triumph of bureaucratic centralism in the Party organization—such is the result of the struggle of the revolutionary Social Democrats against the backward-looking parochialism [*kustarnichestvo*] within the Party. The ideological wrapping is

---

[1] Aksel'rod, 'Ob"edinenie rossiiskoi sotsial'demokratii i eia zadachi', part 1, *Iskra*, no. 55 (December 1903).
[2] Aksel'rod, 'Ob"edinenie', part 2, *Iskra*, no. 57 (January 1904).
[3] Aksel'rod, 'K voprosu', *Iskra*, no. 68, p. 3.

that of revolutionary Social Democracy. But the actual content, in its essence, in its principles, is little more than bourgeois revolutionism [no. 55, p. 5, col. 1].

To begin with, it is necessary to expose the unquestionably erroneous assertions on which Aksel'rod bases his historical evaluation of our Party's history.

(1) It is not true that the so-called Economists deviated in their ideas—consciously—from strictly Marxist foundations. Aksel'rod knows that none of the so-called Economists (none!) has declared himself in agreement with Bernstein or with the 'Credo'. He knows that all the so-called Economists declared themselves in agreement in matters of principle with the Group for the Emancipation of Labour. Hence, whether fundamentally or not, they did not depart in their *ideas*—consciously—from strictly Marxist foundations. Aksel'rod knows that the authors of the 'Credo' had no relation to any organization of the so-called Economists. This was established many times, both at public meetings abroad and in the publications of the so-called Economists, and was never disproved. Hence Aksel'rod is guilty not just of error, but of actual untruth when he says that the so-called Economists were 'ready to sacrifice the fundamental interests of the proletarian movement to the mood of the moment'.

(2) It is also incorrect to say that the authors of the 'Credo' formulated the theories of the so-called Economists. As for the objective significance of the 'practical work' of the so-called Economists, and the 'socio-political implications' of this work, Aksel'rod's assessment ('it cleared the way for the subjection of the masses to the bourgeois democrats . . . and was formulated by the "Credo"') is purely subjective, purely his own. Indeed, it contradicts the fact which Aksel'rod himself points out: 'During the period of so-called Economism, our movement . . . revolutionized the moods and even the consciousness of important sections of the proletariat.' How could the fact that the proletariat was developing a more revolutionary mood and consciousness prepare it for subjection to the bourgeoisie? This thesis is a tribute to Lenin's view that the consciousness of the proletariat is merely trade-unionist, and can become socialist only when the ideas of socialism are introduced into the proletariat from without.

We shall see below that Aksel'rod is still very much under the influence of this view. But granted all this, it is still incomprehensible that Aksel'rod could assert that the revolutionary Social

4. CONFLICTING ORGANIZATIONAL PRINCIPLES

Democrats triumphed over so-called Economism because they relied on the 'close ties, practical and *ideological*, which had developed between the proletariat and our Party during the period of Economism'. It requires a great effort of will to remain calm while analysing Aksel'rod's blatantly untrue statements! Of course, Comrade Aksel'rod will probably prefer not to reply to my comments, just as his friends preferred not to reply to my last booklet. By-passing an opponent's arguments is the usual tactic of those who use unworthy methods in ideological warfare.*

(3) Aksel'rod sees *Iskra*'s war against so-called Economism as a war for 'unity in the programme and organization'. This, again, reveals complete failure to understand the meaning of this war. As I demonstrate in this booklet, the so-called Economists valued the unification of the Party organization and its adherence to the principles of the international Social Democratic movement no less than the *so-called* revolutionary Social Democrats. They clearly recognized the disorganized or rather unorganized character of the Party as their handicap. It was historically inevitable and certainly not their fault. They sought to overcome this misfortune. And if they waged war on the *so-called* revolutionary Social Democrats, on *Iskra*, it was because they were convinced that *Iskra*, with its profoundly erroneous tactics, was doing nothing to overcome this handicap; that, on the contrary, it was destroying the 'gains which had been made at such cost by the past efforts of the Social Democratic movement' (*Two Congresses* [*Dva s"ezda*], p. 32). And is not Aksel'rod compelled today, after three years of *Iskra* tactics, to recognize the fact, 'astonishing' to him but foreseen by the so-called Economists, that it was 'precisely the formal unification' of the Party along the lines laid down by *Iskra* which 'unleashed such chaos in our ideology and organization that by comparison even the anarchic period of *kustarnichestvo* can look like a model of internal unity and order'.[1] It was *Iskra* which opened the door to the disasters ascribed to the so-called Economists.

Since Aksel'rod does not understand the factional struggle which went on before the emergence of the Mensheviks, his attempt to find the basic cause for the downfall of *Iskra*-ism could not succeed. This is why, as we can see from the passages quoted earlier,

---

* Note to the 2nd edition: My fears have, of course, proved justified. I hope, however, that before long Comrade Aksel'rod and his friends will have to abandon those tactics which they use against 'critics'.

[1] Aksel'rod, 'K voprosu', *Iskra*, no. 68, p. 3 n.

events present themselves to Aksel'rod as if in a fantastic kaleido-scope: the movement develops deep roots, revolutionizes the moods and the consciousness of the proletariat, and at the same time the '*majority*' of comrades consciously deviates from the theoretical foundations of our Party. At this moment, revolutionary Social Democrats appear from somewhere and are able to save the movement from the Economists because they rely on the ideological ties of the workers with the Economists. The unification of all forces into one strictly centralized organization becomes an undeniable fact; at the same time, there emerges chaos which far surpasses that of the period of *kustarnichestvo*. But this is inco-herent delirium, a nightmare!

Now that he has become disillusioned with *Iskra*'s organiza-tional and tactical plans, which he supported for three years, Aksel'rod is seeking out the cause of its failures in the basic principles of *Iskra*-ism. This radically distinguishes him and his faction from that of Lenin, which attempts to explain everything as mere 'squabbles'. Let us now turn again to Aksel'rod's words in order to clarify his views on the basic cause of the chaos which has come to reign in the Party.

To develop the class consciousness and political initiative of the labour-ing masses, to unify them into an independent revolutionary force under the Social Democratic banner—that is our basic task. But *before we could start to fulfil this task* [italics mine—V.A.], we had to create the *preliminary* conditions. I am not saying that we had a definite plan, first to achieve this and only then to go on to our true proletarian task. Nothing of the kind! On the contrary, for us this purely proletarian task embraced all the vital problems of contemporary Russian life. It seemed to us that, in practice, our efforts to prepare the ground for a broad organization capable of conducting the proletarian war correctly would merge into one indivisible whole with our efforts to educate the workers to class consciousness.

But history turned out quite differently from what we had expected. It assigned the predominant rôle in our movement not to ends, but to means; not to the fundamental task involving major principles, but to historically more elementary tasks, which had to be at least partially fulfilled in order to make it objectively possible to pursue the primary task. This brought into the development of the Russian Social Demo-cratic movement a contradiction which runs like a scarlet thread through all its phases [no. 57, p. 2, col. 3].

[At that time] the proletariat in Russia was still sunk in profound sleep. Its entry into the arena of political action had to be prepared by men who were not of the proletariat, outsiders—the radical intelligentsia. [In other words] in order to call to life in Russia an independent movement among the labouring masses, it was first necessary to subject them to the ideological and political influence of a stratum socially foreign to them [the intelligentsia—V.A.]. This was the root of the major contradiction between the subjective goal of the founders of our movement and the objective character of the means that history placed at their disposal [no. 57, p. 3, col. 3].

In principle, the proletarian goal of our movement is the same as that of Western Social Democrats, but the circuitous road which history put before us did not lead *straight* to this goal so much as in the opposite direction. In the West, the Social Democratic movement from the very first has been an integral part of the proletariat itself. The proletariat has been at the same time both the subject and the object of its own class education and unification. In the West, it is through a process of self-development that the proletariat has developed class consciousness and initiative. But in our country, the influence of the Social Democrats on the masses meant an influence from without, from an alien social element. The Social Democratic education of the masses actually meant their subordination to the leadership of the radical intelligentsia [no. 57, p. 4, col. 2]. The Russian Social Democratic Party is proletarian in its theories and programme but is still far from proletarian in its social composition and the character of its organization [no. 55, p. 2, col. 1]. When the Social Democratic movement enters the new phase of its development, political leadership will pass to the labouring masses, and the proletariat will have gained its political independence [no. 57, p. 4, col. 3].

I have quoted at such length because it seems to me these passages epitomize all the positive and all the negative aspects of the Menshevik position. On the positive side is the demand that the very '*composition and character*' *of our Party organizations* be transformed; that the workers themselves conduct the work of the Social Democratic Party; that they take its duties upon themselves; and that the Party thus become just a part of the proletariat, its conscious vanguard. This is a most important principle. This recognition of the *principle* of democracy, of the *independent initiative* of the working-class, is the distinguishing trait and the contribution of the Mensheviks. And this idea is excellently expressed by Aksel'rod in the lines quoted above. The practical conclusions which follow from these views were laid down by Comrade Cherevanin, and, still better, by Comrade Rabochii.[1]

However, these views—and the conclusions from them—soon came into conflict with earlier beliefs, with the ideas of the old

[1] See Rabochii, *Rabochie i intelligenty*, and Cherevanin [F. A. Lipkin], *Organizatsionnyi vopros* (Geneva, 1904).

Iskra, from which the Mensheviks find it difficult to free themselves. These negative features of the new *Iskra*, which I shall now examine, are also clearly reflected in Aksel'rod's feuilletons. Aksel'rod is mistaken in saying that the intelligentsia has always rejected the principle which (quite rightly, as I see it) he now advocates for the salvation of the Party. To begin with, what intelligentsia is he talking about? For some reason he calls it the 'radical intelligentsia'. But it is not true that the men at the helm of the Russian Social Democratic Labour Party during the *Iskra* period were radical democrats. They were socialists, 'Social Democrats', albeit much influenced by radicalism.

In Aksel'rod's opinion, 'in order to call to life in Russia an independent movement among the labouring masses, it was first necessary to subject them to the ideological and political influence of the intelligentsia'.[1] This view has long existed among a certain section of our Party comrades, but only among that section to which Comrade Aksel'rod himself belonged. There was also another view, against which Comrade Aksel'rod's group fought. This other group of comrades, also *intelligenty*, had noted as early as 1900 that fact which has only now been recognized by Aksel'rod and the Mensheviks: 'The [Petersburg—*Ed*.] Union, which is made up of *intelligenty*, has really most touching intentions. (It wishes to liberate the working-class.) But it keeps out the actual members of this class. We would like the workers at long last to take their own cause into their own hands!'[2] If such a development had taken place, the Social Democratic organization would have put down roots among the class conscious workers, and the class movement of the labouring masses would have been subjected to their influence rather than to that of the intelligentsia.

I showed in the chapter on Petersburg that this declaration of the Group for the Self-Emancipation of the Working Class expressed the views of an entire section of the Russian Social Democratic movement. Comrade Aksel'rod's section fought against it; branded the Group for the Self-Emancipation of the Working Class as Economist; saw the proclamation I have quoted above as profoundly erroneous and heretical; and confused this proclamation with the 'Credo'.* Therefore, in enumerating the internal

---

[1] Aksel'rod, 'Ob"edinenie', part 2, *Iskra*, no. 57, p. 3.

[2] For the proclamation (somewhat loosely quoted here) of the Group for the Self-Emancipation of the Working Class, see above, pp. 263.

* In his introduction to the pamphlet by Comrade Rabochii, Aksel'rod argues that it is a mistake to demand that control of the Party be transferred to

and external 'factors which impeded the evolution of an organizational structure suited to the tasks and needs of our Party'—those tasks and needs which Aksel'rod himself is now defining—he should have pointed out the harmful effect not of the *radical* intelligentsia, but of that Social Democratic, *Iskra* section to which he had himself belonged.

But how did the intelligentsia understand its tasks—the intelligentsia which, according to Aksel'rod, would have to dominate the labouring masses in order to rouse a class movement among them? The tasks of our Party are formulated by Aksel'rod as follows: 'To develop the class consciousness and political initiative of the labouring masses under the Social Democratic banner—that is our basic task' (no. 57, p. 2, col. 3). A strange thing! One task is omitted here, a task which every worker sets himself, which 'every worker should know and remember', and which, therefore, cannot and must not be forgotten by a workers party, any workers party, least of all a Social Democratic *workers* party. This is the daily, hourly struggle waged by the working-class all along the line with its immediate class enemies for its economic interests and its individual rights! Even if the workers' class *consciousness* does not develop, the class war—the struggle which is peculiarly that of the working-class—can yet go on. Even if the workers are not *politically* active, not united, not independent, the proletariat can still act as a class even if its actions take merely elementary and embryonic forms.

But where there is no fight for the vital, direct interests of the individual, where the worker endures his fate like a slave, there class life does not exist, even though men are aware that sooner or later socialism will establish universal happiness on earth. There can then be an organization of professional revolutionaries working to popularize Social Democratic ideas, but a workers party is impossible. Thus economic warfare is not only 'the best and most widely applicable means of the proletariat's class war', but also a necessary, an essential feature of the very concept of a 'workers

the hands of the workers themselves, because the workers would not necessarily share the views of the Social Democrats. To support this 'original' idea, Aksel'rod even finds it necessary to refer to the example of England where it turns out that the purely labour organizations are a very long way from socialism. These arguments are not merely trivial but also irrelevant, for those who argue that our organizations should be transferred to the hands of the workers are obviously thinking of workers who are Social Democrats. [See P. B. Aksel'rod, 'Pis'mo k tovarishcham rabochim', in Rabochii, *Rabochie i intelligenty*, pp. 6–7.]

party'; everything else—the development of class consciousness and unification into an independent party—emerges only at a definite stage of development in the economic war. Indeed, political warfare itself arises initially only as a form and means of the economic war: the direct struggle for food, for clothing, for leisure time, for 'better treatment', for human dignity, for all those conditions essential to the manifold development of the individual. This is why the Social Democratic movement must take as its basic task the organization and management—not only the leadership, but the actual management—of the economic struggle of the working-class. And this is the task that was forgotten by Aksel'rod.

Similarly, of intrinsic value to the worker as man and citizen are the rights of personal and general freedom and the right to play a part in the law-making process of the modern state. As soon as the working-class reaches the level where it becomes aware of its stake in these rights, it begins to fight for them.

Hence, the economic struggle waged by our Party during the period of so-called Economism and the political demonstrations organized by it during the period of *Iskra*-ism were both correct, albeit transitional, forms of the class war, and so, in their time, both were essential tasks which the proletarian, Social Democratic Party had to face. In Aksel'rod's view, however, these were 'not the real' tasks of the Party, but merely a means to stir up, to 'awaken' the working-class, a means which 'did not lead straight to our goal so much as in the opposite direction'. He sees our methods of action—the 'historically more elementary tasks, which had to be at least partially fulfilled in order to make it objectively possible to pursue the primary task'—as actually contradicting that primary task itself. These tasks, according to him, should have been carried out by radical democrats in Russia, as they had been in Western Europe. Hence Aksel'rod regards this work as foreign to us, a necessary evil, a compromise forced upon our Party by the whim of history.

To the working-class, and hence to the proletarian party, the economic struggle was important for its own sake; besides, it was important as education. Aksel'rod not only refuses to recognize this but says that it only seemed that 'our efforts to prepare the ground for a broad organization capable of conducting the proletarian war correctly would merge into one indivisible whole with our efforts to educate the workers to class consciousness'.[1]

---

[1] Aksel'rod, 'Ob"edinenie', part 2, *Iskra*, no. 57, p. 2 (quoted above, p. 340.)

4. *CONFLICTING ORGANIZATIONAL PRINCIPLES*

But this is just what the Economists really did believe. They saw this fusion of the educational and practical aspects of their activity as the most characteristic feature of Social Democratic tactics.

Thus regarding the question of democratic organization Aksel'-rod has accepted in entirety the views of the 'third period' of our movement's history, but in tactical questions he still retains *in toto* the attitude of the 'fourth period'. Aksel'rod's assessment of the tasks facing the workers party ignores the actual needs of the workers and speaks merely of the tactical considerations of a socialist theoretician. Thus for Aksel'rod, too, the masses continue to be not the subject of Social Democratic action but an object to be influenced by the Social Democratic party—an approach which he himself regards as one of the shortcomings of the old *Iskra*. He therefore arrives once more at conclusions incredible for a veteran writer: the programme and the Organizational Statute adopted by the Second Congress possess, in his view, only a single fault—they are too good for a movement as young as ours! 'A strictly centralized organization and a Social Democratic programme of action based on firm ideological principles are not possible without a class proletarian party. Otherwise, if they do not correspond to the real growth of the party as a whole, both may prove not beneficial but actually harmful' (no. 68, p. 2, col. 3, note). No! A centralized organization and a programme based on firm principles can never be harmful. Only tendentious critics, in the heat of argument, attributed to so-called Economism the paradoxical idea expressed here by Aksel'rod. But the conspiratorial organization and the backward programme of *Iskra* have certainly caused us much damage. And it was evidently the fact that he recognized this damage which led Aksel'rod to make such a monstrously erroneous generalization.

And so the Menshevik faction is at the crossroads: its aims remain on the old road, its methods of action are leading to a new road. Seeing that the ties between our Party and the working-class are breaking, [the new] *Iskra* wants the workers themselves to run the Party. But it seems that the direct interests of the workers are at variance with the objectives of the Social Democrats, that 'the road which history put before us' leads us away from our goals. Under such circumstances, a socialist can come to only one conclusion—a conclusion drawn by the old *Iskra*, by Lenin: the working-class must be diverted from its road. The new *Iskra*, albeit unawares, still adheres to this principle, and therefore it neither can nor will be able to transfer the leading organizations of our Party, its committees, into the hands of workers.

In the eyes of the Menshevik theoreticians our Party has become divided both in its composition—between the 'radical intelligentsia and the working-class'—and in its aims—between the 'proletarian task' itself and 'the creation of the preliminary conditions' which have to be in existence 'before we can start to fulfil' this task. This gives rise to insoluble contradictions in Menshevik tactics. Fortunately, these paradoxical contradictions do not exist in objective reality but only in Menshevik theories. Only if we are aware of these contradictions can we give an answer to the question recently raised in the excellent pamphlet of Comrade Rabochii [*Rabochie i intelligenty*]: 'How, then, can we explain that hesitancy which we find in the latest Menshevik publications?' (pp. 36–7).

I appeal to you, to the comrades of the Menshevik group [continues Rabochii]. You have taken the first step toward a real rapprochement with the labouring masses. You have placed new objectives on the agenda, and now, in your actual practice, you should take the second step toward their realization! Call upon the workers throughout Russia to become the leaders of the movement side by side with the *intelligenty*! (p. 51).

But that, indeed, is the trouble with the Menshevik comrades, and here I must agree with the opinion of my antipode, Comrade Lenin. They have taken two steps forward, but also one step backward. I only disagree with Comrade Lenin about the direction in which we are going. What he considers to be a step 'forward', I see as a step backward.

'Rabochee Delo': the so-called Economists

I shall now attempt to analyse the views on the Party which emerged and developed in the workers' organizations of the Bund, of Petersburg, Kiev, Ekaterinoslav, and other cities. These were formulated in a number of theoretical declarations and organizational statutes, and were most fully reflected in the literature of the Union of Russian Social Democrats Abroad.

Disagreements between the Bolsheviks and the Mensheviks expressed themselves in concrete, practical work, in organizational questions, at a time when the contending factions did not yet understand the ideological differences that divided them.

4. CONFLICTING ORGANIZATIONAL PRINCIPLES

Similarly, the Union of Russian Social Democrats saw in its conflict with the Group for the Emancipation of Labour only an organizational dispute. In reply to Plekhanov's *Vademecum* and Aksel'rod's *Letter*, the editors of *Rabochee Delo* declared that 'at the root of all the past revolts against the Group for the Emancipation of Labour were disputes not about principles but about organization and tactics'. In support of this assertion, the editors briefly cited 'a number of indisputable facts, particularly facts related to the emergence of the most recent revolt, which ended in the reorganization of the Union of Russian Social Democrats along democratic lines'.

Thus, defending a specific type of Social Democratic organization, the Union was aware that it was defending a specific organizational *principle*—democracy—and not just particular organizational details. However, like the present-day contestants, they did not link this particular principle to general theoretical principles. This, it seems to me, was a mistake, as I pointed out in my previous book.

I shall cite several passages from the *Reply* in order to illustrate the first clashes between two organizational principles—the democratic and the conspiratorial.

As early as the end of the 1880s it became apparent that the publishing activity of the Group for the Emancipation of Labour was inadequate to meet the new demands of the developing labour movement in Russia. Popular literature demanded for propaganda among the workers was supplied either inadequately or not at all. This failure became chronic because of the completely closed character of the Group for the Emancipation of Labour, its isolation not only from Russia but also from the young Social Democrats abroad. This situation prompted the 'youngsters' to seek a more direct and active rôle in the publishing work of the Russian Social Democrats abroad.

Such was the origin of the first opposition to the Group for the Emancipation of Labour, which flared up sharply at the congress of 1888. There was no question at the time of ideological or tactical differences. The opposition formed by the 'young' Social Democrats sought the right to participate in deciding what kind of works the Group for the Emancipation of Labour would publish. It insisted that greater attention be paid to the demands from Russia. But this first attempt ended not in the sought-after unification of all the active Russian Social Democrats abroad but in a split [p. 70].

A second, and more broadly based, opposition to the Group for the Emancipation of Labour arose in 1891–2. By then many young Social Democrats without police records had come abroad, especially to

Switzerland. They knew the situation in Russia and the new demands for illegal literature. The circle of young Social Democrats abroad began to refuse to send money and information to the Group for the Emancipation of Labour. They demanded the right to play a more active part in administration, and in shaping the character of the literature published by the Group for the Emancipation of Labour. Total lack of funds and lack of contacts compelled the Group for the Emancipation of Labour to consider reform.

In 1893 there was a congress of representatives from the local groups of young Social Democrats abroad. The spokesmen of the 'youngsters' categorically demanded a more democratic organization in general and the right to participate in the editorial and administrative work of the projected Union of Russian Social Democrats. The constitutional demands advanced by this opposition of the 'youngsters' were very modest. Thus they were entirely willing to see all the Union's publications edited by the Group for the Emancipation of Labour. They merely demanded a place on the editorial board for one of the 'youngsters', who would represent the new demands for literature coming from Russia and speak for the aspirations of the young Social Democrats abroad. But even this modest demand of the 'youngsters' was rejected by the Group for the Emancipation of Labour. A break followed. There was no mention at these congresses of ideological or tactical differences. The total break occurred on purely organizational grounds.[1]

The young comrades who joined the Union in 1898 soon were all without exception in opposition to the Group for the Emancipation of Labour. This was already the third opposition. At the same time, the continual clashes on practical issues between the 'young' and the 'veteran' members of the Union brought to light their divergent ideas about the mass labour movement and about the immediate goals of the Russian Social Democratic movement. The Group for the Emancipation of Labour flatly refused to play any part in the editorial and administrative work of the Union. They left it to the 'youngsters', who had to take upon themselves all of the responsible and difficult duties of the Union of Russian Social Democrats. This decision was taken at the congress in the autumn of 1898, when new members were accepted and a new Statute and publication programme was drawn up for the Union, which was now reorganized along democratic lines (pp. 75–9).

The paragraph of the old Statute most resented by the 'youngsters' was the provision requiring unanimous approval of every new member. In practice, this gave the Group for the Emancipation of Labour the right of veto, and as the Group was anxious to maintain the purity of its principles and so to shut itself off from newcomers, it made wide use of this right. It refused to accept new members merely on the grounds that it did not have sufficient

[1] *Otvet redaktsii 'Rabochego dela'*, pp. 71–3.

information about them. The new Statute opened the Union to an applicant if he was recommended by two old members, received a majority vote in his favour, and was not opposed by anybody. If one-third of the members voted against admission, the applicant was rejected. If less than a third voted against an applicant, these votes had to be explained. A second vote followed, and the matter was then decided by a simple majority.

The 'young' Union regarded itself as the Party committee abroad. This right was granted it by the First Party Congress. Because of this, it felt duty-bound to admit into its ranks all Social Democrats, irrespective of their political leanings and solely on the basis of their revolutionary trustworthiness and experience. That this was actually the case I discovered from my own experience when I came abroad just before the Congress of 1898. The only person who knew me here was Comrade Ivanshin. However, he declared that he could not recommend me for membership in the Union. When asked to explain his attitude toward me, he replied that he had nothing against me as a comrade and a revolutionary, but he thought that I would advocate a 'Plekhanovite' position and would therefore be unsuitable for the 'youngsters'. Comrades objected that such factors could not be considered in admitting new members; otherwise the Union would become a sect similar to the Group for the Emancipation of Labour. I was admitted.

The same thing happened later, in 1900, with Comrade Nevzorov. Rightly or wrongly, we considered him an enemy of the 'youngsters'. We even attributed to Comrade Nevzorov a number of actions hostile to the Union. As a result Ivanshin and I crossed swords with him in some sharp encounters. At that time we were fighting for the Union's very survival against the Group for the Emancipation of Labour, and we were certain that Comrade Nevzorov was on the side of the Group for the Emancipation of Labour. After long discussion, however, we decided that we had *no right* not to admit Comrade Nevzorov if he wanted to work, if he was a Social Democrat by conviction, and if he had a clean record as a revolutionary. The formal right to membership in the Union was merely an acknowledgment of the fact that the person in question did really belong to the Social Democratic movement. The Union Abroad regarded itself not as the autonomous organization of a particular group of people, but as one branch of the Social Democratic movement in Russia. On this issue there was a major disagreement in principle with the Group for the Emancipation of Labour.

Furthermore, the Union saw itself simply as the mouthpiece of the Social Democratic Party in Russia, which, although still unorganized and still engaged in a scattered, partisan struggle, was united in the kind of work it was doing. The Union naturally considered that the main duty of its administrative and editorial officers was to execute the Party's will and decisions, and that these men should therefore be elected and be subject to replacement. For ten years the Group for the Emancipation of Labour would not— and, given its point of view, could not—accept this principle. And now it chose to take no part in the work rather than yield, so sharp was its disagreement on this principle with the young Union. The Union's new Statute gave practical application to the new principles.

Finally, the Union was not ready to give *carte blanche* to act in its name even to its editorial and administrative officers. It drew up a series of instructions to guide its executive organs. Membership in the editorial and administrative committees was open only to those who agreed with the instructions and could pledge to follow them. How sharply, indeed, this differed from the views of the Group for the Emancipation of Labour! The old Statute stated that the editorial committee (non-elective and permanent!) had to comply with the instructions of the congress 'only if they took the form of resolutions adopted unanimously by all the delegates'. In other words, the only thing that was obligatory for the Group for the Emancipation of Labour was what it considered obligatory itself. It was 'a monarchy, which acts according to the letter of the laws issued by the autocratic monarchy itself'.

The fact that a referendum could be initiated by three members of the Union ensured that the organization could keep constant control over its executive organs. I am profoundly convinced that this excellent, broadly democratic Statute, which was developed in greater detail as a result of the practical experience of the Union, will in time become a model for the statutes of our Party committees. After fighting the Union for two years, the League of Russian Revolutionary Social Democrats Abroad adopted a statute at its second congress in 1903 which was very similar to that of the Union.

Among the members and adherents of the Group for the Emancipation of Labour, Plekhanov alone insisted on opposing the new Statute of the League. His isolation could surely be attributed, among other things, to the battle for democracy waged by the 'youngsters' over a period of fifteen years.

Immediately after the Congress of 1898 the Union sent one of its underground members to Russia. The Union's delegate was given a generally sympathetic reception by the committees. The comrades in Russia had long known about the struggle between the 'youngsters' and the Group for the Emancipation of Labour, and the victory of the 'youngsters' was hailed everywhere. 'When you tell us about your fight for a democratic organization,' the Petersburg comrades said to the Union's delegate, 'it seems to us that you are describing the events in Petersburg. We experienced the same thing!' The comrades were referring to their clash with the 'veterans', the members of that earlier Union of Struggle, which Lenin idealizes and holds up as an example both in his *The Tasks* and in *What Is to Be Done?* I have already discussed this conflict in the chapter on Petersburg. Thus the struggle between the two different organizational principles was taking place both in the Russian centres and abroad. From a dispute between groupings, it became a dispute between factions; from a dispute between organizations, it became a dispute between two discordant camps. Neither of the camps was capable as yet of defending its organizational plans in terms of principles and theory. But though still unformulated, these principles were reflected in the general statements of both groups.

The Group for the Emancipation of Labour saw the 'seeds of the future workers party' in the 'workers' circles'. 'Closely linked together in one unit, these organizations . . . would not hesitate at the right moment to go over . . . to a decisive attack on the autocracy . . . and would not stop even at terrorist acts' (draft programme of [1885] 1887).[1] From the point of view of the Group for the Emancipation of Labour, 'the Russian Social Democratic movement was born not in Russia itself, but among a small group of émigrés at a time when reaction, both governmental and social, was at its height' (Aksel'rod, *The Question of the Tasks* [*K voprosu*], November 1897).[2]

From the Union's viewpoint, on the contrary, the embryo of the future workers party was the mass labour movement. And the

---

[1] 'Vtoroi proekt programmy russkikh sotsial-demokratov', in Plekhanov, *Sochineniia*.

[2] Aksel'rod, 'Pervoe pis'mo', in his *K voprosu o sovremennykh zadachakh i taktike russkikh sotsial'demokratov*, p. 3.

Russian Social Democratic movement, as the Union saw it, was born in the large industrial centres, the centres of socio-political life, and its first attempt at organization was the Northern Workers Union, which was formed when the revolutionary struggle and popular enthusiasm were at their height.

True, at the time when the 'young' Union emerged, the workers' movement was still fighting for its most elementary interests. But the Union hoped that 'in the course of the workers' battle for those immediate needs which they themselves already recognize as essential, the mass labour movement in Russia will begin to assume a class character' ('Instructions for the Editorial Committee', November 1898, *Rabochee Delo*, no. 1, p. 2). The mass workers' movement was still almost exclusively 'economic', but the Union regarded 'the political struggle of the working-class' itself as 'only the most advanced, broad, and effective form of economic struggle'. Hence it assumed that 'the exigencies of the purely economic struggle will compel the workers to raise political demands and fight for political freedom' (*ibid.* p. 3).*

* In *What Is to Be Done?*, p. 42, Lenin quotes and comments as follows on these views of the Union Abroad: '"The political struggle of the working-class is only the most advanced, broad, and effective form of economic struggle" (*The Programme of Rabochee delo*, 1898). (The political struggle is not *only* this.) "Today the problem of the Social Democratic movement is how to lend the economic struggle itself a political character" (Martynov in *Rabochee delo*, no. 10, p. 44.) "The economic struggle is the most widely applicable means of drawing the masses into active political warfare" (A resolution adopted at the congress [of the Union—*Ed.*], 1901).' Lenin remarks quite justly: 'All these propositions have permeated *Rabochee Delo* from its first number right up until the most recent "Instructions" for the editors. They all express, it would seem, a single view of political agitation and of the political struggle.'

But Lenin draws an entirely wrong conclusion when he says that the above quotations show that *Rabochee Delo* 'did not take upon itself to organize all-round political campaigns'. That the quotations cited by Lenin do not prove what he is trying to prove is clear even from the fact that the Union's resolutions cited by him were taken by the Union *in toto* from Kautsky's book, *The Erfurt Programme*. On p. 103 of the Russian edition [Stuttgart, 1903—*Ed.*] Kautsky says: 'Political warfare itself is, ultimately, and sometimes even directly, economic warfare. Political warfare is merely a special form of economic warfare—its broadest and most embracing form.'

At the present time I do not share the views cited above. I regard political rights and the rights of personal and general freedom as important in themselves, rather than as a means subordinate to other interests. They encounter independent obstacles too, and not only those connected with the economic dominance of the bourgeoisie. The subordination of all interests to the concept, *salus revolutiae* [sic—*Ed.*], is typical of the school to which Lenin belongs. This is why, in his criticism of the Union's resolutions, Lenin was not just profoundly wrong, but also inconsistent.

4. CONFLICTING ORGANIZATIONAL PRINCIPLES

'Under such circumstances', according to the Union,

the task of the Social Democratic party and its publications is to hasten the transition of the spontaneous mass movement into a conscious class movement. Such a movement would fight for the class interests of the entire proletariat (in contrast to mere strikes which are waged on behalf of particular groups within the proletariat). The Social Democratic party has to develop the class consciousness and the organizations of the Russian proletariat (*ibid.* p. 2).

What party was meant here? The party did not yet exist at the time as a unified organization, and the reference is not by proper name to the Russian Social Democratic Labour Party. Obviously, these words referred to the socio-political movement which was developing then under the Social Democratic banner, and the word 'party' was often used in this sense in the Union's publications before it was defined exactly. The existing revolutionary organization was regarded as no more than the most vitally important branch of the party. This was why the work of the revolutionary organization itself was considered by the Union to be 'useful only if, first, it guides itself not just by the general principles of scientific socialism but also by the concrete relationships between the classes in Russia and by the essential needs of the Russian movement at a given stage of its development; and, second, if it takes into account the different conditions and the different levels attained by the various strata of the working-class' (*ibid.*).

The assertion that the Union based its political propaganda merely on economic warfare is incorrect.* But equally incorrect is

---

* As early as the 'Instructions' of 1898, it was stated that 'political agitation and propaganda should exploit those clashes which arise between the labouring masses and the government during the economic struggle. But they should also exploit those important aspects of Russian life which affect the great masses of the labouring people and which at the same time demonstrate the hostility of the Tsarist government toward those masses. Examples would be the famine, new laws, etc.'

In *What Is to Be Done?* Lenin cites the headings of the articles in the never-published issue of the newspaper of the Petersburg Union of Struggle in 1895 in order to demonstrate how broadly it understood political tasks. I shall cite titles of several articles from *Rabochee Delo* which show the absurdity of the charge that the Union acted solely in the sphere of the economic interests of the working-class. No. 1: 'Secret Report of the Moscow Chief of Police.' 'The Tsarist Government's Fight Against the "Violence and Wilfulness" of the Peasants.' 'Militarism in Russia and the Tsar's "Peaceful" Proposal.' 'How the Government Fights the Labour Movement.' 'Justice and Mercy in Our Courts.' Nos. 2–3: 'The Autocracy's New Crime (About Finland).' 'May Day in Russia.' 'Hunger, Hunger, and Again Hunger.'

the assertion that the Union denied the need for an organization of professional revolutionaries. It merely insisted that every Social Democratic organization should speak for the class movement of the proletariat and show it the way forward. With quotations from the report of the Union's administrative committee to its third congress, I shall demonstrate how much the Union valued both an organization of revolutionaries in general and a united Party organization in particular. The report read:

Comrades! The period [April 1900 to September 1901] for which the administrative committee of the Union must submit its report to you opened with one notable development and is now closing with another, similar in kind yet radically different in quality. Our second congress ended, and the third is opening, with a discussion of the attitude of the Union of Russian Social Democrats to another organization, which is hostile to it even though it pursues the same goals. It is this factor in the life of the Union which exists today just as it did in March of last year.

But at that time we spoke of dividing; today, of uniting. We are confident that this year, as last, we shall find the inner strength to defend that which we value in the Union, whether we unite or whether we divide. We are referring to its organizational principle, democracy, which recognizes that all members have equal rights, and that at the same time all are equally subject to organizational discipline. We are referring also to its tactical principle. It guides itself by the general principles of scientific socialism, but it does not separate off from the masses of the proletariat who are fighting under the Social Democratic banner.

Events in Russia did not permit us to devote ourselves entirely to the defence of our own organization. In response to a summons from Russia, we sent two comrades to a projected congress which was to deal with the Party organization. The congress did not take place. We contacted Russia with great frequency and tried to persuade the comrades to make use of the Paris Congress of the International as a chance to meet. Unfortunately, these efforts also proved unsuccessful. Only one organization sent its delegate; another was represented by chance; a member of a third organization was present, but he had not been empowered to speak in its name.

'What Is Called a Peasant Mutiny in Our Country.' 'Jewish Pogroms in Southern Russia.' 'Student Disorders.' Nos. 4–5: 'To the Memory of Chernyshevskii.' 'Factory Inspection in Russia.' 'The Famine of 1898–99.' 'The Russian Government Commits a New Outrage' (Temporary Rules on Drafting Students into the Army). No. 6: 'The Life and Death of Lavrov.' 'The Tsarist Government's Struggle against the Zemstvo and Public Education.' 'What One Is Forbidden to Write about in Russia.' 'An Address by Petersburg Students to the Dismissed Professors.' No. 7: 'Economic and Political Struggle in the Russian Workers' Movement.' 'Peasant Unrest', etc., etc.

4. CONFLICTING ORGANIZATIONAL PRINCIPLES

In the autumn of 1900 the Union's position was extremely difficult. It seemed impossible to form administrative and editorial committees. The question was even asked whether the organization could continue to exist. Given such conditions, it was necessary to reorganize the Union, not so much to assure the success of its policies as to save it from actual extinction. This was accomplished. The Union did not die. We are handing on our democratic organization to our comrades—not destroyed, but, it seems to us, in a healthier state. And we believe that we now are strong enough to put in first place that which should always be of prime importance in a revolutionary organization—revolutionary action, rather than the defence of one's own section.

Our aim was to *organize* the work of the Union, that is, to entrust specific comrades with specific functions and to unify their work. In this we failed. But this aim must be achieved; the work demanded of the Union's members must be organized. If the administrative committee failed, the congress should find a way.

Compelled as we were to devote all our energies solely to our own organization, we felt all the more keenly the lack of a unifying central organization within our Party. We therefore made a third attempt to convene a Party congress. We sent a circular letter to several organizations in Russia, but found virtually no support.*

Anxious to arrange the celebration of May Day with the organizations in Russia, and also to lay the groundwork for the Second Party Congress, we sent another comrade to Russia in January 1901. This time everybody welcomed the idea of a congress. Though involved in an enormous amount of routine work, we followed eagerly the events which day by day were unfolding in Russia with unprecedented speed. Unfortunately, at this time we were hindered in our work, not by our enemies but by comrades who failed to understand the full importance to our cause of Party discipline.

In the spring of 1902 the Union made another attempt to convene the Congress. But *Iskra* sent its delegate and instructed him to do what he could to prevent the Congress from taking place. Martov tells of the incident in *The Struggle with the State of Siege* [*Bor'ba s osadnym polozheniem*], page 85. This unfortunate assignment went to Comrade Dan. In *Iskra's* view, the time was not ripe for the Congress, and it deliberately hindered the attempts to convene it. This was a reactionary aspect of its activities. *Iskra*, which had spoken so much and so sharply about *kustarnichestvo*, about backward-looking parochialism in our Party, consciously prevented its elimination. It was waiting until that faction which it considered to be the only one worthy became

* This Circular Letter was included in the Report [of the Union] to the Second Congress, which was included in my book, *The Second Congress*. [See above, Appendix I, pp. 188–92].

strong enough to overshadow all others. Thus the choice of methods to be used in building up our Party once again revealed the profound disagreements that divided the attitude of *Iskra* from that of the Union.

This disagreement took the following form. In the 'Instructions for the Editorial Committee' of 1901 the Union recognized as 'its basic characteristic the fact that it stresses the necessity to link the Social Democrats closely to the broad mass movement of the proletariat'.[1] It assumed that 'as the battle of the workers for those interests of which they are already aware develops and expands, the mass movement in Russia will merge with that of the Social Democrats'. These views were upheld by the Union with such persistence and consistency that many people accused it of confusing the concepts of 'class' and 'party', and *Iskra* said that the Union denied the need for a Party organization. I have already shown the emptiness of the latter accusation by quotations which show that the Union expended much effort to create a united Party organization. Nor was the Union guilty of confusing the concepts of party and class. By the 'Social Democratic party' the Union meant not a class, but only the movement within the working-class which develops, fully aware, under the Social Democratic banner.

This view logically led to the idea of building the Party not from above, but from below. But 'below' the Party its foundations —the local organizations—were already in place. The unification of the Party should therefore have begun with a congress attended by the representatives of these organizations. In the article 'Where to Begin?' *Iskra*, no. 4, asserted that the building should be started 'from above', that the entire upper level of the Party, the 'centre', first had to be set up and then given a broader basis of support by the establishment of a network of agents.[2] The Union regarded this as the 'destruction of the gains which had been made at such cost by the past efforts of the Social Democratic movement' (*Two Congresses*, p. 32).

The Union's view of the party as a socio-political movement was reflected in numerous articles and declarations but was not explicitly formulated for a long time. I believe that the first attempt to state this idea was made in the report on the 'unification' congress (of October 1901) in which the concept of the Union was

[1] *Instruktsii dlia redaktsii 'Rabochego dela'* (in Martynov, *Dva s"ezda*, p. 15).
[2] [Lenin], 'S chego nachat'?', *Iskra*, no. 4 (May 1901), p. 1.

contrasted with that of *Iskra*: 'To *Iskra*, the term "Social Democracy" denotes a group of people who have fully assimilated Marxist theory and have thus become the quintessence of the Party. To the Union, this term means an active socio-political force, and its kernel is the proletariat which fights under the Social Democratic banner' (*Two Congresses*, p. 23). However, the definitive statement of this concept was made by Comrade Martynov in the talk which he gave for the Union after the failure of the 'unification' congress in the autumn of 1901. This talk was later published as a pamphlet under the title of *Social Democracy and the Working-Class* [*Sotsial'demokratiia i rabochii klass*]. In it we find the following definition: 'By "party" we mean the proletariat which fights under the Social Democratic banner and is led by the democratically organized, revolutionary vanguard.'

And again, these were not the views of one particular organization, but of an entire section of the movement. They are evident in the 1901 programme of the Petersburg Union of Struggle, in the *Profession de foi* of the Kiev Committee, and in the speech delivered by the chairman of the Congress of Southern Committees and Organizations. This speech is characteristic and interesting in another respect, too: it marked yet another step in the development of a system of party organization. I shall quote a relevant passage to illustrate the particular form of reasoning typical of this school of thought and to recall the way in which our Party was built up and its organization developed.*

Ten years ago the socialist appeal to the workers began and closed with the call: Organize! Today this call inevitably recedes into the background. For today we have to appeal not to hundreds of workers who are being educated in circles, but to tens of thousands of proletarians who have been drawn into active warfare despite the conditions created by a despotic régime. To organize the fighting masses has thus become difficult in the extreme. The systematic, organized unification of the Social Democratic *committees* which *lead* the struggle becomes, therefore, all the more urgent. With the vast geographical diffusion of the Russian movement, with the great diversity of industrial, cultural, and living conditions in the different parts of Russia, the formation of unified organizations for particular regions is urgently demanded by life itself. This, of course, cannot damage the efforts to unify the entire Social

---

* All the resolutions of this congress bear visible traces of the 'third period', of so-called Economism. The main resolution on the economic struggle is wholly derived from the resolutions adopted by the Union of Russian Social Democrats.

Democratic movement in Russia into one Party. The recent emergence of a number of Social Democratic unions—for the Volga area, for Siberia, for North Russia—shows to what an extent the need for such unions is gaining recognition.

The southern region is at least as ripe for such unification as those just mentioned. It includes some of our *strongest* centres and shows every sign of developing a sustained mass political movement. Moreover, this region is sufficiently *homogeneous* both in its industrial structure (no textile industry, highly developed mechanized enterprises, a substantial contingent of craft workers) and in the way of life of its labouring masses. From these facts and considerations, we have to conclude that the congress must and can solve one of the *vitally urgent tasks* facing the revolutionary Social Democratic movement. It may be hoped that the congress will create a viable united organization in the southern region, which, together with the other unions, will serve as a stepping-stone to general Party unification. Thus the Russian Social Democratic Labour Party would soon be of importance not just as an idea, a concept, linking the active Social Democratic committees, but as a major force in the broadly organized battle and victory of the Russian Social Democrats.[1]

Thus within our Party the foundations were being laid for the kind of organization which alone could speak for and lead the class conscious sections of the proletariat. It remained only to crown this structure with a central Party organization. This work, however, was never done, and it therefore still remains on the agenda despite its *formal* completion by the Second Congress. In its present form, the existence of a central organization is significant only as an experiment, which by its very failure may serve the cause of sound organization.

[1] 'S"ezd iuzhnykh komitetov i organizatsii R.S.D.R.P.', *Letuchii listok gruppy 'Bor'ba'*, no. 1 (June 1902), p. 2. This article was published later in the year in Geneva as a separate pamphlet. The chairman, who delivered the speech quoted here, was O. A. Ermanskii. See his *Iz perezhitogo (1887–1921 gg.)* (Moscow, 1927), p. 57.

5. CONCLUSION

I most certainly do not consider that the transfer of the committees into the hands of the workers will in itself cure our Party of all ills. But a change in the organizational principles will inevitably lead to an entire re-evaluation of the accepted philosophy—whether the people setting out upon the 'new road' are aware of it or not.* The feuds about Party organization which now divide the Bolsheviks and the Mensheviks will be solved on the basis of the organizational principles which were defended by the Union and its school of thought. Of this I am deeply convinced. But the philosophy which made possible the events of recent years in our Party must not and cannot continue. The advocates of this philosophy consider themselves 'orthodox' Social Democrats. They consider their faction the most revolutionary in the Social Democratic movement. This is an error. It was that at one time. But in its conservatism it is becoming increasingly obsolete and retrograde. And we must always move forward if we are to remain in the vanguard. It is essential to criticize orthodoxy and to develop the ideas of scientific socialism in the literature of the Russian Social Democratic Labour Party. This is the duty of those men who belong to the 'third period'. In my views I was of this period, and I should like to say a few words here to those who belonged with me to this wing of the Social Democratic movement.

Comrades! We declared that we had no disagreements in principle with the Group for the Emancipation of Labour. And it is true that we were actually in agreement with our party comrades, our factional opponents, about those particular issues which they saw as the centre of dispute. Gradually, however, it became clear that we differed about tactics, theory, and philosophy, although

* In the Supplement to *Iskra*, no. 86, which has just appeared, Comrade Rabochii writes: 'The same thing was said some time in some place by Akimov and *Rabochee Delo*. True, *Rabochee Delo* and Akimov did not ask the workers to deal independently with that broad range of responsibilities which we now assign to them. And the rôle which *Rabochee Delo* expected our Party to play did not guarantee that the working-class would be able to act independently of other classes.' Comrade Rabochii thought that he was at odds with *Rabochee Delo*. Well, what of it! He is one of us anyway. He does our work for us and repeats our words, even if he is not aware of it.

neither we nor they had been aware of these differences three years before.

It was said that we were Economists, that we did not recognize the importance of politics. This was untrue. As early as 1898, when the Union was just setting to work, it declared its task to be the attainment of a democratic constitution for Russia. From the first issue of its journal it chose as its watchword the saying of Marx: 'The social emancipation of the working-class is impossible without its political emancipation.' We were the first to call upon the proletariat to take political action, to demonstrate. We devoted perhaps too much, rather than too little, space in our publications to the problem of Tsarism. It is true, however, that our attitude toward the day-to-day life and interests of the proletariat was very different from that of the orthodox. We saw the battle for these interests as one of our Party's tasks.

It was said that we were *kustari*—backward-looking provincials —that we hindered the Party's unification, the creation of an organization of professional revolutionaries. This was untrue. We were ourselves an organization of professional revolutionaries, and we worked stubbornly, consciously, and long for the creation of a centralized Party organization, for a Congress. It is true, however, that we envisage the rôle of a central organization in a way very different from that of the orthodox. We regarded the professional revolutionaries as men in the service of the movement, and therefore we wanted to build our Party in a particular way—according to democratic principles.

We were called *khvostisty*—men at the tail end, the rear of the mass movement. This was untrue. On the contrary, we were innovators who insisted on putting our ideas into practice despite opposition from the authoritative theoreticians of our Party and from our older comrades. Even those workers who had gone through the socialist propaganda circles were not on our side at first. As for the mass movement, we always tried to advance at its head, and—as subsequent events showed—we did so. It is true, however, that our attitude toward the workers' mass movement was different from that of the orthodox: we saw it as an elemental upsurge with which we consciously wished to fuse. Hence, we have a different idea of how society lives and functions. We could not and did not wish to set instinct and spontaneity against consciousness, for we differ from the orthodox about the actual theory of cognition.

We were called opportunists. This was untrue. We have our

principles—the principles of scientific socialism, and our programme is the programme of the international Social Democratic movement; these we shall not yield in the name of anything. As for that scholastic, doctrinaire vulgarization of Marxism which is served up to us under the title of orthodoxy (and why not translate this Greek term into Russian—*pravoslavie*—the Orthodox Faith), we certainly cannot acknowledge it as a correct representation of scientific socialism. The orthodox regards all attempts at critical thinking, from Bernstein to Bogdanov, as mere varieties of revisionism, and he hates impartially every manifestation of revisionism. This is why every thinking member of the Party suffocates in the atmosphere of the orthodox Social Democratic church.

We must distinguish the general features which mark the events now taking place in our Party. We shall then be able to explain the philosophy which mirrors these events and to oppose it to our own philosophy. For from our philosophical standpoint, the things in which our factional opponents take pride and satisfaction are harmful, false, evil, and intolerable.

But all this will have to be discussed at a later date. As I complete this work in February 1905, the hour sets us pressing tasks and problems which must be met with whatever forces actual developments in Russia permit our Party to muster. These are, first of all, problems of organization. Today we have to deal with them literally under the fire of our enemies, but we cannot postpone them. For thirty years now the Russian socialists have carried their ideas to the working-class. Tens of thousands of lives were lost in this cause. Hundreds of thousands of years in prison, penal exile, and hard labour have paid for those changes through which our country is now about to pass. For twenty years the Russian socialists, as represented by the Social Democrats, have linked their cause to that of the working-class. Today we have men who share our ideas everywhere, tried and true comrades. It is time to draw conclusions.

In all plants and factories, in all trades, wherever our Party has contacts, it is essential to group together immediately the class-conscious workers, the Social Democrats. To these groups— as to the trade councils of the Bund, the Petersburg factory organizations, the Kiev *kassy*—we must entrust the conduct of our work in their plants, factories, and trades. These groups should be made the foundation of our Party. Further, we must unify these cells by assembling their representatives at 'agitators' councils', as the Bund has done, or in 'district organizations', as was done in Petersburg, or in 'factory' or 'trade' committees, as was done in Kiev. Connected with these organizations there should be organizations of professional revolutionaries to lend them their experience, knowledge, and conspiratorial skill, and the advantage of their education.

Further, the authority required to unify and direct the work of all the organizations in a particular centre should be vested in a committee, made up of the elected representatives of these organizations. 'With the vast geographical diffusion of the movement, the formation of unified organizations for particular regions is urgently demanded by life itself.' The committees should therefore be combined in unions which should enjoy the fullest independence of action.

Finally, the Party's central organization should be reorganized to correspond to the democratic structure of the Party as a whole. As in the Belgian Labour Party, a delegate from a union of the local committees should be a member of the Central Committee of the Party. Then the party that represents the Jewish proletariat, the Bund, which is not confined within regional limits, would again find a place in our Party as a union of local committees. This would also be true of the proletarian organizations of other nationalities in Russia.*

Our present Central Committee is modelled on a ministerial cabinet. The Central Committee of the Belgian party is built like the Swiss Cabinet—the Federal Council. This is not the place for an extended defence of these organizational principles; I am therefore merely drawing attention to them. I need only point out that it is possible to defend these principles with all those same irrefutable arguments that our Party uses to defend the idea of a democratically organized state. If we accept that a democratic political organization can best guide the development of an entire nation with all its class contradictions, how much more suitable it must be for the control of a political party. As for the handicaps imposed by Russia's police régime, the experience of the 'third period' demonstrated that a democratic, no less than a conspiratorial, organization can function effectively underground.

---

* Note to 2nd edition: As was noted in the Preface, this plan has already passed into the realm of history. Since the October events, our Party has been in need of a broader organization.

5. CONCLUSION

Despite the major war that the Party is waging against its external enemies, it is still confronted by an internal problem—the problem of its own organization.

In 'The Wall', a story by Andreev, a wall divides heaven and earth from each other, leaving only cruel and unnecessary suffering on the side of humanity. People come together and separate in a mad dance; repulsive as lepers, they poison one another's existence. Hating this life, they butt their heads against the wall, trying to make a breach in it. They seek desperately for some way to destroy it. But the mind is powerless before the fatal obstacle, and those who do not submit to fate perish at the immovable wall. The French sculptor who created a symbolic wall on the occasion of a certain historical event perhaps merely has given us a more concrete conception of this same general idea. 'Give me back my child, my son, my brother, my daughter . . . Murderer! Give me back myself!'[1] cried the lepers before Andreev's wall, which had swallowed so many lives. On the wall of Moreau-Vauthier can be seen the forms of the torn bodies of the defenders of the Commune. As a symbol of an obstacle to freedom and joy, the wall differs from the real obstacle only in that it is formed of dead stones. But the obstacle to the progress of mankind consists of the people themselves, suffering, wretched, pitiful, yet immovable in their inertia. It is this wall of the inert human mass that we must destroy.

We socialists must be the men of the future. We must foresee this future, and by it, by our vision, we must guide our lives and actions! According to our teaching, in every modern civilized nation there is a vital, revolutionary stratum, which creates the future. This is the lowest stratum, the very foundation of the wall—the proletariat. When it comes into motion, then, as the *Communist Manifesto* says, with the force of a geological upheaval it will destroy everything that rests upon it. It will bring down the entire wall.

And now the cornerstones of the wall are already crying out. The proletariat has already begun to stir in search of its freedom. Let us speak for the foundation of the wall! In the ancient legend the walls of Jericho fell at the sound of the trumpets and opened the promised land to the Israelites. So now, at the sound of our voice, the enemies of the proletariat, who press like a dead weight upon it and all the labouring people, will tumble.

This is how I understand the basic idea of the 'third period'.

[1] L. Andreev, 'Stena', in *Pol'noe sobranie sochinenii* (St Petersburg, 1913), I, 144–5.

BIBLIOGRAPHY AND INDEX

BIBLIOGRAPHY

The Bibliography contains works which deal with Akimov's central field of interest in this book—Russian revolutionary Marxism from the late 1880s to 1904. It does not include those works which are cited in the notes but are not directly relevant to this theme.

Akimov, V. P., pseudonym (Vladimir Petrovich Makhnovets). 'K istorii vtorogo s"ezda R.S.D.R. partii', *Minuvshie Gody*, No. 7, 1908, pp. 279–96.

O shifrakh. Izd. Soiuza Russkikh Sotsial'demokratov, published under the pseudonym V. P. Bakharev. Geneva, 1902.

'Pervoe maia v Rossii', *Byloe*, 1906, No. 10, pp. 163–92; No. 11, pp. 78–99; No. 12, pp. 131–57.

'Pervyi s"ezd R.S.D.R. partii', *Minuvshie Gody*, No. 2, 1908, pp. 128–68.

'Stroiteli budushchego', *Obrazovanie*, 1907, No. 4, pp. 91–118; No. 5, pp. 66–98; No. 6, pp. 54–88.

Aksel'rod, Pavel Borisovich. 'Gruppa "Osvobozhdenie Truda" (Neopublikovannye glavy iz vtorogo toma *Vospominanii*)', *Letopisi Marksizma*, No. 6, 1928, pp. 82–112.

Istoricheskoe polozhenie i vzaimnoe otnoshenie liberal'noi i sotsialisticheskoi demokratii v Rossii. Geneva, 1898.

K voprosu o sovremennykh zadachakh i taktike russkikh sotsial'-demokratov. Geneva, 1898.

Pis'mo v redaktsiiu 'Rabochego Dela'. Geneva, 1899.

Aksel'rod, P. B., and L. Martov. *Pis'ma P. B. Aksel'roda i Iu. O. Martova* (ed. F. Dan and B. I. Nikolaevskii). Berlin, 1924.

Aksel'rod-Ortodoks, L. 'Iz moikh vospominanii', *Katorga i Ssylka* (Moscow), No. 2 (63), 1930, pp. 22–42.

Aleksandrov, Mikhail Stepanovich (Galerka; M. S. Ol'minskii, pseudonyms). '"Gruppa Narodovol'tsev" (1891–1894 gg.)', *Byloe*, No. 11, 1906, pp. 1–27.

Aleksandrov, Mikhail Stepanovich, and A. Bogdanov. *Nashi nedorazumeniia*. Published under the pseudonyms Galerka and Riadovoi. Geneva, 1904.

Andreev, Ia. A. '1897–1898 gg. v Kolpine', *Proletarskaia Revoliutsiia*, No. 2 (14), 1923, pp. 77–86.

Andropov, S. V. 'G. V. Plekhanov i Peterb. gruppa *Rabochego Znameni*', *Proletarskaia Revoliutsiia*, Nos. 8–9 (31–2), 1924, pp. 323–4.

(ed.). 'Pis'ma V. P. Nogina k S. V. Andropovu (1900–1906 gg.)', *Proletarskaia Revoliutsiia*, Nos. 8–9 (31–2), 1924, pp. 325–60.

BIBLIOGRAPHY

Angarskii, N. (ed.). *Doklady sots.-demokraticheskikh komitetov vtoromu s"ezdu RSDRP.* Moscow–Leningrad, 1930.

'K istorii I s"ezda RSDRP', *Proletarskaia Revoliutsiia*, No. 3 (74), 1928, pp. 22–48.

Astrov, V. *'Ekonomisty': Predtechi Men'shevikov.* Moscow, 1923.

Babushkin, I. V. *Vospominaniia I. V. Babushkina (1893–1900 gg.).* Leningrad, 1925.

Balabanov, M. *Ocherki po istorii rabochego klassa v Rossii.* Vol. III: *Kapitalisticheskaia Rossiia.* Moscow, 1926.

Baron, S. H. *Plekhanov, the Father of Russian Marxism.* Stanford, 1963.

Baturin, N. 'O "sotsial'nykh korniakh", "ekonomizma" i men'shevizma', *Proletarskaia Revoliutsiia*, No. 2 (25), 1924, pp. 110–13.

Bebel' o Bernshteine: Rech' Avgusta Bebel'ia proiznesennaia na Gannoverskom parteitage 10 oktiabria 1899 goda. London, 1902.

Bernstein, Eduard. *Istoricheskii materializm.* St Petersburg, 1901.

Bonch-Bruevich, V. D. *Izbrannye sochineniia.* Vol. II: *Stat'i, vospominaniia, pis'ma 1895–1914.* Moscow, 1961.

B-ov, M. 'Otvet *Rabochei Gazety* (1898 g.) G. V. Plekhanovu', *Krasnyi Arkhiv*, No. 6 (19), 1928, pp. 207–9.

Broido, E. L. 'Gruppy "Sotsialist" i "Rabochaia biblioteka" 1899–1901 gg.', *Letopis' Revoliutsii*, No. 1, 1923, pp. 126–33.

Memoirs of a Revolutionary. Oxford, 1967.

Brusnev, M. I. 'Vozniknovenie pervykh sotsial-demokraticheskikh organizatsii (Vospominaniia)', *Proletarskaia Revoliutsiia*, No. 8 (14), 1923, pp. 17–32.

Bugaev, N. V., and V. Z. Sergiuk (eds.). *Listovki revoliutsionnykh sotsialdemokraticheskikh organizatsii Ukrainy 1896–1904.* Kiev, 1963.

Bukhbinder, N. A. 'Gruppa "Sotsial-Demokraticheskaia Biblioteka" (po neizdannym arkhivnym materialam)', *Katorga i Ssylka*, No. 2 (31), 1927, pp. 49–54.

'K istorii sotsial-demokraticheskogo dvizheniia v Kievskoi gubernii, I: Kiev (po neizdannym arkhivnym materialam)', *Krasnaia Letopis'*, No. 7, 1923, pp. 263–84.

'K kharakteristike sotsial-demokratii kontsa 90-kh godov', *Katorga i Ssylka*, No. 10 (47), 1928, pp. 85–7.

(ed.). *Materialy dlia istorii evreiskogo rabochego dvizheniia v Rossii.* Moscow, 1923. A publication of the Komissiia po istorii oktiabr'skoi revoliutsii i RKP (b).

Bund. *IV-yi s"ezd Vseobshchego Evreiskogo Soiuza v Litve, Pol'she i Rossii.* Geneva, 1901.

Deiatel'nost' Bunda za polednie 2 goda. London, 1903.

Istoriia evreiskogo rabochego dvizheniia v Rossii i Pol'she. Geneva, 1901.

Nasha blizhaishaia organizatsionnaia zadacha. London, 1903.

V-yi s"ezd Vseobshchego Evreiskogo Rabochego Soiuza. London, 1903.

II s"ezd Rossiiskoi S.D.R. Partii: Otchet delegatsii Bunda. London, 1903.

BIBLIOGRAPHY

Burtsev, V. (ed.). *Za sto let (1800–1896)*. London, 1897.

Chaadaev, O. (ed.). 'Iz istorii rabochego dvizheniia kontsa 90-kh godov i "Soiuzy borby za osvobozhdenie rabochego klassa"', *Krasnyi Arkhiv*, No. 2 (93), 1939, pp. 119–89.

Cherevanin, pseudonym (F. A. Lipkin). *Organizatsionnyi vopros*, with a foreword by L. Martov. Geneva, 1904.

Cherikover, A., A. Menes, F. Kurski, and A. Rozin (eds.). *Di yidishe sotsialistishe bavegung biz der grindung fun Bund: Historishe Shriften*, Vol. III. Vilna and Paris, 1939.

Chernomordik, S. 'K 50-letiiu gruppy *Osvobozhdenie truda*', *Katorga i Ssylka*, No. 10 (107), 1933, pp. 5–35; No. 12 (109), pp. 5–36.

Dan, F., pseudonym (Fedor Il'ich Gurvich). *Proiskhozhdenie Bol'-shevizma*. New York, 1946. [English translation: *The Origins of Bolshevism*. New York, 1964.]

Dan, F. and B. I. Nikolaevskii (eds.). *See* Aksel'rod, P. B., and L. Martov.

Deiateli revoliutsionnogo dvizheniia v Rossii: Bio-bibliograficheskii slovar'. *See* Vilenskii-Sibiriakov, V., and others (eds.).

'Deiateli Soiuza Sovetskikh Sotsialisticheskikh Respublik i Oktiabr'skoi revoliutsii', *Entsiklopedicheskii slovar' T-va Br. A. i I. Granat i Ko*. 7th ed. Moscow, 1927(?). Vols. XL–XLI.

Deich, L. 'Kak G. V. Plekhanov stal marksistom', *Proletarskaia Revoliutsiia*, No. 7, 1922, pp. 97–140.

'Kto prav? (Otvet prof. M. N. Pokrovskomu)', *Gruppa 'Osvobozhdenie Truda'*, V (1926), 255–72.

(ed.). *See* Gruppa 'Osvobozhdenie Truda'.

Deutscher, I. *The Prophet Armed: Trotsky 1879–1921*. Oxford, 1954.

Dimanshtein, S. (ed.). *Revoliutsionnoe dvizhenie sredi Evreev*. Moscow, 1930. With a foreword by S. Dimanshtein.

'Doklad po delu o voznikshikh v Peterburge v 1894 i 1895 godakh prestupnykh kruzhkakh lits, imenuiushchikh sebia "sotsial-demokratimi"', *Sbornik materialov i statei*, Vol. I, pp. 93–178. Moscow, 1921, Glavnoe Upravlenie Arkhivnym Delom.

Doklad predstavlennyi delegatsieiu russkikh sotsial-demokratov Mezhdunarodnomu rabochemu sotsialisticheskomu kongressu v Londone v 1896 godu. Izd. Soiuza Russkikh Sotsial'demokratov. Geneva, 1896.

'Dokumenty G. V. Plekhanova: K 100-letiiu so dnia rozhdeniia (1856–1956 gg.)', *Istoricheskii Arkhiv*, No. 6, 1956, pp. 3–28.

Dva s"ezda: Tretii ocherednoi s"ezd Soiuza i 'ob"edinitel'nyi' s"ezd. *See* Martynov, A. S.

Eidel'man, B. L. 'Kievskaia rabochaia gazeta *Vpered*, I: 1897 g.', *Proletarskaia Revoliutsiia*, No. 6 (65), 1927, pp. 249–71; 'II: 1897–1898 gg.', *Proletarskaia Revoliutsiia*, No. 12 (71), 1927, pp. 216–32.

'K istorii vozniknoveniia Rossiiskoi sots.-dem. rabochei partii', *Proletarskaia Revoliutsiia*, No. 1, 1921, pp. 20–67.

'Literatory Kievskogo sotsial-demokraticheskogo podpol'ia do 1-go s"ezda', *Katorga i Ssylka*, No. 2 (51), 1929, pp. 36–56.

Eidel'man, B. L. 'Ob "ekonomistskikh" tendentsiakh na l s"ezda RSDRP', *Proletarskaia Revoliutsiia*, No. 10 (81), 1928, pp. 137–49.

'Pervyi s"ezd partii v sovremennoi literature', *Proletarskaia Revoliutsiia*, No. 2 (73), 1928, pp. 6–22.

'Po povodu stat'i Akimova', *Proletarskaia Revoliutsiia*, No. 1, 1921, p. 75.

Elizarova, A. I. 'Vladimir Il'ich v tiurme (dekabr' 1895–fevral' 1897)', *Proletarskaia Revoliutsiia*, No. 3 (26), 1924, pp. 107–25.

Engels, Friedrich. See *Perepiska K. Marksa i F. Engel'sa.*

See 'Pis'ma G. Plekhanova k F. Engelsu i R. Fisheru'.

Erfurt programme. See 'Programm der Sozialdemokratischen Partei Deutschlands'.

Ermanskii, O. A., pseudonym (Osip Arkad'evich Kogan). *Iz perezhitogo (1887–1921 gg.)*. Moscow, 1927. With a foreword by P. Lepeshinskii.

Fedorchenko, L. (N. Charov, pseudonym). 'Pervye shagi sotsialdemokratii v Kieve', *Katorga i Ssylka*, No. 6 (27), 1926, pp. 21–33.

[Feinberg, B. L.]. *Rabochee dvizhenie v Khar'kove*. Izd. Soiuza Russkikh Sotsial'demokratov. Geneva, 1900.

Frankel, J. 'Economism: A Heresy Exploited', *Slavic Review*, No. 2, 1963, pp. 263–84.

'Party Genealogy and the Soviet Historians (1920–1938)', *Slavic Review*, No. 4, 1966, pp. 563–603.

Fürstenberg, Ia. See Ganetskii (Hanecki), Ia.

Galerka. See Aleksandrov, Mikhail Stepanovich.

Ganetskii (Hanecki), Ia., pseudonym (Ia. Fürstenberg). 'Delegatsiia SDPiL na II s"ezde RSDRP', *Proletarskaia Revoliutsiia*, 1933, No. 2, pp. 187–200.

Gel'man, S. 'Pervaia podpol'naia tipografiia gruppy *Rabochee Znamia*', *Katorga i Ssylka*, No. 6 (27), 1926, pp. 44–56.

Gershanovich, D. L. 'Vospominaniia o gruppe *Rabochego Znameni*: O Moisee Vladimiroviche Lur'e', *K dvadtsatipiatiletiiu Pervogo s"ezda partii (1898–1923)*, pp. 165–74. Moscow, 1923. A publication of the Komissiia po istorii oktiabr'skoi revoliutsii i RKP (b).

Getzler, Israel. *Martov: A Political Biography of a Russian Social Democrat*. Cambridge, 1967.

Geyer, D. *Lenin in der Russischen Sozialdemokratie*. Cologne, 1960.

Golubev, V. S. 'Stranichka iz istorii rabochego dvizheniia (pamiati N. V. Shelgunova)', *Byloe*, No. 12, 1906, pp. 105–21.

Gorev, B. I., pseudonym (Boris Isaakovich Gol'dman). *Iz partiinogo proshlogo: Vospominaniia, 1895–1905*. Leningrad, 1924.

'Pered vtorym s"ezdom (Vospominaniia)', *Katorga i Ssylka*, No. 1 (8), 1924, pp. 42–65.

Gruppa 'Osvobozhdenie Truda' (iz arkhivov G. V. Plekhanova, V. I. Zasulich i L. G. Deicha), ed. Lev Grigor'evich Deich, 6 vols. Moscow,

1923–8. Relevant correspondence of members of the Group is in Vols. IV–VI.

Gurvich, E. A. 'Evreiskoe rabochee dvizhenie v Minske v 80-kh godakh', *Revoliutsionnoe dvizhenie sredi Evreev* (ed. S. Dimanshtein), pp. 33–64.

Gurvich, Isaak Adol'fovich. 'Pervye evreiskie rabochie kruzhki', *Byloe*, No. 6, 1907, pp. 65–77.

Haimson, Leopold. *The Russian Marxists and the Origins of Bolshevism.* Cambridge, Mass., 1955.

Hertz, Y. Sh. and others (eds.). *Di geshichte fun Bund*, 2 vols. New York, 1960–2.

Istoriia Kommunisticheskoi partii sovetskogo soiuza, Vol. I: *Sozdanie bol'shevistskoi partii 1883–1903 gg.* (ed. P. N. Pospelov and others). Moscow, 1964.

Istoriia SSSR: Ukazatel' sovetskoi literatury za 1917–1952 gg. Vol. II: *Istoriia SSSR v period kapitalizma (1861–1917).* Moscow, 1958.

Istoriko-revoliutsionnyi sbornik, ed. by V. I. Nevskii, 3 vols. Moscow, 1924–6. A publication of the Komissiia po istorii oktiabr'skoi revoliutsii i RKP (b).

Ivanov, B. 'N. L. Sergievskii kak istorik partii russkikh sotsial-demokratov', *Katorga i Ssylka*, No. 1 (74), 1931, pp. 59–122.

Ivanov, L. M. (ed.). *See* Rabochee dvizhenie v Rossii.

'Iz perepiski *Iskry* s mestnymi organizatsiiami' (ed. Ts. Bobrovskii), *Proletarskaia Revoliutsiia*, 1928, Nos. 6–7 (77–8), pp. 93–178; No. 8 (79), pp. 50–63.

Iz rabochego dvizheniia v Odesse i Nikolaeve. See [Stekov, Iu. M., and L. Trotskii].

Kamenev, Iu. (L. Kamenev), pseudonym (Lev B. Rosenfeld). *Russkaia politicheskaia literatura zagranitsei*, Vol. I: *Sotsial'demokraticheskie izdaniia: Ukazatel' sotsial'demokratischeskoi literatury na russkom iazyke 1883–1905 gg.* Paris, 1913.

(ed.). See *Leninskii Sbornik.*

Katin-Iartsev, V. 'Teni proshlogo', *Byloe*, No. 25, 1924, pp. 101–18.

Kautsky, K. *Osnovnye polozheniia Erfurtskoi programmy.* Kolyma, 1894.

Sotsial'naia revoliutsiia (ed. N. Lenin). Izd. Ligi R.R.S.-D. Geneva, 1903.

Kazakevich, R. A. *Sotsial-demokraticheskie organizatsii Peterburga.* Leningrad, 1960.

Kazakevich, R. A., and F. M. Suslova. *Mister Paips fal'sifitsiruet istoriiu.* Leningrad, 1966.

K dvadtsatipiatiletiiu Pervogo s"ezda partii (1898–1923). Moscow, 1923. A publication of the Komissiia po istorii oktiabr'skoi revoliutsii i RKP (b).

Keep, J. L. H. *The Rise of Social Democracy in Russia.* Oxford, 1963.

Kharitonov, V. 'Iz vospominanii uchastnika gruppy Blagoeva', *Proletarskaia Revoliutsiia*, No. 8 (79), 1928, pp. 152–66.

24-2

Kopel'zon, T. M. 'Evreiskoe rabochee dvizhenie kontsa 80-kh i nachala 90-kh godov', *Revoliutsionnoe dvizhenie sredi Evreev* (ed. S. Dimanshtein), pp. 65–80. Moscow, 1930.

See 'Materialy k istorii pervogo s''ezda'.

'Stranichka iz vospominanii', *O Lenine vospominaniia* (ed. N. L. Meshcheriakov). Vol. III, pp. 19–30. Moscow, 1925–30.

Koz'min, B. P. *Rabochee dvizhenie v Rossii do revoliutsii 1905 goda.* Moscow, 1925.

Krasin, G. B. 'Stepan Ivanovich Radchenko', *Staryi Bol'shevik*, No. 2 (5), 1933, pp. 186–9.

[Kremer (Kramer), Arkadii]. *Ob agitatsii.* With an afterword by P. Aksel'rod. Geneva, 1897. Dated 1896.

'Osnovanie Bunda', *Proletarskaia Revoliutsiia*, No. 11, 1922, pp. 50–6.

Krovatskii, A. 'Moi vospominaniia', *K dvadtsatipiatiletiiu Pervogo s''ezda partii (1898–1923)*, pp. 79–83. Moscow, 1923.

Krupskaia, N. K. 'Piat' let raboty v vechernikh Smolenskikh klassakh', in her *Pedagogicheskie sochineniia.* Vol. I, pp. 38–55. Moscow, 1957. *Vospominaniia o Lenine.* Moscow, 1933.

Kudelli, P. F. *Narodovol'tsy na pereput'i: Delo Lakhtinskoi tipografii.* Leningrad, 1925.

Kuskova, Ekaterina Dmitrievna. *See* 'Materialy k istorii pervogo s''ezda'.

Laliants, I. 'O moikh vstrechakh s V. I. Leninym za vremia 1893–1900 gg. (Otryvki iz vospominanii)', *Proletarskaia Revoliutsiia*, No. 1 (84), 1929, pp. 38–70.

Lenin, N. (V. I. Lenin), pseudonym (Vladimir Il'ich Ul'ianov). *Chto delat'? Nabolevshie voprosy nashego dvizheniia.* Stuttgart, 1902.

Pis'mo k tovarishchu o nashikh organizatsionnykh zadachakh. Geneva, 1904.

Polnoe sobranie sochinenii. 5th ed., 55 vols. Moscow, 1958–65. Relevant correspondence is in vols. XLVI and LV.

Shag vpered, dva shaga nazad: Krizis v nashei partii. Geneva, 1904.

Sochineniia. 2nd ed., 30 vols. Moscow–Leningrad, 1927–32.

Sochineniia. 4th ed., 40 vols. Moscow, 1941–62. [English translation: *Collected Works.* 39 vols. Moscow, 1960–8.]

Sochineniia. 5th ed. *See* Lenin, N., *Polnoe sobranie sochinenii.*

Zadachi russkikh sotsial'demokratov. With a foreword by P. Aksel'rod. Geneva, 1898.

Leninskii Sbornik (ed. L. Kamenev). 35 vols. Moscow, 1924–45. A publication of the Institut Lenina pri Ts.K.V.K.P. (b). Relevant correspondence is in vols. I–IV, VI–VIII, X, XI, XIII.

Lepeshinskii, P. *Na povorote.* 3rd ed. Moscow, 1935.

Levitskii, V., pseudonym (Vladimir Osipovich Tsederbaum). *Za chetvert' veka*, Vol. I, Part 1: *Revoliutsionnaia podgotovka 1892–1901 gg.* Moscow, 1926.

Lichtheim, G. *Marxism. An Historical and Critical Study.* London, 1961.

Listovki Peterburgskogo 'Soiuza bor'by za osvobozhdenie rabochego klassa'. See Valk, S. N., and I. Tovstukhi (eds.).

Listovki revoliutsionnykh sotsialdemokraticheskikh organizatsii Ukrainy. See Bugaev, N. V., and V. Z. Sergiuk (eds.).

Logacheva-Piletskaia, M. 'Soiuz bor'by za osvobozhdenie rabochego klassa v 1900–1901 godakh', *Byloe*, No. 3 (31), 1925, pp. 93–107.

Makhnovets, Vladimir Petrovich. See Akimov, V. P.

Manilov, V. 'Ocherk iz istorii sotsial-demokraticheskogo dvizheniia v Kieve (80-ye–90-ye gody)', *Letopis' Revoliutsii* (Khar'kov), No. 3, 1923, pp. 116–37.

Martov, L. (Iu. O. Martov), pseudonym (Iulii Osipovich Tsederbaum). *Bor'ba s 'osadnym polozheniem' v Rossiiskoi sotsial'demokraticheskoi rabochei partii (otvet na pis'mo Lenina).* Geneva, 1904.

'Iz neopublikovannykh vospominanii', *Leninskii Sbornik* (ed. L. Kamenev), Vol. iv, pp. 49–61.

Zapiski Sotsialdemokrata. Vol. i. Berlin, 1922.

Martov, L. (Iu. O.), and P. B. Aksel'rod. See Aksel'rod.

Martov, L. (Iu. O.), P. Maslov and A. Potresov (eds.). *Obshchestvennoe dvizhenie v Rossii v nachale XX veka.* 4 vols. St Petersburg, 1909–14.

[Martynov, A. S., pseudonym (Aleksandr Samoilovich Piker)]. *Dva s"ezda: Tretii ocherednoi s"ezd Soiuza i 'ob"edinitel'nyi' s"ezd.* Izd. Soiuza Russkikh Sotsial'demokratov. Geneva, 1901.

Sotsial'demokratiia i rabochii klass: Dva techeniia v russkoi sotsial'-demokratii. Geneva, 1901.

'Vospominaniia revoliutsionera', *Proletarskaia Revoliutsiia*, No. 11 (46), 1925, pp. 262–83.

Marx, Karl. See *Perepiska K. Marksa i F. Engel'sa*.

Masanov, I. F. *Slovar' psevdonimov russkikh pisatelei, uchenykh i obshchestvennykh deiatelei.* 4 vols. Moscow, 1956–60.

Materialy dlia istorii evreiskogo rabochego dvizheniia v Rossii. See Bukhbinder, N. A. (ed.).

'Materialy k istorii pervogo s"ezda', *Proletarskaia Revoliutsiia*, No. 3 (74), 1928, pp. 152–69. Letters of Kuskova, Kopel'zon, etc., 1898.

'Materialy po delu M. I. Brusneva', *Ot gruppy Blagoeva k 'Soiuzu bor'by'* (*1886–1894 gg.*), pp. 79–96.

Menes, A. 'Di yidishe arbeter-bavegung in Rusland fun onhaib 70-en biz sof 90-er yoren', *Di yidishe sotsialistishe bavegung biz der grindung fun Bund: Historishe Shriften* (eds. A. Cherikover, A. Menes, F. Kurski and A. Rozin), Vol. iii, pp. 1–59.

Menshchikov, L. P., *Okhrana i revoliutsiia: K istorii tainykh politicheskikh organizatsii, sushchestvovavshikh vo vremena samoderzhavia,* 3 vols. Moscow, 1925–32.

(ed.). *Russkii politicheskii sysk zagranitsei.* Vol. i. Paris, 1914.

Meshcheriakov, N. L. (ed.). *O Lenine vospominaniia,* Vol. iii. Moscow, 1925–30.

Meyer, A. G. *Leninism*. Cambridge, Mass., 1957.

Mikhailova, E. 'Iz kommentariev k *Chto delat'?*, "Gruppa samo-osvobozhdeniia rabochego klassa"', *Krasnaia Letopis'*, No. 1 (12), 1925, pp. 239–48.

Moshinskii (Moszinski), I. N., pseudonym (Iuz. Konarskii). 'Devianostye gody v Kievskom podpol'e', *Katorga i Ssylka*, 1927, No. 5 (34), pp. 7–24; No. 6 (35), pp. 36–53; No. 7 (36), pp. 101–11; No. 8 (37), pp. 52–67. This series of articles was published in slightly different form: see entry that follows.

Na putiakh k 1-mu s"ezdu R.S.-D.R.P.: 90-tye gody v Kievskom podpol'e. Moscow, 1928.

Moskalev, M. A. 'Bor'ba za sozdanie marksistskoi rabochei partii v 90-kh godakh XIX veka', *Voprosy Istorii*, No. 8, 1956, pp. 91–104.

Nettl, J. P. *Rosa Luxemburg*. 2 vols. Oxford, 1966.

Nevskii, V. I. 'Gruppa Osvobozhdenie Truda v period 1883–1894 gg.', *Istoriko-revoliutsionnyi sbornik* (ed. V. I. Nevskii), Vol. II, pp. 7–85.

—— (ed.). *Istoriko-revoliutsionnyi sbornik.* See *Istoriko-revoliutsionnyi sbornik.*

'K voprosu o pervom s"ezde Rossiiskoi sotsial-demokraticheskoi partii', *Proletarskaia Revoliutsiia*, No. 1, 1921, pp. 82–113.

—— (ed.). *Materialy dlia biograficheskogo slovaria sotsial-demokratov vstupivshikh v rossiiskoe rabochee dvizhenie za period ot 1880 do 1905 g.*, Vol. I. Moscow–Petrograd, 1923.

Ocherki po istorii Rossiiskoi Kommunisticheskoi Partii. 2nd ed., Vol. I. Leningrad, 1925.

Nikitin, I. 'Peterburgskii Soiuz bor'by za osvobozhdenie rabochego klassa.' Moscow, 1950.

[Nikolaevskii, B. I.]. 'Iz epokhi *Iskry* i *Zari*', *Katorga i Ssylka*, 1927, No. 6 (35), pp. 7–35; No. 7 (36), pp. 83–100. Published under the initials B.N.

'K istorii Peterburgskoi sotsial-demokraticheskoi gruppy "starikov"', *Letopisi Marksizma*, No. 3, 1927, pp. 61–6.

'Pis'mo G. V. Plekhanova v redaktsiiu *Rabochei Gazety'*, *K dvadtsatipiatiletiiu Pervogo s"ezda partii (1898–1923)*, pp. 284–7. Moscow, 1923. Published under the name B. N——skii.

'Programma pervogo v Rossii s.-d. kruzhka', *Byloe*, No. 7 (13), 1918, pp. 38–52.

—— (joint ed.). See *Sotsial-demokraticheskoe dvizhenie.*

Nikolaevskii, B. I., and F. Dan (eds.). *See* Aksel'rod, P. B., and L. Martov.

Ob agitatsii. See [Kremer (Kramer), Arkadii].

Ocherki istorii Leningrada, Vol. III: *Period imperializma i burzhuazno-demokraticheskikh revoliutsii, 1895–1917 gg.* (ed. B. M. Kochakov and others). Moscow, 1956. A publication of the Akademiia Nauk SSSR: Institut istorii.

BIBLIOGRAPHY

Olenin, Boris. 'Po povodu poslednikh peterburgskikh proklamatsii', *Nakanune: Sotsial'no-revoliutsionnoe obozrenie*, Nos. 26–7 (February–March 1901), pp. 314–16.

Ol'minskii, M. S. *See* Aleksandrov, Mikhail Stepanovich.

Ot gruppy Blagoeva k 'Soiuzu bor'by' (*1886–1894 gg.*). Rostov, 1921. A publication of the Komissiia po istorii oktiabr'skoi revoliutsii i RKP (b).

Otvet redaktsii 'Rabochego Dela' na 'Pis'mo' P. Aksel'roda i 'Vademecum' G. Plekhanova. Izd. Soiuza Russkikh Sotsial'demokratov. Geneva, 1900.

Ovsiankin, V. A. (ed.). *See* Suslova, F. M.

Ovsiannikova, S. *Gruppa Blagoeva*. Moscow, 1959.

Paialin, N. 'V. I. Lenin i rabochie Semiannikovskogo zavoda v 90-e gody', *Krasnaia Letopis'*, No. 1 (58), 1934, pp. 48–56.

Pavlovich, pseudonym (Petr Ananevich Krasikov). *Pis'mo k tovarishcham o vtorom s"ezde RSDRP*. Geneva, 1904.

Perepiska G. V. Plekhanova i P. B. Aksel'roda (ed. P. A. Berlin, V. S. Voitinskii, and B. I. Nikolaevskii). 2 vols. Moscow, 1925.

Perepiska K. Marksa i F. Engel'sa s russkimi politicheskimi deiateliami. Moscow, 1947.

Pervoe maia 1891 goda: Chetyre rechi rabochikh proiznesennye na tainom sobranii v Peterburge. With a foreword by G. Plekhanov. Geneva, 1892.

Pervoe maia 1892 goda: Chetyre rechi evreiskikh rabochikh. With a foreword. Geneva, 1893. A publication of the Tipografiia Sotsial'-demokraticheskoi Biblioteki.

Peterburzhets, pseudonym (Konstantin Mikhailovich Takhtarev). *Ocherk peterburgskogo rabochego dvizheniia 90-kh godov.* London, 1902.

Pipes, R. 'Russian Marxism and Its Populist Background: The Late Nineteenth Century', *The Russian Review*, No. 4, 1960, pp. 316–37.

Social Democracy and the St Petersburg Labor Movement 1885–1897. Cambridge, Mass., 1963.

'Pis'ma G. Plekhanova k F. Engel'su i R. Fisheru'. *See* Plekhanov, Georgii Valentinovich.

Pis'ma P. B. Aksel'roda i Iu. O. Martova. See Aksel'rod, Pavel Borisovich.

Plamenatz, J. *German Marxism and Russian Communism*. London, 1954.

Plekhanov, Georgii Valentinovich. 'Buki Az-Ba', *God na rodine*, Vol. II, pp. 257–68. Paris, 1921.

Nashi raznoglasiia. Geneva, 1885. [English translation in his *Selected Philosophical Works*. Moscow, 1961, pp. 122–399.]

See Otvet redaktsii 'Rabochego Dela'.

See Perepiska.

O zadachakh sotsialistov v bor'be s golodom v Rossii. Geneva, 1892.

'Pis'ma G. Plekhanova k F. Engel'su i R. Fisheru', *Pod Znamenem Marksizma*, No. 11–12, 1923, pp. 13–30.

375

BIBLIOGRAPHY

Sochineniia (ed. D. Riazanov). 24 vols. Moscow, 1923–7.

Plekhanov, G. V. (ed.) *Vademecum dlia redaktsii 'Rabochego Dela', Sbornik materialov*. With a foreword by G. Plekhanov. Geneva, 1900.

Vserossiiskoe razzorenie. St Petersburg, 1906. First published Geneva, 1892.

Polevoi, Iu. Z. *Zarozhdenie marksizma v Rossii 1883–1894*. Moscow, 1959.

Polonskii, P. 'Na zare sotsial-demokraticheskogo dvizheniia v Kieve', *Katorga i Ssylka*, No. 3 (40), 1928, pp. 11–22.

Pospelov, P. N. (ed.). See *Istoriia Kommunisticheskoi partii*.

Programma periodicheskogo organa Soiuza Russkikh Sotsialdemokratov, 'Rabochee Delo'. Geneva, 1899.

'Programm der Sozialdemokratischen Arbeiterpartei in Oesterreich', *Protokoll über die Verhandlungen der Sozialdemokratischen Arbeiterpartei in Oesterreich Abgehalten zu Wien, 2.–6. November 1901*. Vienna, 1901.

'Programm der Sozialdemokratischen Partei Deutschlands', *Protokoll über die Verhandlungen des Parteitages der Sozialdemokratischen Partei Deutschlands Abgehalten zu Erfurt, 14.–20. October 1891*. Berlin, 1891.

Protokoly 2-go ocherednogo s"ezda Zagranichnoi ligi russkoi revoliutsionnoi sots.-demokratii, ed. I. Lesenko and F. Dan, pseudonyms (Inna Germogenovna Smidovich and Fedor Il'ich Gurvich). Geneva, 1904.

Protokoly. See *Vtoroi ocherednoi s"ezd Ross. Sots.-Dem. Rabochei Partii*.

Rabinowitsch, Sara. *Die Organisationen des Jüdischen Proletariats in Russland*. Karlsruhe, 1903.

Rabochee Delo. See *Otvet redaktsii 'Rabochego Dela'*.

Rabochee dvizhenie v Ivanovo-Voznesenskom raione. Izd. Soiuza Russkikh Sotsial'demokratov. Geneva, 1900.

Rabochee dvizhenie v Khar'kove. See [Feinberg, B. L.].

Rabochee dvizhenie v Rossii: Sbornik dokumentov i materialov. Vol. IV: *1895–1900*. 2 books (ed. L. M. Ivanov). Moscow, 1961–63.

Rabochii, *Rabochie i intelligenty v nashikh organizatsiiakh*. With a foreword by P. Aksel'rod. Geneva, 1904.

Radchenko, I. I. 'Stepan Ivanovich Radchenko', *Staryi Bol'shevik*, No. 2 (5), 1933, pp. 177–86.

Rakhmetov, V. 'K voprosu o men'shevistskikh tendentsiiakh v gruppe "Osvobozhdenie truda"', *Proletarskaia Revoliutsiia*, No. 9 (80), 1926, pp. 26–56.

Rappoport, C. 'The Life of a Revolutionary Emigré' (translation), *Yivo Annual* (New York), No. 6, 1951, pp. 206–36.

Riazanov, N. (D. Riazanov), pseudonym (David Borisovich Gol'dendakh). *Materialy dlia vyrabotki partiinoi programmy*, Vol. II: *Proekt programmy 'Iskry' i zadachi russkikh sotsial'demokratov*. Geneva, 1903.

(ed.). See Plekhanov, G. V. *Sochineniia*.

BIBLIOGRAPHY

Rubach, M. (ed.), *Istoriia Ekaterinoslavskoi Sotsialdemokraticheskoi Organizatsii, 1889–1903*. Ekaterinoslav, 1923.

Sbornik materialov i statei, Vol. I. Moscow, 1921. Glavnoe Upravlenie Arkhivnym Delom.

Schapiro, L. *The Communist Party of the Soviet Union*. London, 1960.

Schapiro, L., and P. Reddaway, *Lenin: The Man, the Theorist, the Leader— A Reappraisal*. London, 1967.

Semenov, K. 'Pervyi god Peterburgskoi "Rabochei Organizatsii"', *Minuvshie Gody*, No. 12, 1908, pp. 265–94.

Sergievskii, N. L. 'Gruppa "Osvobozhdenie Truda" i marksistskie kruzhki', *Istoriko-revoliutsionnyi sbornik* (ed. V. I. Nevskii). Vol. II, pp. 86–266. 2 vols. Leningrad, 1924.

'Kogda i po kakomu povodu byl napisan Plekhanovym *Proekt programmy russkikh sots.-demokratov*', *Proletarskaia Revoliutsiia*, No. 1 (72), 1928, pp. 85–101.

Partiia russkikh sotsial-demokratov: Gruppa Blagoeva. Moscow– Leningrad, 1929. A publication of the Komissiia po istorii oktiabr'- skoi revoliutsii i RKP (b).

Shcheglo, L. '*Rabochaia Mysl*', *Katorga i Ssylka*, Nos. 4–5 (101–2), 1933, pp. 64–94.

Shcheprov, S., *Na puti k sozdaniiu partii*. Moscow, 1959.

Shelgunov, V. A. *See* 'Vospominaniia V. A. Shelgunova'.

Sil'vin, M. A. 'K biografii V. I. Lenina (iz vospominanii)', *Proletarskaia Revoliutsiia*, No. 7 (30), 1924, pp. 66–81.

Lenin v period zarozhdeniia partii. Leningrad, 1958.

Skrobot, S. S. 'Stachechnaia bor'ba peterburgskikh rabochikh v 1891– 1895 gg.' *Istoriia SSSR*, No. 6, 1958, pp. 105–14.

Sorin, V. G. *Pervye shagi Lenina po sozdaniiu partii*. Moscow, 1934.

Sotsial-demokraticheskoe dvizhenie v Rossii: Materialy (ed. A. N. Potresov and B. I. Nikolaevskii), Vol. I. Moscow–Leningrad, 1928. Letters from Lenin, Potresov, Akimov, Kopel'zon, etc., 1895– 1904.

Sponti, Evg. 'Vstrechi s Leninym', *Zapiski Instituta Lenina*, No. 3, 1928, pp. 71–3.

Steklov, Iu. M., pseudonym (Iurii Mikhailovich Nakhamkes). 'V ssylke i v emigratsii (ideinye konflikty)', *Proletarskaia Revoliutsiia*, No. 5 (17), 1923, pp. 193–250.

Otkazyvaemsia-li my ot nasledstva? Geneva, 1902.

[Steklov, Iu. M., and L. Trotskii, pseudonyms (Iurii Mikhailovich Nakhamkes and Lev Davidovich Bronshtein)]. *Iz rabochego dvizheniia v Odesse i Nikolaeve*. Izd. Soiuza Russkikh Sotsial'- demokratov. Geneva, 1900.

Stepniak, S., pseudonym (Sergei Mikhailovich Kravchinskii). *Chego nam nuzhno i nachalo kontsa*. London, 1892.

Struve, Peter. 'My Contacts and Conflicts with Lenin', *The Slavonic Review*, No. 36 (1934), pp. 573–95; No. 37 (1934), pp. 66–84.

BIBLIOGRAPHY

Suslova, F. M. 'Peterburgskie stachki 1895–1896 godov i ikh vliianie na razvitie massovogo rabochego dvizheniia', *Istoriia rabochego klassa Leningrada* (ed. V. A. Ovsiankin), Vol. II, pp. 49–91. Leningrad, 1963.

Sviatlovskii, V. V. 'Na zare Rossiiskoi sotsial-demokratii', *Byloe*, No. 19, 1922, pp. 139–60.

Takhtarev, Konstantin Mikhailovich. *See* Peterburzhets.

Tatarov, I. 'I s"ezd RSDRP v istorii nashei partii', *Proletarskaia Revoliutsiia*, No. 3 (74), 1928, pp. 3–21.

Teodorovich, I. 'Karl Marks i revoliutsionnoe dvizhenie v Rossii', *Katorga i Ssylka*, No. 3 (100), 1933, pp. 7–81.

Thun, A. *See* Tun (Thun), A.

Tikhomirnov, G. 'Pervye agitatsionnye listki Lenina', *Proletarskaia Revoliutsiia*, No. 8, 1937, pp. 124–36.

Tovstukhi, I. (joint ed.). *See* Valk, S. N., and I. Tovstukhi (eds.).

Treadgold, D. W. *Lenin and his Rivals: The Struggle for Russia's Future, 1898–1906*. London, 1955.

Trotskii, peudonym (Lev Davidovich Bronshtein). *Nashi politicheskie zadachi*. Geneva, 1904.

[Trotskii, L., and Iu. M. Steklov]. *See* [Steklov, Iu. M., and L. Trotskii]. *Iz rabochego dvizheniia v Odesse i Nikolaeve.*

Tuchapskii, P. L. *Iz perezhitogo: Devianostye gody*. Odessa, 1923.

Tun (Thun), A. *Istoriia revoliutsionnykh dvizhenii v Rossii*. Geneva, 1903.

Ulam, A. B. *The Bolsheviks*. New York, 1965.

Ustinovich, N. 'Pervaia tipografiia Peterburgskogo Soiuza bor'by za osvobozhdenie rabochego klassa v 1900 g.', *Krasnaia Letopis*, No. 2 (11), 1924, pp. 93–102.

Vaganian, V. G. *V. Plekhanov. Opyt kharakteristiki sotsial'no-politicheskikh vzrenii*. Moscow, 1924.

Valentinov, pseudonym (Nikolai Vladislavovich Vol'skii). 'Tragediia G. V. Plekhanova (K 30-letiiu so dnia ego smerti)', *Novyi Zhurnal*, No. 20, 1948, pp. 270–93.

Vstrechi s Leninym. New York, 1953. [English translation: *Encounters with Lenin*. Oxford, 1968.]

Valk, S. N. 'K dokumental'noi istorii *Rabochego Znameni*', *Krasnaia Letopis*, Nos. 2–3, 1922, pp. 333–46.

'K istorii Belostokskoi konferentsii 1902 g.', *Proletarskaia Revoliutsiia*, No. 6 (101), 1930, pp. 132–48.

'Obshchestvennoe dvizhenie v Peterburge v 90-kh i nachala 900-kh godov. Leninskii "Soiuz za osvobozhdenie rabochego klassa"'. *Ocherki istorii Leningrada*. Vol. III, pp. 147–222.

'Peterburgskaia gruppa "Rabochego Znameni"', *Istoriko-revoliutsionnyi sbornik* (ed. V. I. Nevskii), Vol. I, pp. 127–69.

Valk, S. N., and I. Tovstukhi (eds.). *Listovki Peterburgskogo 'Soiuza bor'by za osvobozhdenie rabochego klassa': 1895–1897 gg*. Moscow, 1934.

BIBLIOGRAPHY

Varentsova, O. A. 'Organizatsionnyi komitet po sozyvu II s"ezda RSDRP', *Proletarskaia Revoliutsiia*, No. 2, 1933, pp. 37–71.

Severnyi Rabochii Soiuz. Moscow, 1935.

Varskii, A. (ed.). 'Perepiska G. V. Plekhanova, P. B. Aksel'roda i V. I. Zasulich s L. Iogikhes (Grozovski, Tyshkoi) (1891–1892 g.)', *Proletarskaia Revoliutsiia*, Nos. 11–12 (82–3), 1928, pp. 255–85.

Varzar, V. E. *Spisok fabrik i zavodov evropeiskoi Rossii*. Izd. Ministerstva Finansov. St Petersburg, 1903.

Vienna programme. *See* 'Programm der Sozialdemokratischen Arbeiterpartei in Oesterreich'.

Vilenskii-Sibiriakov, V., and others (eds.). *Deiateli revoliutsionnogo dvizheniia v Rossii: Bio-bibliograficheskii slovar'*. Vol. I (Books 1–2); II (1–4); III (1–2); V (1–2). Moscow, 1927–34. A publication of the *Vsesoiuznoe obshchestvo politicheskikh katorzhan i ssyl'noposelentsev*.

Voden, A. 'Na zare "legal'nogo marksizma" (okonchanie)', *Letopisi Marksizma*, No. 4, 1927, pp. 87–96.

'Vospominaniia V. A. Shelgunova', *Ot gruppy Blagoeva k 'Soiuzu bor'by' (1886–1894gg.)*, pp. 52–9.

Vtoroi ocherednoi s"ezd Ross. Sots.-Dem. Rabochei Partii: Polnyi tekst protokolov. Geneva, 1903.

Vtoroi s"ezd RSDRP: Protokoly. Moscow, 1959.

V zashchitu Soiuza: otchet Komissii Soiuza russkikh sotsial'demokratov o zakhvate tipografii i sklada Soiuza. Izd. Soiuza Russkikh Sotsial'-demokratov. Geneva, 1900.

Walkin, J. 'The Attitude of the Tsarist Government toward the Labor Problem', *The American Slavic and East European Review*, No. 2, 1954, pp. 163–84.

Wildman, Allan K. 'Lenin's Battle with "Kustarnichestvo": the *Iskra* Organization in Russia', *Slavic Review*, No. 3, 1964, pp. 479–503.

Making of a Workers' Revolution: Russian Social Democracy 1891–1903. Chicago, 1967.

Wolfe, B. *Three Who Made a Revolution*. Boston, 1948.

Zalevski, E. *Mouvements ouvriers et socialistes: Chronologie et bibliographie. La Russie:* Tome 1, *1725–1907*. Paris, 1956.

Zasulich, V. *Desiatiletie Morozovskoi stachki*. Geneva, 1897.

Zeman, Z. A. B., and M. B. Scharlau. *The Merchant of Revolution, the Life of Alexander Israel Helphand (Parvus) 1867–1924*. Oxford, 1965.

INDEX

Abramovich, Emilii Abramovich, 205–6, 285

Adler, Viktor, 93, 117–18, 123, 128–9, 133, 151, 155

Aizenshtat, Isai L. (pseudonym: Iudin), 20, 104

Akimov, V. P., pseudonym (Vladimir Petrovich Makhnovets)
childhood, education, arrest, 74–5, 254 n.
in the 1905 Revolution and after, 80–3
and Lenin, 3, 6–7, 80–1, 83–96, 111, 156, 172–5, 176, 322 n.
and Party historiography, periodization, 82, 86–9, 91, 175–6, 202–4, 236, 245–6, 263–4, 281–4, 291, 299, 315, 320, 336, 351–2, 359–61
and Plekhanov, 6–7, 75–7, 91–5, 97–8, 156–8, 175–8
and the Union Abroad, *Rabochee Delo*, 75–9, 188, 349, 359 n.
at the Second Party Congress, 59, 79, 84, 90, 104, 106, 111–12, 155–78, 188, 330–1, 333–4
on democracy and proletarian dictatorship, 6, 81–2, 94–6, 133–53, 170–1, 171–2 n., 173, 179–80, 344, 352 n.
on Party organization, 6, 81–2, 89–91, 152–3, 356–8, 361–2; in the Bund, 223–30; in St Petersburg, 235–6, 243–5, 251–4, 259–67; in Kiev, 291–3, 303–5
on proletarian consciousness, 6, 83–5, 89, 112–25, 174, 308–11, 342, 345–6
on the effects of capitalist development and the 'theory of pauperization', 92–3, 112–13, 125–33, 177–8, 182
on the peasant and agrarian question, 93–4, 160–9

Aksel'rod, Pavel Borisovich, 6, 13, 23 n., 24–5, 27–30, 32–42, 57, 61, 65–6, 71, 74, 86–7, 96, 185, 232, 262 n., 298–9, 298–9 n., 306 n.,

315, 317, 317 n., 331, 334 n., 335–45, 347, 351

Aleksandrov, Mikhail Stepanovich (pseudonyms: Ol'minskii; Galerka), 231 n., 234, 235 n., 252, 314–15, 335

Aleksandrova, Ekaterina Mikhailovna, 106

Alekseev, Nikolai Aleksandrovich, 76

Alekseev, Petr Alekseevich, 322

Aleksinskii, Grigorii Alekseevich, 81

Alexander III, Tsar, 13, 15

Andreev, Leonid Nikolaevich, 363

Andropov, Sergei Vasil'evich, 259 n., 266 n.

Arabazhin, Konstantin Ivanovich, 285 n.

Arbeter Shtime [*Labour Voice*], 88, 216, 217, 225, 273

Babushkin Ivan Vasil'evich, 245 n., 250 n.

Bakunin, Mikhail Aleksandrovich; Bakuninism, 4, 6, 7, 28, 67, 74

Barabanshchikov, Nikolai L'vovich, 262 n.

Baranov, Nikolai Mikhailovich, 237–8

Baranskaia, Nadezhda Nikolaevna, 250 n.

Bastiat, (Claude) Frédéric, 125

Bauman, Nikolai Ernestovich, 254 n.

Bebel, August, 131, 148–9

Belevskii, Aleksei Stanislavovich (pseudonym: Belorussov), 253

Bellamy, Edward, 161

Bernstein, Eduard; Bernsteinian, 32, 42, 44–5, 63, 72, 92, 94–5, 131–2, 140, 143, 146–51, 153, 155, 157, 169, 170, 174, 338, 361

Bervii, Vasilii Vasil'evich (pseudonym: Flerovskii, N.), 208

Bezrukova, Aleksandra Georgievna, 262 n.

Bismarck, Otto, Fürst von, 13.

Blagoev, Dmitrii Nikolaevich, 232 n.

381

INDEX

Weitling, Wilhelm, 116
Witte, Sergei Iul'evich, 250
Workers Will (Odessa), 103
Young *Narodovol'tsy, see* Group of *Express Review*
Zaichnevskii, Petr Grigor'evich, 152 n.
Zaretskaia, Sofiia M., 279 n.
Zasodimskii-Vologdin, Pavel Vladimirovich, 207 n.
Zasulich, Vera Ivanovna, 8, 13–14, 23 n., 24–5, 27–30, 32–3, 36–9,

49, 57, 61–2, 64, 66, 72, 97, 247, 262 n.
Zborovskii, M. S. (pseudonym: Kostich), 104
Zemlia i Volia, 8, 181
Zheliabov, Andrei Ivanovich, 322
Zionism, 210
Zobov, Nikolai Matveevich, 207
Zubatov, Sergei Vasil'evich, 34, 220
Zundelevich, Aaron Isaakovich, 210 n.
Zvezdochetova, Ol'ga Appolonovna, 266 n.

CAMBRIDGE STUDIES IN THE HISTORY AND THEORY OF POLITICS

TEXTS

LIBERTY, EQUALITY, FRATERNITY *by James Fitzjames Stephen*. Edited, with an introduction and notes, by *R. J. White*

VLADIMIR AKIMOV ON THE DILEMMAS OF RUSSIAN MARXISM 1895–1903. Two texts in translation, edited and introduced by *Jonathan Frankel*

TWO ENGLISH REPUBLICAN TRACTS. Plato Redivivus or, A Dialogue concerning Government (*c.* 1681) *by Henry Neville*. An Essay upon the Constitution of the Roman Government (*c.* 1699) *by Walter Moyle*. Edited by *Caroline Robbins*

STUDIES

1867: DISRAELI, GLADSTONE AND REVOLUTION. THE PASSING OF THE SECOND REFORM BILL, *by Maurice Cowling*

THE CONSCIENCE OF THE STATE IN NORTH AMERICA, *by E. R. Norman*

THE SOCIAL AND POLITICAL THOUGHT OF KARL MARX, *by Shlomo Avineri*